SharePoint® 2007 Disaster Recovery Guide

John Ferringer and Sean McDonough

Charles River Media

A part of Course Technology, Cengage Learning

COURSE TECHNOLOGY
CENGAGE Learning™

Australia, Brazil, Japan, Korea, Mexico, Singapore, Spain, United Kingdom, United States

COURSE TECHNOLOGY
CENGAGE Learning™

SharePoint® 2007 Disaster Recovery Guide
John Ferringer and Sean McDonough

Publisher and General Manager,
Course Technology PTR: Stacy L. Hiquet

Associate Director of Marketing: Sarah Panella

Content Project Manager: Jessica McNavich

Marketing Manager: Mark Hughes

Acquisitions Editor: Mitzi Koontz

Project and Copy Editor: Karen A. Gill

Editorial Services Coordinator: Jennifer Blaney

Interior Layout: Shawn Morningstar

Cover Designer: Mike Tanamachi

Indexer: Jerilyn Sproston

Proofreader: Mike Beady

For product information and technology assistance, contact us at

Cengage Learning Customer and Sales Support, 1-800-354-9706.

For permission to use material from this text or product, submit all requests online at **cengage.com/permissions**.

Further permissions questions can be e-mailed to **permissionrequest@cengage.com**.

Library of Congress Control Number: 2008929235

ISBN-13: 978-1-58450-599-0

ISBN-10: 1-58450-599-0

Course Technology
25 Thomson Place
Boston, MA 02210
USA

Cengage Learning is a leading provider of customized learning solutions with office locations around the globe, including Singapore, the United Kingdom, Australia, Mexico, Brazil, and Japan. Locate your local office at **international.cengage.com/region**.

Cengage Learning products are represented in Canada by Nelson Education, Ltd.
For your lifelong learning solutions, visit **courseptr.com**.
Visit our corporate Web site at **cengage.com**.

Printed in Canada
1 2 3 4 5 6 7 11 10 09

To Gretchen and Tracy,
for their infinite patience and support.

Acknowledgments

John Ferringer would like to acknowledge the following people:

- Becky Isserman, for giving me this opportunity.
- David Zinsmeister, for asking me all those years ago if I had ever considered writing something of my own; it's a question I never forgot.
- Ben Frame, Kelly Pfledderer, and all my coworkers at Apparatus for the encouragement and support throughout this process.
- Jeremy Gunter, for starting me down this road in so many ways.
- All the folks on Twitter who chipped in with great advice, information, and verifications: @autosponge, @emilysc, @greenearings, @greghughes, @hipslu, @itchysanchez, @JDWade, @joeloleson, and @Sadalit.
- Steve Pietrek, for all the helpful resources and one unbelievable referral.
- Jennifer Blaney, for her patience and support of a first-time writer.
- Karen Gill, for making it look like I write so purty, offering encouragement, and laughing at all my terrible jokes.
- Sean McDonough, for being a great mentor, keeping me sane, providing great feedback, encouraging my terrible jokes, writing like a madman, and going above and beyond at all times.
- The two amazing women in my life every day. Piper for making all the late nights, headaches, and long hours that much easier with every smile, giggle, and laugh; and my beautiful wife Gretchen, for suffering through the late nights, headaches, and long hours with me and providing so much encouragement, strength, support, and love.

Sean McDonough would like to acknowledge the following people:

- Andy Layton and Nate Peterson, for cutting me a desperately needed break here and there to get this book done; my sanity would have left me were it not for their flexibility in how I got some aspects of my job done while writing in my so-called "spare time."

- My friends and coworkers, for their willingness to listen to me talk about the book and for tolerating the half-asleep answers I sometimes gave them to questions they would ask.

- My SharePoint team at Cardinal, for their tolerance and support as I gave them the play-by-play on everything that was happening with regard to the book; I took up a fair bit of time during several of our team lunches and during my one-on-ones with them, but they have remained fantastically supportive throughout the entire process.

- Steve Pietrek, for introducing me to John after asking me that fateful question, "Would you consider tech editing a book?"

- Jen Blaney, for her feedback, encouragement, even-handed manner, exploration of creative solutions to problems, and decision to pull the plug when some things simply couldn't be made to work.

- Karen Gill, for her pragmatic outlook, kind words for a first-time author, ability to whip any chapter into shape, lighthearted nature, and willingness to explain where prepositions can go and what they are for. (Or should the sentence end as "that for which they are?")

- John Ferringer, for his witty humor, his ability to keep things on track and in focus, his razor-sharp attention to detail, his wealth of technical knowledge, the patience and willingness to engage me in dialogue and chat so often, his unbelievably strong work ethic, and for simply being the best writing partner a guy could hope to have.

- My nothing-short-of-incredible wife Tracy, for her willingness to support me through yet another project that ultimately pushed well beyond the bounds I had originally described; without her help, support (particularly with our two children), open ear, ability to cope with my staggering around the day after a long night of writing, and love, I would have spontaneously burst into flames halfway through the writing process.

About the Authors

John L. Ferringer is a solutions architect for Apparatus, Inc. in Indianapolis, Indiana, with over four years of experience administering and supporting SharePoint technologies. He is a Microsoft Certified Technology Specialist (MCTS) in the areas of SharePoint and System Center Operations Manager (SCOM), in addition to being a Microsoft Certified Application Developer (MCAD). John's blog can be found at http://www.SharePointBlogs.com/ForTheUser. He also operates http://SearchForSharePoint.com, a custom search engine for all things SharePoint. John lives in Indianapolis, Indiana, with his wife and daughter. He is an avid reader who enjoys golf and barbequing.

Sean P. McDonough is a managing consultant for Cardinal Solutions Group, Inc., a Microsoft Managed Partner in Cincinnati, Ohio. He is the team lead for Cardinal's group of SharePoint professionals, responsible for the development and delivery of custom software and infrastructure solutions based on SharePoint technologies. Sean has over a decade of experience in the IT industry and has served as the application architect in the creation of a corporate disaster recovery implementation for a Fortune 500 financial institution. Sean carries several Microsoft Certified Technology Specialist (MCTS) certifications for SharePoint and other areas, and he is a Microsoft Certified Professional Developer (MCPD). Sean resides in Cincinnati, Ohio, with his wife and two children. In his spare time, he enjoys practicing Hapkido, experiencing new electronic music, and hosting regular online gaming sessions for friends.

Contents

ON THE BOOK'S WEB SITE (HTTP://WWW.COURSEPTR.COM/DOWNLOADS)

Appendix A   **Third-Party Backup and Restore Tools**

Appendix B   **Chapter Review Q&A**

Introduction

If you've done any previous research on SharePoint disaster recovery topics, such as content recovery, backup and restore, and high availability, you've probably found quite a bit of information on the subject. That was certainly what we discovered as we investigated the subject in preparation for this book. But what we also found was that much of the discussion did one of two things: either it just scratched the surface of SharePoint disaster recovery, or it covered such a narrow focus that it was only applicable in certain situations. So we set out to create a resource for SharePoint disaster recovery that comprehensively examined the ins and outs of the various technical options available to back up and restore your SharePoint environment and demonstrated how to build those options into a successful disaster recovery plan.

WHAT YOU'LL FIND IN THIS BOOK

Microsoft's SharePoint platform is a complex, diverse technical tool designed to meet a range of business needs and uses. It requires several other platforms and applications for implementation, and it can be integrated with other external line-of-business applications. This diversity also applies to the numerous methods, tools, and approaches that can be used to preserve your SharePoint farm if it becomes affected by a catastrophic event. The majority of this book introduces you to those methods, tools, and approaches for backing up and restoring SharePoint. Once we've covered all the crucial technical aspects of preserving SharePoint with the tools Microsoft provides for it, we introduce you to the key concepts and activities necessary to develop a disaster recovery plan to implement those technical practices.

Listed next are some of the main concepts this recovery guide discusses:

- Preserving and recovering content, as well as tracking how it changes over time within a site
- Backing up and restoring sites with SharePoint Designer
- Backing up and restoring a SharePoint farm and its components through the Central Administration Web site
- Backing up and restoring a SharePoint farm and its components through STSADM.exe
- Developing your own custom backup and restore tools for SharePoint
- Backing up and restoring SQL Server 2005 and making it highly available
- Backing up and restoring Windows Server 2003 and making it highly available
- Learning the concepts and terminology of SharePoint disaster recovery planning
- Designing and documenting a SharePoint disaster recovery plan
- Testing and maintaining a SharePoint disaster recovery plan

WHO THIS BOOK IS FOR

In general, this book is geared toward readers who are worried about the long-term health and viability of their SharePoint environment and the valuable business information stored in it. It's assumed that readers are at least familiar with SharePoint as end users, and most of the technical content inside is best suited for those who have experience deploying, configuring, and administrating SharePoint. The examples, walkthroughs, and advice in this recovery guide are intended to be general and can be applied to a variety of situations and SharePoint environments.

HOW THIS BOOK IS ORGANIZED

Each chapter has relevant visual aids such as screenshots, diagrams, and example documents to guide you through the topics being discussed. You'll also find special breakout sections to call your attention to items of note, tips and tricks, and areas of caution that we have found particularly relevant. Finally, each chapter ends with a series of review questions intended to test your understanding of what you've completed and help you think about some of the chapter's key concepts. Don't worry, though; we're providing answers to those questions in Appendix B, "Chapter Review Q&A," on the book's Web site at http://www.courseptr.com/downloads.

Because you can't have an Appendix B without first having an Appendix A, we decided to go ahead and write one. Appendix A, "Third-Party Backup and Restore Tools," alphabetically lists some of the SharePoint backup and restore, replication, and disaster recovery–related tools currently available for download or purchase in the marketplace today. As much as we would have liked to cover each of these tools in the same depth we devoted to out-of-the-box options from Microsoft, it just wasn't possible given timelines and space constraints we were already up against. But that doesn't mean that these tools are unworthy of mention, so in Appendix A you'll see a quick synopsis of each tool's attributes as provided by their manufacturer and direction on where you can find out more. This appendix is also available online at the book's Web site, so we'll continue to update it with new information and tools as we come across them.

1 Getting Started with SharePoint Disaster Recovery

Why read a book about SharePoint disaster recovery? Hopefully, your answer to that question is *not* your quest to end your insomnia. (There are so many other technology books out there that could try to fit that bill.) That is not to say that the rest of this book is full of explosions, sirens, or thunderclaps, but those sounds and the events associated with them are definitely something that should get your attention. But while the contents of this book may not rivet you to your seat, they can help you to prevent things like explosions, sirens, thunderclaps, or Joe User deleting a file and causing disastrous effects.

What if you are a SharePoint administrator for a Fortune 500 company and the sole purpose of your job is to watch and monitor the SharePoint servers? If the SharePoint server is down for even one second during the day, your company will lose business from the United States, Korea, or Canada. What would you do if the servers crashed? You would need to use some form of disaster recovery, but you might not know where to start.

Disasters can come in all sorts of shapes and sizes. Look at a natural disaster, such as a tornado. What happens when a tornado hits? Tornadoes are relentless and can level a building without remorse. In an area of the United States known as Tornado Alley (consisting of parts of Missouri, Kansas, and Oklahoma), residents know that it is not a question of *if* a tornado is going to strike, but *when*. This means they have to establish emergency procedures for when one strikes and lay out contingency plans for how they are going to pick up the pieces once the tornado has moved on. They determine the location of their nearest shelter area so that they can safely survive the storm. Residents regularly practice tornado drills so that everyone knows what they should do in case a twister touches down in their vicinity. They evaluate the cost and benefits of purchasing the proper insurance so their belongings can be replaced if they are damaged.

As a SharePoint administrator, you most likely have a responsibility to not only build a system that adds value to your business's processes and practices, but to keep that system healthy, available, and functional for its users for as long as it is in use.

But the reality of today's information technology (IT) landscape is that it is no longer just enough to plan on applying the latest patches to your systems and simply rebuild anything that breaks down or gets deleted accidentally. Current IT systems, especially ones like SharePoint and the systems it depends on, are complex, broad, and tightly integrated into the daily business practices of its users. Not to mention, these systems are bound by the Sarbanes-Oxley Act of 2002 if they are a publicly traded company, so data retention is important in the event of a government audit. You are going to find yourself surrounded by more and more reasons why, like the residents of Tornado Alley, you need to be prepared should disaster strike.

Do you know what actions to take if your database's files are deleted from the server or your data center is washed away in a flood? How quickly can you bring your SharePoint environment back online? These are some of the questions that the coming pages address, to help you think about the best way to solve them for your unique situation and requirements. Now, this book isn't trying to equate the value of a SharePoint farm with that of a human life or one's personal assets. Rather, it is illustrating that planning to successfully survive a catastrophic event such as a tornado, hurricane, or fire is something that everyone does on a regular basis, so you should take the thought process behind that planning and apply it to your SharePoint environment. Also, keep in mind that SharePoint disaster recovery is not a "one size fits all" kind of situation. There are a range of options, solutions, and tools available for use in this area, and each one appeals to such a broad audience that it is not possible to say that any given approach is the only thing you'll need to preserve your system when disaster strikes. This book aims to introduce you to the majority of these options and describe their attributes, uses, pros, and cons so you can decide which one works best for you. So find shelter from the tornado in your bathroom or basement, and continue on to Chapter 2, "End User Resources."

2 End User Resources

Contributions by Becky Isserman

In This Chapter

- Assumptions
- Recycle Bins
- Version Control (Versioning)
- Alternative Solutions

The majority of people using SharePoint (Windows SharePoint Services [WSS] version 3 and Microsoft Office SharePoint Server [MOSS] 2007) do not touch administrative tools like the SharePoint Central Administration Web site or STSADM.exe. If a disaster should strike, such as the loss of a server data center or a network backbone outage, it is not the users' responsibility to restore service. They do not need to worry about disaster recovery preparedness; that is the responsibility of their information technology (IT) support staff. Most of these people are focused on managing their content, whether it is in document libraries, lists that they set up, or collaboration sites created by an administrator. To them, the most important aspects of SharePoint are the documents, conversations, and information they are storing in it, not the environment itself. These people are the general users of SharePoint known as end users, or information workers in information technology speak.

In the previous releases of SharePoint, WSS v2 and SharePoint Portal Services (SPS) 2003, there were not a lot of options available in the area of disaster recovery for the end user. Microsoft IT did release a recycle bin add-on for WSS v2 and SPS 2003 that now resides on CodePlex (http://www.codeplex.com), but it was not fully supported or integrated with the platform. In WSS v2 and SPS 2003, like WSS v3 and MOSS 2007, end users normally posted their content, shared it with others in document libraries and lists, and could set up an alert to notify them of changes in the lists or libraries. Unlike WSS v3 and MOSS 2007, WSS v2 and SPS 2003 had no ability to create major and minor versions of content to track drafts as well as full versions, nor could they version the contents of their SharePoint lists.

In SharePoint, end users are empowered out of the box with options such as recycle bins and detailed version control, as well as creative alternative solutions using list templates and Web Distributed Authoring and Versioning (WebDAV). They no longer have to fully rely on their SharePoint environment's administrators to ensure that all their content is safe. This chapter discusses the end user options available in SharePoint and how you can leverage those options to empower information workers to better update, preserve, and restore their vital content.

ASSUMPTIONS

The visual examples provided in this chapter were generated in a testing environment using the platforms and components listed next. Depending on how your environment is configured, your experiences may vary slightly. Unless a specific item indicates that it is unique to MOSS, the features and functionality covered in this chapter apply to both WSS and MOSS in the same fashion.

- **Operating system.** Microsoft Windows Server 2003 R2 Enterprise Edition Service Pack (SP) 2
- **Microsoft .NET Framework.** Versions 1.1, 2.0 SP1, 3.0 SP 1, and 3.5
- **Database.** Microsoft SQL Server 2005 Developer Edition Service Pack 2
- **Web server.** Microsoft Internet Information Services (IIS) 6.0
- **SharePoint.** MOSS 2007 Enterprise Edition
- **SharePoint Site Template.** Collaboration—Team Site
- **SharePoint Site Permissions.** Contribute

In the current release of SharePoint, the only content that will be displayed to a user is content that the user has the right to access. If a user does not have the privileges necessary to access content, regardless of its location, SharePoint does not give the user any indication that the content exists. This practice, known as security trimming, is applied in areas throughout SharePoint such as document libraries, collaboration sites, search results, and recycle bins.

RECYCLE BINS

The latest release of SharePoint offers a much-needed feature that was previously only available through add-ons. Now users can delete an item within a SharePoint site yet still recover it as easily as checking a box and clicking a button. This feature is called a *recycle bin*.

The recycle bin comes in two flavors:

■ End User Recycle Bin
■ Second Stage Recycle Bin (Site Collection Recycle Bin)

The End User Recycle Bin allows users to recover any content that they delete within a set period. For example, if users delete a document and need to recover it, they can quickly click on the recycle bin icon on that site and retrieve the item. By default, the files in this recycle bin are migrated to the Site Collection Recycle Bin 30 days after deletion. Farm administrators can change this option in the Central Administration site, which is covered later in this chapter in the section "How to Change the Recycle Bin Settings in Central Administration."

HOW TO ACCESS THE END USER RECYCLE BIN

If a user with Contribute access or above accidentally deletes a list, list item, document, or document library, he can access the End User Recycle Bin by following these steps:

1. Open up the main site collection in Internet Explorer.
2. On the left side of the page in the Quick Launch menu is a recycle bin icon, as seen in Figure 2.1.

   By default in most SharePoint site templates, the recycle bin appears on the same side of the browser that the Quick Launch menu bar resides for users with Contribute access and above.

In some SharePoint site templates, such as the Publishing Portal, the Quick Launch bar is not displayed on every page.

CAUTION

3. Click on the recycle bin icon to open the End User Recycle Bin, shown in Figure 2.2.

FIGURE 2.1 This is an example of what the End User Recycle Bin looks like on the default theme in SharePoint.

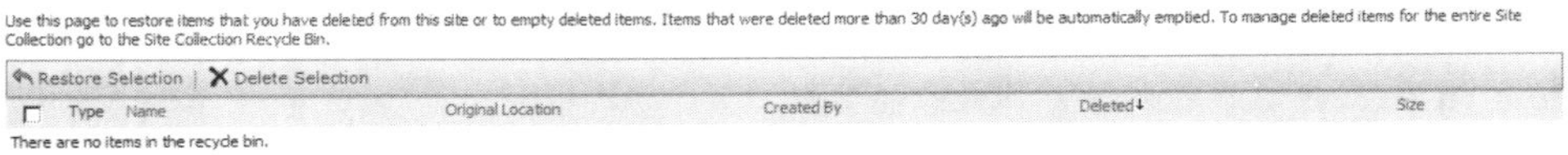

FIGURE 2.2 This is what the default End User Recycle Bin looks like in SharePoint.

HOW TO RESTORE A DELETED DOCUMENT FROM A RECYCLE BIN

A user with Contribute access who deletes a document and wants to recover the item within the 30-day limit can follow these steps to retrieve the items:

1. Open a site collection and navigate to a recycle bin using the steps in the previous section, "How to Access the End User Recycle Bin."

If you are in the End User Recycle Bin, you should see items deleted by the current user account. If you are inside the Site Collection Recycle Bin, you should see items from all end users' recycle bins.

2. If you want to restore an item from a recycle bin, check the box next to the item, as shown in Figure 2.3, and click the Restore Selection link located above the list of items within the recycle bin.

Use this page to restore items that you have deleted from this site or to empty deleted items. Items that were deleted more than 30 day(s) ago will be automatically emptied. To manage deleted items for the entire Site Collection go to the Site Collection Recycle Bin.

	Type	Name	Original Location	Created By	Deleted↓	Size
☑		Test Document.doc	/Documents	Isserman, Becky M.	3/30/2008 2:08 PM	26.7 KB

FIGURE 2.3 In this example, notice how boxes are checked
next to the item that you want to restore.

Remember the original location, because this area lists where the item was deleted and where it will be restored. Unfortunately, users do not have the option to restore an item to any area other than the original location.

3. Click the Restore Selection link. A prompt appears asking Are you sure you want to restore <*Your Item's Name*>? For an example, please see Figure 2.4.
4. Click the OK button to restore the item.
   If you navigate to the original location that you saw in step 2, you see the item fully restored.

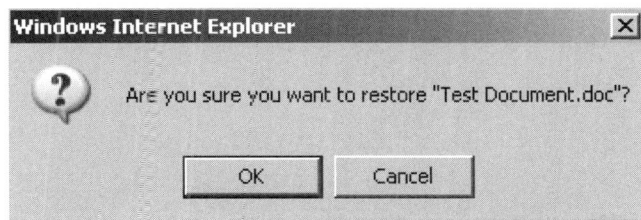

FIGURE 2.4 Remember to select the OK button and not the Cancel
button when this message pops up when restoring an item.

If you attempt to restore an item to its original location and an item exists in that location with the same name as the item in your recycle bin, SharePoint displays an error page with the following message: A file with this name <Your Item Name> already exists in <Your Original Location>. To restore the file, rename the existing file and try again.

The Site Collection Recycle Bin is not as easy to access as the End User Recycle Bin. This recycle bin resides in the Site Settings page of the top-level site within each site collection under the Site Collection Administration section. Only site collection administrators for this site collection can access this area. This recycle bin is great as a second stage to the End User Recycle Bin, because users delete files from the End User Recycle Bin, and they are thrown into the Site Collection Recycle Bin.

If you look at the process, the first stage is the End User Recycle Bin, and the second stage is the Site Collection Recycle Bin. If a site collection administrator needs to recover a file for a user who no longer exists, this recycle bin has a copy of all End User Recycle Bins with all deleted items. Therefore, site collection administrators can restore items from any recycle bin, not just the Site Collection Recycle Bin. This recycle bin is also set to expire 30 days after items are deleted from the End User Recycle Bin, so if users delete a file from their own recycle bin, they have another 30 days from deletion to recover a file by requesting that it be restored by the site collection's site collection administrator. Therefore, an item expires after 60 days of deletion from the source library on default. The item sits in the End User Recycle Bin for 30 days, is sent to the Site Collection Recycle Bin, and gets permanently deleted after 30 more days under normal circumstances. When a site collection is created in SharePoint, a quota can be established by the farm administrator creating the site application. The Site Collection Recycle Bin operates off of this quota, so if the data within this recycle bin exceeds the quota, a user's information may not stay for the full 30 days.

HOW TO GET TO THE SITE COLLECTION RECYCLE BIN

If a user has Site Collection Administrator access to a site collection, he can follow these steps to view the Site Collection Recycle Bin:

1. Open the main site collection in Internet Explorer.
2. Click on the Site Actions menu and then the Site Settings option. When the Site Settings page opens, click the Modify All Site Settings link, as seen in Figure 2.5.
3. If you look under the Site Collection Administration Area, there should be an area labeled Recycle Bin, as seen in Figure 2.6.

If you click on the icon, you see an area with two links to the side for End User Recycle Bin Items and Deleted from End User Recycle Bin, as shown in Figure 2.7.

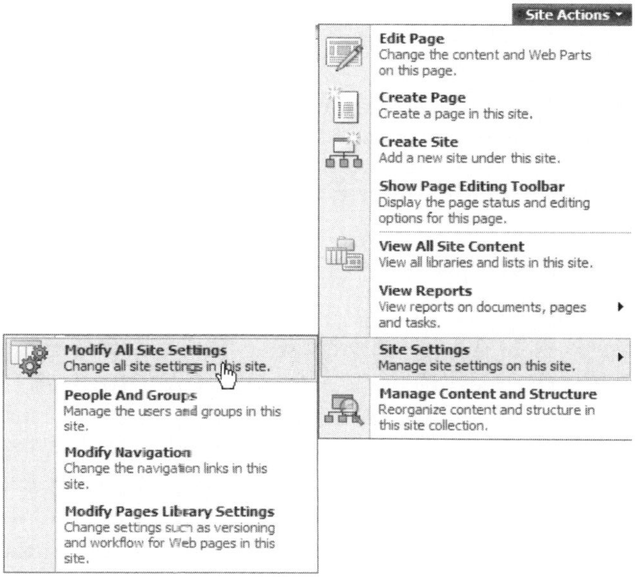

FIGURE 2.5 This menu option allows site collection administrators to access site settings for this site collection.

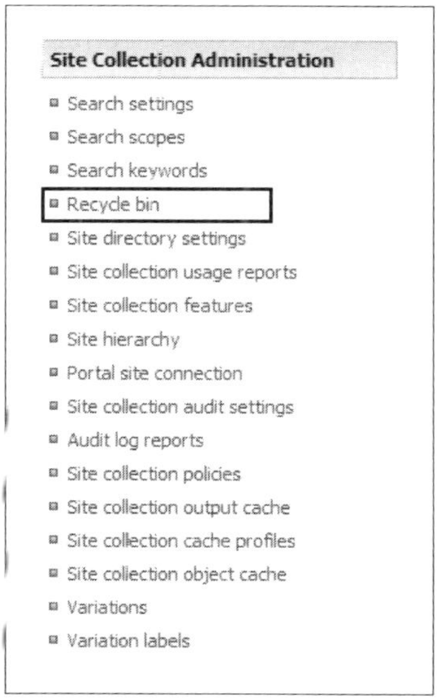

FIGURE 2.6 Here the Recycle Bin option is highlighted. This is the area where site collection administrators can access items deleted by end users that have been migrated from the site collection's End User Recycle Bins to the Site Collection Recycle Bin.

FIGURE 2.7 This recycle bin is similar to the End User Recycle Bin. However, notice that there are two options: End User Recycle Bin Items and Deleted from End User Recycle Bin.

How to Change the Recycle Bin Settings in Central Administration

Several configurable settings are available for SharePoint's recycle bins that can be modified to meet the specific requirements of your organization and how it uses SharePoint. These settings must be updated by a user with Farm Administrator access rights within your SharePoint environment; they are not available to end users or even site collection administrators. If a user has Farm Administrator access rights, he can follow these steps to change the settings in the Site Collection Recycle Bin:

1. Open the Central Administration site for your SharePoint environment in Internet Explorer.
2. Click on the Application Management tab, and you see an area called SharePoint Web Application Management. Click the Web Application General Settings link to proceed. For an example, please see Figure 2.8.

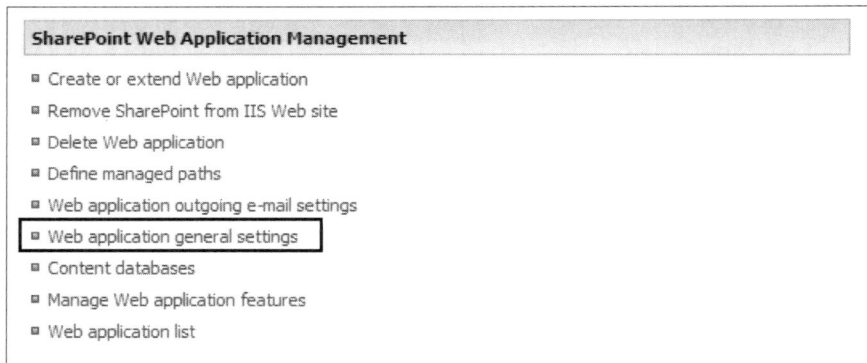

FIGURE 2.8 This is the area in the Central Administration site where a farm administrator changes the settings for recycle bins and other areas of a Web application in SharePoint.

3. At the top of the Web Application General Settings page, you should see the Choose a Web Application drop-down menu. If the desired Web application is not chosen by default, click on the arrow and select the Change Web Application option. A pop-up window appears, allowing you to select the desired Web application.

4. Scroll down to the bottom of the page, to the Recycle Bin section. For an example, please see Figure 2.9.

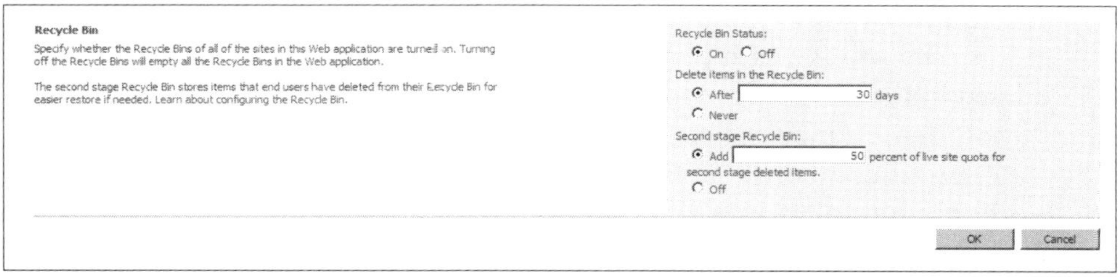

Recycle Bin

Specify whether the Recycle Bins of all of the sites in this Web application are turned on. Turning off the Recycle Bins will empty all the Recycle Bins in the Web application.

The second stage Recycle Bin stores items that end users have deleted from their Recycle Bin for easier restore if needed. Learn about configuring the Recycle Bin.

Recycle Bin Status:
  ○ On   ○ Off
Delete items in the Recycle Bin:
  ○ After [30] days
  ○ Never
Second stage Recycle Bin:
  ○ Add [50] percent of live site quota for second stage deleted items.
  ○ Off

[OK] [Cancel]

FIGURE 2.9 This section resides at the bottom of the General Settings section.

In this area, you can turn off the recycle bins, choose an expiration period for items within the recycle bins, or adjust the space allocated to each Site Collection Recycle Bin (or, as it is called in this area, Second Stage Recycle Bin). Changes made to these settings affect all site collections within the target Web application; they do not impact every site collection or Web application within your SharePoint farm. If your farm contains multiple Web applications where you want to change the recycle bin configuration settings, you must repeat the preceding steps for each Web application to change the settings throughout your farm.

Recycle bins are great for quick restores, but they are not a complete safety net for all of your content and settings within a SharePoint site. The most glaring weakness of the built-in recycle bin is its inability to retrieve a site or subsite that has been deleted. When a site is deleted, you will not find it in the recycle bin of its parent site. To recover that site, you have to have made a backup of the site and perform a restore using that backup.

NOTE

Chapters 3, 4, and 5 discuss SharePoint's out-of-the-box options for backing up and restoring your SharePoint sites. Additionally, the recycle bin does not easily cover some of the elements of a SharePoint site, such as alerts. If you delete an alert attached to a document library, the alert is not placed in the recycle bin. Instead, it is completely deleted and is no longer retrievable without going to a site's backup. So it is important to evaluate each decision to delete a component within your SharePoint site; you can't assume that the recycle bin will automatically retain your item if you go ahead with the action.

Appendix A, "Third-Party Backup and Restore Tools," discusses a site deletion capture feature available from MSIT. You can find Appendix A on the book's Web site at http://www.courseptr.com/downloads.

The same rules apply if you delete an attachment before you delete the list item that holds this attachment, because you cannot retrieve the attachment. However, both recycle bins can retrieve list items, documents, forms, pictures, and all other forms of content in addition to the items already mentioned. You cannot use a recycle bin to retrieve a solution or feature package that has been uninstalled and deleted from SharePoint. All files that expire in the Site Collection Recycle Bin are gone permanently unless the administrator made a backup prior to the expiration. This means that the administrator would need to get involved, and the restoration process could take hours or days depending on what kind of backup solutions your company is using. Essentially, these recycle bins are great for quick recovery by the end users (stage 1) and site collection administrators (stage 2) as long as they remember to recover the data within the expiration period.

VERSION CONTROL (VERSIONING)

Version control, or *versioning*, is the ability to keep a set number of drafts for an item, so that the end user can revert to a previous draft. This option is available in all lists and libraries within SharePoint. Versioning was available in SPS 2003; however, you had only one type of version and could not limit the number of versions.

Versioning is available in every type of SharePoint list and library, but it is disabled by default. To enable versioning, open the list or library's Settings page and click the Versioning Settings link in the General Settings section. At this point, users can configure versioning settings so that major and minor versions of an item are kept. Users are prompted to choose a major or minor version when an item is checked back into the library where it exists. A *minor version* is a draft version that is not automatically available to all users. In the settings, users can allow or deny other users the ability to see minor versions of an item. A *major version* is a full published version of a document or form. Site administrators can set how many major or minor versions they want to save within a document or form library.

SharePoint only tracks major and minor versions for items in document libraries. Versioning is available for all types of SharePoint lists, but the ability to create major and minor versions is only available in document libraries. For lists other than document libraries, only major versions of items can be created.

There are functions associated with versioning that are not available in every edition of SharePoint. To have automatic content approval workflows and visibility of draft versions integrated with the versions you create in a SharePoint list or library, you must at least be running the Standard licensed version of MOSS 2007. Also, these functions are not available by default in MOSS 2007; you must enable the Publishing Infrastructure Feature within your target site collection to make this functionality available within your site.

TIP

HOW TO TURN ON VERSIONING IN A DOCUMENT LIBRARY FOR SITE ADMINISTRATORS

A user with Design access rights or above in a document library can set up versioning for that document library by following these steps:

1. Open your target site collection and navigate to the document library where you desire to enable versioning.
2. Click on the Settings drop-down menu and then select the Document Library Settings option. For an example, please see Figure 2.10.
3. Under the General Settings area, click on the Versioning Settings link. For an example, please see Figure 2.11.
4. Choose the desired settings from the menu. For an example, please see Figure 2.12.

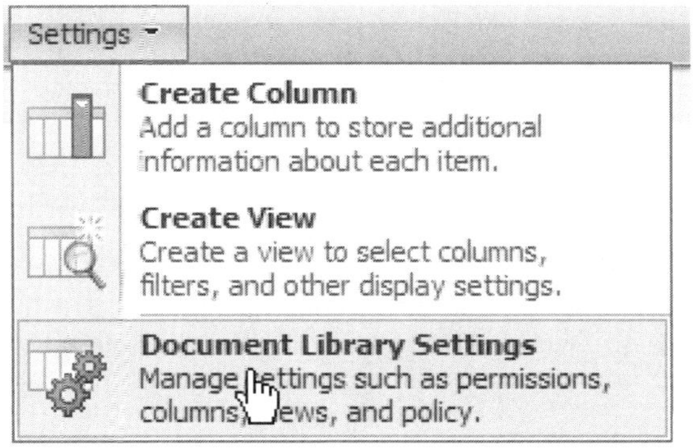

FIGURE 2.10 The Document Library Settings menu is located on the Settings menu in a document library.

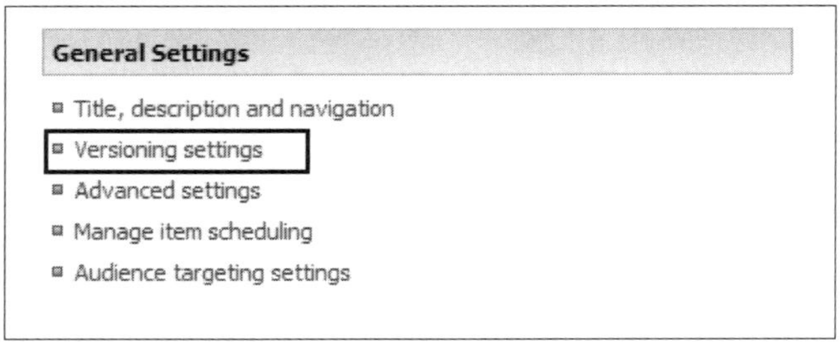

FIGURE 2.11 Versioning Settings is the second link under the General Settings section in a document library's Settings page.

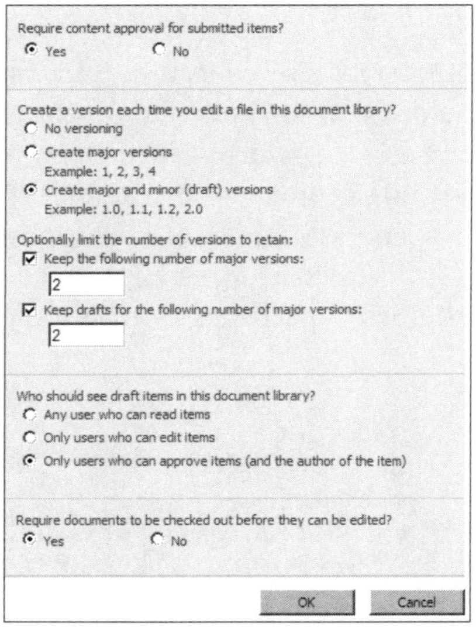

FIGURE 2.12 Site administrators can set up a document library to allow major and minor versions and specify a number of each type of version that the document library keeps.

In this area, the user can turn on content approval, allow major and minor versions, set how many drafts of major and minor versions to keep, specify whether other users who did not create the document can edit a minor (draft) version, and specify whether checkout is required. Users with WSS v3 do not have the content approval option because this feature is available only in MOSS. However, content approval is not automatically available in MOSS unless the site administrator or above activates the feature.

In MOSS, users can create sites using the Publishing template. The Publishing template is a site template with a page library that has versioning automatically activated. When a user makes a change to one of the pages in this library a Publishing button appears, so that users can check in the latest version of the page by clicking the button.

HOW TO PUBLISH A PAGE

A user with Contribute access or above can edit a page and publish the final product by following these steps:

1. Open Internet Explorer and navigate to the page that you would like to modify.
2. If this toolbar does not appear as in Figure 2.13, click on the Site Actions menu, and then select the option Show Page Editing Toolbar, as shown in Figure 2.14.

FIGURE 2.13 This is an example of what a publishing toolbar looks like on a Publishing template in MOSS.

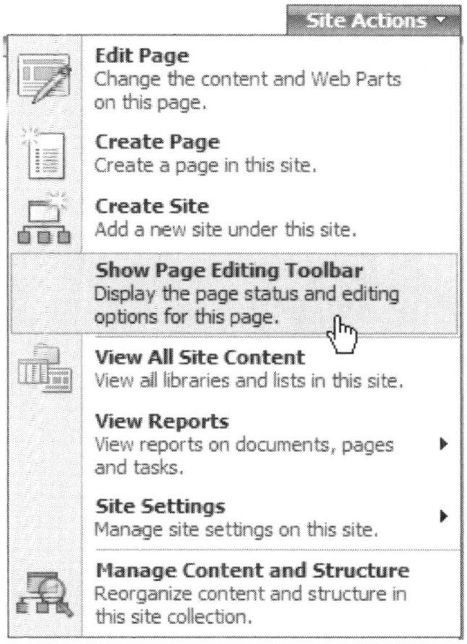

FIGURE 2.14 If a user with Contribute access or above wants to view a publishing toolbar, he can access this menu option on the right-hand corner of a site.

3. At this point, you have two options available:
   a. You will see a toolbar as in Figure 2.13. You can click on the Edit Page button, change the content of the page, and then click on Publish a Major Version of a Document.
   b. Alternatively, you can click on the Page button. A JavaScript drop-down menu appears where you can click on the Check Out button. For an example, see Figure 2.15.

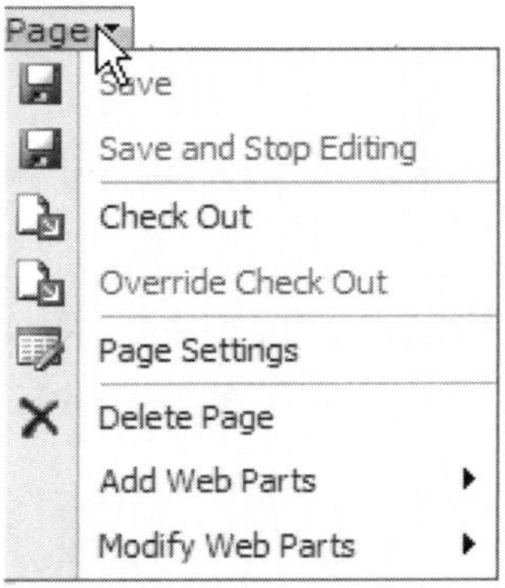

FIGURE 2.15 This is the Page button menu in the Page Editing toolbar in a site created using the MOSS Publishing template.

4. When you are finished adding content on the page, you can check in the item by clicking the Check In button on the menu in Figure 2.16. This opens the Check In page, as shown in Figure 2.17.

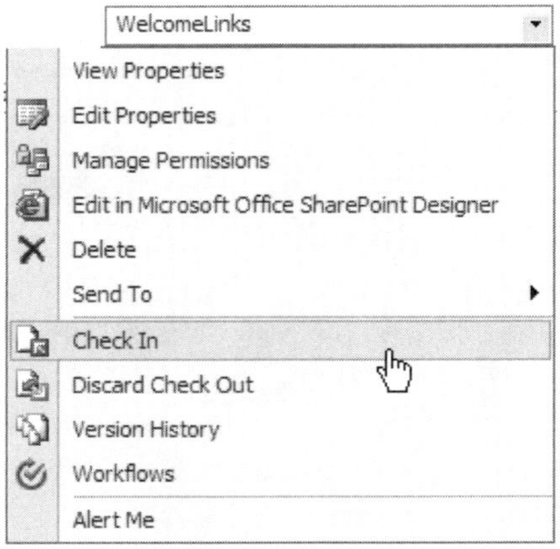

FIGURE 2.16 This is an example of what the Check In option looks like on a document library menu.

Step 3b is the same as if you were in a document library and you wanted to publish a major version of a document. However, you would click on the drop-down menu for the document and then select the Check In or Check Out option, depending on your desired activity.

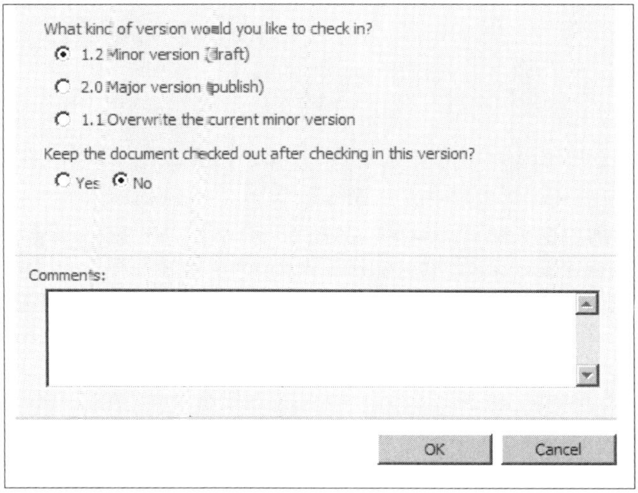

What kind of version would you like to check in?

    ◉ 1.2 Minor version (draft)

    ○ 2.0 Major version (publish)

    ○ 1.1 Overwrite the current minor version

Keep the document checked out after checking in this version?

    ○ Yes ◉ No

Comments:

OK   Cancel

FIGURE 2.17 The Check In page of a Publishing site in MOSS. If major-only versioning is set, the menu does not show options related to minor versions.

HOW TO REVERT TO AN OLD VERSION

A user with Contribute access or greater can follow these steps in any SharePoint list, regardless of SharePoint's edition or the site template used, and revert an item to an older version:

1. Open Internet Explorer and navigate to the site and list or library containing the item that needs a previous version restored.
2. Find the target item in the list or library and click the arrow to the right of the item's name to bring up the JavaScript drop-down menu displaying the options available to modify the item.
3. In the drop-down menu, click on the Version History option, as shown in Figure 2.18.
4. You now see a page that has various versions of the page that you are editing. You can view the differences in each version in Figure 2.19.

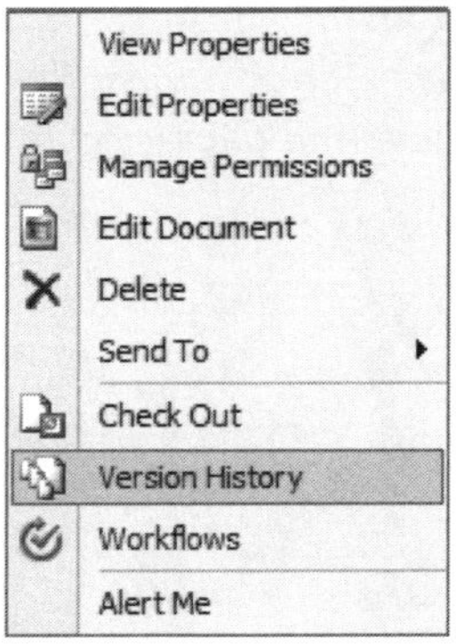

FIGURE 2.18 This is an example of an item's JavaScript drop-down menu in a document library with versioning enabled. If a user has Contribute access or greater, he can view this menu with the options listed.

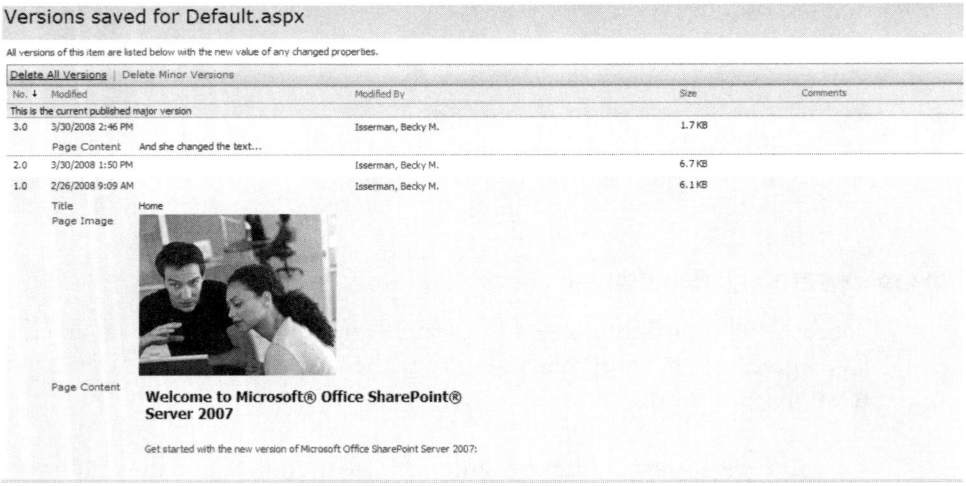

FIGURE 2.19 This is an example of a Version History page for an item in a document library.

If you want to revert to an old version, hover over the Modified field of each version, click on the arrow to open the drop-down menu, and choose the Restore option, as shown in Figure 2.20. If the version is minor and the changes in the version have not yet been published, the menu shows options to view the version or restore it.

If the changes in a prior major or minor version have been published, the three options shown are View, Restore, and Delete. After you select the Restore option, a confirmation dialog box is displayed. Click OK, and the library is updated to make the selected version the current one.

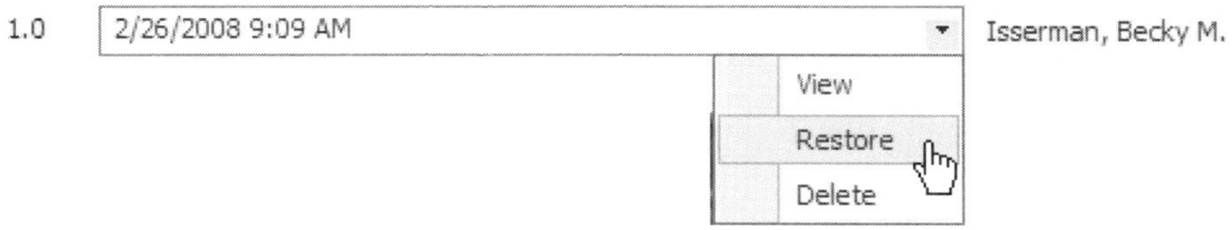

1.0   2/26/2008 9:09 AM   ▼   Isserman, Becky M.

View
Restore
Delete

FIGURE 2.20 The drop-down menu options available for a version of a document in a SharePoint document library.

If you navigate to the actual page in Internet Explorer, you see the old version of the page.

Versioning is a useful content recovery tool for end users, allowing them to restore an old item with the click of a button. Users with Contribute rights or greater in the site can choose between all the major and minor versions saved within the library if they need to recover an item. Unfortunately, versioning can bloat your SharePoint server if the users are storing a substantial number of documents in SharePoint. For example, if there are 5 document libraries on each of 10 sites, and each of these document libraries had 20 documents saved in these libraries, there are 1,000 documents saved on your SharePoint instance. As a more drastic example, what if in each of these 1,000 documents there were 2 major and 2 minor versions saved? That would create 4,000 copies of the documents saved within your SharePoint environment's content database! In a large enterprise environment, those numbers can really start to add up and directly impact the storage available to your content databases.

Users should take caution when using this feature, because one version of a document can multiply exponentially in a matter of days. For this reason, you should think twice before fully turning on versioning in every list and library of the SharePoint Site Collection and consider setting a default quota for Web applications. By only tracking major versions of your list items or documents, you cut your storage utilization by half, which is nothing to sneeze at. If you want to set up a default quota on your Web application, please see the section that follows titled "How to Set Quotas for a Web Application." Quotas are a good way to make sure that users do not exceed the amount of space allotted to a Site Collection, because farm administrators can set a specific size limit in a quota template. Quota templates can determine how much storage space a Site Collection can use. Every time a site administrator creates an item with versioning, he cannot create a quota for an individual library or list, because it is not possible to limit the size of individual libraries or lists in SharePoint. If farm administrators understand that quotas can help manage overall Site Collection storage and create some form of tracking system, they should be able to avoid problems with versioning.

HOW TO SET QUOTAS FOR A WEB APPLICATION

A farm administrator can set a default quota for a Web application by following these steps:

1. Open the Central Administration site for your SharePoint environment in Internet Explorer.
2. Click on the Application Management tab. You see a section called SharePoint Web Application Management. This is the area in Central Administration where a farm administrator changes the settings for recycle bins, quotas, and other areas of an application in SharePoint. Click on the Web Application General Settings link. For an example, refer to Figure 2.8.
3. At the top of the Web Application General Settings page, you see a drop-down menu titled Choose a Web Application displaying the current Web application available to modify. If the desired Web application is not currently displayed, click on the arrow and choose the Change Web Application option. A pop-up window appears allowing you to select a new target Web application. Click on the desired Web application and click the OK button to save your changes.
4. After you choose a Web application, notice that the third option has a drop-down list under the heading Default Quota Template, as seen in Figure 2.21.

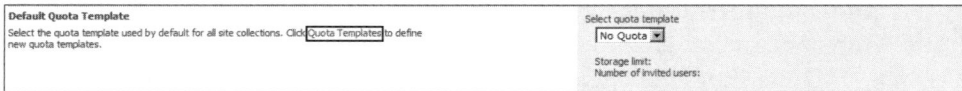

FIGURE 2.21 If the farm administrators create quota templates, they can choose one in this drop-down list and associate it to the Web application.

5. If quota templates are available, skip to step 7. If no quota templates are available, the farm administrators must click on the Quota Templates link highlighted in Figure 2.21 to create a new quota template. A screen appears that looks like Figure 2.22.

You can also access the Quota Templates page from the Application Management page in the Central Administration site by clicking the Quota Templates link.

NOTE

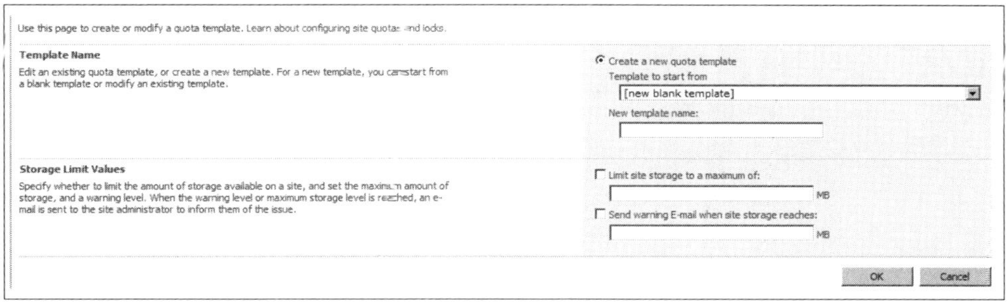

FIGURE 2.22 This page is the area where a farm administrator can set up a new quota template.

6. Type in a name for the template and check the box next to Limit Site Storage to a Maximum Of. Then type in the megabyte amount for the quota, as shown in Figure 2.23. If the check box next to Send Warning E-Mail When Storage Reaches is selected, site collection administrators receive a warning e-mail alerting them to the fact that the storage threshold has been met. Click OK and follow steps 3 and 4 to navigate back to set quota templates on an application.

TIP

When creating quota templates, it is important to carefully weigh your available storage against the amount of content you anticipate your users will use in target Site Collections you assign the template to. Your goal is to create a balance where you are efficiently using your storage and giving your users the freedom to upload their desired content without administrative intervention.

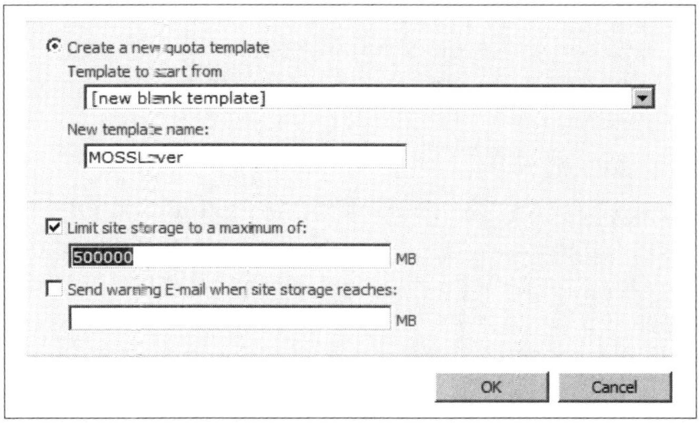

FIGURE 2.23 In this area, farm administrators can create a series of quotas that can be attached to applications and site collections.

If your configuration database is set to Active Directory Creation mode, a farm administrator can limit the number of invited users; otherwise, this option is not available on a quota template.

7. Select the quota template from the drop-down list under Select Quota Template, as seen in Figure 2.24. Click the OK button, which is available at the top and bottom of the Web Application General Settings page.

Select quota template

MOSSLover ▾

Storage limit: 500000 MB
Number of invited users: Not applicable

FIGURE 2.24 In this area, farm administrators can attach a quota that exists so that the amount of data posted can be controlled.

ALTERNATIVE SOLUTIONS

The recycle bin and versioning functionality built into SharePoint are not the only tools available to end users for protecting and recovering their vital content. The approaches discussed in this section use features in SharePoint that are intended primarily for purposes outside of backing up or restoring content. The great thing about SharePoint's broad capabilities and flexibility is how you can apply them in creative and often unconsidered uses to meet your own personal requirements. So even though list templates and WebDAV access to SharePoint lists are not designed as end user content protection and recovery tools, they do provide alternative solutions when recycle bins or versioning simply don't work.

LIST TEMPLATES

Lists are the base unit for content within SharePoint. Everything is a list, including document libraries, discussions, and blogs. Each has specific interfaces and unique functionality, but they are all lists. SharePoint list templates allow users to take an existing list within a SharePoint site and create a reusable template based on the columns and design of that original site. The list template can then be used to create one or more new lists in any SharePoint site that the user can upload the list template into, each list starting with the same configuration and contents as the original list. List templates are intended to make SharePoint lists reusable and more repeatable throughout an environment, but because you can also include a list's content in a template when it's created, they can also be used to preserve your content at a specific point in time. If you want to create a quick backup of a document library or a list of links, you can create a list template based on your target and save it to your workstation for safekeeping; then you can restore it later if needed.

The following steps describe how to create a list template based on an existing SharePoint list. The example uses a document library, but any type of SharePoint list offers the ability to create a template from it. To create a list template, the user must have the Manage Lists right for the list (the Web Designer and Administrator groups have this right by default) and have the right to add items to the list template gallery for the list's parent site collection.

1. Navigate to the target list in SharePoint, and click the Settings drop-down menu above the contents of the list. Select the Document Library Settings option, as shown in Figure 2.25.

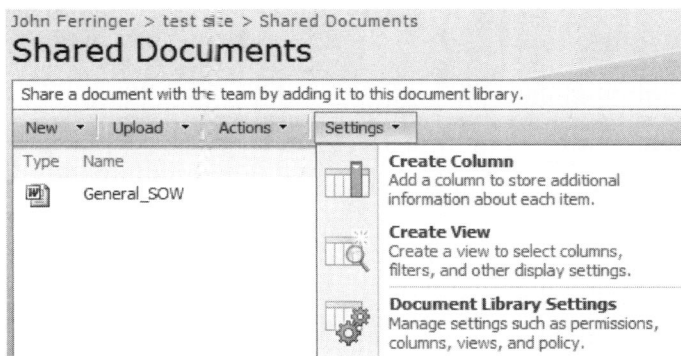

FIGURE 2.25 The Settings drop-down menu in a SharePoint document library.

2. When the Customize [*List Name*] page opens, click the Save [*List Type*] as Template link in the Permissions and Management section. Figure 2.26 has an example of the Customize page for a document library titled Shared Documents.

3. In the Save as Template page (see Figure 2.27), enter a file name for the .stp (template) file, a template name that is displayed when it is used to create new lists, and a template description. (This field is optional.) Make sure to select the Include Content check box to preserve your list's contents. Click the OK button to create the list.

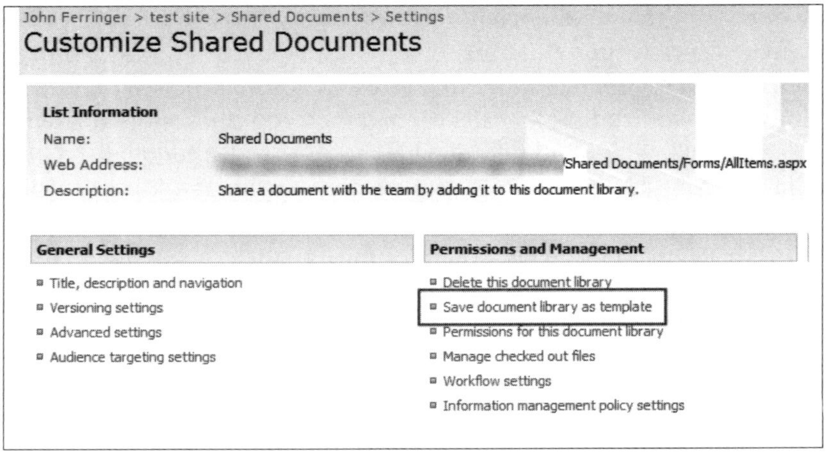

FIGURE 2.26 In the Customize [*List Name*] page, click the link highlighted here to create a template based on the list.

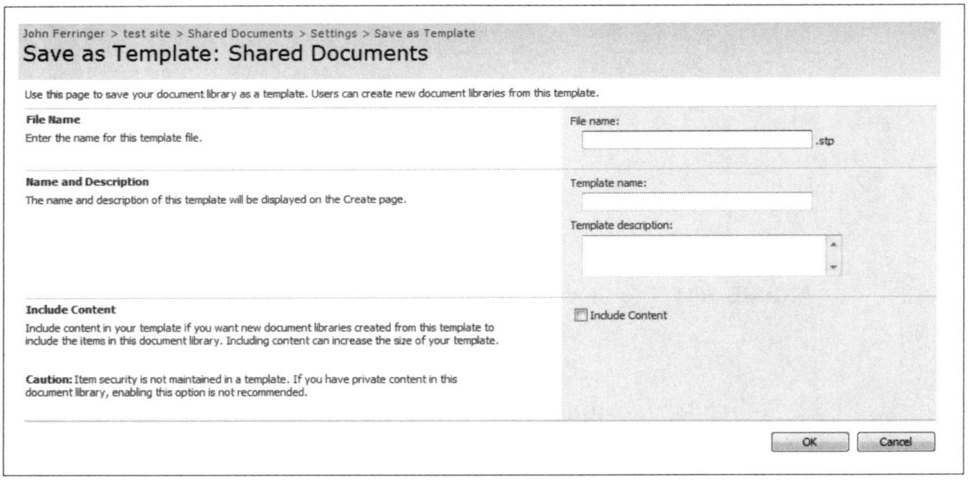

FIGURE 2.27 The Save as Template page.

By default, SharePoint's Save as Template functionality is limited to the creation of template files that are no greater than 10MB. You can adjust this limit upward to a maximum of 500MB, but doing so affects all sites within a SharePoint farm. The process for performing this change is beyond the scope of this book, but you can find additional information describing the procedure (and items you should consider before attempting it) at http://technet.microsoft.com/en-us/library/ cc424962.aspx.

4. When the operation completes, SharePoint displays a page stating `Operation Completed Successfully`, as shown in Figure 2.28. To save the newly created template, click the List Template Gallery link.

John Ferringer > test site > Operation Completed Successfully
Operation Completed Successfully

The template has successfully been saved to the list template gallery. You can now create lists based on this template.

To manage templates in the gallery, go to the list template gallery.

To return to the list customization page, click **OK**.

OK

FIGURE 2.28 After the list template has been created, a page is displayed stating that the operation completed successfully.

5. The Link Template Gallery page is opened in the browser. To save the list template to your workstation, right-click on the linked name of the template and select the Save Target As option from the menu. (If you are using a browser other than Internet Explorer, this option may be named differently.) Select the desired storage location and save the file.

The newly created list template is stored in a gallery within the parent site collection for the list, regardless of whether the list resides in a subsite within the site collection.

NOTE

Because list templates are stored in a list template gallery within SharePoint, you can manage them like any other document in any other library within Share-Point. As you have already seen, you can download them to your local computer and upload them from your computer when you need to restore the list and its contents. After the list template is stored in the site collection's gallery, you can use it to create a list within any subsite in the site collection. The preserved contents of the list are present in the restored list, along with the columns and metadata for those contents.

There are drawbacks to backing up content via a list template export. First, this is a manual process that must be executed by a user and cannot be systematically executed without creating a custom application. So you cannot schedule this action to run on a regular basis; a user has to personally create the list template to preserve its contents. Just as importantly, aspects of the list are not retained when you export its contents to a template, such as security and attachment settings for the list as well as any columns containing lookup data from other lists. Keep these drawbacks in mind when considering this option to back up and restore your SharePoint lists. Although the option is appealing in many ways for end users, it isn't well suited as an enterprise-level solution.

WEBDAV AND EXPLORER VIEW

One interesting, yet often overlooked, method to access the contents of a Share-Point site and its lists is through Windows Explorer, using either the Explorer View option available on SharePoint lists or a protocol known as WebDAV. SharePoint's Explorer View functionality opens a SharePoint library or list in Windows Explorer so that you can manage files in a SharePoint list in the same way you manage files in a folder in a Windows operating system. WebDAV allows users to access those contents within the familiar folder structure of Windows Explorer via a Universal Naming Convention (UNC) path.

The ability to access a SharePoint site, document library, or other type of list via Windows Explorer is pretty powerful, because it allows end users to easily manage the files and items in those repositories like they would any other folders in their Windows workstation's operating system, rather than using the limiting and tedious tools available through a browser. With the Windows Explorer interface, a user can drag a document into a SharePoint list to add it, rather than clicking through multiple Web pages, and do the same to copy that file back down to his workstation. Even more importantly, this can be easily done with multiple files, which can save a great deal of time.

To access a SharePoint resource, such as a document library, in Explorer View, navigate to the target resource in a Web browser and click the list's Actions drop-down menu. If your SharePoint environment and client workstation are properly configured to enable Explorer View, an option labeled Open with Explorer View is visible and enabled in the menu. Select the option to open the resource in Windows Explorer and begin managing its contents.

To open a SharePoint resource via WebDAV, you must translate the resource's SharePoint URL into a Windows Explorer–friendly UNC path. You can accomplish this by copying the target URL into a text file. (Don't include the `.aspx` file name at the end of URL; focus only on the folder objects above that file so you can open the containing object for the resource and not an item within it.) Remove http:// at the beginning of the address and replace it with \\. Replace all forward slashes (/) with backslashes (\). Then copy the address, paste it into the address bar of a Windows Explorer window, and press Enter to load the address. The SharePoint resource now opens as a folder within Windows Explorer on your desktop.

Like the list template, Explorer View and WebDAV let you easily copy the contents of a SharePoint list down to your local workstation for backup purposes and likewise restore them to the resource as needed. They use a familiar interface, and the commands to manage the files within them are simple and common to Windows operating systems. But, like list templates, end users must manually execute them, and they are better suited to one-time actions whereby an end user wants to create a copy of crucial content.

Another drawback to these tools is their difficulty to configure and be usable on a consistent basis. An end user's ability to use Explorer View is greatly impacted by the combination of his client's operating system, Web browser, and the versions of both items. Even when those are configured optimally (which can be difficult in environments with a variety of workstation configurations), Explorer View has been found to be slow, prone to crashing, or simply unusable at times.

Explorer View and WebDAV suffer from additional dependencies on client configuration. For WebDAV to work, for example, the WebClient service must be running on the client workstation you're using to access the SharePoint resource. The list of server-side configuration requirements is even longer. (For example, target resources must not reside within a Web application running on a custom TCP port if they are to be accessed via the WebDAV redirector.) Because these items can be tricky to configure and troubleshoot within your SharePoint environment, it is not recommended that you view Explorer View and WebDAV as viable disaster recovery options, but rather as potential tools for your users to preserve their content without having to engage an administrative resource or tool.

CONCLUSION

As an end user, you now have the power to harness the tools in this chapter. You can partake in the disaster recovery process by managing how changes to your content are stored and tracked. Open SharePoint, and try to use some of the tools listed in this chapter. That way, you can gain a better understanding of disaster recovery from the end user perspective. If you feel comfortable with the lessons that you have learned in this chapter, feel free to move on Chapter 3, "SharePoint Designer's Backup and Restore Tools." To test your comfort level, here is a list of questions that you should be able to answer after reading this chapter. You can find the answers to these questions in Appendix B, "Chapter Review Q&A," on the book's Web site at http://www.courseptr.com/downloads.

1. Who can view the End User Recycle Bins? Where is the Site Collection Recycle Bin? Who can turn on recycle bins in Central Administration?
2. What is the difference between the End User Recycle Bin and the Site Collection Recycle Bin?

3. Where are quotas set for an application? What access level does a user need to set these quotas? Can quotas exist on a document library or list?
4. When setting up versioning, can minor versions only exist?
5. Who can set up versioning on a list or library?
6. Is versioning automatically turned on in a document library?
7. How many major and minor versions are allowed at a given point in time on a document library or list?
8. If a person with Contribute access deletes an item in the Version History section, is the item moved to the End User Recycle Bin?

3 | SharePoint Designer's Backup and Restore Tools

Contributions by Becky Isserman

In This Chapter

- SharePoint Designer Backup and Restore
- SharePoint Designer Backup Options
- How to Back Up and Restore with SharePoint Designer
- Pros and Cons of SharePoint Designer Backups

As a SharePoint administrator, you may find that it is not always a good idea to back up an entire site collection in SharePoint, especially if you are targeting only a small subset of the content contained within the entire site collection. Sometimes you may just want to back up and restore a single list, library, or site without the subsites attached. Although it is not possible to get that kind of granularity with the out-of-the-box tools available when you install SharePoint, Microsoft does provide a tool that, among other things, allows you to back up and restore those smaller items within a site collection. That tool is Microsoft Office SharePoint Designer 2007 (or simply "SharePoint Designer").

In SharePoint Designer, site collection administrators can back up single sites, lists, or libraries, unlike tools like the Central Administration site's backup and restore tool and STSADM.exe, which can only back up and restore items to the site collection level. This chapter introduces you to the three options in SharePoint Designer to back up items, the process for backing up and restoring these items, and the benefits and drawbacks of using each option.

The visual examples provided in this chapter were generated in a testing environment using the platforms and components listed next. Depending on how your environment is configured, your experiences may vary slightly. Unless a specific item indicates that it is unique to Microsoft Office SharePoint Server 2007 (MOSS), the features and functionality covered in this chapter apply to both Windows SharePoint Services version 3 (WSS) and MOSS in the same fashion.

- **Operating system.** Microsoft Windows Server 2003 R2 Enterprise Edition Service Pack (SP) 2
- **Microsoft .NET Framework.** Versions 1.1, 2.0 SP1, 3.0 SP 1, and 3.5
- **Database.** Microsoft SQL Server 2005 Developer Edition Service Pack 2
- **Web server.** Microsoft Internet Information Services (IIS) 6.0
- **SharePoint.** MOSS 2007 Enterprise Edition

In addition to the aforementioned server and associated components, a copy of SharePoint Designer with Microsoft Office 2007 Service Pack 1 must be installed and available for use. Though SharePoint Designer can be installed on the server alongside MOSS for attachment to the local SharePoint environment, it is more commonly installed on a client workstation for end-user, designer, and remote administrator access.

NOTE *SharePoint Designer is not included in the same licensing package as MOSS or WSS 3.0. This product is a standalone tool that Microsoft created to complement SharePoint as part of the Office 2007 Suite. Please contact Microsoft for information on licensing for this product.*

SharePoint Designer Backup and Restore

SharePoint Designer is a tool that affords users (specifically, those with some form of contribution rights) the ability to design, customize, administer, and affect various other powerful changes upon SharePoint sites. This chapter is designed to discuss only the backup and restore capabilities of SharePoint Designer within the context of disaster recovery planning and execution. For more details on the full set of SharePoint Designer's design and management capabilities, see Microsoft's product documentation or any of several books on the market devoted to the product.

A Brief History of SharePoint Designer

Prior to 2007, the SharePoint Designer product line was known by a different name: FrontPage. Obtained in the acquisition of Vermeer Technologies Incorporated in January 1996, Microsoft quickly pressed FrontPage into service as its flagship tool for managing Web sites in an end-user-friendly what-you-see-is-what-you-get (WYSIWYG) fashion. In its original form, FrontPage was not associated with SharePoint. By 2003, however, FrontPage had grown into something of a Swiss army knife of Web functionality—and that functionality included the ability to customize Windows SharePoint Services 2.0 and SharePoint Portal Server 2003 sites.

While the strategy for the SharePoint 2007 server line was being considered and planned in 2006, Microsoft was reevaluating its approach with regard to FrontPage and Web editing in general. Rather than continue forward with "one tool to rule them all," Microsoft made the decision to instead break FrontPage's functionality into two distinctly different products. Microsoft Expression Web Designer (not covered in this book) was ordained the next-generation, standards-based, WYSIWIG Web site editor, while SharePoint Designer was established to specifically address the site design and customization needs of those working within SharePoint environments.

Even today, a number of conventions from the Vermeer approach to Web technology can still be found across Microsoft product lines, including SharePoint. The _vti prefix (for Vermeer Technologies Incorporated) within the server-side file system directories of SharePoint Web sites is but one example of this.

Accessing a Site in SharePoint Designer

To use SharePoint Designer to back up and restore a site to another farm's site collection or area in the same site collection, you must have access to both site collections as a site collection administrator. As mentioned earlier, you can install SharePoint Designer on a server in your SharePoint farm, or for greater convenience, locally on your client workstation. To connect to a SharePoint site, open SharePoint Designer and click on the File menu. Then click Open a Site, type in your site collection's Uniform Resource Locator (URL), and click the Open button. Notice a series of folders that look like the site's lists and libraries open in SharePoint Designer, as seen in Figure 3.1.

NOTE

If you receive an error message and cannot access a site in SharePoint Designer, you may need to contact the Farm Administrator for the SharePoint environment or the site collection's primary administrator for assistance. You may not have the correct rights within the site to manage it with SharePoint Designer, or the farm may be configured to prevent sites from being accessed by the tool. The latter is a common step that administrators take to ensure design consistency throughout a SharePoint farm and aid with future upgrades to the system.

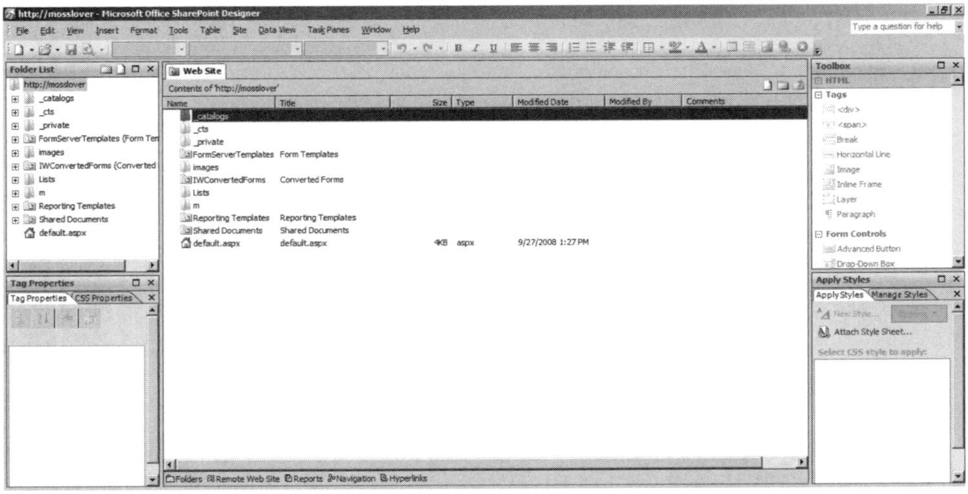

FIGURE 3.1 A site opened in SharePoint Designer.

SHAREPOINT DESIGNER BACKUP OPTIONS

SharePoint Designer has three options available to back up all or part of a site collection and its subsites in SharePoint Designer. These options are shown in Figures 3.2 and 3.3. Figure 3.2 shows the Export menu on the File menu in SharePoint Designer. Figure 3.3 shows the Administration menu underneath the Site menu in SharePoint Designer. The options included in both menus combined are

- Personal Web Package
- SharePoint Site Template
- Backup Web Site

These three options and how to perform a backup and restore using each option are discussed in further detail later in this chapter.

PERSONAL WEB PACKAGE

The Personal Web Package menu item appears on the File Export menu. The creation of a Personal Web Package results in a single file that contains one or more reusable elements that have been extracted from a SharePoint site. When a Personal Web Package is exported, the file that is created is assigned an extension of `.fwp` (for "FrontPage Web Package"—a legacy carryover from the previous incarnation of SharePoint Designer). This file can then be opened later within SharePoint Designer and its contents imported into one or more sites of the user's choosing.

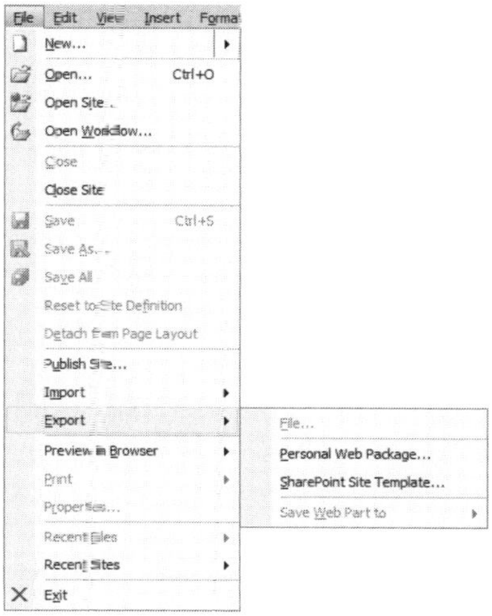

FIGURE 3.2 The File Export menu in SharePoint Designer.

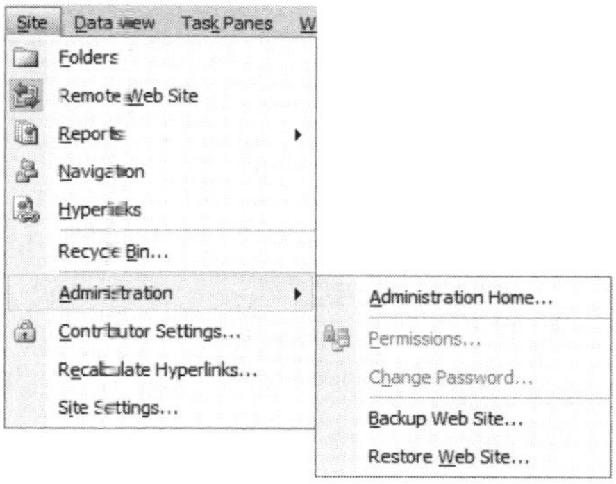

FIGURE 3.3 The Site Administration menu in SharePoint Designer.

Personal Web Packages have numerous characteristics that distinguish them from the other backup methods described in this chapter. First, Personal Web Packages focus on structural reuse, not data reuse. Personal Web Packages can be used to export site elements such as lists, libraries, and pages. They can also be used to export documents residing within lists and libraries. They cannot, however, be used to export list data and other nonstructural items (e.g., security information, alerts, etc.) This notion of a "structural template" makes a Personal Web Package the ideal building block for the implementation of identical functionality across one or more SharePoint sites.

Another noteworthy aspect of Personal Web Packages is the relative flexibility you have when selecting the items to be included in them from within SharePoint Designer. Some backup methods, like the Backup Web Site method (discussed soon), insist on an all-or-nothing approach by requiring you to back up the entire site. Others enforce a hierarchical approach where the element selected is the starting point for the backup; that is, the selected element is included, plus all its child elements, plus all their child elements, and so on. In contrast to these approaches, Personal Web Packages allow users to pick and choose structural items from within a site to be included in the resultant export file in a rather freeform fashion. An entire site could be exported, a single element could be exported, or any combination of elements in between. Users simply pick and choose the items they want to include from a tree view control, and those items are the ones that are exported.

Finally, Personal Web Packages offer several options for the identification of dependencies, or those items required for proper functioning of the exported content once it is imported into a new site. As part of the Personal Web Package creation process, internal dependencies (items that exist within the site and upon which the exported content depends) can be automatically included within the exported Personal Web Package file. External dependencies, on the other hand, can be identified but cannot actually be packaged within the exported file.

Personal Web Packages are ideal for exporting structural elements, but there are some guidelines that should be observed when using them. Generally speaking, you should base the destination site for the contents of a Personal Web Package on the same platform (WSS or MOSS) and site definition (Team Site, Collaboration Portal, and so on) as the originating site. Moving content across platforms or between site types may result in aberrant behavior (for example, attempting to import a WSS Personal Web Package into a MOSS My Site). If you're going to perform cross-platform or cross-site type exports/imports, test them in a nonproduction environment first.

From a disaster recovery perspective, Personal Web Packages can be used to granularly store site elements to expedite the rare recovery plan that involves the manual regeneration of SharePoint sites. Although data would have to be handled through some other mechanism, sites could potentially be "snapped together" through carefully organized and documented Personal Web Packages. Such an approach is not advised, however. Because a significant number of follow-up steps would be required to add users, apply permissions, import data, and more, there is little to recommend the use of Personal Web Packages in any formal disaster recovery capacity. Well-written disaster recovery plans seek to avoid manual intervention wherever possible, so at best this makes the use of Personal Web Packages a fallback plan in the event that a better, more complete, primary recovery strategy goes awry.

Simply put, Personal Web Packages serve best in their intended role: copying structural elements between sites and as a quick, granular backup of site structures on a limited subfarm scale.

SHAREPOINT SITE TEMPLATE

The other option that appears on the File Export menu, SharePoint Site Template, affords the user the capability of exporting an entire site as a standard SharePoint Site Template file. Site Template files are single-file exports that possess an .stp file extension and can be downloaded from a site collection's Site Template Gallery following generation. To create a SharePoint Site Template, a user must have both administrative rights to the target site and write access to the parent site collection's Site Template Gallery.

NOTE

Despite the fact that template generation originates within SharePoint Designer, the process of creating a SharePoint Site Template file doesn't actually occur within SharePoint Designer; it occurs within the system's default browser. After you select the SharePoint Site Template menu item from the File Export menu, a browser window is launched and you're directed to the savetmpl.aspx *admin page within the target SharePoint site. The functionality of this admin page was discussed in the "List Templates" section of Chapter 2, "End User Resources." All features and constraints that are attributed to the List Templates in that section apply equally to the SharePoint Site Templates described in this section; beyond the scope of what they include, there is no appreciable difference between the two.*

TIP

If Internet Explorer is not your default browser, you may encounter problems attempting to export a SharePoint Site Template from SharePoint Designer. For example, the message A world wide web browser, such as Windows Internet Explorer, is required to use this feature *is commonly seen when Firefox is the default system browser. Older versions of Opera commonly report* The server requested a login authentication method that is not supported, *though newer versions properly handle authentication. If browser issues are encountered, the easiest path to resolution is to make Internet Explorer the default system browser.*

SharePoint Site Templates differ from Personal Web Packages in a couple of important ways. First, SharePoint Site Templates (as originated from within SharePoint Designer) are an all-or-nothing proposition; the only option is to package up the entire target site and export it as an .stp file. No option exists for the partial export of some of a site's elements; everything in the site must be included.

Another important distinction between SharePoint Site Template and Personal Web Packages centers on content. Whereas Personal Web Packages can only export the structural elements of a site, SharePoint Site Templates can be used to export both the structure and content (list items, custom workflows, and so on) of a site. The export of content is optional.

Although they can package site content along with structure, SharePoint Site Templates do carry a couple of significant disadvantages. Like Personal Web Packages, SharePoint Site Templates do not capture security information, alerts, and other information that is tied to specific users. The inclusion or exclusion of content within the SharePoint Site Template export does not alter this behavior.

SharePoint Site Templates are not supported for use with publishing sites (sites for which the Office SharePoint Server Publishing Infrastructure Feature is enabled). This is primarily because the template export process does not capture the page layouts that publishing pages use.

CAUTION

Practically speaking, the biggest constraint to the use of Site Templates comes in the form of the default 10MB limit on SharePoint template exports. As described in Chapter 2, attempts to export a template file in excess of 10MB result in failure. This makes the SharePoint Site Template export operation impractical for many sites; this is doubly true if the intent is to export content along with the structural site information.

Although extremely limited in their usefulness as a disaster recovery tool, Site Templates could still be leveraged in roughly the same fashion as Personal Web Packages in the rare recovery strategy that is based on the manual recreation of sites and site structures. As was mentioned with Personal Web Packages, though, proven disaster recovery strategies seek to minimize the number of manual steps required during recovery stages. For this reason, it is recommended that Site Templates be relegated to the ranks of "secondary strategies" (in a disaster recovery sense) and be left to do what they do best: act as templates for the creation of a particular type of site, with or without content.

BACKUP WEB SITE

SharePoint Designer's final backup option, Backup Web Site, is available from the Administration submenu within the application's main Site menu. The Backup Web Site functionality is the closest mechanism to a full-fidelity backup option within SharePoint Designer. To perform a Backup Web Site operation, you must have administrative rights within the site that is to be backed up. Execution of the Backup Web Site operation results in the generation of a single backup file possessing a `.cmp` (for Content Migration Package) extension.

For additional information on content migration packages, see the "STSADM Backup/Restore versus STSADM Export/Import" section of Chapter 5, "STSADM.exe's Backup and Restore Operations."

Like the SharePoint Site Template export option, the Backup Web Site operation is an all-or-nothing proposition. No option exists to back up specific items or a portion of the site in the same way that Personal Web Packages do.

The Backup Web Site operation distinguishes itself from both the Personal Web Package and Site Template mechanisms in one important way, though; whereas Personal Web Packages and Site Templates can only target one site within a site collection (be it the site collection root or an individual site lower in the site hierarchy), the Backup Web Site operation can recursively target a site and all its subsites. This feature of the Backup Web Site operation is typically leveraged to back up a site collection (starting at the root site) and capture all sites/subsites within just one pass, but it can also be used to back up a single site (and everything below it) within a site collection.

As mentioned earlier, the Backup Web Site operation is the closest thing Share-Point Designer offers to a full-fidelity backup. Once underway, the backup captures structural information such as lists and libraries; it also captures all list data within the site. Additionally, the Backup Web Site operation captures security settings, user information, personalized content, SharePoint Designer–originated customizations, and more. There are a handful of items that aren't captured by this operation, but the list is relatively small: custom data view Web parts, workflow tasks, and any associated state, alerts, recycle bin items, change log history, and audit trails.

Whereas the Personal Web Backup and SharePoint Site Template export options are geared toward the construction of building blocks and their reuse, the Backup Web Site operation is oriented toward copying or moving an entire site from one location to another. You might use the Backup Web Site option, for instance, to move whole sites between farm environments.

Behind the scenes, the Backup Web Site operation is actually executed by SharePoint as an export through the Content Migration (PRIME) API. This fact is mentioned here for one important reason: under normal circumstances, the maximum file size on a file exported using the Content Migration API is limited to 24MB. Because SharePoint Designer doesn't offer a way to adjust this value or save multiple files, 24MB becomes the practical limit on the size of content that can be backed up using the Backup Web Site operation.

The Backup Web Site operation is the most useful of the SharePoint Designer backup methods from the perspective of a disaster recovery plan. Unlike the other two export methods previously described, this operation captures most of the information (for example, user information and permission assignments) that the other methods don't. It also allows the capture of an entire site collection, including subsites. Not all information is captured, though, and the operation must still be carried out manually through the SharePoint Designer interface. The Backup Web Site operation can't match the power and flexibility of the SharePoint platform's intrinsic backup functions (discussed in Chapter 4, "The Central Administration Site's Backup and Restore Tools," and Chapter 5), but it can afford some peace of mind to site administrators seeking to do something on their own for the purposes of disaster recovery.

There are specific (and sometimes unusual) circumstances under which a backup of larger than 24MB can be generated, and there are unsupported tricks that can be leveraged to stretch SharePoint Designer's capabilities in this area. If you're using the Backup Web Site operation to back up content larger than 24MB, you may encounter inconsistent results and should test your results as much as possible. For mission-critical backups, it's recommend that 24MB be regarded as the functional limit for Backup Web Site operations.

HOW TO BACK UP AND RESTORE WITH SHAREPOINT DESIGNER

The previous section discussed the three options available in SharePoint Designer. This section discusses how to use these options to back up and restore your files using the Personal Web Package, SharePoint Site Template, and Backup Web Site options.

HOW TO PERFORM A BACKUP AND RESTORE USING A PERSONAL WEB PACKAGE

This section illustrates the process of creating, and then importing, a Personal Web Package. To work through the examples that follow, ensure that SharePoint Designer is open. Make sure you have two SharePoint sites available to you: one with content that can be exported as a Personal Web Package, and another site into which you can import the elements stored within your Personal Web Package.

Backing Up a Site with the Personal Web Package Option

To illustrate how to employ a Personal Web Package, this section begins by illustrating the steps needed to create such a package from within SharePoint Designer.

1. To perform a backup, open SharePoint Designer and open the site where you want to back up the items.
2. Click on File, Export, Personal Web Package, as seen in Figure 3.4.
3. Figure 3.5 shows the menu that pops up after you choose the option in step 2. Highlight the items that you want to back up and click the Add button.

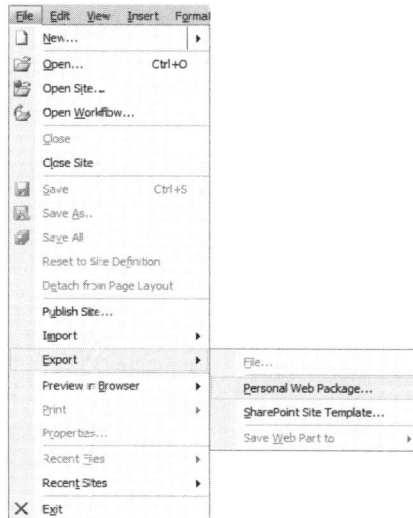

FIGURE 3.4 The Personal Web Package menu option in the File menu under Export in SharePoint Designer.

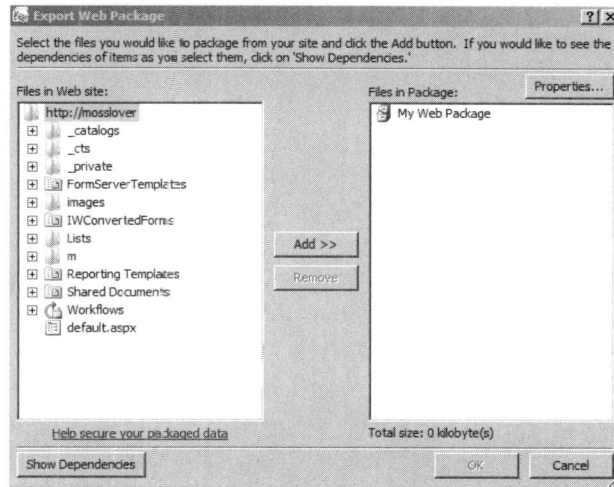

FIGURE 3.5 Export Web Package dialog box in SharePoint Designer.

4. SharePoint Designer pauses for a minute (depending on the number of files copied), and then you see the items move to the other side of the menu, as in Figure 3.6.

If a folder containing one or more items is selected for inclusion, a prompt appears after the folder has been added to the package. The prompt gives you the option of adding the contents of the folder to the package in addition to just the folder itself.

NOTE

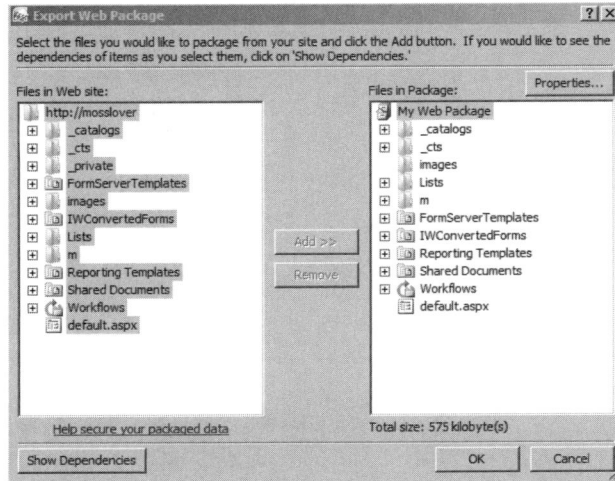

FIGURE 3.6 Export Web Package dialog box in SharePoint Designer after items are added to backup.

5. You can use the Show Dependencies button at the bottom left of the dialog to toggle the display of items that the package depends on for proper functioning. These internal dependencies are included in the Personal Web Package during export to ensure that the selected elements (from step 3) operate as desired when imported into a new site. The internal dependencies area also includes a drop-down list box that permits the selection of the extent to which dependency checking is performed. Through this drop-down, you can override dependency checking and inclusion altogether; by default, though, all dependent items (except hyperlinks) are detected and included in the export package. See Figure 3.7.

6. After you've selected all files for inclusion within the package, click the Properties button near the upper-right corner of the dialog box. This launches the Web Package Properties dialog seen in Figure 3.8. It is in this dialog that you can specify additional information describing the Personal Web Package, including title, description, author, and company. The dialog also supplies a couple of useful pieces of information—specifically, the size of the data to be packaged and any external dependencies upon which

the final exported package will depend. Unlike the internal dependencies described previously, external dependencies shown in this dialog are not included within the package that is exported. For this reason, you should verify that the dependencies cited are present and available within the target environment when a Personal Web Package import is performed in a new site.

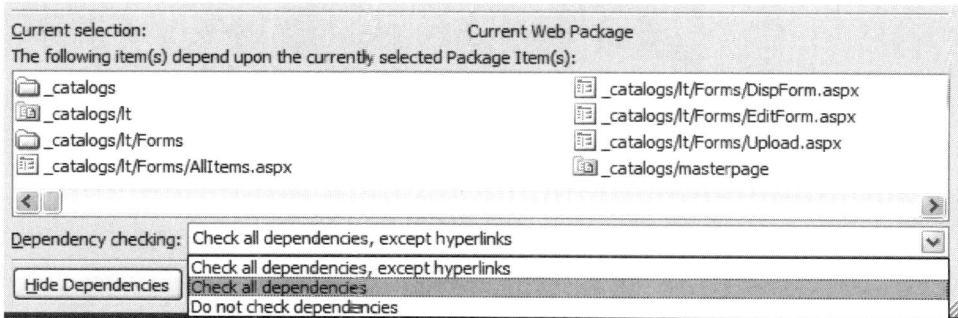

FIGURE 3.7 The internal dependencies area of the Export Web Package dialog box.

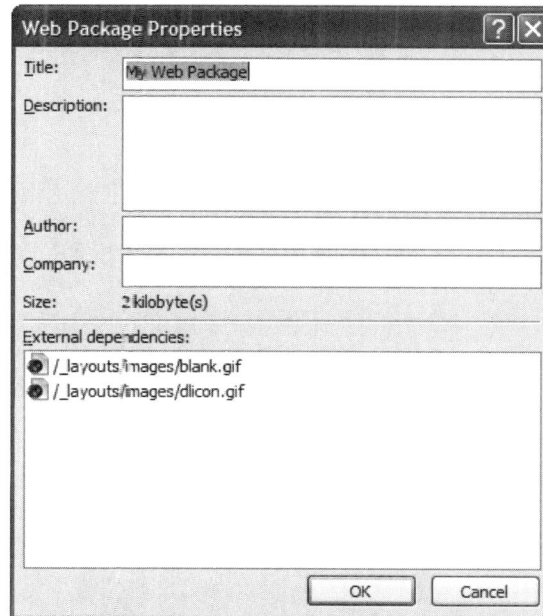

FIGURE 3.8 The Web Package Properties dialog box.

7. Once all files have been selected and Web package properties have been specified, click the OK button on the Export Web Package dialog. A window pops up, as in Figure 3.9, and you can choose an area to save your export. Choose the directory on a network or local drive to save the file, type in a name for the file, and click on the Save button.

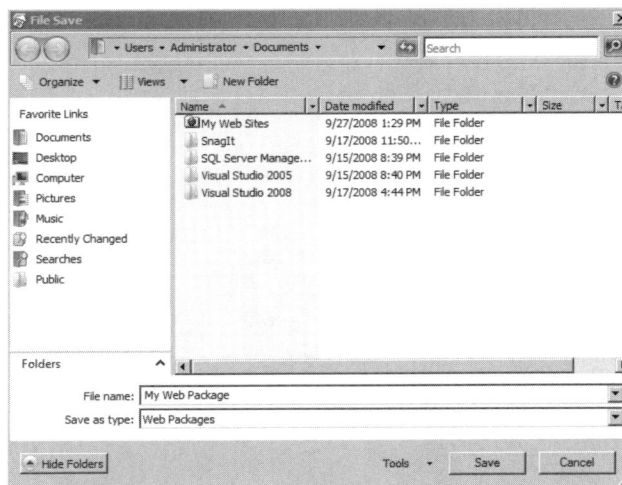

FIGURE 3.9 SharePoint Designer's File Save dialog box.

Once the Save button is clicked, the export of the Personal Web Package begins. The aggregate size of the elements to be packaged determines how long the export operation takes to complete. A few kilobytes may appear to export almost instantaneously, whereas 100MB may take several minutes. Keep this in mind if it appears that the system has hung or become nonresponsive.

8. When the backup is complete, a dialog box appears, as in Figure 3.10. Click OK.

FIGURE 3.10 The Web Package save completion dialog box.

Restoring a Personal Web Package Backup

At this point, it is assumed that a Personal Web Package file (with an .fwp extension) is available for the deployment of one or more elements exported from a source site. The following steps describe the process of importing the desired elements into the target site.

1. To perform a restore, open SharePoint Designer and open the site where you want to restore the items.
2. Click on File, Import, Personal Web Package, as seen in Figure 3.11

FIGURE 3.11 The Personal Web Package menu option in the File menu under Import in SharePoint Designer.

3. You see the File Open window, like the one in Figure 3.12. Navigate to the .fwp file that you want to restore and double-click on it.
4. You see a list of the items included in the Web package, as shown in Figure 3.13. Check the boxes next to the items that you want to restore and click Import. The Destination URL that is shown can also be altered to perform an asymmetric import (that is, an import of the package contents to a higher or lower location in the namespace hierarchy of the target site than may have existed in the source). For example, a document library that existed at http://oldsite/documents in the source site could be imported to http://newsite/differentlevel/documents. In this example, if the differentlevel folder didn't exist in the target site, it would be created during the import process.

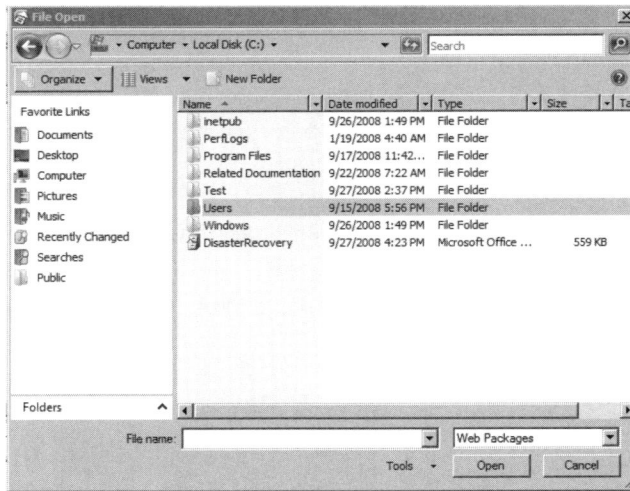

FIGURE 3.12 File Open dialog box.

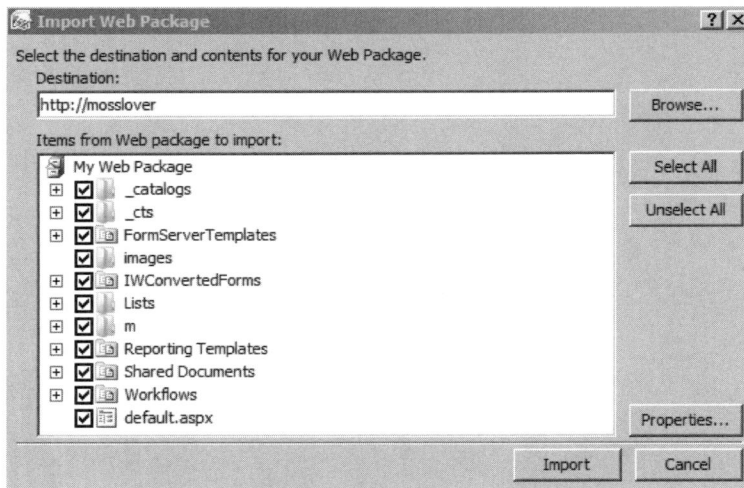

FIGURE 3.13 Import Web Package window.

After you click the Import button, a security warning dialog box appears. This dialog box appears because Personal Web Packages can contain scripting and code that could negatively impact your site or worse. As a general rule of thumb, you shouldn't import a Personal Web Package unless you're familiar with its contents and trust its source/originator.

The Property button shows package information (such as the title and description) that was assigned when the Personal Web Package was created. Additionally, the package's external dependencies are displayed. These files don't exist within the Personal Web Package, so it's the responsibility of the individual performing the import to ensure that the listed files are available within the target site or environment.

5. The dialog box shown in Figure 3.14 is displayed, depicting the progress of the restore operation. When you see a dialog box pop up like in Figure 3.15, click OK. The import is complete, and you can now navigate to the restored item within your SharePoint site.

If a conflict is encountered during the import process (that is, a file being imported would overwrite an existing file within the target site), a dialog box asks you whether you want to overwrite the existing file or have it renamed so that the imported file can be used in its place. This prompt appears each time you encounter a conflict.

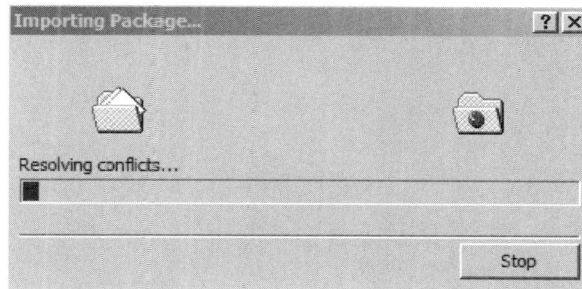

FIGURE 3.14 The Importing Package dialog box.

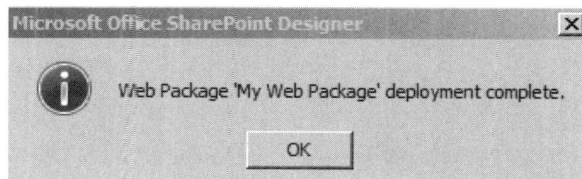

FIGURE 3.15 Web Package deployment completion dialog box.

How to Perform a Backup and Restore Using a Site Template

The next set of examples focuses on the creation of a Site Template in a source site and its subsequent export, followed by an import of the Site Template and its use within a target site. For these examples, it's recommended that you have two Share-Point sites available to you: one with content that you can generate a Site Template from, and another that you can import and apply your Site Template into. You must have site administrator access in both sites, and you need read/write permissions to each site collection's Site Template Gallery.

Backing Up a Site with a Site Template

The process begins with the generation of a Site Template from an existing site you want to export for later use.

1. Open SharePoint Designer and navigate to File, Export, SharePoint Site Template, as seen in Figure 3.16.

FIGURE 3.16 The SharePoint Site Template option on the Export section of the File menu.

2. After you select the SharePoint Site Template menu item, a browser window opens (as seen in Figure 3.17) to the current SharePoint site's Save as Template page (`savetmpl.aspx`). Enter a name for the Site Template file in the File Name field, making sure that the value provided does not include spaces. Fill out the Name and Description fields with text that makes the resultant Site Template easily recognizable, because these are the fields

that are displayed when the Site Template is presented for possible selection on the New SharePoint Site page. Note that spaces are permitted (and encouraged) in the Template name and description fields. Check the check box next to Include Content if you want to include content on the site, and then click OK to start the Site Template creation operation.

By default, the exported Site Template and any content it may contain is limited to 10MB. Attempting to generate a Site Template that contains more than 10MB will fail with an error.

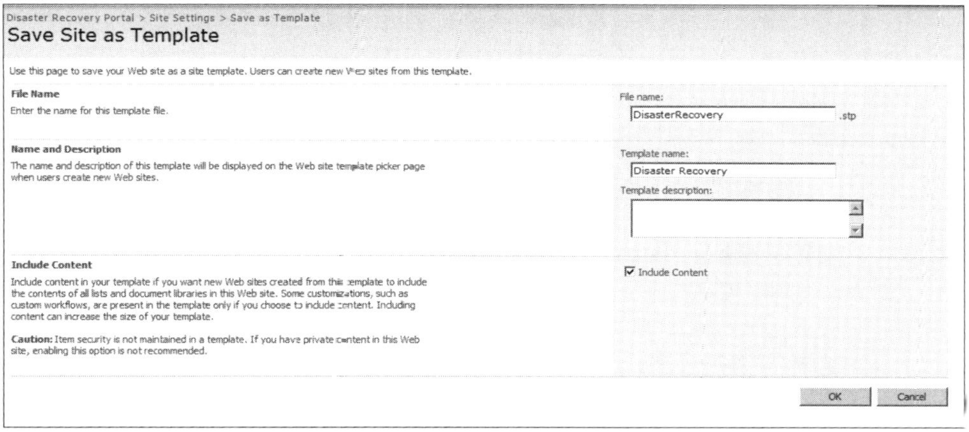

NOTE

FIGURE 3.17 Save Site as Template form.

3. Upon successful completion of the Site Template generation process, a success page is displayed, as seen in Figure 3.18. At this point, the Site Template is available within the parent site collection's Site Template Gallery. Click the site template gallery link on the page to direct the browser to the gallery.

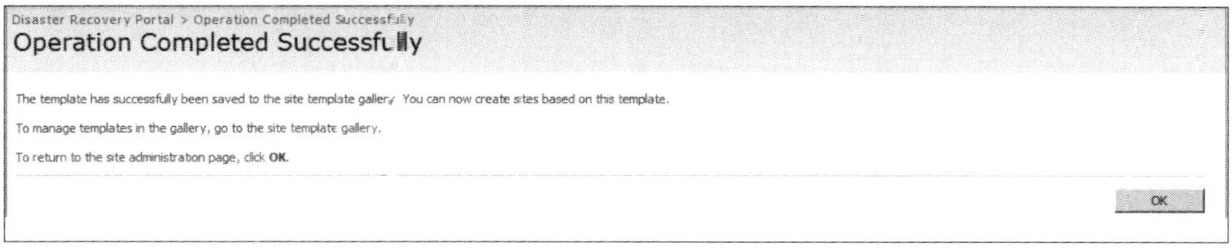

FIGURE 3.18 Operation Completed Successfully page after saving a site template.

4. Navigating to the site collection's Site Template Gallery presents a page similar to Figure 3.19. The addition of the DisasterRecovery template link is easily seen, complete with the !New tag next to it. To download the Site Template from the gallery for local storage, right-click on the Disaster-Recovery link and select Save Target As from the pop-up menu that appears.

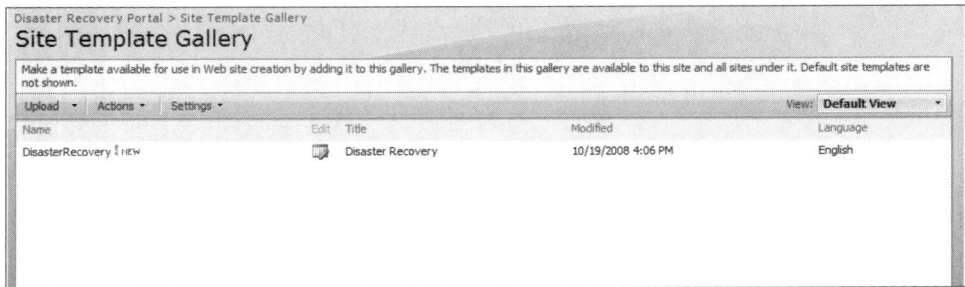

FIGURE 3.19 The Site Template Gallery.

5. A Save As dialog box appears, as seen in Figure 3.20. Navigate to the location on the local system where the Site Template file (named DisasterRecovery.stp by default) should be saved, and then click the Save button. This brings the template from the SharePoint site down to your local system. Remember the location where the file is saved for use in the next exercise. At this point you can move or copy the .stp file from your local system to anywhere you want so it can be preserved according to your requirements.

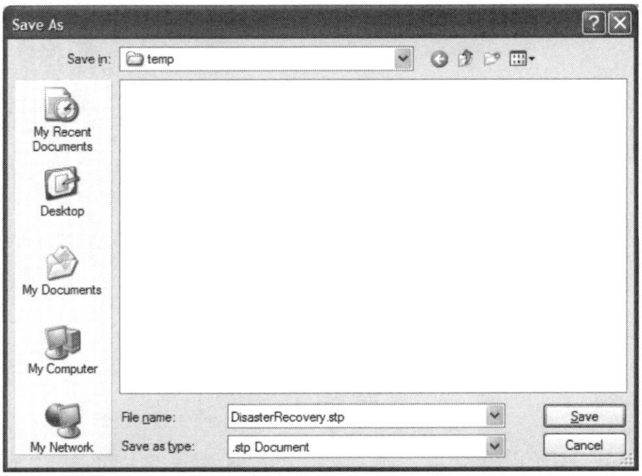

FIGURE 3.20 The Save As dialog box for the Site Template file.

Restoring a Site Template

The process of restoring a Site Template for use is basically the reverse of what was performed in the previous exercise. Restoration begins with a Site Template import and is concluded with the creation of a new subsite from the imported Site Template.

1. Open a browser and navigate to the root site of the SharePoint site collection that the Site Template will be imported into. Once there, select the Site Settings option from the Site Actions menu, as seen in Figure 3.21.

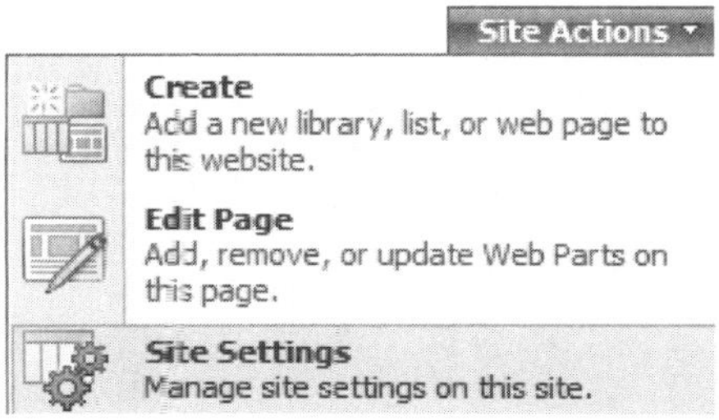

FIGURE 3.21 Selecting Site Settings from the Site Actions menu.

2. The Site Settings administration page appears. Locate the Site Templates link under the list of Galleries options near the middle of the page (see Figure 3.22). Follow this link to open the Site Templates Gallery page.

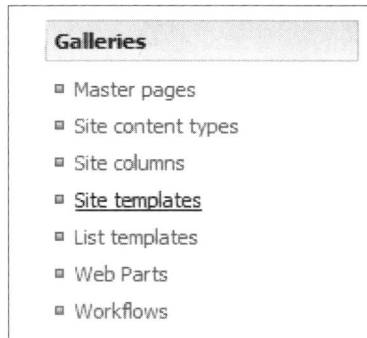

FIGURE 3.22 The Site Templates link under the Galleries column.

3. When the Site Templates Gallery page appears, select the Upload Document menu item from within the Upload menu (see Figure 3.23). This directs the browser to the Upload Template: Site Template Gallery page, as seen in Figure 3.24. Once there, click the Browse button.

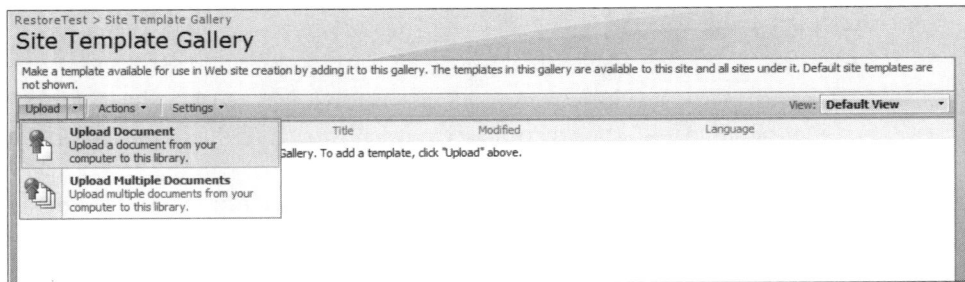

FIGURE 3.23 The Upload menu within the Site Template Gallery.

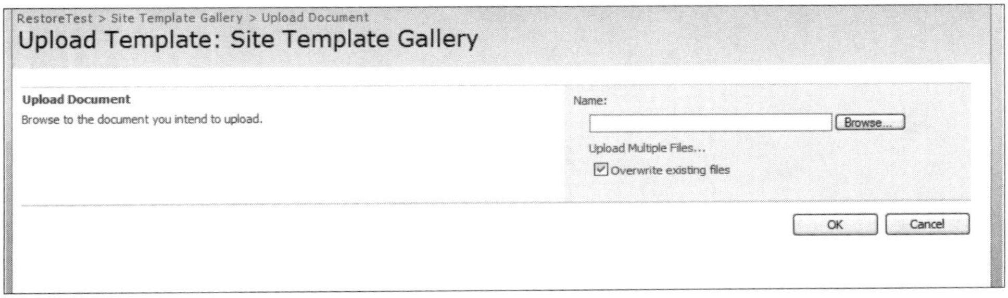

FIGURE 3.24 The Upload Template page for the Site Template Gallery.

4. When the Choose File dialog box appears, as seen in Figure 3.25, navigate to the location on the local system where the Site Template was saved in the previous exercise. Select the Site Template by clicking on it or typing its name in the File Name text box, and then click the Open button.

5. The Name text box in the Upload Document area now contains the fully qualified path to the Site Template that will be uploaded (see Figure 3.26). To continue the upload process, click the OK button; the template is then uploaded to the Site Template Gallery.

6. After the Site Template is uploaded, you're given the option of updating the metadata associated with the Site Template that was uploaded in the previous step; see Figure 3.27. The text boxes for the properties that were specified at the time of Site Template creation are populated, and the only required field is Name. As previously mentioned, though, it's recommended that both the Title and Description fields contain information that makes the Site Template easily recognizable when presented. When you're satisfied with the text box values on the page, click OK.

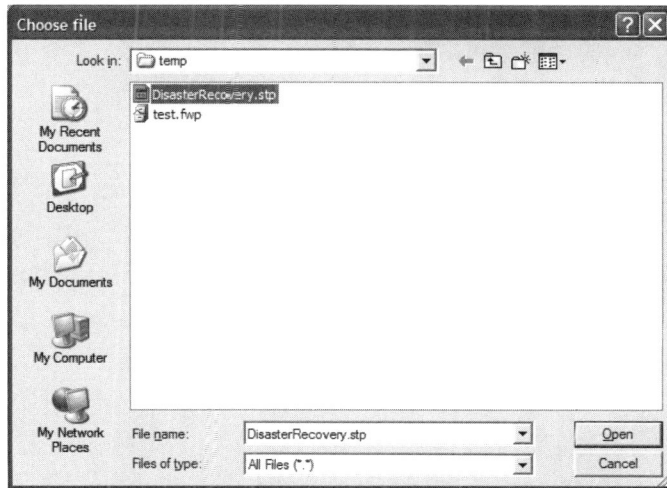

FIGURE 3.25 The Choose File dialog box.

FIGURE 3.26 The Upload Template page with the populated Site Template file name.

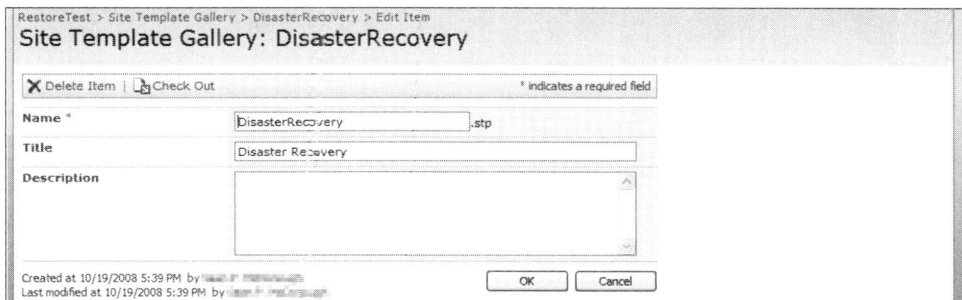

FIGURE 3.27 Updating the metadata for the uploaded Site Template.

7. As Figure 3.28 shows, the Site Template is now available for use within the target site collection, including all subsites it may have. To create a new subsite from it, click on the Site Actions button and click on Create, as seen in Figure 3.29.

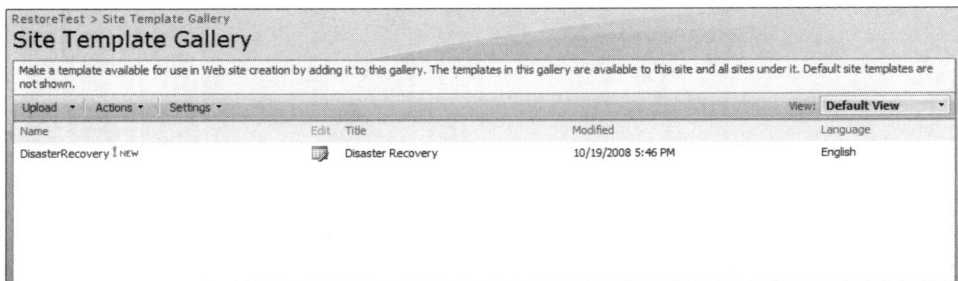

FIGURE 3.28 The Site Template Gallery with the uploaded Site Template.

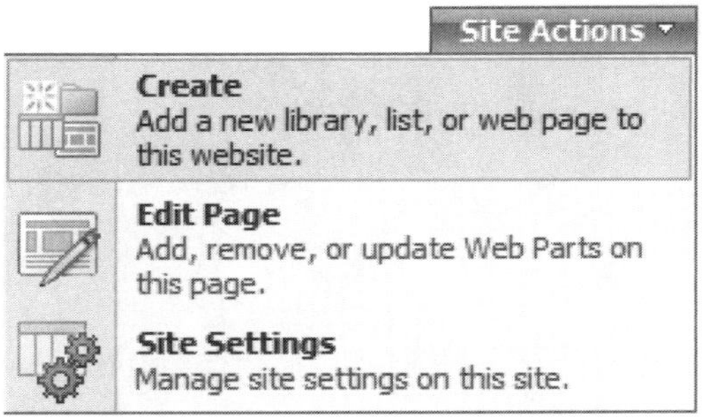

FIGURE 3.29 The Site Actions menu Create option.

8. A page similar to the one shown in Figure 3.30 is displayed in your browser. Click on the Sites and Workspaces option.
9. The Site Creation page opens in your browser, as shown in Figure 3.31. Enter a title and a URL in the appropriate fields in the page to configure the location and name of the new site to your specifications. In the Template section, click on the Custom tab and choose the template that you just saved. Add the appropriate security, because security is not replicated, and click the Create button. A progress bar page is displayed; once the operation is completed, you are redirected to the new site.

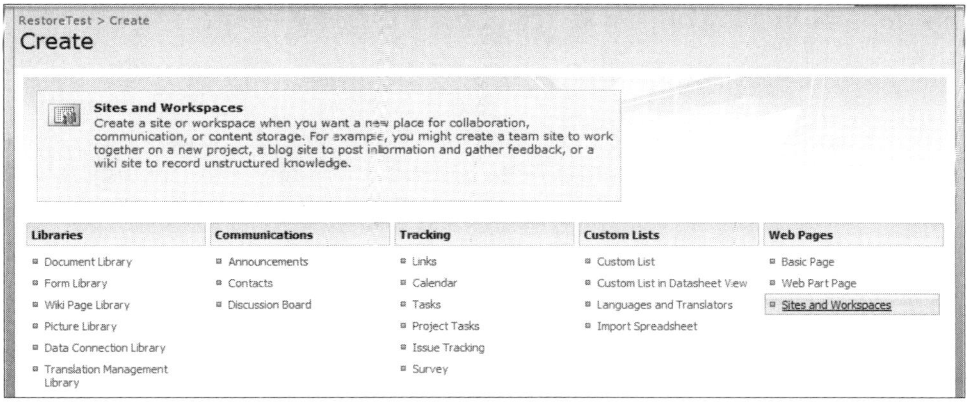

FIGURE 3.30 Create page.

If you are creating a new site from a site template to replace a corrupted site, make sure to delete the old site before creating a replacement with the original site's address information. Not doing so can cause an error in your request; SharePoint does not overwrite the original site if a new one is requested with the same data.

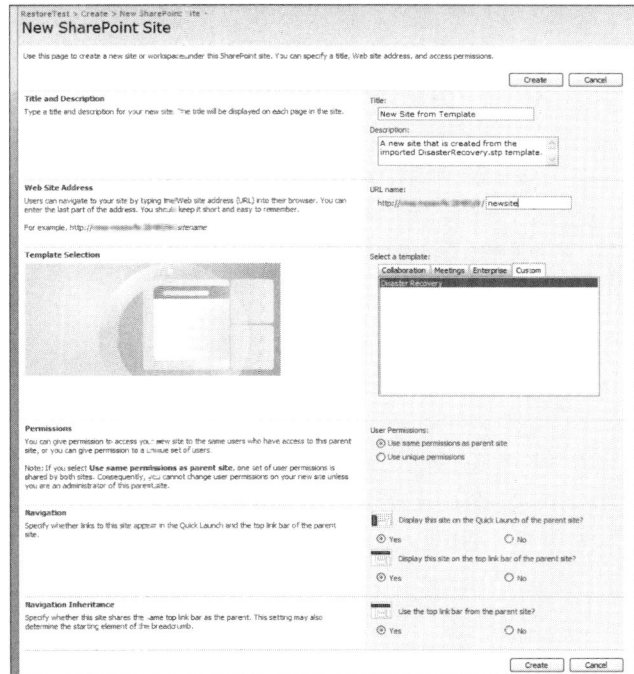

FIGURE 3.31 The New SharePoint Site creation page.

HOW TO PERFORM A BACKUP AND RESTORE USING A BACKUP WEB SITE

The final examples in this chapter cover the creation and restoration of a SharePoint site using SharePoint Designer's Backup Web Site option. To carry out the exercises that follow, you'll need two sites: one containing data that serves as the backup target, and another "empty" site to serve as the target for the subsequent restore operation. You are also required to possess site administrator rights to both sites.

Backing Up a Site with a Backup Web Site

The first exercise in this series begins with the backup of the Web site containing the structure and data you want to capture.

1. Open SharePoint Designer and open the site that you want to back up. Click on Site, Administration, Backup Web Site, as seen in Figure 3.32.

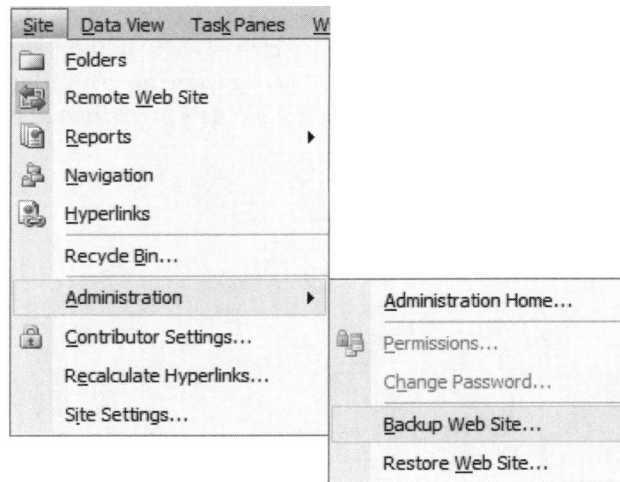

FIGURE 3.32 The Backup Web Site option under the Administration section of the Site menu in SharePoint Designer.

2. When you see the Backup Web Site dialog box, as in Figure 3.33, check the box next to Include Subsites in Archive (if desired), and then click on the Advanced button.

Checking the Include Subsites box isn't a requirement, but failing to do so negates one of the significant advantages of the Backup Web Site method: a fully recursive site (or site collection) backup. Leaving this box unchecked results in a backup of the current site only without any of its subsites—much like the export behavior of the Personal Web Package and Site Template options.

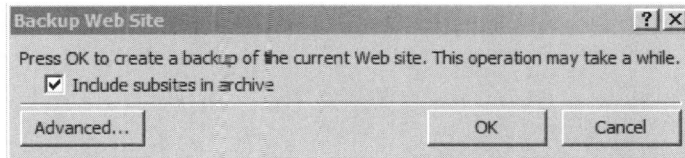

FIGURE 3.33 Choose the properties for your site's backup in the Backup Web Site dialog box.

3. The Advanced dialog box shown in Figure 3.34 appears. If the site or site collection being backed up is nearing its quota limit and doesn't have enough free space to hold the working backup file as it is created, this dialog box gives you an opportunity to specify another site (to which you must also have site administrator permissions) to act as the temporary holding area during backup file generation. As a rule of thumb, the location specified in this text box must have an amount of free space at least equal to the size of the site being backed up. When you are satisfied with the path specified, click the OK button to return to the Backup Web Site dialog box and OK once again to proceed.

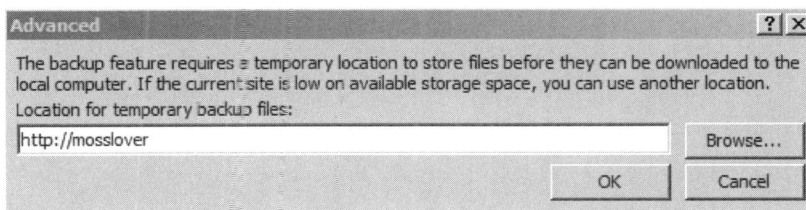

FIGURE 3.34 The Advanced area of the SharePoint Designer Backup Web Site option.

4. The File Save area is now displayed (see Figure 3.35). Navigate to the appropriate location in the file system of the computer running SharePoint Designer, type in a file name, and click Save.

5. The Backup Web Site Progress box is displayed while SharePoint Designer prepares your backup files, as in Figure 3.36, and then it's replaced by a dialog box stating that the backup has completed successfully.

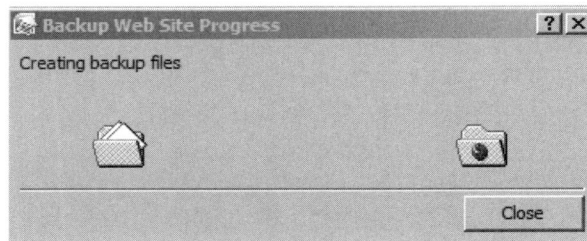

FIGURE 3.35 The File Save dialog box for content migration packages.

FIGURE 3.36 The Backup Web Site Progress dialog box.

When the progress box appears, SharePoint Designer begins the content migration export process behind the scenes. As content is exported from the target site, it is written to the temporary location specified in step 3. Only after all content has been exported is the content migration package (`.cmp` file) transferred from the temporary working location to the local file system. As mentioned earlier, the size of the file generated on the content export must be 24MB or less; anything larger results in additional export files being generated by the export process. Because SharePoint Designer is only able to transfer one `.cmp` file to the local file system, any exported content over 24MB is effectively lost.

When the Backup Web Site operation concludes, SharePoint Designer may leave one or more temporary files with globally unique identifier (GUID)–based file names in the root of the site being backed up. These temporary files (commonly with `.cmp` *or* `.snt` *extensions) are an artifact of the backup process and can be safely deleted.*

Restoring a Site Backed Up with the Backup Web Site Option

In the previous exercise, a content migration package (`.cmp` file) was generated as a result of a backup operation that was performed. In this exercise, the `.cmp` file that was created is used to restore the site.

1. To restore a site that has been backed up using the Backup Web Site option in SharePoint Designer, open in SharePoint Designer the location where you want to restore the site and click on the Site menu. Then click on Administration, Restore Web Site, as seen in Figure 3.37.

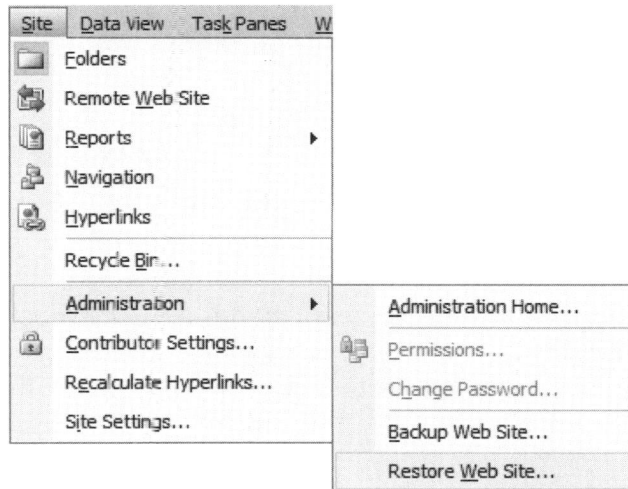

FIGURE 3.37 The Restore Web Site menu option in SharePoint Designer.

2. The File Open dialog box is displayed, as seen in Figure 3.38. Navigate to the `.cmp` file that you want to use to restore the site, and double-click on it to open it.
3. The Restore Web Site dialog box is displayed (see Figure 3.39). Click on the Advanced button to further configure the restoration operation.

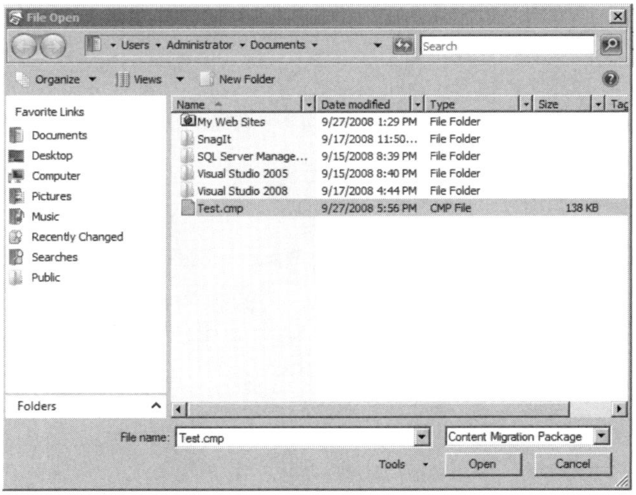

FIGURE 3.38 The File Open dialog box for content migration packages.

FIGURE 3.39 The Restore Web Site dialog box.

4. Figure 3.40 is an example of the Advanced dialog box. Here you can choose where you want to store the working archive and import logs. If you click either of the Browse buttons, you see an area as in Figure 3.41. You can choose a location and click Open to use the selected location in lieu of the default.

As with the Advanced dialog box in the previous backup exercise, the Advanced dialog box that is available during restoration (here) allows you to specify a temporary working location for the contents to be imported/restored. As a rule of thumb, the temporary location specified must have enough free space to accommodate an uploaded copy of the content migration package (.cmp) file. Additionally, the import .log that is generated by the restore operation can be written to a different location by specifying that location here. By default, both the working copy of the content migration package and the import log are written to the site where the restore operation is occurring.

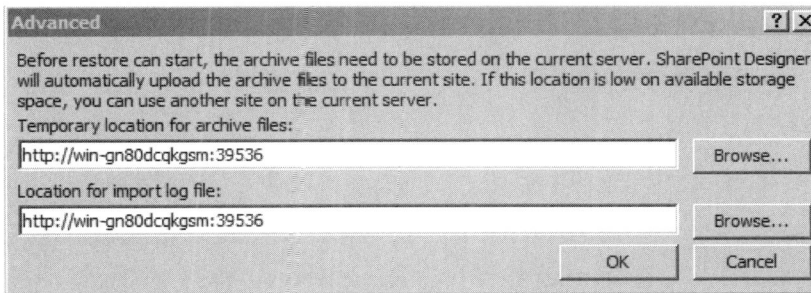

FIGURE 3.40 The Advanced dialog box.

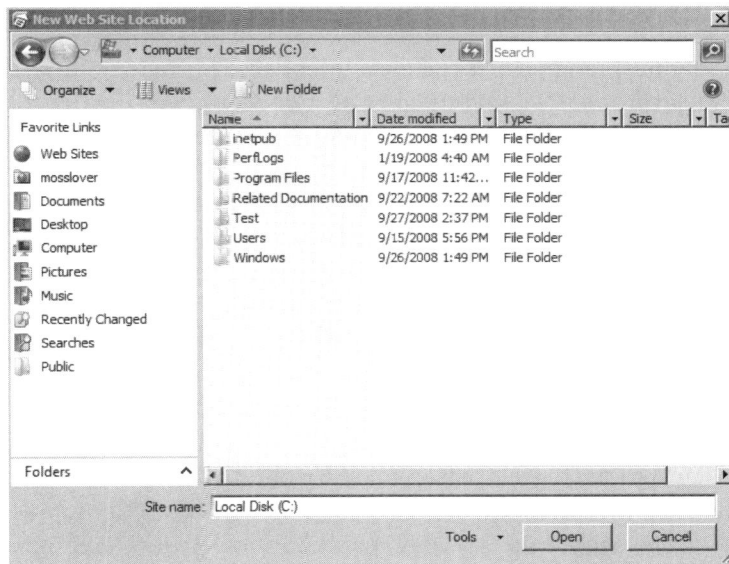

FIGURE 3.41 The New Web Site Location dialog box.

5. Click the OK button to close the the Advanced dialog box; this returns control to the Restore Web Site dialog box. Click the OK button on this dialog box to proceed to the Restore Web Site Progress dialog box, as shown in Figure 3.42. This box provides a visual indicator of progress being made on the upload of the content migration package and the restoration of the desired sites and subsites from within the package. When the restoration is complete, you see a Web Site Restore Completed Successfully dialog box. You can then navigate to the restored site.

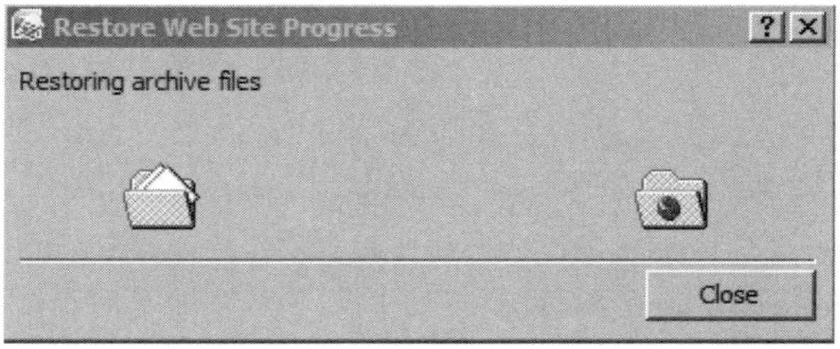

FIGURE 3.42 The Restore Web Site Progress dialog box.

PROS AND CONS OF SHAREPOINT DESIGNER BACKUPS

SharePoint Designer backups are intended to provide quick, simple options for backing up small SharePoint sites or individual items within a site, not to be used as your only disaster recovery solution. Because most of the backup and restore options available with SharePoint Designer do not address all aspects of a target site, such as security configurations, they are not a good solution for your comprehensive disaster recovery problem. They are, however, attractive options offered in concert with other SharePoint backup and restore tools, such as STSADM.exe. For example, if a single subsite within a large site collection needs to be restored, a backup made with STSADM.exe could be restored to a separate environment, such as a development or testing farm. After you've restored the site collection, you can back up the target subsite with SharePoint Designer and then restore it to the original environment, leaving the rest of the site collection unmodified.

Perhaps the biggest reason that SharePoint Designer does not make sense as an enterprise-level disaster recovery tool is the size restrictions it places on the content that can be backed up by it. Microsoft only supports SharePoint Designer backups (via the Backup Web Site function) to a maximum of 24MB, and attempts to stretch past this limit are likely to encounter serious errors preventing the backups from completing. This limit pales in comparison to the size restrictions of similar options available through STSADM.exe (15GB) and SQL Server 2005 (200GB). Furthermore, most SharePoint sites that warrant backup and restore coverage are well over the 24MB threshold without batting an eyelash. This limitation underscores the fact that SharePoint Designer is a good option for small, one-off backup and restore activities but should not be considered as an enterprise-level disaster recovery tool.

Another major drawback to SharePoint Designer is the fact that it is not included in the install of WSS 3.0 or MOSS. To use SharePoint Designer, you must purchase separate licenses for each person using the tool. Although it certainly is a useful tool and offers far more functionality beyond its backup and restore options, the fact remains that it does require additional spending on your part to use it. If you plan to purchase SharePoint Designer solely for its backup and restore functionality, consider some of the other, more fully featured options discussed in the coming chapters of this Recovery Guide. If you plan to acquire SharePoint Designer based on its full range of SharePoint design and management functions, the backup and restore options it provides can be helpful on a small scale or when used in coordination with additional tools in a comprehensive disaster recovery strategy.

CONCLUSION

After reading this chapter, you should now have an understanding of three backup processes in SharePoint Designer: Personal Web Package, SharePoint Site Template, and Backup Web Site. You understand that SharePoint Designer is a disaster recovery solution only when used alongside another backup solution, such as STSDAM.exe or the Central Administration's backup and restore tools. The following chapters provide an introduction and education on those options and their full range of features and functionality. Now that you are finished with this chapter, you should be able to answer the following questions. You can find the answers to these questions in Appendix B, "Chapter Review Q&A," on the book's Web site at http://www.courseptr.com/downloads.

1. How do you open a site in SharePoint Designer?
2. How is site security and permission-related data addressed by each of the three backup options (Personal Web Package, Site Template, and Backup Web Site)?
3. When should you use a SharePoint Designer backup?
4. What is included in a Web site backup? What is not included in a Web site backup?
5. Is SharePoint Designer included with MOSS or WSS?
6. Can you use SharePoint Designer on your computer?

4 The Central Administration Site's Backup and Restore Tools

In This Chapter

- SharePoint Central Administration Backup and Restore
- How to Perform a Backup via the Central Administration Site
- How to Restore a Backup via the Central Administration Site
- The Backup History Page
- How to Back Up and Restore SSO Encryption Keys
- The Benefits and Drawbacks of Using the Central Administration Site

Administering an information technology platform is a difficult and sometimes thankless task. A common complaint of the IT professional is that no one notices when everything is working as it should; it is only when something breaks or shuts down that the professional gets noticed. SharePoint is no different in that regard. When your SharePoint environment is up and running smoothly, it is the contents of the document libraries or the meeting workspaces that get all the attention. Until something breaks, and those document libraries and their precious contents become unavailable. At that point, you as an administrator are going to get noticed. Someone is going to want to know what you are going to do to bring back their collaboration site from the dead, and you need to be ready.

The good news is that every edition of the latest version of SharePoint is shipped with built-in administrative tools designed to back up and restore your SharePoint sites, databases, and even farms. This chapter covers the first of SharePoint's two built-in backup and restore tools specifically for administrators: the Central Administration site's Backup and Restore section. You will see how to create backups with the Central Administration site's tool, learn what the tool can back up, and discover how to restore backups. After finishing this chapter, you should have a working understanding of the Central Administration site's tool's prerequisites, activities, outputs, and results.

Later, Chapter 5, "STSADM.exe's Backup and Restore Operations," covers SharePoint's other administrative backup and restore tool: the Backup and Restore operations of the STSADM.exe command-line tool. Subsequent chapters discuss advanced situations for using SharePoint's built-in tools, the pros and cons of using these tools, when each is best suited for your needs, and how the tools fit into a comprehensive SharePoint disaster recovery plan. Although Microsoft has done quite a bit for SharePoint administrators by including these useful backup and restore tools in SharePoint, understanding how and when to use each tool can be a challenge. This chapter is designed to help you understand how to use the Central Administration site's powerful backup and restore tools and determine when it is best to use them in your own environment.

The visual examples provided in this chapter were generated in a testing environment using the following platforms and components listed next. Depending on how your environment is configured, your experiences may vary slightly. Unless a specific item indicates that it is unique to Microsoft Office SharePoint Server 2007 (MOSS), the features and functionality covered in this chapter apply to both Windows SharePoint Services version 3 (WSS) and MOSS in the same fashion.

- **Operating system.** Microsoft Windows Server 2003 R2 Enterprise Edition Service Pack (SP) 2
- **Microsoft .NET Framework.** Versions 1.1, 2.0 SP1, 3.0 SP 1, and 3.5
- **Database.** Microsoft SQL Server 2005 Developer Edition Service Pack 2
- **Web server.** Microsoft Internet Information Services (IIS) 6.0
- **SharePoint.** MOSS 2007 Enterprise Edition

SHAREPOINT CENTRAL ADMINISTRATION BACKUP AND RESTORE

With the release of WSS version 3 and MOSS 2007, administrators of SharePoint have a new backup and restore tool available: the Backup and Restore section of the SharePoint Central Administration Web site. The backup and restore functionality of the Central Administration site allows administrators to preserve several components of their environment through a graphical user interface (GUI) and restore those backups to a configuration of their choosing. Through the WSS and MOSS Central Administration site, you can back up individual content databases, Web applications, shared services providers (SSPs), search databases and indices, and much more, all the way up to your entire SharePoint farm.

ACCESSING THE CENTRAL ADMINISTRATION SITE

To use the Backup and Restore section of the Central Administration site, you must have access to the site as a SharePoint farm administrator. Typically, the Central Administration site is running on one of the Web Front End servers in your SharePoint farm on a port number greater than 10,000, but it can also be hosted on its own dedicated application server within your farm. If you have a single server environment, the site is hosted by your server running SharePoint. If you have a multiserver environment, you can determine the exact address for your environment's Central Administration site by opening the IIS Manager management console snap-in on the server hosting the site and checking in the listed Web sites for a site named something similar to SharePoint Central Administration v3. If you cannot successfully log into the site after you have determined its address, you may need to contact another SharePoint or Active Directory administrator for assistance.

NOTE

This is by no means the only way that you can access the Central Administration site on a server running SharePoint. By default, the installer creates a shortcut to the site that can be found in the Start menu under Programs, Microsoft Office Server titled SharePoint 3.0 Central Administration. You can find a second shortcut in the Start menu at Programs, Administrative Tools with the same name. Either shortcut runs the executable psconfigui.exe with the -cmd showcentraladmin *parameter to open the SharePoint Central Administration site in Internet Explorer. These shortcuts are certainly more efficient for regular use, but it is also a good idea to know the specific address for your Central Administration site, because it is typically not hosted on an easily determined URL.*

When you have successfully logged into the Central Administration site, you are presented a welcome page displaying Web parts for Administrative Tasks, Farm Topology, and Resources (see Figure 4.1). Click on the Operations tab to open the Operations page of the Central Administration site.

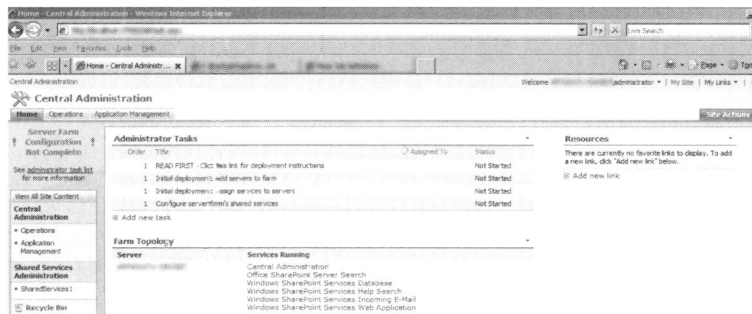

FIGURE 4.1 The SharePoint Central Administration site.

The Operations page is designed to assist you in the management of your SharePoint environment, farm, or servers in your farm. The actions available in the Operations page allow you to make changes or additions to your SharePoint configuration that can impact multiple applications running in your SharePoint environment, such as enabling services in the farm, configuring usage analysis processing, or creating alternate access mappings. Its links are grouped into several sections, based on functionality. See Figure 4.2 for an example of the Operations page. The page's organizational sections are as follows:

- Topology and Services
- Security Configuration
- Logging and Reporting
- Upgrade and Migration
- Global Configuration
- Backup and Restore
- Data Configuration
- Content Deployment

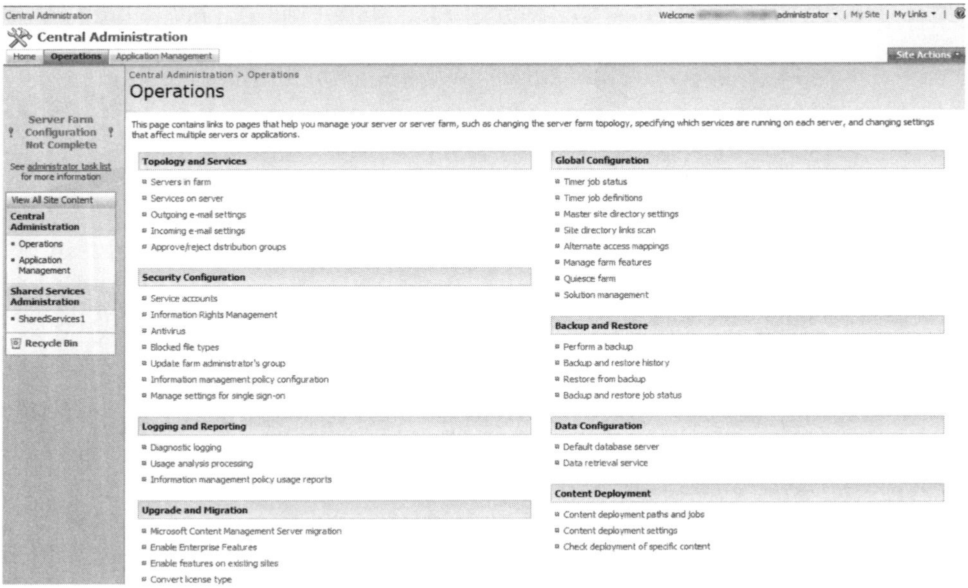

FIGURE 4.2 The Central Administration site's Operations page.

The Backup and Restore section contains the following links:

- Perform a Backup
- Backup and Restore History
- Restore from Backup
- Backup and Restore Job Status

ABOUT THE CENTRAL ADMINISTRATION BACKUP AND RESTORE TOOLS

With the backup and restore tools of the Central Administration site, you can preserve a variety of SharePoint components and restore those components to your existing environment (or a new one). The following items are available for backup and restore operations through the Central Administration site:

Some items on this list are exclusive to MOSS 2007 and are marked accordingly.

NOTE

- Top-level site collections
- Content databases
- Web applications (including SSPs, which are MOSS only)
- Content publishing Web services, also known as collections of Web applications
- Search databases and indices
- Single sign-on (SSO) keys (MOSS only)
- SSO databases (MOSS only)
- Your entire SharePoint farm

You can programmatically configure custom components for inclusion in SharePoint backup and restore operations, but you must take specific custom development steps to ensure that availability. These custom development steps are covered in Chapter 7, "Custom Development and Scripting for SharePoint Disaster Recovery."

TIP

When a backup or restore operation is executed in the Central Administration site, it runs as a WSS Timer Service job. (This service is also known as OWSTIMER or SPTIMER.) The Timer Service is responsible for running crucial jobs across a SharePoint farm, such as profile synchronizations, workflow execution, solution deployments and much more. This means you should take special care when planning to execute a backup or restore through the Central Administration site so you can avoid conflicts with other timer jobs. Also, closely monitor backup and restore operations through the Central Administration site in case they run too long or begin to consume a dangerous amount of a server's memory or CPU resources.

Finally, remember that the more storage space your SharePoint components use, the longer it will take to complete both backup and restore operations for them. Chapter 12, "SharePoint Disaster Recovery Planning and Key Concepts," covers the recommended approach to take when backing up and restoring your environment as it grows larger.

> *When viewing a list of running processes from a dialog box such as the Windows Task Manager, the SharePoint Timer Service is listed as OWSTIMER.exe. When starting or stopping the Timer Service from the Windows Command Shell, it must be referred to as SPTIMERv3.*

NOTE

CENTRAL ADMINISTRATION BACKUP AND RESTORE PREREQUISITES

You need to take other considerations into account before initiating a backup or restore through the SharePoint Central Administration site. The tool requires you to store backup files in a file system location designated by a Universal Naming Convention (UNC) path (formatted as \\<shared drive name>) or local drive (formatted as C:\<backup directory name>) on the server hosting the Central Administration site. This means that you cannot directly record the backup files to a tape backup drive, a storage medium traditionally used for disaster recovery backups. For those backup files to be stored on a tape drive, an administrator must move the files to the tape drive manually or move them systematically via a scheduled custom script.

> *To use a local drive as a backup storage location, your environment must have SharePoint and its backend database installed on the same server. If they are running on separate servers, you can only use a UNC path as the backup file location.*

TIP

The target backup location must also have enough space available to store the backup files that the Central Administration site's backup tool creates. You should expect to require storage space equal to at least 1.2 times the size of your SharePoint components targeted for backup, and at least 1.5 times is highly recommended. So if you are backing up a 500MB content database, you need, at a minimum, 600MB of free space in your storage location to hold the backup files. It is also strongly advised that you back up this file location so that multiple copies of the SharePoint files are available in case of a hardware failure such as a network outage or a corrupted hard drive.

For the Central Administration site backup tool to successfully write the SharePoint backup files to the designated target location, specific permissions in that target location must be granted to some of the service accounts associated with SharePoint. The service account serving as the identity of the Central

Administration site's application pool in IIS must be granted the ability to write to the backup file target location. If the backup file target location is a shared UNC path, the service account must be granted Read and Change permissions for the directory. See Figure 4.3 for an example of the Permissions dialog box for a file share where these can be selected. If the backup file target location is a local directory on the server, the service account must be granted Read and Write permissions for the directory. Figure 4.4 shows the Security tab of a target directory's Properties dialog box with the desired permissions.

FIGURE 4.3 The Permissions dialog box for a shared directory targeted for backup file storage.

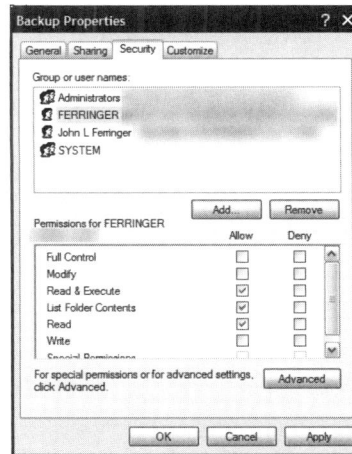

FIGURE 4.4 The Security tab of the Properties dialog box for a directory in the file system targeted for backup file storage.

If you do not know the identity of the Central Administration site's application pool, execute the following steps to determine it:

By default, the name of the Central Administration site's application pool is the same as the name of the Central Administration site.

1. Log on to the MOSS server hosting the Central Administration site via a Remote Desktop Connection (RDC) as an administrator as shown in Figure 4.5.

In Windows XP, Server 2003, and Vista, you can access the Remote Desktop Connection dialog box by opening the Start menu and then selecting the Run option. When the Run dialog box opens, type `mstsc.exe` *in the text field and click the OK button to open the Remote Desktop Connection dialog box.*

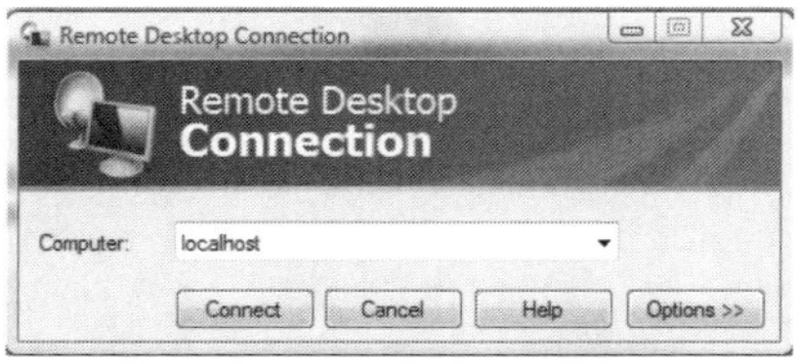

FIGURE 4.5 The Remote Desktop Connection dialog box.

2. After you have connected to the target MOSS server, open its Start menu and select the Run option.
3. When the Run dialog box appears, as shown in Figure 4.6, enter `inetmgr` and click the OK button.

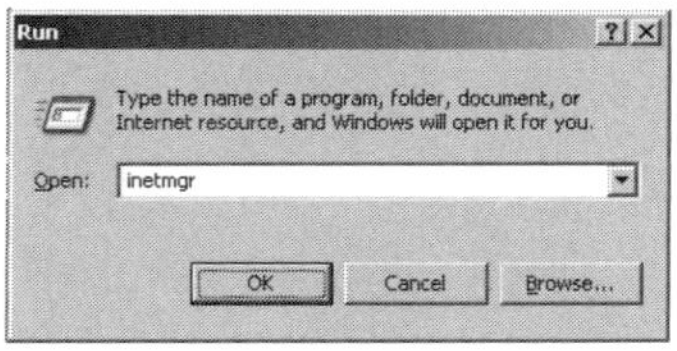

FIGURE 4.6 The Start Menu's Run dialog box,
used to open the IIS Manager console.

4. When the Internet Information Services Manager management snap-in opens, similar to Figure 4.7, click to expand the Web Sites entry in the left pane of the console.

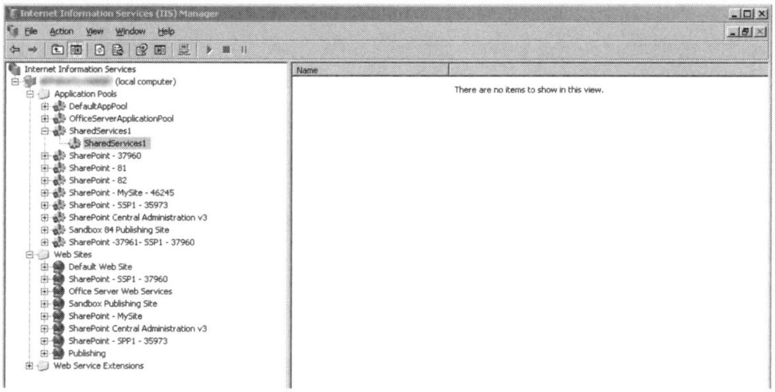

FIGURE 4.7 The IIS Manager console.

5. Right-click on the Central Administration site, and select the Properties option from the menu.

6. When the Central Administration site's Properties window opens, click the Home Directory tab, displayed in Figure 4.8.

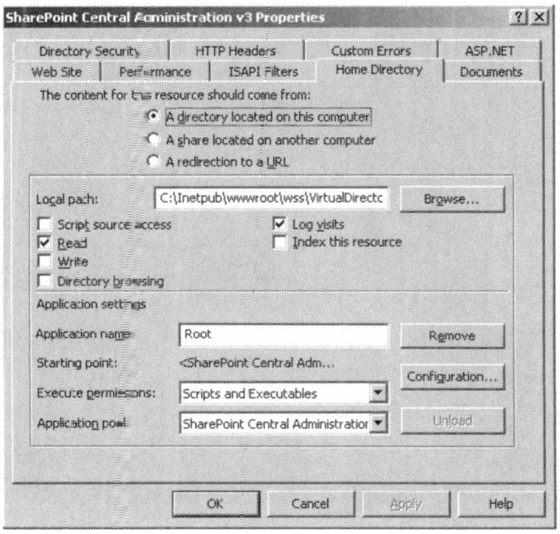

FIGURE 4.8 The Home Directory tab in the Properties dialog box of the Central Administration site.

7. The site's application pool is listed in the Application Pool pull-down menu field.

8. Click to expand the Application Pools entry in the left pane of the management console. Right-click on the Application Pool that the Central Administration site is running in, and select the Properties option from the menu.

9. When the Central Administration application pool's Properties windows opens, click the Identities tab. The service account listed on this tab is the identity of the Central Administration site's application pool. See Figure 4.9 for an example.

The identity of the Central Administration site's application pool is also the account used to run the SharePoint Timer Service. You can determine that account by noting the user name associated with the OWSTIMER.exe process in the Windows Task Manager on the SharePoint server or the identity of the SharePoint Timer Service in the Services management console snap-in.

NOTE

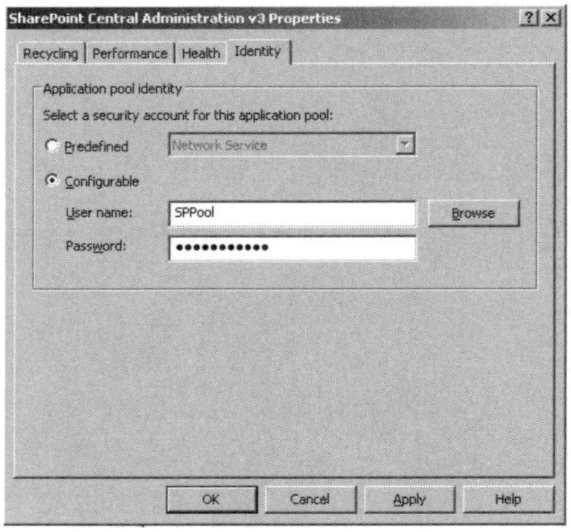

FIGURE 4.9 The Identity tab in the Properties dialog window of the Central Administration application pool.

The other service account that requires the ability to write to the backup file location is the service account used to run SQL Server services on the SharePoint database server. If you do not know the identity of the SQL Server service account, you can find it by taking the following steps:

The following two sets of instructions assume SQL Server 2005 is being used as the backend database provider for your environment and that the SharePoint databases are being hosted in the default database instance in SQL Server 2005. For named instances, replace MSSQLSERVER with the name of the target database instance.

CAUTION

1. Log on to the SQL Server 2005 server hosting your SharePoint environment's databases via an RDC.
2. Click the Start button, and select the Run option.
3. When the Run dialog box opens, enter `services.msc` into the text field, and click the OK button.
4. When the Services management snap-in opens, scroll down to the entry named SQL Server (*MSSQLSERVER*), like the one shown in Figure 4.10.
5. Note the Log On As value for the service; this is the SQL Server service account.

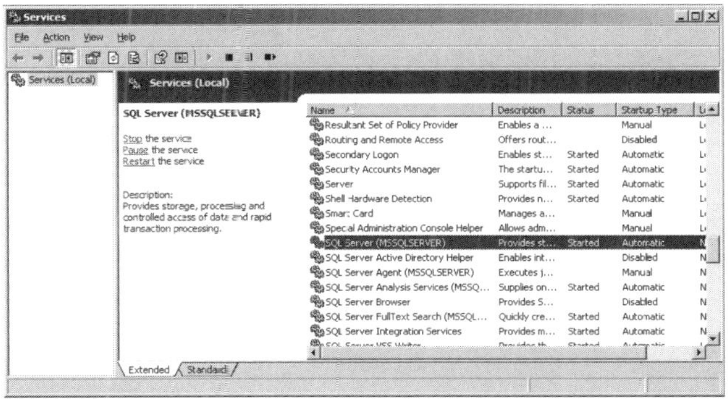

FIGURE 4.10 The SQL Server service in the Services management console.

If you do not see an entry named SQL Server in the Services console, take the following steps:

1. Click the Start button and navigate to Programs, Microsoft SQL Server 2005, Configuration Tools, SQL Server Configuration Manager, as shown in Figure 4.11.

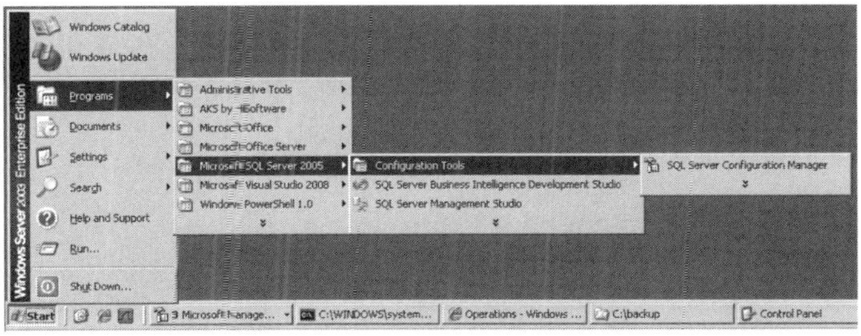

FIGURE 4.11 The SQL Server Configuration Manager's entry in the Start menu.

2. When the SQL Server Configuration Manager opens (see Figure 4.12 for an example), click the entry in the left pane for SQL Server 2005 Services.

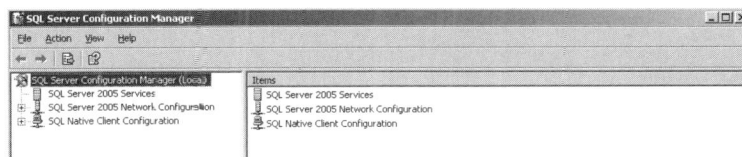

FIGURE 4.12 The SQL Server Configuration Manager.

3. In the right pane, find the line item with a Service Type value of SQL Server. This is the SQL Server service. The account shown in the Log On As field is the SQL Server service account. Figure 4.13 depicts an example account in the SQL Server Configuration Manager.

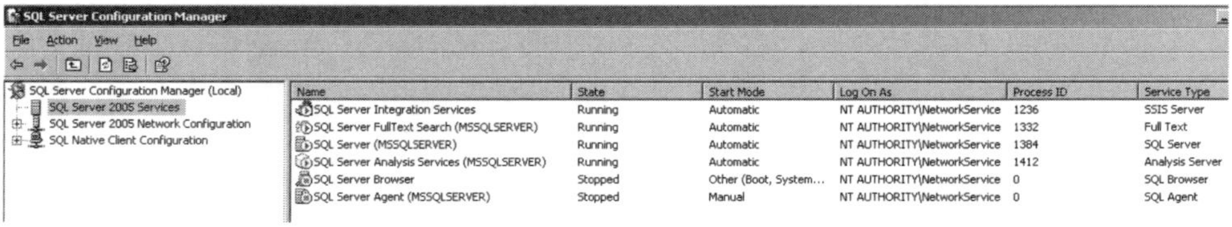

FIGURE 4.13 The SQL Server service account's identity in the SQL Server Configuration Manager.

After you have implemented the necessary prerequisites, you can begin backing up or restoring your SharePoint farm's components through the Central Administration site tools.

HOW TO PERFORM A BACKUP VIA THE CENTRAL ADMINISTRATION SITE

Log into your SharePoint farm's Central Administration site in a browser and open the Operations page. Click the Perform a Backup link in the Backup and Restore section to initiate a backup operation.

LOCKING A SITE COLLECTION PRIOR TO BACKUP

One highly recommended activity before generating a site collection backup, regardless of the tool that you use to do it, is to lock the site so that users cannot attempt to update the site while the backup operation is running. Site collection administrators can lock the site via the Site Settings menu of the site collection, or they can lock the site via STSADM.exe's GetSiteLock and SetSiteLock operations. SharePoint farm administrators can also lock a site collection from the Central Administration site by following these steps:

1. Open the SharePoint Central Administration site for your farm and click on the Application Management tab.
2. Click the Site Collection Quotas and Locks link in the SharePoint Site Management section of the Application Management page, as depicted by Figure 4.14.

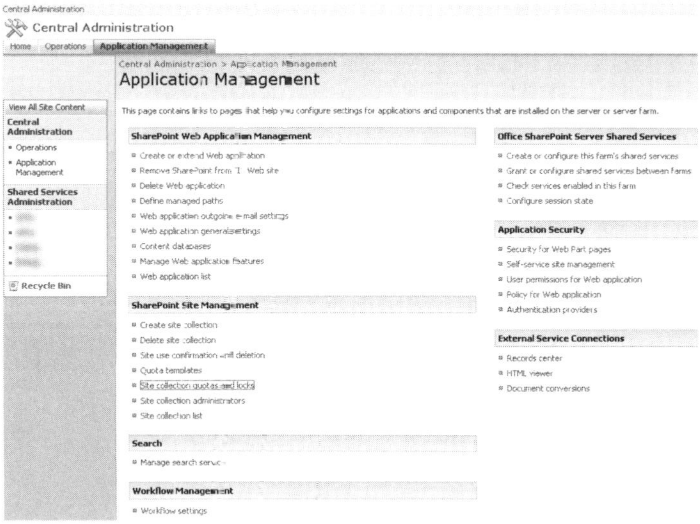

FIGURE 4.14 The Application Management page of the Central Administration site.

3. When the Site Collection Quotas and Locks page opens (see Figure 4.15 for an example), check the value of the Site Collection drop-down menu to determine if it is the site collection you want to lock. If it is not, click the arrow next to the name of the site collection and select the Change Site Collection option to select the correct site collection.

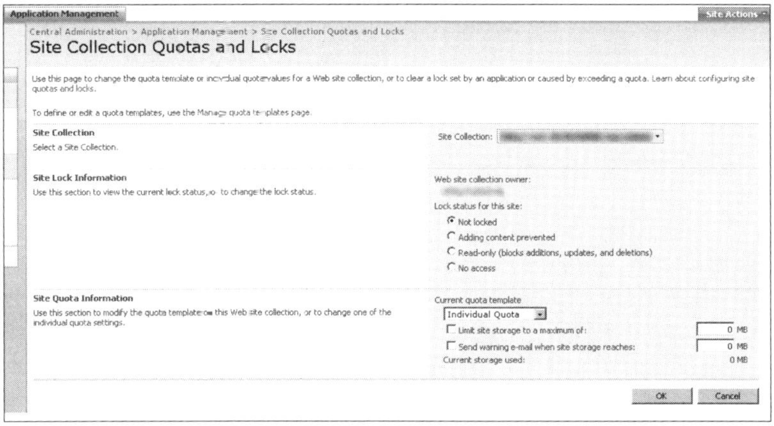

FIGURE 4.15 The Site Collection Quotas and Locks page.

4. In the Site Lock Information section, select the option button next to the type of lock you want to apply to the site collection. For best results, select No Access to completely lock the site and keep it from being used while the backup operation is in progress.

By default, if the site collection is not locked, the Not Locked option in the list will be selected. The Adding Content Prevented option allows for existing content to be modified, but no new content can be added to the site. Read-Only leaves the site up and accessible to users but prohibits them from modifying content in the site. The No Access option prevents users from opening the site in any way and displays a status message stating that the site has been locked.

5. Click the OK button to lock the site and close the page.

SELECT YOUR COMPONENTS TO BACK UP

After clicking the link, a page titled Perform a Backup—Step 1 of 2: Select Component to Backup is displayed. In this page, you have the ability to select one, some, or all of the components of your SharePoint farm that are available for backup through the tool. The page consists of two links (Continue to Backup Options and View History) followed by a table listing the SharePoint components in your farm available for backup. Each component is displayed with a check box, its name, what type of component it is, and a brief description of it. As Figure 4.16 shows, you can select the components by clicking the check box to the left of the desired SharePoint component. For detailed descriptions of each type of SharePoint component made available to the Backup tool, see the sections that follow.

Some components may not be displayed by default. If a plus sign (+) is displayed to the left of a component, clicking on it expands a tree view and displays the child component(s) available for backup.

It is a recommended best practice when creating your SharePoint databases to always name them with a relevant description of their purpose, so that this is readily apparent to anyone who views them in the future. This is especially applicable to backup and restore situations when you need to be certain that the components you are selecting are the actual items you want to work with.

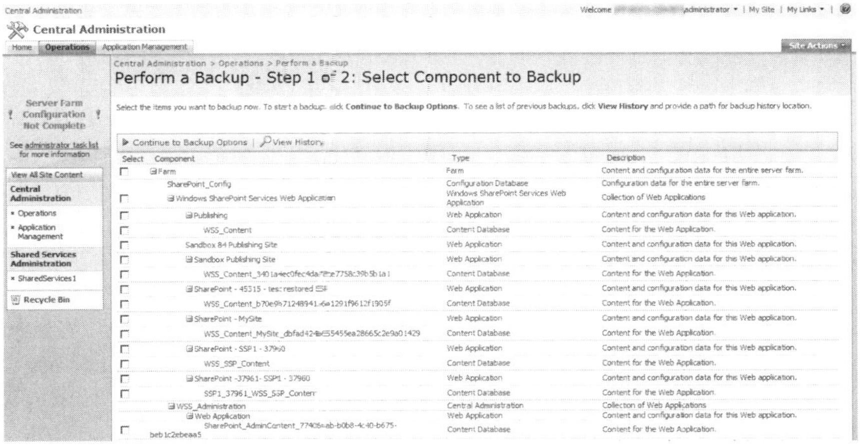

FIGURE 4.16 Select the check box next to the desired object to back up and click the Continue to Backup Options link to proceed.

Your SharePoint Farm

By selecting the check box next to the Farm entry in the table, you are choosing to back up every available component within your farm that can be covered by the tool. It is important to keep in mind that this option does not truly back up every aspect of your SharePoint farm; you are still bound by the limitations of the Central Administration backup tool. It does not back up the registry keys, file system, or IIS metabases of your SharePoint servers, or the farm's configuration database. If you select your SharePoint farm for backup, the Central Administration site automatically selects all the farm's child Web applications, databases, and configurations for backup. See Figure 4.17 for more detail.

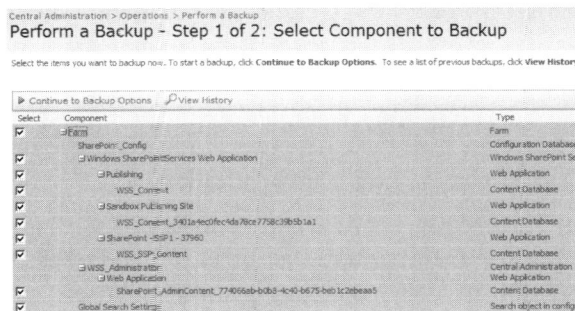

FIGURE 4.17 You can select the entire SharePoint farm for backup by selecting only the check box next to the Farm line item.

If you select a parent component (such as the farm or a Web application) for backup, you cannot deselect child objects to exclude them from the backup; they must be included. In addition, only one parent component can be selected per backup operation through the Central Administration site; if you want to back up multiple Web applications, you must either back up the entire farm or run the tool multiple times.

Configuration Databases

Although your farm's configuration database is displayed as a component by the backup tool, it cannot be individually selected for backup or restore. The only way to back up or restore your farm's configuration database through the Central Administration site is by backing up and restoring your entire farm.

It is not recommended to back up or restore your farm's configuration database through any other means besides as a part of a full farm operation. If you are restoring your environment's databases from SQL backups, you should not restore your configuration database, because this could cause conflicts between globally unique identifiers (GUIDs) and other data stored in those databases. Chapter 8, "SQL Server 2005 Backup and Restore," covers how to create a new SharePoint farm and reattach your restored content databases to that new farm. This restores all your sites without creating data conflicts or corruption.

Sometimes restoring a farm's configuration database from a backup is the right thing to do, such as for a nonproduction farm, an environment where users are not regularly updating content or configuration information, or a production farm that has not gone live to its full user base yet. It may be quicker to restore your configuration database than to rebuild your farm, or you may not have the resources necessary to build out a new environment. You can restore a farm from backup in its entirety, including its configuration database. But in addition to the risk noted earlier, be aware that this action is not supported by Microsoft. Weigh those risks against your need to have your farm in its previous condition.

Windows SharePoint Services Web Applications

This SharePoint component encompasses all the SharePoint Web applications in your farm and their content databases. It can be selected as a target for backup and restore, but if a WSS Web application is chosen, most Web applications and content databases contained within it are automatically included in the backup and restore operations. This selection cannot be overridden through the Central Administration tool.

The Web application for the Central Administration site is one exception to the statement in the previous paragraph. The content database for the Central Administration site can be backed up by itself, but its Web application cannot.

Web Applications

You can individually select each Web application in your SharePoint farm for backup or restore through the Central Administration site. Note that the name displayed for the Web application in the backup tool corresponds to the name of the Web application in the Web Application List page (available from the Application Management tab of the Central Administration site) and the name of the Web application's Web site in IIS Manager. Automatically selecting a Web application for backup or restore includes its associated content database as a backup target; that selection cannot be overridden.

Content Databases

Individual content databases can be selected for backup and restore, independent of their parent SharePoint Web applications. This includes the content database for the Central Administration site of your SharePoint farm. This allows you to back up the content of your SharePoint environment without its associated configuration data, which can be useful if you need to migrate a Web application from one farm to another.

The name of the content database displayed corresponds to the name of that database within SQL Server, which you were able to specify when you created its SharePoint Web application. Chapter 8 discusses how to identify those databases within SQL Server's management console, as well as how to alternatively back them up using SQL Server–specific tools.

Central Administration

The Central Administration site is one WSS site that cannot be backed up or restored via the Central Administration tool. You cannot select its WSS Web application or the specific Web application for the Central Administration, but its content database is available for backup or restore. The Central Administration site's Web application components are included in a full farm backup, so you can back them up and restore them via the Central Administration tool, just not individually.

Shared Services Provider (SSP)

If you have a MOSS 2007 farm, the Web applications associated with your farm's SSPs can be backed up or restored via the Central Administration site just like any other Web applications in your environment. Selecting the SSP's group as your component to back up targets the content and configuration information for the SSP's site and automatically selects its child content database.

SSP Database

Just as you can back up or restore SSP Web applications like standard SharePoint Web applications, SSP content databases follow the same rules for backup and restore via the Central Administration site as other SharePoint content databases.

User Profiles

If your farm is running on MOSS 2007, you can back up or restore any user profiles created for your environment via the Central Administration tool, but you cannot select them individually as a target. You must select the parent SSP to include your user profiles in the backup or restore operation.

TIP

Along the lines of user profiles and SSPs, there's another aspect of personalization from the perspective of backup and restore operations: MySites. Because MySites can proliferate and grow quickly as usage of your SharePoint environment becomes more popular, one highly recommended best practice is to host your MySites in a Web application separate from the one hosting the administration site for your SSP. This gives you more flexibility and granularity when backing up and restoring your users' MySites.

Session State

The only way to back up the session state components of an SSP is via a backup of your environment's SSP. Although it is listed as an available component within your SSPs, you cannot individually select the Session State Shared Application for backup or restore.

Search Indices and Databases

You can back up and restore the search indices and databases of your SSP via the Central Administration site, but like the SSP's user profiles and session state, you can only back them up or restore them when you request a backup of their parent SSP. Search indices are stored on the file system of the server in your farm with the Indexer role, not in a SharePoint database. The Central Administration tool backs up and restores the files associated with your indices just as it does data stored in SharePoint's databases. The recommendation is to always back up and restore your indices in tandem with their associated SSP via the same tool, whether it is the Central Administration site, STSADM, or a third-party product. SharePoint tightly couples its search indices to the data stored in the SSP content database. Attempting to restore an index from a file system backup or other tool that does not tightly couple the two sources in the backup and restore process can lead to inconsistent search data or worse.

Search Objects in the Configuration Database

This component is identified in the Central Administration site as Global Search Settings and can be selected individually for backup and restoration via the Central Administration site. You cannot back up this component as part of the SSP; you must specifically select the search objects to back up this component via the Central Administration site unless you select its parent farm component.

SSO Database

You can individually back up the SSO database or include it as part of a farm backup. If SSO has not been configured in your farm, no SSO databases are displayed in the list of components that can be backed up. To fully back up your SSO configuration, you also need to back up your SSO encryption key, as described later in this chapter.

TIP

The farm content access service account must have the right to access the contents of the SSO database to back it up.

By selecting the check boxes of one to many of the components for backup, you are ready to move on to the next step of the backup process. As Figure 4.18 shows, if you click the Continue to Backup Options link without selecting components for backup, an error message stating Select a component to backup is displayed in red text.

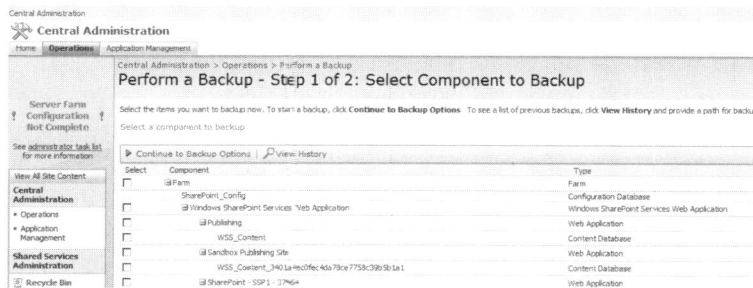

FIGURE 4.18 If you fail to select a component to back up and try to proceed, the Central Administration displays an error message instructing you to Select a component to backup.

You can also view the results of previous backup and restore operations saved to your target directory by clicking on the View History link. To perform a backup of a component in your SharePoint farm, ensure that the check box for the desired item(s) is checked and click the Continue to Backup Options link. For more information on the page that the View History link leads to, see the section "The Backup History Page" later in this chapter.

CONFIGURE YOUR BACKUP

After clicking the Continue to Backup Options link, a page titled Start Backup—Step 2 of 2: Select Backup Options is displayed. In this page, you can review your components selected for backup and configure the settings of your backup's operation. The page is divided into three sections:

- Backup Content
- Type of Backup
- Backup File Location

The Backup Content section displays the item(s) that you selected for backup. The component you selected for backup is listed under the text `Backup the following component` as a clickable link with an indicator arrow for a drop-down menu next to it. Clicking the component brings up the option Change Backup Component; you can opt to change your selected component by clicking it. This action returns you to the first step of the process, the Select Component to Backup page. Review your selected items before initiating a backup to confirm that you have chosen the components you intended to back up.

> *It is better to find out prior to starting the backup process that you have omitted a necessary component or included too much content to back up than after the fact.*

TIP

The Type of Backup section allows you to select if you want to perform a full or differential backup. As the page describes it, a full backup backs up the selected content with all history, whereas a differential backup backs up all changes to the selected content since the last full backup.

By default, the radio button next to the Full option is selected.

> *You must perform at least one full backup of the target component before you can request a differential backup for it. Note that you cannot differentially back up search indices. If you select a search index for backup, SharePoint generates a full backup for it regardless of whether you select the Differential option.*

TIP

If you attempt to request a differential backup and have not performed a full backup of the target component, after you click the OK button, the Central Administration site displays an error page stating A differential backup cannot be started or restored because no full backup exists. You must run a full backup instead. You must have run a full backup for the specific target component. If you have run a full backup for your target's parent component (such as a Web application when targeting a content database) and try to request a differential backup for the child component, SharePoint does not recognize the full backup of the parent component. If you are shown an error page, go back to the previous page in your browser and request a full backup of your target component.

Finally, in the Backup File Location section, you can specify where the Central Administration site's backup tool stores the backup files for your selected components in the Backup File Location section. Remember, you need to enter this location as a UNC path, and you are not able to browse through the server's file system to your desired location. In addition, the tool does not check ahead of time to see if the selected file location exists or if the required service accounts have write privileges for the file location. For the backup to run as smoothly as possible, you should confirm ahead of time that these prerequisites have been met. You must enter a valid UNC or file path into the Backup location field to proceed with the backup.

Below the Backup File Location field, the Central Administration backup tool displays an estimate of how much disk space the backup files require to be available in the target backup file location. Keep in mind that this is only an estimate; its accuracy varies from system to system. The Backup File Location section also provides a Help link titled Learn About Backup Locations, which when clicked opens a new browser window displaying an article from the SharePoint help file titled Backup a farm, Web application, database, or other components, as shown in Figure 4.19.

NOTE

Although the Help resources provided with SharePoint are useful, you should take them with a grain of salt. For example, the page referenced earlier makes the following statement: "A differential backup backs up data created or changed since the last backup. If you are performing a combination of full and differential backups, restoring will require you to have the last full backup, the last differential backup, and intervening differential backups."

The problem is that the definition provided for a differential backup is incorrect. As noted previously in this chapter, a differential backup includes all changes since the last full backup, regardless of whether or not other differential backups have been made since that full backup. What the help page describes is known as an incremental backup, which is not possible with SharePoint's built-in backup and restore tools. Incremental backups are discussed in more detail in Chapter 10.

Regarding the help files in general, keep in mind that in most cases the information in them has not been updated since SharePoint was initially released in November 2006. These files are not necessarily flawed or completely incorrect, but be mindful of their limitations when reading them and confirm their information if at any point in time you question their validity.

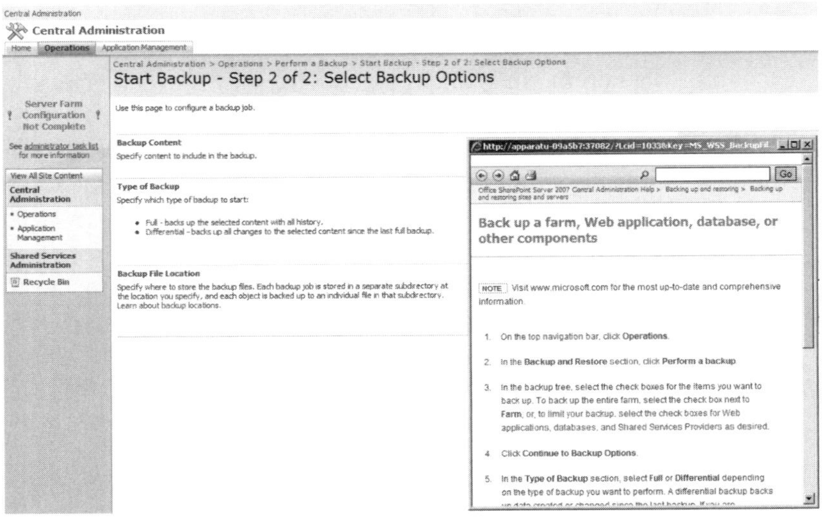

FIGURE 4.19 The SharePoint help file on backups available from within the Central Administration site.

If your SharePoint service accounts do not have the required privileges in the target backup file directory, the Central Administration backup tool does not inform you of that fact until you click the OK button to start the backup process. The tool still attempts to run the backup process, only to report that the directory is not configured with sufficient privileges when it tries to write the first file to the directory. You cannot return to the Select Backup Options page to choose a new directory (or correct the permissions for the directory) because the Central Administration tool has submitted a timer job as part of the backup process, which you have to delete before successfully backing up SharePoint.

You must delete the Backup/Restore timer job after any failed backup or restore operation (such as an access denied error) before you can submit a new backup or restore request. SharePoint reports a conflict with the existing timer job until you delete it, preventing you from proceeding. You can view SharePoint timer jobs in the Central Administration site's Timer Job Definitions page, shown in Figure 4.20, which you can access in one of two ways:

- By clicking the Timer Job Definitions link on the Backup and Restore Status page
- By clicking the Timer Job Definitions link in the Global Configuration section on the Operations page

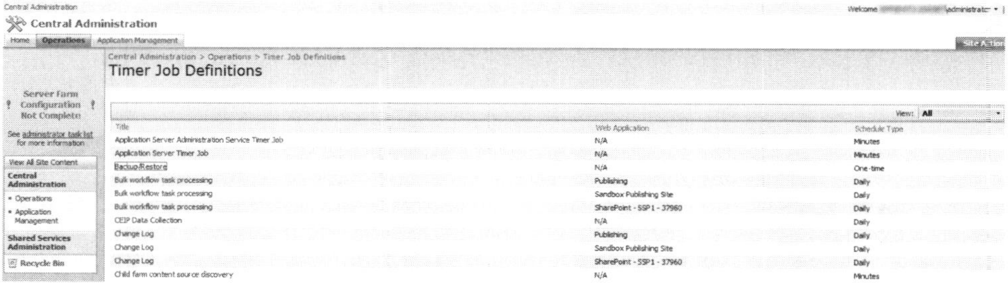

FIGURE 4.20 The Timer Job Definitions page.

After you open the Timer Job Definitions page a linked entry is displayed in the page titled Backup/Restore with a Scheduling Type of One-Time. Click on the title for this entry to open its details in the Edit Timer Job page, shown in Figure 4.21, and then click the Delete button to remove the failed backup timer job. Remember, you still need to get your SharePoint service accounts the right privileges in the target backup directory before you can resubmit your backup request.

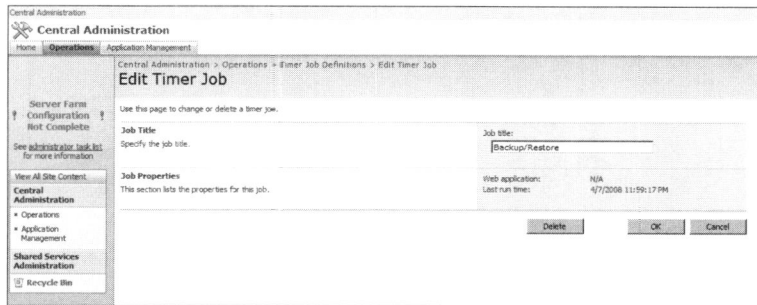

FIGURE 4.21 The Edit Timer Job page.

After you have selected the desired type of backup and entered your target UNC path for the backup file location, click the OK button to initiate the backup process. The amount of time required to complete the backup operation depends on the size of the SharePoint components you selected to back up and your network configuration. Results from testing by Microsoft's internal IT support group have shown throughputs of up to 35MB a second over a gigabit Ethernet connection, but this should only be used as a reference point, because your network configuration is sure to vary.

Even though SharePoint starts the backup process immediately after you click the OK button, the Central Administration's backup status page may not initially display information about your backup request. In some cases it can take over a minute for status data about the backup operation to be published on the page, depending on the speed of your server, what other timer jobs are running on the server, and the usage of your farm in general. If you do not see the status of your request listed, patiently give it 30 seconds or so and refresh the page in the browser.

YOUR BACKUP FILES

When your backup request has been successfully executed, the Central Administration tool generates your backup package, consisting of several files and directories, to the target file location you specified. See Figure 4.22 for an example of a backup storage directory containing the results of several backup operations. Specifically at the root level of that location, you find two items related to that completed backup: a file called `spbrtoc.xml` and at least one directory named `spbrNNNN`. (NNNN designates a sequential four-digit number that SharePoint uses as a unique numeric identifier for your backup files.) SharePoint automatically increments the NNNN number as you save additional backups to this directory, starting at 0000. If you change your target backup location to a new directory, SharePoint starts the numeric identifier back at 0000. SharePoint `Spbrtoc.xml` is an XML file storing the history information for the backups stored in the target file location.

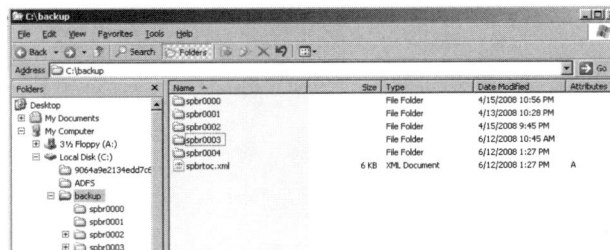

FIGURE 4.22 SharePoint backup files created via the Central Administration's backup tool.

`Spbrtoc.xml`'s file name is an acronym for SharePoint Backup Restore Table of Contents. If you change your target backup file storage location in the future, SharePoint creates a new `Spbrtoc.xml` in that location as well.

It is not recommended that you manually update or modify the files in your backup packages. This action can potentially corrupt your backup files or your SharePoint components when you restore the package. Microsoft does not support writing to, moving, deleting, or renaming any of the files in SharePoint backup packages.

Spbrtoc.xml (shown in Figure 4.23) contains SPHistoryObject elements within the top-level SPBackupRestoreHistoryelement; you see one SPHistory Object for each backup package stored in the backup location, sorted in descending order by date. The file will also contain entries for each restore operation run using backup packages stored in the location. Each SPHistoryObject contains the following child elements describing the backup package:

```xml
<?xml version="1.0" encoding="utf-8" ?>
<SPBackupRestoreHistory>
  <SPHistoryObject>
    <SPId>13d4f608-1cae-4dbd-a17c-7f0b692f5d51</SPId>
    <SPRequestedBy>              \Administrator</SPRequestedBy>
    <SPBackupMethod>Full</SPBackupMethod>
    <SPRestoreMethod>None</SPRestoreMethod>
    <SPStartTime>06/12/2008 17:27:40</SPStartTime>
    <SPFinishTime>06/12/2008 17:27:48</SPFinishTime>
    <SPIsBackup>True</SPIsBackup>
    <SPBackupDirectory>\\              \backup\spbr0004\</SPBackupDirectory>
    <SPDirectoryName>spbr0004</SPDirectoryName>
    <SPDirectoryNumber>4</SPDirectoryNumber>
    <SPTopComponent>Farm\Windows SharePoint Services Web Application\Publishing\WSS_Content</SPTopComponent>
    <SPTopComponentId>e85de5d9-b037-4027-a79e-81b6287fc820</SPTopComponentId>
    <SPWarningCount>0</SPWarningCount>
    <SPErrorCount>0</SPErrorCount>
  </SPHistoryObject>
</SPBackupRestoreHistory>
```

FIGURE 4.23 An example of the contents of Spbrtoc.xml.

- **SPId.** This is a GUID that SharePoint generates automatically.
- **SPRequestedBy.** Displayed in DOMAIN\User format, this is the SharePoint administrator who submitted the backup.
- **SPBackupMethod.** Options are Full or Differential.
- **SPRestoreMethod.** Options are None, Overwrite, or New. None indicates that the backup has not yet been restored. Overwrite indicates that the Same Configuration option was used to restore the backup, and New similarly maps to the New Configuration restore option. For more information, see the section regarding restore options Same Configuration and New Configuration later in this chapter.
- **SPStartTime.** This is the date and time that the backup process was initiated, displayed in MM/DD/YYYY HH:MM:SS format. The time is displayed in Coordinated Universal Time (UTC), not the local time zone of the server.

■ **SPFinishTime.** This is the date and time that the backup process completed, displayed in MM/DD/YYYY HH:MM:SS format. The time is displayed in UTC, not the local time zone of the server.

■ **SPIsBackup.** Options are True or False. If the entry in the file is for a backup this value is True. If the entry is for a restore, this value is False.

■ **SPBackupDirectory.** This is the UNC path to the folder containing the files for the backup package.

■ **SPDirectoryName.** This is the name of the folder containing the files for the backup package.

■ **SPDirectoryNumber.** This is the sequential number assigned to the backup package. The first package in the directory has a value of 0 (zero).

■ **SPTopComponent.** This is the highest component in the tree view of the Backup Target Selection page that was checked as a target for backup or restore.

■ **SPTopComponentId.** This is a GUID identifying the top component backed up.

■ **SPWarningCount.** This is the number of warnings generated during the backup process.

■ **SPErrorCount.** This is the number of errors generated during the backup process.

Within each backup package's directory (see Figure 4.24 for an example), SharePoint creates several files that make up your environment's backed up components.

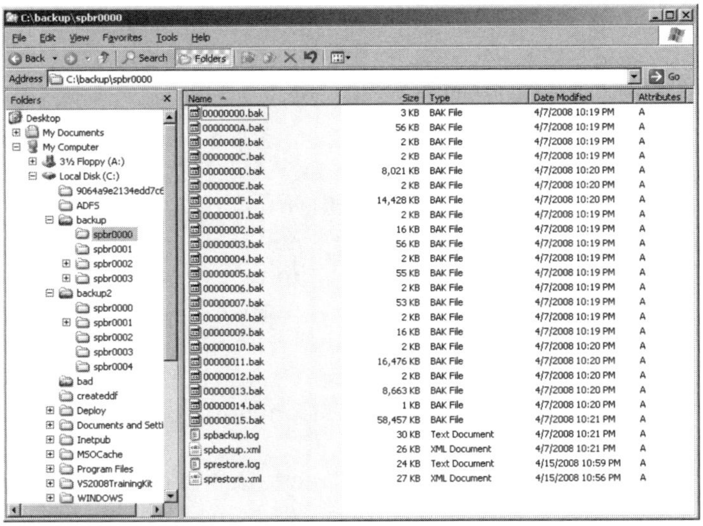

FIGURE 4.24 The contents of a SharePoint backup package created by the Central Administration site's backup tool.

Every directory contains the following elements:

- **One to many .bak files.** These files make up the contents of your backed up SQL Server databases. Figure 4.25 shows an example .bak file.

```
<object type="Microsoft.SharePoint.Administration.SPFarm, Microsoft.SharePoint, Version=12.0.0.0, Culture=neut
  <sFld type="Int32" name="m_PersistedFileChunkSize">4194304</sFld>
  <fld name="m_PairConnectionString2" type="null" />
  <fld type="Microsoft.SharePoint.Administration.Pairing, Microsoft.SharePoint, Version=12.0.0.0, Culture=neut
  <sFld type="Boolean" name="m_SqmEnabled">False</sFld>
  <sFld type="Boolean" name="m_WatsonEnabled">True</sFld>
  <sFld type="Boolean" name="m_DownloadErrorReportingUpdates">False</sFld>
  <sFld type="Boolean" name="m_bUpgradeFinalized">True</sFld>
  <sFld type="Boolean" name="m_bCommandLineUpgradeRunning">False</sFld>
  <sFld type="Boolean" name="m_regHostOnUpgrade">False</sFld>
  <fld type="System.Collections.Generic.Dictionary`2[[System.Guid, mscorlib, Version=2.0.0.0, Culture=neutral,
    <sFld type="Guid">00000000-0000-0000-0000-000000000000</sFld>
    <sFld type="Version">12.0.0.4518</sFld>
    <sFld type="Guid">77e7f90e-1989-46c2-ad65-361a53dcb2e0</sFld>
    <sFld type="Version">3.0.4.0</sFld>
    <sFld type="Guid">6ac833ea-3f8d-46b6-8b30-92ac4553a742</sFld>
```

FIGURE 4.25 An example of the contents of a .bak file.

> *There is not a one-to-one mapping of* .bak *files to databases; the contents of those databases are broken across many* .bak *files.*

- **Spbackup.log.** This text file contains the details of what occurred during the backup operation that created this backup package. Figure 4.26 shows an example of an Spbackup.log file.

```
[4/7/2008 10:19:49 PM]: Verbose: Using directory: \\               \backup\spbr0000\.
[4/7/2008 10:19:49 PM]: Verbose: The backup/restore process included the following objects:
[4/7/2008 10:19:49 PM]:     Farm\
    [SharePoint_Config]\
    Windows SharePoint Services Web Application\
        Publishing\
            WSS_Content\
        Sandbox Publishing Site\
            WSS_Content_3401a4ec0fec4ba78ce7758c39b5b1a1\
        SharePoint - SSP1 - 37960\
            WSS_SSP_Content\
    [WSS_Administration]\
        [Web Application]\
            SharePoint_AdminContent_77606ab-b0b8-4c43-b675-beb1c2ebeaa5\
    Global Search Settings\

[4/7/2008 10:19:49 PM]: Progress: Starting Backup.
[4/7/2008 10:19:49 PM]: Start Time: 4/7/2008 10:19:49 PM.
[4/7/2008 10:19:49 PM]: Verbose: Requested by              Administrator.
[4/7/2008 10:19:49 PM]: Verbose: Backup/Restore Settings:
    Backup
    Backup Method: Full
    Top Component: Farm
    Directory: \\               backup
    Progress updated: 5
[4/7/2008 10:19:49 PM]:     Backup threads created: 1

[4/7/2008 10:19:49 PM]: Verbose: Adding Farm to Backup list.
[4/7/2008 10:19:49 PM]: Verbose: Adding SharePoint_Config to Backup list.
[4/7/2008 10:19:49 PM]: Verbose: Adding Windows SharePoint Services Web Application to Backup list.
[4/7/2008 10:19:49 PM]: Verbose: Adding Publishing to Backup list.
[4/7/2008 10:19:49 PM]: Verbose: Adding WSS_Content to Backup list.
```

FIGURE 4.26 An example of the contents of the Spbackup.log file.

All time stamps in this file are saved based on the local time zone of the server hosting the Central Administration site, not UTC.

NOTE

■ **Spbackup.xml.** This XML file provides all the data and inputs that SharePoint requires for a successful backup operation, see Figure 4.27 for an example. Each file contains a single `SPGlobalInformation` node that provides data on the overall backup, similar to the package's `SPHistoryObject` data in its associated `Spbrtoc.xml` file, followed by `SPBackupNode` nodes for each component included in the backup. If the backup package contains parent and child SharePoint components, `SPBackupNode` entries for those components are nested in the `spbackup.xml` file to reflect those relationships.

```xml
<?xml version="1.0" encoding="utf-8" ?>
- <SPBackup>
  - <SPGlobalInformation>
      <SPId>743923ff-da83-4f49-8b2e-3b8a4b3a246f</SPId>
      <SPRequestedBy>         \Administrator</SPRequestedBy>
      <SPCurrentPhase>Done</SPCurrentPhase>
      <SPNetworkServices>false</SPNetworkServices>
      <SPBackupMethod>Full</SPBackupMethod>
      <SPDirectoryNumber>0</SPDirectoryNumber>
      <SPDirectoryName>spbr0000</SPDirectoryName>
      <SPTopComponent>Farm</SPTopComponent>
      <SPTopComponentId>6c392f62-4f58-4a46-bc0f-5b67c07c89dd</SPTopComponentId>
      <SPCurrentItem>13</SPCurrentItem>
      <SPTotalItems>13</SPTotalItems>
      <SPStartTime>04/08/2008 02:19:49</SPStartTime>
      <SPFinishTime>04/08/2008 02:21:28</SPFinishTime>
      <SPUpdateProgress>5</SPUpdateProgress>
      <SPWarningCount>0</SPWarningCount>
      <SPErrorCount>0</SPErrorCount>
    </SPGlobalInformation>
  - <SPBackupNode>
    - <SPBackupObject Name="Farm">
        <SPBackupRestoreClass>Microsoft.SharePoint.Administration.SPFarm, Microsoft.SharePoint, Version=12.0.0.0, Culture=neutral,
          PublicKeyToken=71e9bce111e9429c</SPBackupRestoreClass>
        <SPBackupSelectable>True</SPBackupSelectable>
        <SPRestoreSelectable>True</SPRestoreSelectable>
        <SPName>SharePoint_Config</SPName>
        <SPId>6c392f62-4f58-4a46-bc0f-5b67c07c89dd</SPId>
        <SPCanBackup>True</SPCanBackup>
        <SPCanRestore>True</SPCanRestore>
        <SPCurrentProgress>100</SPCurrentProgress>
        <SPLastUpdate>04/08/2008 02:21:18</SPLastUpdate>
        <SPCurrentPhase>Done</SPCurrentPhase>
      - <SPParameters>
        - <SPParameter Key="SPDescription">
            <![CDATA[ Content and configuration data for the entire server farm. ]]>
          </SPParameter>
```

FIGURE 4.27 An example of the contents of the `Spbackup.xml` file.

In some situations, SharePoint may create additional files within the backup package's directory depending on the components selected for backup or any subsequent actions taken regarding the backup package:

■ **One to many folders with GUIDs for names.** You see folders like this if the components selected for backup have SharePoint Search functionality associated with them. Within these folders, you find a `Config` directory containing `Search Noise` and `Thesaurus` files, a `Projects` directory containing the backed up Search indices for your environment, and a registry file named `RegistryBlob.reg`, which is a backup of your environment's Windows Registry settings for Search.

- **Sprestore.log.** SharePoint generates this text file if you have used the backup package for any restore operations. The log file contains the details of what occurred during the restore process using this backup package.
- **Sprestore.xml.** This file is similar in content and purpose to Spbackup.xml, the main difference being that it is associated with a restore operation and not a backup.

All time stamps in these files are saved based on the local time zone of the server hosting the Central Administration site, not UTC.

How to Restore a Backup via the Central Administration Site

If you do not already have it open, log into the Central Administration site and open the Operations page. Click Restore from Backup to restore your SharePoint components from a backup file.

Select Backup File Location

After you click the Restore from Backup link, a page titled Restore from Backup— Step 1 of 4: Select Backup Location opens. You must enter a UNC path in the Backup Location text field to designate the location of your desired backup files for restoration. You cannot browse through your server's file system to select the backup file location; you must manually enter the UNC path or paste it from another window. Figure 4.28 shows the Restore from Backup Step 1 of 4 page with the field where you must enter the path to your backup storage location. When you have entered the correct path into the Backup Location field, click the OK button to proceed to the next step of the restore process.

FIGURE 4.28 Enter the path for the directory containing the desired backup package in the Backup Location field to continue.

*If you have previously executed a backup in the Central Administration site, the
Backup location text field is prepopulated with the UNC path you used in the previous operation.*

SELECT BACKUP FILES

When the Restore from Backup—Step 2 of 4: Select Backup Package to Restore
page opens, a table is displayed showing a list of the backup packages available in
your target file location (see Figure 4.29). The table shows the following information about each package in the table:

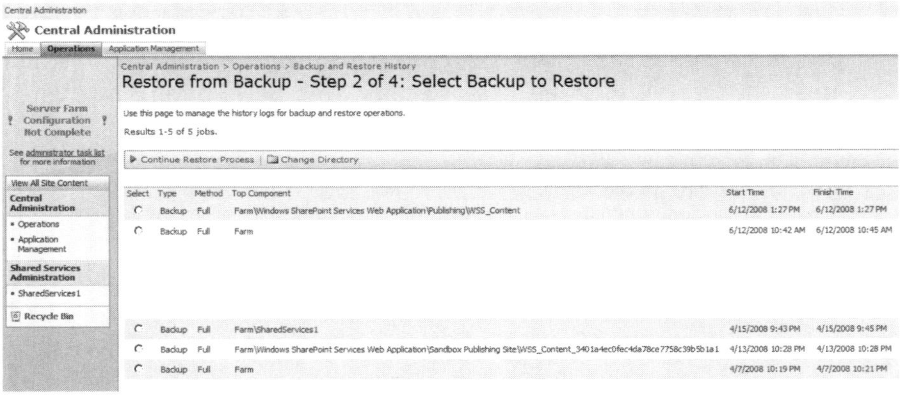

FIGURE 4.29 Select the radio button next to the target backup package
and click the Continue Restore Process link to continue.

- **Type.** Backup or Restore. Your target backup package should have a type of
  Backup. A type of Restore indicates a previous restoration operation.
- **Method.** Select Full or Differential for backups, or Overwrite or New for
  restores.

*If you chose to restore a differential backup, check to confirm that the full backup
made prior to it is in the same directory as the differential's package. SharePoint
automatically combines the differential backup with the last full backup made
before it to build the full set of components to restore. If the full backup is not available, SharePoint reports a* `File Not Found` *error.*

- **Top Component.** This is the highest SharePoint component within the backup
  package.

- **Start Time.** Displayed in MM/DD/YYYY format, this is the local time on the server that the backup process for the file was initiated.
- **Finish Time.** Displayed in MM/DD/YYYY format, this is the local time on the server that the backup process completed.
- **Failure Message.** If there were errors associated with the backup, messages associated with the errors are shown here.
- **Requested By.** Displayed in DOMAIN\User format, this is the user ID of the administrator who requested the backup or restore.
- **Backup ID.** This is a GUID to identify the specific backup package associated with the operation.
- **Directory.** This is the UNC path for the specific backup package associated with the operation.

If a backup package was created prior to a patch, hotfix, service pack, or other type of update being applied to your SharePoint farm, you can't restore it into your updated farm. For more information on this issue, see Chapter 6, "Tips and Tricks for SharePoint's Built-in Administrative Backup and Restore Tools."

CAUTION

From the list, select the radio button next to the backup package you want to restore, and click the Continue Restore Process link to proceed. Next to the Continue Restore Process link is the Change Directory link. Clicking this link returns you to the Select Backup Location page to select a new location for the backup package to restore. Be sure to review all the attributes of the target backup package to confirm that you have selected the correct package before moving to the next step of the process; selecting the wrong backup package may result in outdated or incorrect data being restored to your SharePoint environment.

You may only select one package at a time to restore.

NOTE

SELECT COMPONENTS TO RESTORE

After you have selected your target backup package, the Restore from Backup—Step 3 of 4: Select Component to Restore page opens, as shown in Figure 4.30. This page is formatted similarly to the component selection page of the backup process, with two links (Continue Restore Process and Select a Different Backup Package) located above a table displaying the SharePoint components related to the backup package. All associated SharePoint components are listed in an expandable tree view, with the components available to be restored via the Central Administration tool listed in black text with a check box displayed to the left of their name.

Components not available to be restored are listed in gray text without a check box. For the available components, the same selection rules apply as the backup component selection page; you must restore all of a component's children if you choose to restore it. Clicking the Select a Different Backup Package link returns you to the previous page, which you can also access via the Back button in your browser. After you have selected a component to restore, clicking the Continue Restore Process link opens the last page in the Restore process.

FIGURE 4.30 Select the check box next to the desired SharePoint component to restore and click the Continue Restore Process link to proceed.

SELECT RESTORE CONFIGURATION AND RESTORE YOUR BACKUP

When the Restore from Backup—Step 4 of 4: Select Restore Options page opens, you can configure the final options of the restore before submitting your request. See Figure 4.31 for an example of this page. The Restore Options page has at least three sections: Restore Component, Restore Options, Login Names and Passwords (depending on the component being restored), and New Names. A link to a help file on restoring backups is displayed above the sections, containing a walkthrough detailing the restoration process. One item of note in the help file is If you are using SQL authentication, you will be asked during the restore to provide a user name and password. This means that if you configured SharePoint to connect to SQL Server via SQL Authentication (user accounts stored in SQL Server) rather than Windows Authentication (user accounts stored in Active Directory or locally on the server), you need to provide a SQL Server user name and password when prompted.

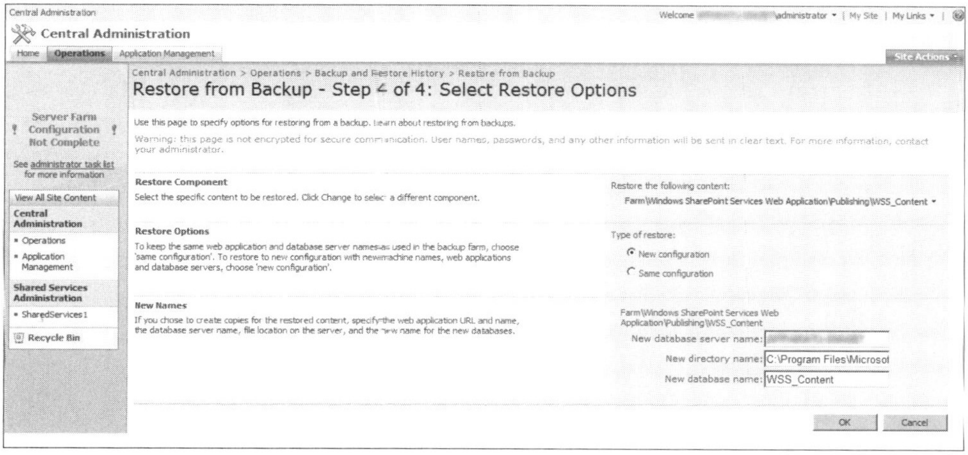

FIGURE 4.31 Enter your desired configuration information about how to restore the backup package, and click the OK button to start the restore process.

The component you selected in the previous page is displayed in the Restore Component section as a selectable link, which displays the drop-down menu option Change Backup Component to Restore if you click it. Selecting the Change Backup Component option returns you to the previous page to select a new component to restore. Review the item displayed here to confirm that you have selected the correct SharePoint component to restore into your environment; this is the last opportunity available to change your selection before starting the SharePoint restore operation.

The Restore Options section allows you to choose to restore your component to a new SharePoint configuration or to your existing SharePoint environment via the radio buttons next to New Configuration and Same Configuration. By default, the New Configuration option is selected. Choosing to create a new configuration allows you to specify a new location for your selected component to be stored, whereas the same configuration option overwrites the existing items in your SharePoint farm with the backup components.

Following the Restore Options section are two sections that require completion, depending on the components that are being restored: the Login Names and Passwords section and the New Names section. The Login Names and Passwords section is used to provide the account and password information that SharePoint uses to update your SQL Server database(s) with the data that you are restoring from backup.

If you do not provide credentials prior to starting the restore operation, SharePoint connects to SQL Server via Windows authentication using the identity information you supplied when you logged into the Central Administration site.

If the credentials provided do not have proper rights within SQL Server, the operation fails. Depending on what components you are restoring, you may see one to many sets of account and password entry fields for each database selected for restoration, or the section may not be displayed at all.

The New Names section is always displayed in the Select Component to Restore page, but what is displayed and whether it can be modified can vary. Much like the Login Names and Passwords section, you may see one to many sets of text fields displayed depending on the components you are attempting to restore. Unlike the Login Names and Passwords section, if there are no text fields to display for the New Names section, it is not hidden. Instead, it is shown as a blank section with no modifiable fields. The New Names section is used to provide SharePoint with new URLs, application names, database storage locations on the server hosting the target SQL Server database instance, and database names in the event that you decide to restore your backup to a new SharePoint environment rather than the existing one. If you have selected the Same Configuration option in the Restore Options section, the text fields in the New Names section are visible but disabled. You must select the New Configuration option to enter data in the text fields in the New Names section.

You do not need to manually create new Web applications or databases for the restored components before running your restore operation; SharePoint automatically generates the objects based on the new names you provide in this section.

After you have entered the desired configuration data about how the backup package should be restored, click the OK button to initiate the restore process. The Central Administration site displays a temporary status page (shown in Figure 4.32) as a placeholder until the process has completed.

You can click the Refresh link to manually update the page with the most recent status for the restoration operation, shown in Figure 4.33. If you do not click the Refresh link, the page automatically refreshes periodically to display the latest status.

Once the operation is completed, the Phase field on the Backup and Restore Status page is updated to Completed, as is the Progress column for all the components in the backup package, as depicted by Figure 4.34.

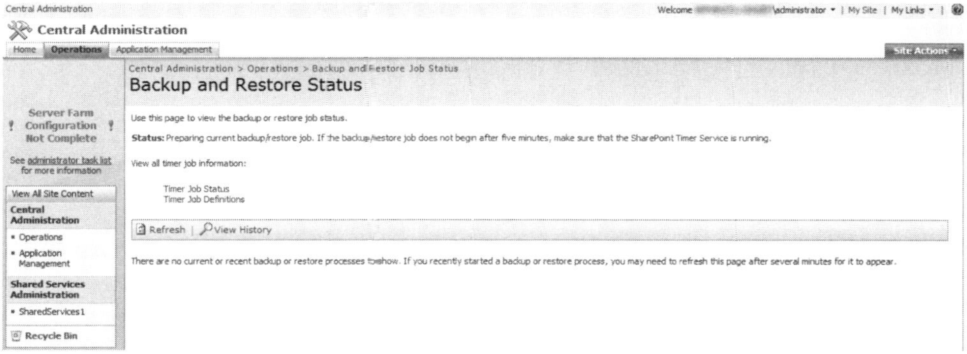

FIGURE 4.32 The Backup and Restore Status page.

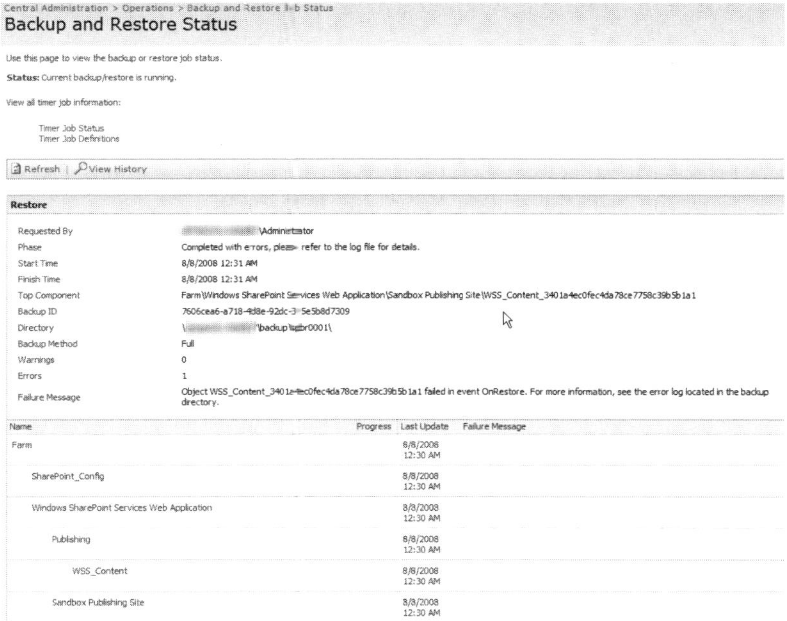

FIGURE 4.33 The Backup and Restore Status page displaying a running restore operation.

Central Administration > Operations > Backup and Restore Job Status
Backup and Restore Status

Use this page to view the backup or restore job status.

Refresh | View History

Restore

Requested By	\Administrator
Phase	Completed
Start Time	8/8/2008 12:37 AM
Finish Time	8/8/2008 12:37 AM
Top Component	Farm\Windows SharePoint Services Web Application\Publishing
Backup ID	c3838d80-51f8-4b84-b739-0cbdac286b2f
Directory	\backup\spbr0005\
Backup Method	Differential
Warnings	0
Errors	0

Name	Progress	Last Update	Failure Message
Farm		8/8/2008 12:36 AM	
SharePoint_Config		8/8/2008 12:36 AM	
Windows SharePoint Services Web Application		8/8/2008 12:36 AM	
Publishing	Completed	8/8/2008 12:37 AM	
WSS_Content	Completed	8/8/2008 12:37 AM	
Sandbox 84 Publishing Site		8/8/2008 12:36 AM	
Sandbox Publishing Site		8/8/2008 12:36 AM	
WSS_Content_3401a4ec0fec4da78ce7758c39b5b1a1		8/8/2008 12:36 AM	
SharePoint - 45315 - test restored SSP		8/8/2008 12:36 AM	
WSS_Content_b70e9b7124894156b1291f9612f1905f		8/8/2008 12:36 AM	

FIGURE 4.34 A completed restore operation displayed in the Backup and Restore Status page.

When to Use the Same Configuration Option

The usage scenario for the Same Configuration is pretty straightforward. By selecting this option, you are choosing to restore your backup to your existing SharePoint environment that the backup originated in. This means that you are overwriting the current components in your farm with the components you selected in the previous step of the process. Any changes made to those components since you made the backup are discarded and cannot be retrieved after you have started the restore operation in the Central Administration site, so it is highly recommended that you review your selections and confirm that there is no content or configurations that need to be preserved before you proceed with the restore.

Keep in mind that in some circumstances you are not able to use the Same Configuration option to restore a backup, such as when recovering a deleted site collection. When a site collection is created in SharePoint, it is assigned a GUID, which is also recorded when the site collection is backed up. SharePoint retains the association between that GUID and its parent Web application after a site is deleted. This means that when attempting to restore with the Same Configuration option, SharePoint errors out and prevents you from restoring to the same Web application. In this case, you must select the New Configuration option and create a new Web application to restore the site to in order to proceed.

In some circumstances, SharePoint may not display an error message during the restore process, but when the restored object is examined, you do not see sites contained within it. This issue is also caused by a conflict between a GUID in the restored backup package and an existing GUID in your target Web application. You must resolve this conflict (either by deleting the existing item in your Web application or by restoring the backup package to a new Web application) before you can access the contents of your backup package.

When to Use the New Configuration Option

Use the New Configuration option when the components in the backup package you are restoring do not currently exist in your environment. For example, if you need to move a site collection from one farm to another or are restoring a farm to a new hardware configuration, you should use the New Configuration option to execute your restore operation. Using this option does not overwrite existing components in your SharePoint environment; instead, SharePoint automatically creates new versions of the components you are restoring from the backup package and applies the backup files to them.

A good rule of thumb to remember is that, when using the New Configuration option, at a minimum, you need to restore your components to a new content database to avoid issues with duplicate GUIDs.

RESTORE A SHARED SERVICES PROVIDER VIA THE CENTRAL ADMINISTRATION SITE

If you are restoring an SSP from backup through the Central Administration site, you must take additional steps once the SSP site has been restored to connect the SSP with its previously associated Web applications. Complete the following steps to renew those connections between your environment's restored SSP and your Web applications that consume its services:

The Web application hosting the SSP must have already been restored from its backup prior to the execution of these steps for them to be successful.

1. Open the Application Management page in the Central Administration site.
2. Click the Create or Configure This Farm's Shared Services link in the Office SharePoint Server Shared Services section.
3. Click the Restore SSP link in the menu bar of the Manage This Farm's Shared Services page, as shown in Figure 4.35.

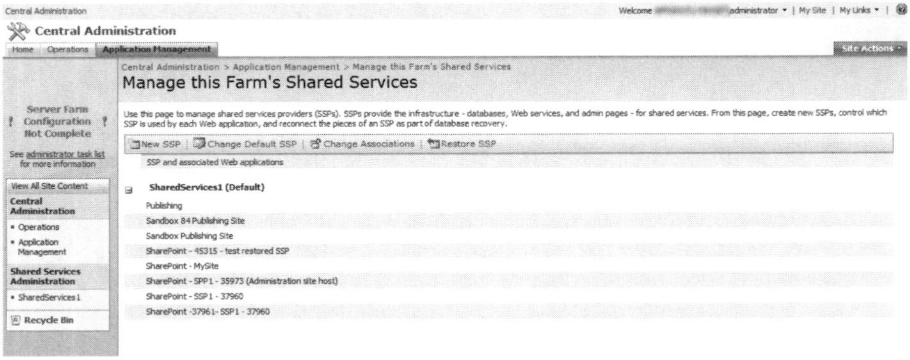

FIGURE 4.35 Click the Restore SSP link to connect the SSP with its previously associated Web applications.

4. In the Restore Shared Services Provider page (see Figure 4.36), you need to provide several configuration settings and values. In the SSP Name section, you must enter a name for your new SSP and select a Web application to host the SSP's administration site. To successfully restore the SSP to its previous state, this must be the Web application that previously hosted the SSP's administration site.

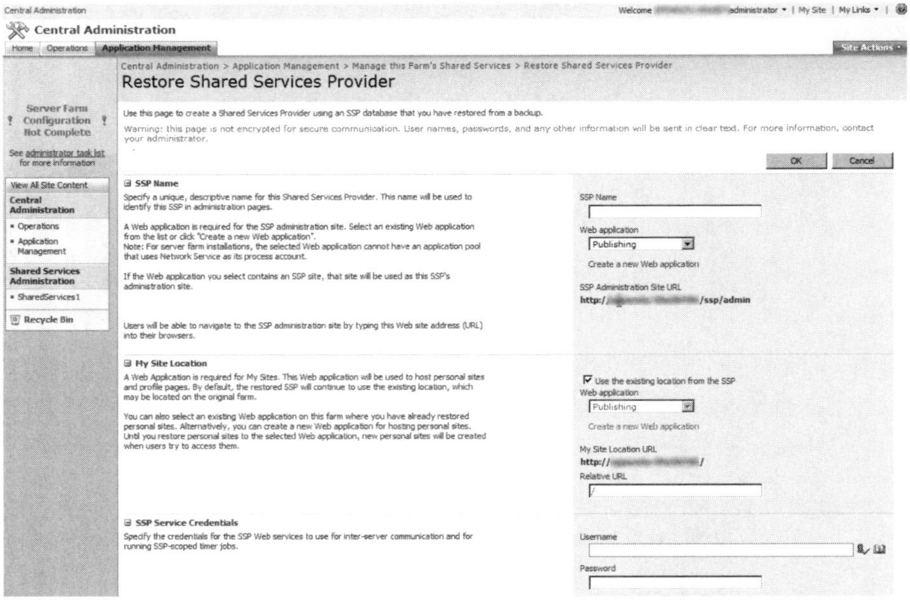

FIGURE 4.36 The Restore Shared Services Provider page.

Keep in mind that you cannot associate the Web application you specify with an application pool using the Network Service as its identity.

If you want to retain the previous location for MySites that the SSP hosts, make sure the Use the Existing Location from the SSP Web Application check box is selected in the My Site Location section. Otherwise, you can configure the SSP to use an existing or new Web application for hosting MySites. In the SSP Service Credentials section, enter the service account used to run the SSP service in the Username field (format must be DOMAIN\username) and its password in the Password field. In the SSP Database section, enter the database server you have selected to host the restored SSP's database and the name that the restored SSP's database should be given within the target database server. Again, this must be the database server and name that previously hosted the SSP's database to successfully restore the SSP to its previous state. If the Windows Authentication option button is selected, no further information is required on this page. If the SQL Authentication option button is selected, you must provide an account assigned the dbcreator and securityadmin SQL Server roles in the target database instance and its password to proceed. You are again prompted for database information in the Search Database section, except that this is used to create the SSP Search database. After you have entered that data, you can specify the Index Server that the SSP's Search functionality uses to crawl its content sources and the path where its index file is stored in the Index Server section. Finally, the SSL for Web Services section allows you to choose whether you want to require SharePoint's Web services to use Secure Sockets Layer (SSL) to protect their communication by selecting the appropriate radio button option. Click the OK button to restore your SSP.

If the Web application you select to host the SSP's administration site already hosts other site collections, SharePoint displays a warning page indicating that proceeding with your request automatically associates those site collections with your restored SSP instead of their current SSP. Because it is fairly simple to change a SharePoint Web application's SSP association within the Central Administration site, this is not a major issue, but it can cause a short-term disruption of your environment's service and your understanding of its configuration. If you want to prevent that association from occurring, click the Cancel button to return to the Restore Shared Services Provider page, and select a different Web application or create a new one. If you want to proceed, click the OK button to continue.

If the Web application you select to host the SSP's administration site also hosts MySites, SharePoint displays a warning page recommending that you change the target Web application so the two are hosted independently of each other. If you want to prevent that from occurring, click the Cancel button to return to the Restore Shared Services Provider page, and select a different Web application or create a new one. If you want to proceed, click the OK button to continue.

5. If your request completes without error, SharePoint displays a message stating that the SSP was restored successfully. If it encounters an error, the results page displays information about the error to aid in troubleshooting the problem. After you have resolved the issue, execute the SSP restoration process again to retry. When SharePoint says that the SSP has been restored, open the SSP's administration site to confirm that all your configurations were restored successfully and are functioning as expected.

THE BACKUP HISTORY PAGE

Within the Operations tab of the Central Administration site, the Backup and Restore History page, shown in Figure 4.37, is available as a link within the Backup and Restore section and can also be accessed via links in the Select Component to Backup page (step 1 of the Central Administration backup tool) and the Backup and Restore Status page (the final page of the Central Administration backup tool. In all cases, the same page is loaded and displays a full history of every completed backup and restore operation in the Central Administration site. The entries are displayed in descending order by their date and time of execution, and the table contains the same columns as the Select Backup to Restore page (step 2 of the Central Administration restore tool).

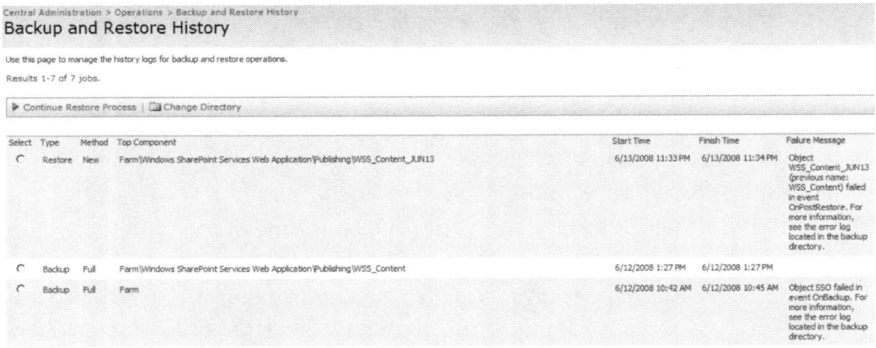

FIGURE 4.37 The Backup and Restore History page.

The main difference between the Backup and Restore History page and the Select Backup to Restore page lies in what items are displayed in the main table. The Backup and Restore History page displays all backup and restore operations for the SharePoint farm, whereas the Select Backup to Restore page only displays the backup packages stored in the chosen backup directory. So if you have used two different directories for storing backups in your farm, the Backup and Restore History page displays the backup packages in both directories but only the contents of a single directory in the Select Backup to Restore page. In addition, the Backup and Restore History page lists items with types of both Backup and Restore, whereas the Select Backup to Restore page only displays items with a type of Backup.

You can initiate a restore operation via the Backup and Restore History page by selecting the radio button to the left of your desired backup package and clicking the Continue Restore Process link above the table. This opens the Select Component to Restore page. From that point, you take the same steps to restore your backup as you do when clicking the Restore from Backup link on the main Operations page.

HOW TO BACK UP AND RESTORE SSO ENCRYPTION KEYS

To completely back up your environment's SSO configuration, you must back up your encryption key in addition to the SSO database.

A removable drive is required on your server to save the encryption key, because you cannot save it to a local or mapped hard drive.

TIP

Because you can use the SSO credentials to access sensitive resources, you should store the removable drive containing the encryption key backup in a secure location.

CAUTION

Execute the following steps to back up the encryption key associated with your environment's SSO configuration:

1. Open the Central Administration site, and click the link on the Operations tab.
2. In the Security Configuration section, click the Manage Settings for Single Sign-On link.
3. When the Manage Settings for Single Sign-On page opens (see Figure 4.38), click the Manage Encryption Key link in the Server Settings section.

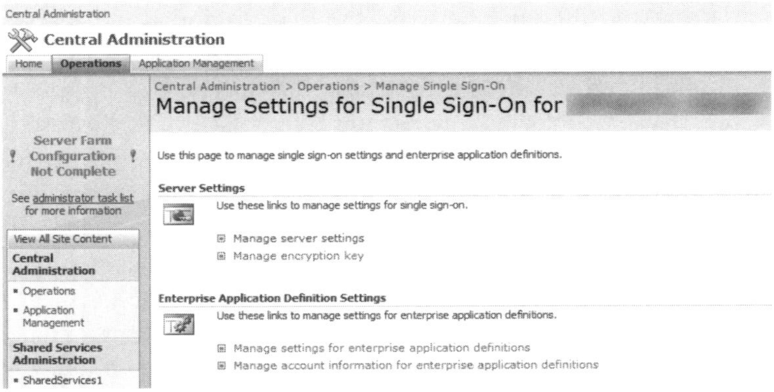

FIGURE 4.38 The Manage Settings for Single Sign-On page.

4. In the Encryption Key Backup section, as shown in Figure 4.39, select the target removable drive to store the backup files on, and click the Back Up link.

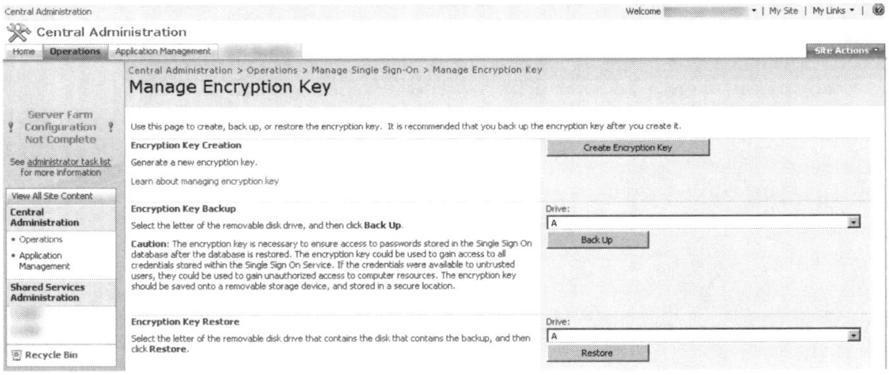

FIGURE 4.39 The Manage Encryption Key page.

Execute the following steps to restore the encryption key associated with your environment's SSO configuration:

1. Open the Central Administration site, and click the link on the Operations tab.

2. In the Security Configuration section, click the Manage Settings for Single Sign-On link.

3. When the Manage Settings for Single Sign-On page opens, click the Manage Encryption Key link in the Server Settings section.
4. In the Encryption Key Restore section, select the target removable drive containing the backup files for the encryption key, and click the Restore link.

The Benefits and Drawbacks of Using the Central Administration Site

The backup tools of the Central Administration site are best used preemptively prior to major state or configuration changes to your SharePoint environment. Through the Central Administration site, you can easily select your entire farm for backup or specifically earmark a Web application, site collection, SSP, or other components to create a backup. This gives you a great deal of flexibility in preserving the conditions and content of your SharePoint site, but the drawback is that you have to know when changes to your environment might need to be rolled back. Make the creation of a backup (regardless of the tool you use) a standard step in your change management process for SharePoint. You can certainly accomplish this with the Central Administration site's backup and restore tool, but there are some limitations of the Central Administration site's tool that can impact your systems.

The biggest drawback to the Central Administration backup tool is your inability as an administrator to schedule regular backups with it. The site provides no interface to schedule your backups to be run on a regular basis without being initiated by an administrator. Without scheduled backups of your SharePoint environment, you are at risk of losing content, data, and configuration settings in the event of a catastrophic event by not having the ability to restore an up-to-date backup package, because not every damaging change or update to your system is the result of a planned change. That is not to say that you should not use the Central Administration backup and restore tools; they are an important piece of your overall Disaster Recovery strategy. But you should not count on the manual backups created via the Central Administration site in the case of a catastrophic event in SharePoint, because they do not necessarily contain current data.

Not only is SharePoint a broad platform, but it is built on or depends on several other Microsoft technologies to function properly. Unfortunately, the backup and restore tools of the Central Administration site cannot cover every dependency that SharePoint has, meaning that a backup created through the Central Administration site does not contain all the content and configuration data required to fully restore a SharePoint farm or server to its previous state. You need to take additional steps outside of the Central Administration site to back up the IIS metabases of your Web server(s), your server(s)'s Windows registry, and the SharePoint template files stored in the file system of your server(s). Chapter 10, "Windows Server 2003 Backup and Restore," covers how and when to back up and restore those components later, but it is important to understand that the Central Administration site is not a comprehensive backup and restore solution in the case of a disaster if you require a full recovery of your system.

A popular feature of SharePoint is its granularity. With SharePoint, you have the ability to nest sites within sites and to place content several levels deep within a site collection. You also have the power to set specific user access rights on content all the way down to an item in a list, no matter how deep within a site collection that item may be. But that level of granularity is not available for backups and restores in the Central Administration site. You cannot target that item specifically for backup or restoration. In fact, the smallest component you can back up or restore via the Central Administration tools is a site collection. This means that if you want to only restore a specific list or subsite, the only way to do so is to restore its entire parent site collection, either to a new configuration and copy the target item to your current environment or to overwrite the entire site collection.

Another drawback to using the Central Administration site's backup and restore tools is its lack of ability to manage the files associated with your backups once they have been created. When you specify a backup package and its designated storage location at a UNC path, SharePoint creates the complete backup package and allows you to use it to restore your components when you chose to. But as you continue to make more backups and store them, you may find yourself wondering how to manage these backup packages and which ones you do or do not need, especially as your system grows and you need more capacity to store your backups. The problem here is that the Central Administration site does not provide administrators with any mechanisms to manage their backup files once they have been generated. The Backup and Restore History page does show useful historical information and tell you if a backup has been used for a restore operation, but it does not allow you to archive or delete a backup package when you no longer need it. This means you lack a SharePoint-based and tested means to delete unneeded backup files to conserve storage space and have to manually do it yourself through the file system.

Any steps you take to archive or delete your stale backup files must be taken with extreme care. As was mentioned earlier, modification of the XML files that SharePoint creates to track your backups is not supported by Microsoft, and if you remove the backup packages listed in those files, SharePoint does not update them to reflect those changes. This means that the archived backup packages are still displayed in the Central Administration Backup and Restore History page even though they are no longer available. Attempting to restore one of those missing packages results in the Central Administration site displaying a `File Not Found` error, with no other information provided by SharePoint regarding the error. Differential backups add complexity to the archival process because, to successfully restore a differential backup, you need the differential package and the last full backup package completed for the target component. Before archiving a full backup package, you need to confirm that no differential backups depend on it, because without both pieces, SharePoint displays a `File Not Found` error if you attempt to restore the differential backup.

CONCLUSION

Taking the limitations of the Central Administration site's backup and restore tools into account, it sometimes makes a lot of sense to use them to back up and restore your SharePoint environment. As mentioned earlier, the tool is useful for backing up your farm or components within it prior to a planned change or update to your environment. For example, it is a best practice to back up SharePoint before you apply any patches or hotfixes to your installed SharePoint system. The biggest reason for this is because the majority of Microsoft updates to SharePoint do not provide any mechanism to undo changes in the case of an error or conflict caused by the update. This is caused by SharePoint's heavy reliance on its backend databases to store content and configuration data. If the tables or schemas of SharePoint's databases are modified by an update, those changes cannot be reverted without the loss of the data in those databases. So the only way to recover from an error caused by an update or patch is to rebuild your SharePoint installation and restore a backup of your content. The backup and restore tools of the Central Administration site can be a valuable component of your change management process, allowing you to easily preserve your business-critical SharePoint content prior to an upgrade and restore it in case complications arise.

Another advantage to using the Central Administration backup and restore tools is the flexibility and feedback they give administrators while using them. The tool automatically enumerates the SharePoint components in your environment available for backup and allows you to make your selection through a graphical interface rather than the command line. Similarly, the tool shows you the backup packages in your storage location and important historical data about those packages to assist you in selecting the proper target for restoration. Finally, along every step of the way, the Central Administration site's backup and restore tools give you the opportunity to review and confirm your selections before initiating an operation, an important feature to take advantage of given the impact your actions can have on your environment.

To more deeply explore these advantages and how they can fit into your comprehensive disaster recovery methodology for SharePoint, please take a close look at Chapter 13, "SharePoint Disaster Recovery Design and Implementation." Upon completing this chapter, you should feel comfortable answering the following questions about the Central Administration site's backup and restore tools. You can find the answers to these questions in Appendix B, "Chapter Review Q&A," on the book's Web site at http://www.courseptr.com/downloads.

1. Which SharePoint and SQL Server service accounts must be granted rights to your target backup directory to successfully generate a backup through the Central Administration site? For bonus points, exactly what rights must be granted to those accounts?

2. What is the only way that you can back up or restore your SharePoint farm's Central Administration site?

3. If a backup or restore operation fails, what actions must you complete in the Central Administration site to submit a request to initiate a new backup or restore operation?

4. What are the differences between the Same Configuration and New Configuration options that you must choose between when restoring a backup?

5. What additional steps must you take to fully restore an SSP from a backup?

6. How do you back up or restore your environment's SSO settings?

7. What are the major drawbacks to relying on the Central Administration site as the only tool used to back up your SharePoint environment?

5 STSADM.exe's Backup and Restore Operations

In This Chapter

- Assumptions
- Accessing STSADM.exe
- STSADM.exe Backup and Restore Prerequisites
- How to Perform a Backup via STSADM.exe
- How to Restore a Backup via STSADM.exe
- STSADM Backup/Restore versus STSADM Export/Import

Since the initial release of SharePoint Team Services in 2001, the primary command-line tool available to administrators for configuring SharePoint's servers, sites, and databases has been STSADM.exe. In Windows SharePoint Services (WSS) v3 and Microsoft Office SharePoint Server (MOSS) 2007, STSADM.exe has been updated and extended to provide an even richer array of functionality, including new tools for backing up and restoring your SharePoint environment. STSADM.exe offers many of the same features and limitations as the Central Administration site's graphical user interface (GUI) backup and restore tool, including the requirement for a Universal Naming Convention (UNC) path for backup files, allowing for the backup of search indices, full or differential backups, no option to include Microsoft Internet Information Services (IIS) configurations and files in backups, and the inability to clean up old or expired backup files. STSADM.exe can create backups with the same granularity as the Central Administration site's backup and restore tool, and its backups can be restored in the same usage scenarios as the Central Administration site's GUI tool.

One difference between STSADM.exe and the Central Administration site's backup and restore tool is that STSADM.exe does not rely on the SPTimer service to execute its functions; it runs independently of that service on the target server.

The Central Administration site's tool actually uses the same functionality as STSADM.exe to run a backup or restore, but as mentioned in Chapter 4, "The Central Administration Site's Backup and Restore Tools," the Central Administration site's backup and restore operations run as timer jobs executed via the SharePoint farm's database access service account. This means that directly using STSADM.exe reduces the chance that it could affect the performance of other timer jobs, because it runs in its own process on the server and does not immediately impact the other SharePoint processes running on the server.

CAUTION

Although backup and restore operations requested via the Central Administration site are run using the identity of the farm database access account, backup and restore operations with STSADM.exe are run using the security credentials of the user running the Windows Command Shell session used to call STSADM.exe. This means that the account used to run the Windows Command Shell must be assigned the db_creator *and* securityadmin *roles in the SQL Server database instance hosting the farm's database and dbo rights in the SharePoint databases targeted by the STSADM.exe operation. For more information, see http:// support.microsoft.com/default.aspx?scid=kb;EN-US;896148.*

The biggest advantage to using STSADM.exe is that it is a command-line executable program; it can be configured as a Scheduled Task in Windows on its own or as a part of a batch script. This means that it can be set up to run as an automatic task that does not require manual intervention to run. This is an important component of properly protecting your environment in the case of a disaster and one not directly offered by SharePoint out of the box without some additional development and configuration by an administrator. Chapter 7, "Custom Development and Scripting for SharePoint Disaster Recovery," covers automating the execution of backup operations with STSADM.exe in more detail, but this chapter explains the specifics of executing backup and restore operations with STSADM.exe.

ASSUMPTIONS

The visual examples provided in this chapter were generated in a testing environment using the platforms and components listed next. Depending on how your environment is configured, your experiences may vary slightly. Unless a specific item indicates that it is unique to MOSS, the features and functionality covered in this chapter apply to both WSS and MOSS in the same fashion.

■ **Operating system.** Microsoft Windows Server 2003 R2 Enterprise Edition Service Pack (SP) 2

Whenever possible, restore your site collection backup package to a site collection within the same Active Directory (AD) domain as the original site. Restoring the backup to a different AD domain can result in the loss of your site's user and permissions data, such as the site collection's Users list and individual permissions for list items.

Locking a Site Collection Prior to Backup

One highly recommended activity before generating a site collection backup, regardless of the tool that you use to do it, is to lock the site so that users cannot attempt to update the site while the backup operation is running. Site collection administrators can lock the site via the Site Settings menu of the site collection, or the site can be locked via STSADM.exe's GetSiteLock and SetSiteLock operations. Because this section covers the use of STSADM.exe for backup and restore, it focuses on using the STSADM.exe locking operations in conjunction with its backup and restore operations. The first thing you should do to properly lock a site with STSADM.exe is to check its current status; if it is already locked, you do not have to take actions prior to initiating your backup or restore operation.

Figure 5.3 uses the GetSiteLock operation to check the lock status of the http://foo site collection by passing the site's URL as an input parameter. This is the only parameter or switch used for this operation; it simply returns a message stating whether the site collection is locked. If the site is already locked, you can move on to backing it up. If it is not locked, you need to lock it yourself through the SetSiteLock operation.

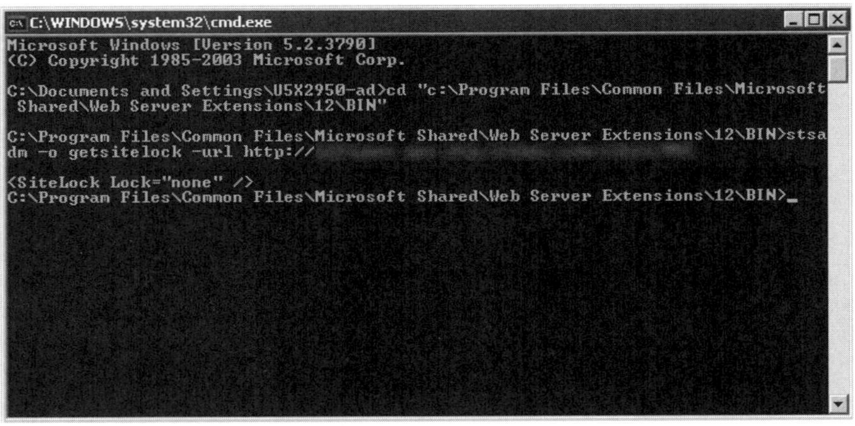

FIGURE 5.3 An example of STSADM.exe's GetSiteLock operation.

- **Microsoft .NET Framework.** Versions 1.1, 2.0 SP1, 3.0 SP 1, and 3.5
- **Database.** Microsoft SQL Server 2005 Developer Edition Service Pack 2
- **Web server.** Microsoft IIS 6.0
- **SharePoint.** MOSS 2007 Enterprise Edition

ACCESSING STSADM.EXE

In Windows Server 2003, command-line tools like STSADM.exe are accessed via the Windows Command Shell (see Figure 5.1), a simple text-based dialog box designed to allow users to interact with and update the operating system. To open a new instance of the Windows Command Shell, execute the following steps:

1. Open a Remote Desktop connection to your SharePoint server.
2. Click the Start button and select the Run option.
3. When the Run dialog box opens, type cmd.exe and click the OK button.
4. A new window titled Command Prompt opens and displays a directory path followed by a text prompt. This is the Windows Command Shell.

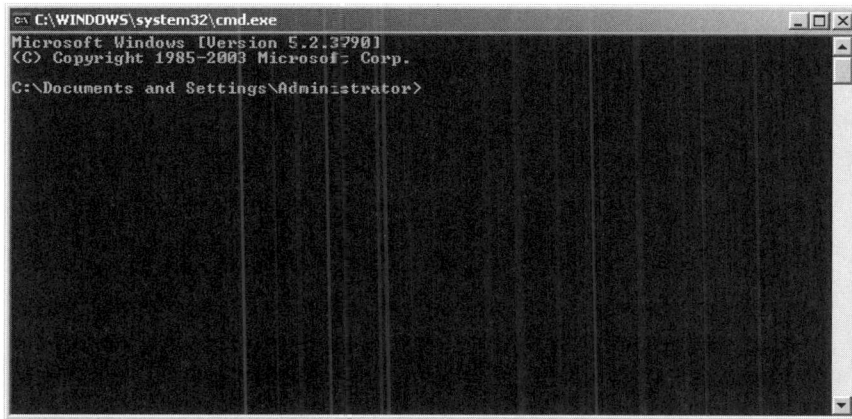

FIGURE 5.1 The Windows Command Shell.

STSADM.exe is installed by default on all servers where you have installed SharePoint. For an example of the directory that contains STSADM.exe, see Figure 5.2. It is located on the drive SharePoint was installed on at the following path:

```
%COMMONPROGRAMFILES%\Microsoft Shared\Web Server Extensions\12\Bin
```

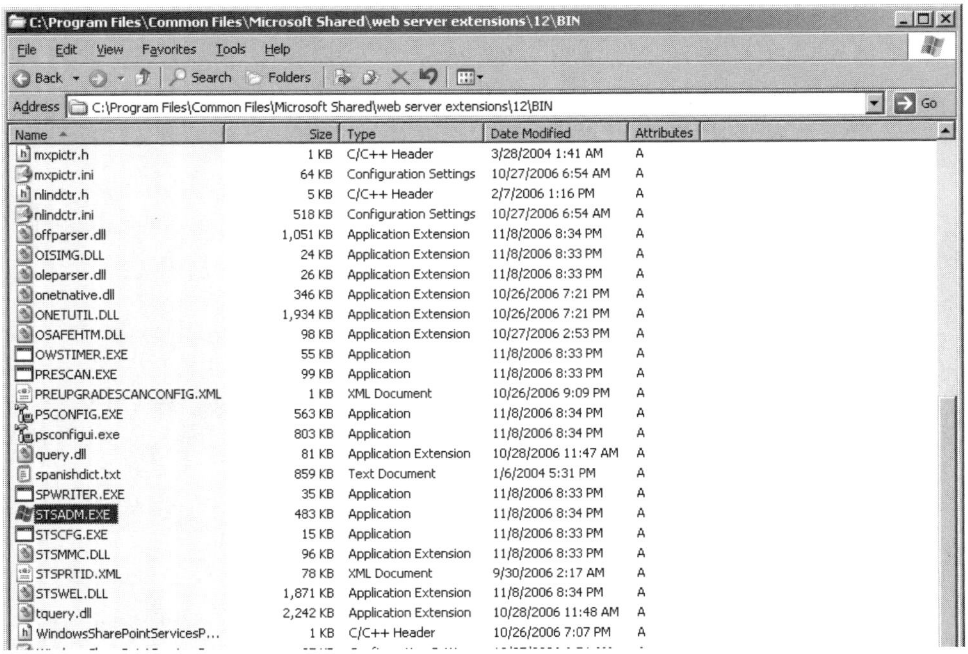

FIGURE 5.2 STSADM.exe in its default location on a 32-bit server.

TIP

The exact location of the %COMMONPROGRAMFILES% *variable listed in the previous example path is determined by the use of 32- or 64-bit hardware, 32- or 64-bit versions of the Windows operating system, or 32- or 64-bit versions of SharePoint. If you are running a 64-bit version of Windows Server on 64-bit hardware, you should see two Program Files directories in your system drive:* Program Files *and* Program Files (x86). *The former is for 64-bit native applications, whereas the latter is for 32-bit applications.*

The PATH environment variable allows the Windows Server operating system to store a predefined set of directory paths it can search for executables whenever a request is submitted to run an executable without an explicit path to it. When you run a program such as iisreset.exe in the Windows Command Shell from any directory without specifying a path to the application, Windows uses the PATH variable to determine what program needs to be executed. SharePoint does not register a system PATH variable for STSADM.exe, so you need to navigate to the directory containing the application to run it. You can, however, add STSADM.exe's directory path to the PATH variable, allowing you to run the application from any directory on the server.

According to Microsoft, to run STSADM.exe, your account, at a minimum, must be a member of the local Administrators group on your SharePoint server. To successfully execute most tasks with STSADM.exe, you need to have rights in your SharePoint environment's databases equivalent to your farm's SharePoint database access service account or be running STSADM.exe as the database access service account. STSADM.exe is executed by typing the name of the application into the Windows Command Shell followed by one to many arguments and pressing the Enter key, as in this example:

```
STSADM.exe -o backup -url http://foo/bar -filename c:\foo.bak
```

Before covering the various arguments that can be used to run backup and restore operations, it's important to examine the structure of the previous example to understand how to use STSADM.exe. Directly following the name of the application is the operator (–o) switch and its input parameter, (backup), which defines the operation that STSADM.exe is being requested to perform. In this example, it is a backup operation, but it could also be a restore, a solution deployment, or many other operations. The switches that you can use with the operation switch vary depending on the operation requested. Some switches require that an input parameter be provided to further clarify their intent, whereas others do not. For a complete description of STSADM.exe and the operations it can be used for, see http://technet.microsoft.com/en-us/library/cc261956.aspx. If you cannot find the page, search Microsoft's TechNet Web site (http://technet.microsoft.com) for the string STSADM Command Line tool (Office SharePoint Server).

STSADM.exe is not case sensitive; you can execute it using all caps, all lowercase, or a combination of the two. It does not behave differently depending on the casing used.

NOTE

One useful feature of the STSADM.exe application is its built-in Help operation. A call to STSADM.exe's Help operation for information on a desired operation results in a display of all the switches and input parameters that can be used when running the target operation. Simply provide the name of the target operation after the listed Help operation, and the results will be printed to the Windows Command Shell window:

TIP

```
STSADM.EXE -help backup
```

STSADM.exe Backup and Restore Prerequisites

Although Microsoft states that the user must be a local administrator on the SharePoint server to execute STSADM.exe, in actuality elevated rights are required to successfully complete many operations with the tool, including the backup and restore operations. For the backup and restore operations, the account logged into the Windows Command Shell to run STSADM.exe must be an owner of the SharePoint databases impacted by the operation. (The account should be granted the db_owner role in SQL Server.) This can lead to a difficult situation for administrators, because according to Microsoft's recommended best practices, this level of permission should really only be granted to the SharePoint database access service account. It's best to run STSADM.exe as the SharePoint database access service account when performing backup and restore operations.

> *Be careful about the rights granted to SharePoint administrators within your SharePoint databases in SQL Server. From an administrative standpoint, the best practice is to grant each account the least privileges necessary to complete the user's assigned tasks, and this is especially important with SharePoint. Granting elevated database privileges to administrators can increase the risk that unintended and disastrous changes can be made to your databases and impact not only the ongoing service of your SharePoint farm, but your ability to patch and update it as well.*

The account you are using to execute STSADM.exe must also have the right to read from the directory used as the target storage location for the backup files that will be created, as well as to write and update files in the directory. Depending on your SharePoint farm's configuration, the directory you use as the target storage location can be mapped via a file system path such as C:\backups or a UNC path such as \\backups. The individual sections of this chapter outline when each mapping option can or cannot be used based on the type of backup or restore operation you are performing.

> *As with the Central Administration site's backup and restore tool, the amount of storage space available in your target storage location is important to consider before backing up your SharePoint farm with STSADM.exe. The tool does not automatically compress files or archive older files to free up additional space as needed. You must ensure that the selected storage location is large enough to hold your backup files. For more information, see the "Central Administration Backup and Restore Prerequisites" section in Chapter 4.*

How to Perform a Backup via STSADM.exe

As you saw with the previous example of how STSADM.exe can be called, you can configure and submit SharePoint backup requests through STSADM.exe by creating a text string of commands and options. Because you have already seen how to access and execute STSADM.exe, you can move on to the two different types of backups that can be completed via the tool: site collection backups and catastrophic backups.

Site Collection Backups via STSADM.exe

As its name states, STSADM.exe's site collection backup operation is used to back up SharePoint site collections. Administrators can back up site collections with STSADM.exe by calling the backup operation and specifying the –url, followed by the URL of the target site collection as an input parameter.

```
STSADM.exe -o backup -url http://foo/bar -filename \\backups\foo.bak
```

The previous example request is configured to completely back up the SharePoint site collection http://foo/bar and save it to a file named foo.bak in the backups shared directory. STSADM.exe automatically creates one to many backup files in your target location, based on the size of the site collection you have selected to back up.

The list that follows details each switch that you can use in a site collection backup operation and its purpose:

■ **URL.** When you back up a site collection, this parameter is required and must be a valid URL for the target site collection.

■ **Filename.** When you back up a site collection, this parameter is required and must be a valid UNC or Windows directory path to a file that the backup is saved in. The account logged into the Windows Command Shell to run STSADM.exe must have permission to write to the directory specified for this input.

No required extension must be used when specifying the file name for your backup. Use something easily identifiable as a backup file, such as .bak. Regardless of the extension you specify, SharePoint creates your backup at the selected path and restores it if needed.

TIP

■ **Overwrite.** When you back up a site collection, this switch is not required. Using it instructs STSADM.exe to overwrite any existing backup file matching the value of the -filename parameter.

As you can see in Figure 5.4, the SetSiteLock operation uses the URL input parameter to define the target site collection, but it also takes a Lock parameter to
configure how the site collection is locked by STSADM.exe. In this case, the
NoAccess input parameter is used to completely block users from accessing the site
while it's being backed up.

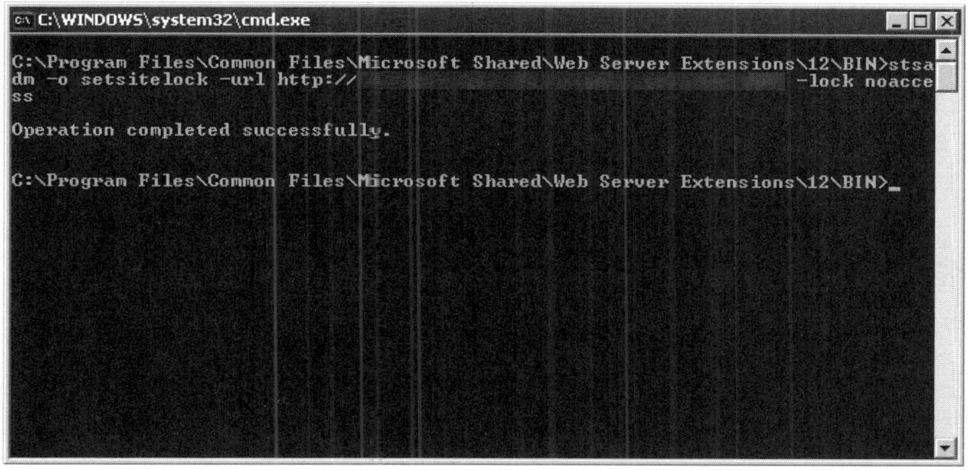

FIGURE 5.4 An example of STSADM.exe's SetSiteLock operation.

Following are the acceptable values for the Lock parameter and their impact on
the operation:

- **None.** This value unlocks the site collection if it was previously locked. The text
value for this input is actually None, not blank text. You must actually provide
the text None as the input parameter value to unlock a site collection.
- **NoAdditions.** This setting allows the site collection to be modified as long as
the modification reduces the size of the data retained by the site. If a user
wanted to delete an existing item in a list, this setting would allow him to do so
while at the same time prevent him from adding new content to the list.
Attempting an action prohibited by this setting results in a page displaying a
message stating Access to this Web site has been blocked. Please
contact the administrator to resolve this problem.
- **ReadOnly.** This value places the site in read-only mode, allowing its contents to
be viewed but not updated. Any user attempting to update the site in any way
is displayed a page with a message stating Access to this Web site has
been blocked. Please contact the administrator to resolve this
problem.

■ **NoAccess.** Use of this value blocks all access to the site, displaying a message stating `Access to this Web site has been blocked. Please contact the administrator to resolve this problem.`

You should only use the SetSiteLock operation on URLs that map to Web applications or site collections within SharePoint; if a URL for a subsite within a site collection is submitted, STSADM.exe locks the entire site collection, not just the subsite. After the backup operation is complete, you can re-run the SetSiteLock operation with a `Lock` input parameter of `None` to unlock the site again for users.

Although it's recommend that you lock a site prior to backing it up, it's up to you to decide what approach is the best fit for your environment and needs. If you choose to lock the site or place it in read-only mode before backing it up, the first thing you should do after restoring a site collection backup is run the GetSiteLock operation to determine if the restored site collection is still in that state. If it is, you need to run a SetSiteLock operation with a Lock input parameter of None for the restored site collection before modifying it in any way. If you fail to do so, your users may not be able to access the site, or you may encounter issues making configuration changes to the site collection as a site collection administrator and getting those changes saved to the SharePoint databases.

CAUTION

CATASTROPHIC BACKUPS VIA STSADM.EXE

You can use STSADM.exe's catastrophic backup operation to back up a wide range of SharePoint components, much like the Central Administration site's backup tool. With it, you can back up SharePoint site collections, databases, Web applications, or your entire farm. The STSADM.exe tool generates a catastrophic backup when the backup operation is called using the `-backupmethod` switch followed by a valid input parameter.

```
STSADM.exe -o backup -directory \\backups -backupmethod full -item
"farm\windows sharepoint services web application\foo web
application\foo_content_database" -percentage 10 -backupthreads 3
```

In the previous example, a backup of the `foo_content_database` is being requested and written to the `backups` shared directory. The example operation displays progress updates at 10 percent intervals of completion and uses three processor threads to complete the backup. The switches and inputs that you can use in a catastrophic backup operation are as follows:

■ **Directory.** When you're performing a catastrophic backup, this parameter is required. The target directory can be on the file system if SharePoint is installed on the same server as its backend database; otherwise, it must be a UNC shared directory.

■ **Backupmethod.** When you're performing a catastrophic backup, this parameter is required. Acceptable input parameter values are `full` or `differential` and determine what type of backup is made for the target SharePoint component. For more information on the differences between full and differential backups, see the "Configure Your Backup" section in Chapter 4.

■ **Item.** When you're performing a catastrophic backup, this parameter is not required. By default, if no item is specified, the entire farm is backed up. If an `Item` input parameter is provided to specify the SharePoint component to be backed up, it must be a valid item in the farm. If the item has spaces in its name, the entire item must be enclosed within quotation marks (" "). If the exact name or path for the desired component is not known, you can use the `ShowTree` switch to list the components available within the farm.

■ **ShowTree.** When you're performing a catastrophic backup, this switch is not required. If the `ShowTree` switch is included with the call of STSADM.exe for a backup, the tool does not complete a backup of any SharePoint components. Instead, it displays the components in the farm so that their names can be used to request a backup. If a value is specified via the `Item` parameter, any components that are not children of that input are excluded and marked with an asterisk (*). Any components that cannot be backed up are enclosed within square brackets ([ ]).

■ **Percentage.** When you're performing a catastrophic backup, this input parameter is not required. If a value is specified for the `Percentage` input parameter, it must be an integer between 1 and 100 and is used to determine the frequency with which STSADM.exe reports progress of the backup operation to the Windows Command Shell. For example, specifying a value of 20 displays the progress of the backup operation for every 20 percent of the operation that is completed. If no `Percentage` parameter is specified, STSADM.exe defaults to reporting progress every 5 percent. This input parameter has no impact on the outcome of the backup operation; it only affects the amount of information that STSADM.exe reports about its activities during the operation. SharePoint is not able to calculate the percent completed of the backup operation with 100 percent accuracy. You may find that your actual progress updates do not appear with exactly the requested frequency.

For large SharePoint components, Microsoft recommends that a Percentage input of 1 be used to provide the best status data about your backup operation.

TIP

THE BACKUP OPERATION'S SHOWTREE SWITCH

If you have a large farm with multiple Web applications and site collections, you may find it difficult to view the results of an STSADM.exe backup operation with the ShowTree switch in the default console for the Windows Command Shell. To easily view the items displayed by the ShowTree switch, you can configure the Windows Command Shell to write its output to a text file instead of the screen. This allows you to open the text file, search its contents for the item you are looking for, and copy its data to the Clipboard for reuse elsewhere. To write the output of any command in the Windows Command Shell to a text file, append a greater than character (>) followed by a space and the target file (including its full path; if no path is provided, the file is written to the directory on your server containing the STSADM.exe executable) for which you want to store the operation's output. The example that follows depicts a sample call of the STSADM.exe backup operation with the ShowTree switch configured to write its output to a text file:

```
STSADM.exe -o backup -showtree > c:\backup_items.txt
```

In addition, all other standard Windows Command Shell commands that can be used to modify or reroute output, such as pipes and filters, can be used with STSADM.exe. For example, you can apply the MORE.exe filter to paginate STSADM.exe's output so that you can view it at a pace that the user defines.

```
STSADM.exe -o backup -showtree | MORE
```

Or if you wanted to show only objects containing the string "Web" in their name, the following command could be used:

```
STSADM.exe -o backup -showtree | FIND "Web"
```

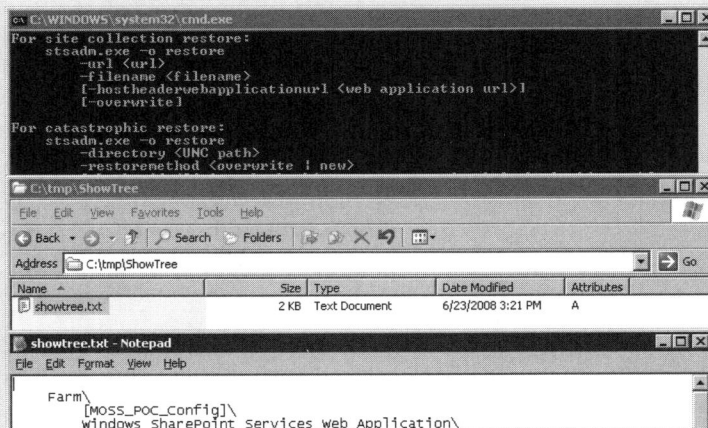

FIGURE 5.5 A request of the STSADM.exe backup operation with the ShowTree switch in the Windows Command Shell window designed to write its output to a file named showtree.txt.

■ **Backupthreads.** When you're performing a catastrophic backup, this input parameter is not required. It determines the number of threads SharePoint uses to complete the backup operation and must be an integer from 1 to 10. If no Backupthreads value is provided, SharePoint defaults to one thread.

For WSS 3.0, Microsoft recommends using three threads to complete backups but does not provide a recommendation specific to MOSS 2007. The use of additional threads adds more data to your backup logs and makes them more difficult to read. It's recommend that you use one thread unless you are experiencing long-running backup operations and can do so without impacting the performance of the SharePoint server hosting the backup operation.

■ **Quiet.** When you're performing a catastrophic backup, this switch is not required. If the Quiet switch is specified, it suppresses all output about the backup operation to the Windows Command Shell until the final backup status message is displayed. STSADM.exe still logs data about the operation to other normal SharePoint sources, but administrators do not receive a status until the operation is completed. If the switch is not listed in the call to STSADM.exe, all normal output is reported to the Windows Command Shell.

Although STSADM.exe's site collection backup operation usually creates a single file to store the backup data, the catastrophic backup operation uses a directory to hold the backup files, much like the Central Administration site's backup tool. In fact, the backup packages created by STSADM can actually be stored in the same place as backup packages created through the Central Administration site, and each tool can restore packages created by the other. STSADM.exe creates a folder named SPBR*NNNN* (where *NNNN* is an incremental, unique three-digit number) that follows the same structure for its contents as the folders created by the Central Administration site. For more information on its contents, see the "Your Backup Files" section in Chapter 4.

How to Restore a Backup via STSADM.exe

Restoring a backup with STSADM.exe is completed in much the same manner as the process you followed to create the backup in the first place. The permissions required to complete the operations are the same, and both operations use many of the same switches and parameters. The main difference is that now instead of specifying backup as the input parameter for the –o operation switch, you must enter a value of restore, followed by several other parameters and switches to configure the restoration. As with STSADM.exe's backup operation, the restore operation is broken into two different use cases: restoring a site collection backup and restoring a catastrophic backup.

RESTORING A SITE COLLECTION BACKUP WITH **STSADM.EXE**

Restoring a site collection backup with STSADM.exe restores the site collection in a backup to a requested URL within your SharePoint environment. Keep in mind that you can only use backups created with STSADM.exe's site collection backup operation for this type of restore operation. If you are restoring a catastrophic backup created with STSADM.exe or a backup created through the Central Administration site, you must use the restore operation for catastrophic backups. Following is an example of a requested site collection restore operation with STSADM.exe:

```
STSADM.exe -o restore -url http://foo/sites/bar -filename
\\backups\foo.bak
```

As you can see, the only difference between this site collection restoration example and the previous site collection backup request is the use of the `restore` operation input parameter. This example is requesting that SharePoint restore the backup file `foo.bak` to the URL http://foo/sites/bar and assumes that there is not an existing site collection at that URL.

The list that follows details each switch that can be used in a site collection restore operation and its purpose:

- **URL.** When you're restoring a site collection backup, this parameter is required and is the URL that you want users to enter when accessing your restored site collection. The use of this parameter indicates to STSADM.exe that you are restoring a site collection backup and not a catastrophic backup. The value submitted for the URL parameter is not required to match the URL of the backup package's original site collection. You can restore STADM.exe's site collection backups to a new URL and attempt to update all the paths within the backup package to reflect the new URL for the site collection. Make sure to fully test the restored site collection's resources that depend on this information, such as links, navigation controls, and search results, to confirm that all the collection's data was correctly updated to the new path. Although this is a legitimate usage of the tool and it is supported by Microsoft, experience has shown that it is not a perfect process and its output needs to be validated before users are allowed into the site collection.
- **Filename.** When you're restoring a site collection, this parameter is required and must be a valid UNC or Windows file path to a backup package created via an STSADM.exe site collection backup operation.

If STSADM.exe created more than one backup file when you originally created your site collection backup, simply provide the name of the first file STSADM.exe created. (It should have the name you provided when the backup was created.) STSADM.exe automatically includes all files associated with the backup and restores their contents to the target site collection.

- **HostHeaderWebApplicationURL.** When you're restoring a site collection backup, this parameter is not required. You use it if you want to restore your site collection to a Web application with a different URL than the value specified for the URL input parameter. This parameter is explained in more detail later.
- **Overwrite.** When you're restoring a site collection backup, this switch is not required. Using it instructs STSADM.exe to overwrite any existing site collection matching the value of the –URL parameter. If you are restoring a site collection backup to the same Web application as the site it was based on, you must either delete the original site prior to the restore or use the Overwrite switch. Otherwise, STSADM.exe detects a conflict between the GUID of the original site and the GUID of the site you are attempting to restore and reports an error stating No content databases are available for this operation. Create a content database, and then try the operation again.

When you're restoring a site collection using the overwrite operation, you must execute STSADM.exe using the identity of a site collection administrator for the target site collection.

You can use the HostHeaderWebApplicationURL parameter to restore a site collection to a URL different from the URL of its parent Web application. If you pass a value of http://bar for the HostHeaderWebApplicationURL parameter as an addition to the previous example, the restore operation creates a site collection for the foo address under the bar Web application even though they have different URLs. When it runs the restore operation, STSADM.exe generates a host header for the target Web application in IIS so that requests submitted to the server for http://foo are mapped to the restored site collection even though it is within a Web application with a different URL (http://bar).

SharePoint site collections created using a host header in this fashion are called host-named site collections. (In the previous release of SharePoint, this approach was known as scalable hosting mode.) Unlike normal site collections, host-named site collections use IIS host headers to direct traffic to the correct site collection instead of managed paths. This allows multiple site collections within a single Web application to have a unique URL that can be used to access its content independent of the other site collections in the Web application. For more information on host-named site collections and their impact on the architecture and administration of your SharePoint farm, review this article from the Microsoft Knowledge Base: http://technet.microsoft.com/en-us/library/cc424952.aspx.

RESTORING A CATASTROPHIC BACKUP WITH **STSADM.EXE**

When used properly, with the correct combination of input parameters and switches, restoring a catastrophic backup package can be easy with STSADM.exe. The problem is that it is often difficult to accurately compile that correct combination of input parameters and switches and execute the restore operation without error. STSADM.exe is a powerful tool, but it is uncompromising; it does not prompt you if you enter erroneous data as an input or omit a required switch. It does not notify you that there is an error until you attempt to initiate the restore operation. The good news is that you can use several options with STSADM.exe's restore operation to collect the data you need to correctly format a request to restore a catastrophic backup package. But before getting into these advanced options, you must examine a basic request to restore a catastrophic backup.

Restoring a Catastrophic Backup over the Current Version of the Site

```
STSADM.exe -o restore -directory \\backups -restoremethod overwrite
```

In this example, the user is requesting that the most recent backup stored in the Backups shared directory be restored over the current version of the component included in the backup files. This is a basic restore request; quite a few other options are available to be used when restoring a catastrophic backup package, as shown here:

- **Directory.** When you're restoring a catastrophic backup, this parameter is required. The target directory can be on the file system if SharePoint is installed on the same server as its backend database; otherwise, it must be a UNC shared directory. The use of this input parameter indicates to STSADM.exe that you are restoring a catastrophic backup and not a site collection backup.
- **RestoreMethod.** When you're restoring a catastrophic backup, this parameter is required. The only two acceptable values for this parameter are Overwrite and New. A value of Overwrite requests that the SharePoint component(s) in the catastrophic backup package be restored to their original location, overwriting any content or settings that have been modified since the backup was taken. If Overwrite is specified as the value of the RestoreMethod parameter, a confirmation prompt is displayed unless the SuppressPrompt switch is included in the call of STSADM.exe.

■ **BackupID.** When you're restoring a catastrophic backup, this parameter is not required. When used, this input parameter must be a valid GUID associated with a backup package in the location specified in the `Directory` input. You can find the GUIDs associated with the backup packages in a directory via STSADM.exe's BackupHistory operation or by viewing the `spbrtoc.xml` file in the target directory. If this parameter is not provided, STSADM.exe selects the most recent full backup package in the target directory to be restored.

Take note that if a `BackupID` is not provided, STSADM.exe uses the most recent full backup package in the target directory. If any differential backups were made after the latest full backup, those changes are not included in the restore operation.

CAUTION

■ **Item.** When you're restoring a catastrophic backup, this parameter is not required. The `Item` input parameter specifies what component within the backup package STSADM.exe should restore. The value provided must be a valid name for a component within the backup package, which can be displayed by using the `ShowTree` switch (see the later bullet) or by viewing the `spbrtoc.xml` file in the target directory. If no `Item` is specified, all the components in the target catastrophic backup package are restored.

If the name of the target component within the backup package contains one or more spaces, enclose the name within quotation marks when listing it as an `Item` input parameter.

TIP

■ **Percentage.** When you're restoring a catastrophic backup, this parameter is not required. If a value is specified for the `Percentage` input parameter, it must be an integer between 1 and 100 and is used to determine the frequency with which STSADM.exe reports progress of the restore operation to the Windows Command Shell. For example, specifying a value of 20 displays the progress of the backup operation for every 20 percent of the operation that is completed. If no `Percentage` is specified, STSADM.exe defaults to reporting progress every 5 percent. SharePoint cannot calculate the percent of the restore operation completed with 100 percent accuracy. You may find that your actual progress updates do not appear with exactly the requested frequency.

For large SharePoint components, such as farms or databases over 20GB, Microsoft recommends that a `Percentage` input of 1 be used to provide the best status data on your restore operation.

TIP

■ **ShowTree.** When you're restoring a catastrophic backup, this switch is not required. If the ShowTree switch is included in an STSADM.exe restore operation, the tool does not complete a restore of any SharePoint components. Instead, it displays the components in the farm that were present at the time the backup package was created so their names can be used to request a restore. The path provided as input for the –directory parameter of an STSADM.exe restore operation with the ShowTree switch determines which backup package should have its farm's contents be displayed, but only the components originally selected for the backup will be available to be restored. If a value is specified via the Item parameter, any components that are not children of that input are excluded and marked with an asterisk (*). Any components that cannot be restored are enclosed within square brackets ([ ]).

■ **SuppressPrompt.** When you're restoring a catastrophic backup, this switch is not required. Adding this switch to the restoration of a catastrophic backup with STSADM.exe prevents the Windows Command Shell from displaying a prompt such as Warning: All selected items will be overwritten. Do you want them to be overwritten (Y/N)?

This switch should only be used when a value of Overwrite is provided as an input parameter to the RestoreMethod switch. This switch is especially useful when automating restore operations via a scripted call of STSADM.exe, which are discussed in Chapter 7.

■ **Username.** When you're restoring a catastrophic backup, this parameter is not required. The value provided for the Username input parameter must be a valid and active SQL Server login name that has sufficient permissions (at a minimum, the db_creator and security_admin roles are required) within the target SQL Server environment to restore the requested components. A Username must only be provided if your SharePoint environment is using SQL authentication to connect to its backend SQL Server databases.

■ **Password.** When you're restoring a catastrophic backup, this parameter is not required. The value provided for the Password input parameter must be the exact password associated with the username value supplied for the Username input parameter. A Password must only be provided if your SharePoint environment is using SQL authentication to connect to its backend SQL Server databases.

■ **NewDatabaseServer.** When you're restoring a catastrophic backup, this parameter is not required. The NewDatabaseServer input parameter indicates the SQL Server instance that should be used to host any databases being restored when a value of New is specified for the RestoreMethod input parameter. The Windows Command Shell prompts you for a database server instance for each restored database within the target catastrophic backup package. This input parameter is not valid when a value of `Overwrite` is specified for the `RestoreMethod` input parameter; STSADM.exe displays an error if that combination is attempted, stating `Restore option newdatabaseserver can only be used when restoremethod is new`.

■ **Quiet.** When you're restoring a catastrophic backup, this switch is not required. If you specify the `Quiet` switch, it suppresses all output about the restore operation to the Windows Command Shell until the final restore status message is displayed. STSADM.exe still logs data about the operation to other normal SharePoint sources, but administrators do not receive a status until the operation is completed. If the switch is not listed in the call to STSADM.exe, all normal output is reported to the Windows Command Shell.

As the list shows, some of the input options for the restore of a catastrophic backup via STSADM.exe are used for informational purposes, whereas others actually configure and request an actual restore operation. Before you attempt to restore a catastrophic backup package, you should use the informational options for the STSADM.exe restore operation to determine exactly what inputs are required to restore your SharePoint component to their required state. Next, you will see examples of the process to follow to correctly restore a SharePoint component, one in which an existing SharePoint content database is overwritten and one in which the backup is restored from an existing SharePoint farm to a new SharePoint farm.

The first example assumes that you recently created a full backup of your entire SharePoint farm through STSADM.exe and have been asked to overwrite a single site collection in your production SharePoint farm with the saved version in the most recent full backup file. Because SharePoint does not allow for the individual backup of subsites within a site collection, you may find that this is a common request when a site is unintentionally deleted from within a site collection and needs to be fully restored. Although the information provided for this example request is enough to identify what you want to restore, it is not enough to tell STSADM.exe exactly how to restore that site collection to the proper location within your farm. So you use STSADM.exe and the `ShowTree` switch to figure out the exact values necessary to restore your desired site collection from backup. You can see an example call to STSADM.exe's restore operation with the `ShowTree` switch in Figure 5.6.

When the restore operation with the `ShowTree` switch is completed, as seen in Figure 5.7, the Windows Command Shell outputs a list of the components within your SharePoint farm and their availability for restoration. To restore the target site collection, you must note its full name in the output of the `ShowTree` call, as well as the full name of its parent components. After you have obtained that information, you can move on to the operation that actually restores your target site collection.

FIGURE 5.6 This example shows an STSADM.exe restore operation in the Windows Command Shell, including the ShowTree switch.

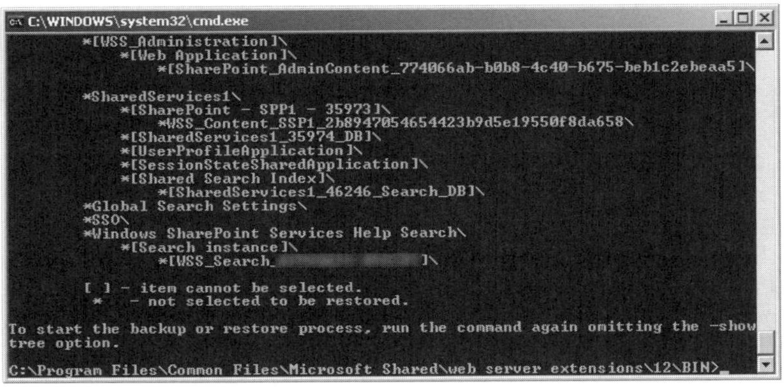

FIGURE 5.7 The output of the STSADM.exe restore operation, using the ShowTree switch to display the contents of the target SharePoint farm.

Because you are restoring your site collection from your most recent full backup, you do not have to specify a BackupID parameter to restore your target site collection because STSADM.exe automatically selects its most recent backup from within the target directory by default. You do, however, need to correctly provide the full name of the target site collection as it exists within your farm.

Based on the data from the ShowTree call, you can now compile the STSADM.exe call to restore your target site collection from the backup and submit it, as depicted in Figure 5.8.

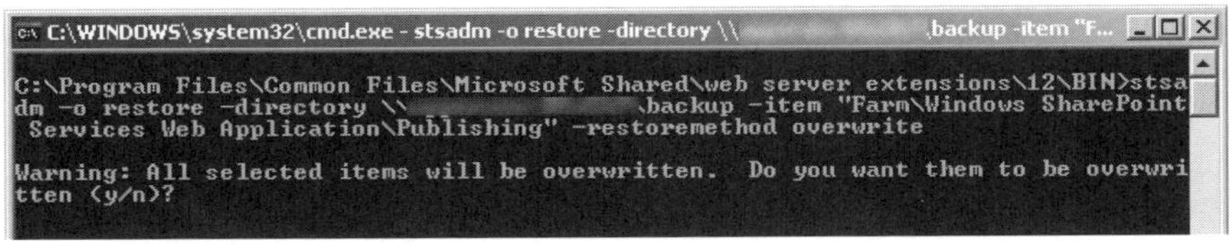

FIGURE 5.8 An example STSADM.exe restore operation requesting the restoration of a backup of the Publishing site collection over the current Publishing site collection in the target SharePoint farm.

Be careful to submit the same backup directory that you used in the ShowTree call, so that you use the same backup file as the source for the restoration of the site collection. Because you now know the name of the target site collection, you are submitting it as the Item parameter, exactly as it is listed in the results of the ShowTree call. This is important, not only because you want to make sure that you select exactly the right site collection to restore, but because it determines which site collection is to be overwritten by the restore operation.

*Do not submit values for the Item input parameter beginning with a backslash (\).
The restore operation fails to complete and displays an error stating that the target
Item was not found.*

CAUTION

As the restore operation runs, the Windows Command Shell displays its progress as streaming text (see Figure 5.9). As it enumerates through the contents of the backup package, you may be prompted for additional information needed by STSADM.exe to complete the operation, such as the target Web application's IIS application pool identity and its password. The operation also creates a log file (sprestore.log) containing this output in the directory of the backup package used to restore the site collection. If your restore operation encounters errors, examine the sprestore.log file for more information about what caused the operation to fail.

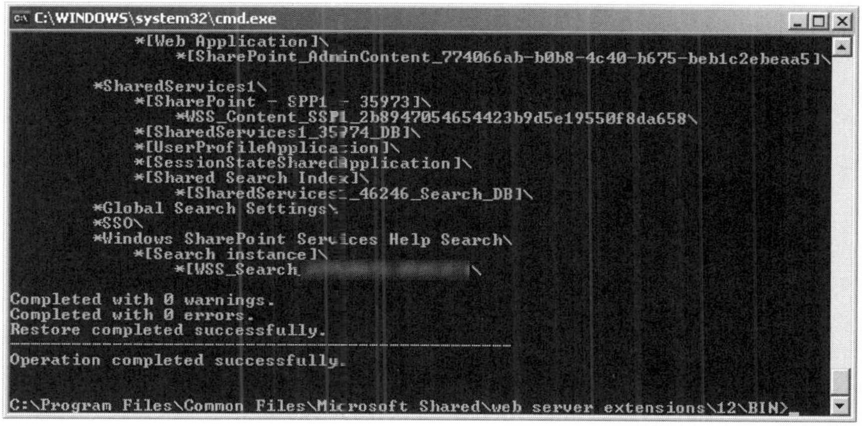

FIGURE 5.9 An example of the STSADM.exe's restore operation's final output.

Restoring a Catastrophic Backup to a New SharePoint Farm

Because you have successfully used STSADM.exe to restore a site collection into an existing SharePoint farm from a catastrophic backup package, you can now look at the second example: restoring a catastrophic backup to a new SharePoint farm with STSADM.exe. In this example, it is assumed that you have been asked to restore a specific catastrophic backup package created three weeks ago to a new SharePoint environment so that it can be compared to the current version of the environment.

> **CAUTION**
>
> *When you're restoring a backup file to a new SharePoint environment, it must match the environment that was backed up. It must use the same version of SharePoint (including service packs, hotfixes, and patches, not just the major version of the platform), the same version of SQL Server, and if any custom code (items deployed via SharePoint solution packages such as site templates, master pages, page layouts, or Web parts) was used in the original environment, it must also be deployed to the new one prior to the restore operation to avoid errors when it is completed.*

This example is a bit trickier than the previous one, not only because it requires more inputs in the restoration call with STSADM.exe, but because it involves more moving parts, components, and variables. Again, it is vital that you make an investigative request with STSADM.exe to get a better handle on some of these pieces before you submit your actual restore request in the command line. This time, however, because you need a backup that was generated three weeks ago and you do not know if another full backup had been made between then and now, you are using the Backuphistory operation for STSADM.exe, as shown in Figure 5.10. For more information on how to use the Backuphistory operation, see the related sidebar.

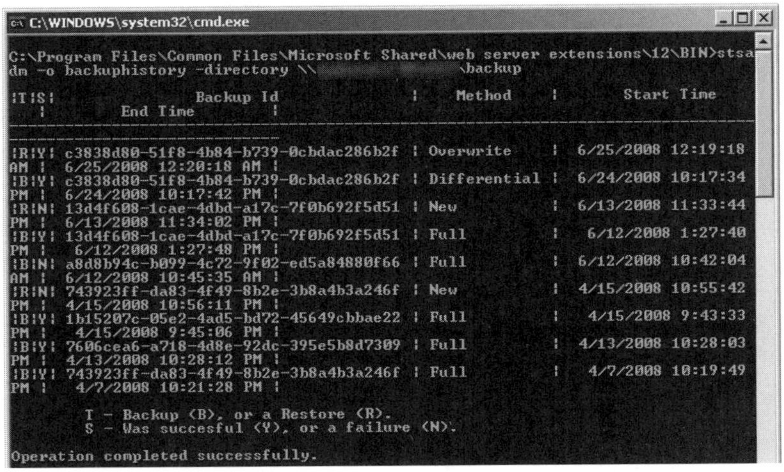

FIGURE 5.10 An example of STSADM.exe's Backuphistory operation and its output.

The STSADM.exe Backuphistory Operation

The purpose of the Backuphistory operation for STSADM.exe is pretty self-explanatory. It outputs a listing of the various backup and restore operations that have been conducted using the files in the specified directory. The Backuphistory operation uses the `spbrtoc.xml` file stored within the target backup storage directory to determine and display information.

The Backuphistory operation can only be used to display information on full or differential catastrophic backups created via STSADM.exe or the Central Administration site's backup tool. It does not work for other types of backups, such as site collection backups via STSADM.exe or backups created with other tools like SharePoint Designer or the Volume Shadow Copy Service (VSS). For more information on VSS and how you can integrate it with SharePoint as a disaster recovery tool, see Chapter 7.

A sample STSADM.exe Backuphistory operation request is listed next. You can also see an example in Figure 5.10:

```
stsadm.exe -o backuphistory -directory \\backups
```

You can use the following switches and input parameters with the Backuphistory operation:

- **Directory**. This input parameter is required when running a Backuphistory operation with STSADM.exe. The same rules apply to this parameter as the `Directory` input parameters for the restore and backup STSADM.exe operations discussed earlier.
- **Backup**. This input switch is not required when running a Backuphistory operation with STSADM.exe. When used, it filters the output of the operation so that only backup operation history data is displayed by STSADM.exe.
- **Restore**. This input switch is not required when running a Backuphistory operation with STSADM.exe. When used, it filters the output of the operation so that only restore operation history data is displayed by STSADM.exe.

If both the Backup *and* Restore *switches are omitted from the Backuphistory operation request, the history data for all backup and restore operations is displayed by STSADM.exe. If both the* Backup *and* Restore *switches are used with the Backuphistory operation, the history data for all backup and restore operations is displayed by STSADM.exe.*

Now that you have successfully run the Backuphistory operation, you can determine which backup you need to use for your restore operation and its BackupID. The only other input you need to consider is the target SQL Server database instance hosting your new farm's databases. In addition to determining the name of the database server, the account you use to run the STSADM.exe restore operation must have rights equivalent to the new farm's database access account. After you determine that information, you need to make sure that you are logged into the server hosting the Central Administration site for your new farm, not the old farm's Central Administration server, and you can proceed with the restore operation, as shown in Figure 5.11.

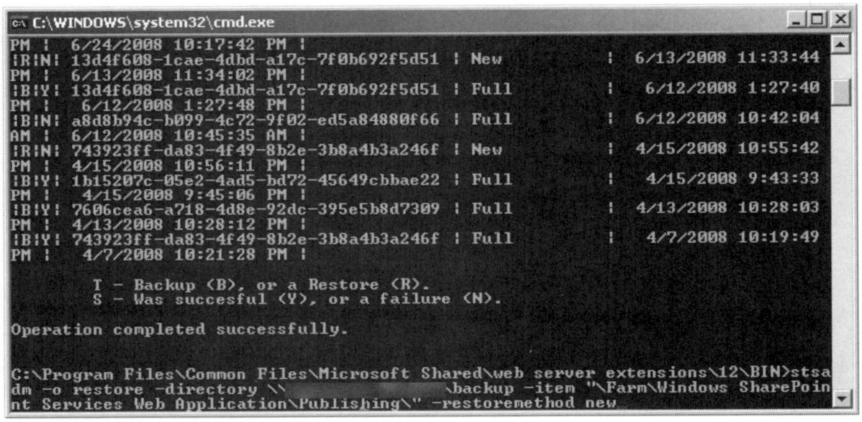

FIGURE 5.11 An STSADM.exe restore operation with a RestoreMethod of New and a GUID selected from a previous Backuphistory operation.

This operation restores your new SharePoint environment from backup files and deploys its databases to the specified SQL Server instance. Because you do not specify values for the Item and Percentage parameters or the Quiet switch, STSADM.exe uses the default behaviors for its actions and output. This means that all the components within the backup file are restored, the status of the operation is reported approximately every 5 percent, and all output is displayed in the Windows Command Shell. When the operation is completed, the farm should be ready to test and verify prior to normal usage to confirm that the backup was restored without error.

You may have noticed that a Username and Password were not provided for a SQL Server login in the previous restore operation. This is because the farm in the example uses Windows authentication rather than SQL authentication to connect SharePoint to SQL Server. This configuration is recommended by Microsoft and is the most likely choice for the majority of SharePoint environments. If you are using

SQL authentication to grant your SharePoint service account access to your databases in your target farm, you are required to submit values for the Username and Password inputs. Be careful when entering the value for the Password parameter; it is displayed in clear text to any users reading your screen while you have the Windows Command Shell open. You should close your Windows Command Shell session immediately after you are done with it to prevent that password from being stolen without your knowledge.

Restoring a Shared Services Provider via STSADM.exe

Similar to the process to fully restore a shared services provider (SSP) through the Central Administration site, there is an additional STSADM.exe command that you must execute to completely restore your SSP after you have restored a catastrophic backup. This process requires a completely different operation; instead of the Restore operation, you must use the RestoreSSP operation to direct STSADM.exe to properly associate your restored SSP with the Web applications in your environment. The RestoreSSP operation requires several input parameters and optional inputs. The list that follows describes the various components of the STSADM.exe operation.

NOTE

SSPs can be created only for SharePoint environments running MOSS 2007. WSS v3 does not offer the ability to create SSPs.

- **Title.** This input parameter is required when running a RestoreSSP operation through STSADM.exe and should be a character string containing only numbers and letters. STSADM.exe sets the submitted Title input value as the name of the new SSP.
- **URL.** This input parameter is required when running a RestoreSSP operation through STSADM.exe and should be formatted as a valid URL address string. The URL provided must be the correct URL for the SSP Web application in SharePoint that is hosting the restored SSP's administration site. Keep in mind that the Web application you specify cannot be associated with an application pool using the Network Service as its identity.
- **SSPLogin.** This input parameter is required when running a RestoreSSP operation through STSADM.exe. It must be a valid login for your environment, in the format of DOMAIN\username. This account is used as the identity for the SSP timer job and Web services.
- **MySiteURL.** Similar to the URL input, this parameter is required when running a RestoreSSP operation through STSADM.exe and should be formatted as a valid URL string. The URL provided should map to a SharePoint Web application that is used to host personal sites and user profiles for the users of your SharePoint environment.

Microsoft recommends that the value provided for MySiteURL *map to a Web application specifically created for hosting personal sites and user profiles. Sharing a SharePoint Web application with other SharePoint site collections can create the potential for performance issues and prevent you from backing up and restoring your MySite site collections independent of the other sites in the Web application.*

- **IndexServer.** This input parameter is required when running a RestoreSSP operation through STSADM.exe. The value provided should be a text string that maps to a valid computer or fully qualified domain name for a server in your SharePoint environment. STSADM.exe instructs the restored index server in your farm named in the IndexServerparameter to crawl content in all SharePoint Web applications associated with the restored SSP. The target server for the IndexServer parameter must have the Office SharePoint Server Search service enabled and running to be valid.
- **IndexLocation.** This input parameter is required when running a RestoreSSP operation through STSADM.exe. The text submitted must be a valid folder location on your environment's target index server in the form C:\Folder1\. This parameter determines where your environment's search index files are stored. Be sure to use a storage location on your server with enough disk space to store search data for all the content sources your SharePoint environment is going to crawl.
- **KeepIndex.** This switch is not required when running a RestoreSSP operation through STSADM.exe. This switch instructs STSADM.exe not to create a new search index or reset the existing index when the SSP has been restored and you are associating it with your environment's other Web applications.

Microsoft recommends that you use the KeepIndex *switch only when you are able to restore your search index and search databases at the same time using a backup and restore application from a third-party vendor.*

- **SSPPassword.** This input parameter is only required for the RestoreSSP operation if the account provided for the SSPLogin parameter has a password. (Some system accounts, such as Network Service, do not have a password associated with them.) If the account supplied for SSPLogin does have a password, it must be accurately entered here for the RestoreSSP operation to be successful. If a value is supplied for the SSPLogin parameter and the SSPPassword parameter isn't used in the call to STSADM.exe, you're prompted to enter a password value when the operation is executed.
- **SSPDatabaseServer.** This input parameter is not required when running a RestoreSSP operation through STSADM.exe. The value provided should be a text string that maps to a valid computer or fully qualified domain name for a

server with an installed SQL Server instance or directly to the name of the installed instance.

- **SSPDatabaseName.** This input is not required when running a RestoreSSP operation through STSADM.exe. The value provided should be a text string that identifies the SSP's backend database. The SSPDatabaseName value should not use words reserved in SQL Server for special activities, such as UPDATE or DELETE.

- **SSPSQLAuthLogin.** This input is only required for a RestoreSSP operation if SharePoint's service accounts use SQL authentication to connect to the farm's backend databases; if Windows authentication is used, this parameter is unnecessary. If used, the value submitted should be a valid and active SQL login account.

- **SSPSQLAuthPassword.** This input is only required for a RestoreSSP operation if SharePoint's service accounts use SQL authentication to connect to the farm's backend databases; if Windows authentication is used, this parameter is unnecessary. If used, the value submitted should be a valid password for the SQL login account provided for the SSPSQLAuthLogin parameter.

- **SearchDatabaseServer.** This input parameter is not required when running a RestoreSSP operation through STSADM.exe. The value provided should be a text string that maps to a valid computer or fully qualified domain name for a server with an installed SQL Server instance or directly to the name of the installed instance.

- **SearchDatabaseName.** This input is not required when running a RestoreSSP operation through STSADM.exe. The value provided should be a text string that identifies the SSP's backend database. The SearchDatabaseName value should not use words reserved in SQL Server for special activities, such as UPDATE or DELETE.

- **SearchSQLAuthLogin.** This input is only required for a RestoreSSP operation if SharePoint's service accounts use SQL authentication to connect to the farm's backend databases; this parameter is unnecessary if Windows authentication is used. If used, the value submitted should be a valid and active SQL login account.

- **SearchSQLAuthPassword.** This input is only required for a RestoreSSP operation if SharePoint's service accounts use SQL authentication to connect to the farm's backend databases; this parameter is unnecessary if Windows authentication is used. If used, the value submitted should be a valid password for the SQL login account provided for the SSPSQLAuthLogin parameter.

- **SSL.** This switch is not required for a RestoreSSP operation through STSAMD.exe. Adding the SSL switch to a RestoreSSP operation configures the SSP's Web services to use Secure Sockets Layer (SSL) encryption for all communication to and from those Web services.

If you choose to use SSL for your SSP's Web services, you must configure and add an SSL certificate to every server in your farm via the Internet Information Services (IIS) v6 certificate deployment tool, found in the IIS 6 Resource Kit Tools download from Microsoft.

At this point, you are going to examine an example call to STSADM.exe with the RestoreSSP operation to get an idea of how you might use the operation in a restored SharePoint environment.

```
Stsadm.exe -o RestoreSSP -title SSPAdminSite -url http://foo:8000 -
ssplogin FOOBAR\SSPServiceAcct -mysiteurl http://foo:9000 -indexserver
bar -indexlocation e:\indices —ssl
```

The previous example is a call you might make to restore your environment's SSP and associate it with your existing Web applications. In the example, you are restoring the SSP to a site named SSPAdminSite with a URL of http://foo:8000. (The digits trailing the server name indicate the port number that the SSP Web application is listening on in IIS.) You are requesting that the SSP's services run with the FOOBAR\SSPServiceAct as their identity and that the SSP's MySites and user profiles be hosted on the http://foo:9000 Web application. The environment's Index server is going to be set up on the Bar server, and its indices are stored in the Indices folder on its E:\ drive. Finally, you are configuring the SSP's Web services to be encrypted via SSL for additional security.

The example uses the —ssplogin input parameter to provide the identity for the SSP timer job service, but it does not supply a value for the —ssppassword input parameter. When this STSADM.exe request is submitted, the Windows Command Shell prompts you to provide the password and does not write the value entered to the screen. If you're not comfortable entering account passwords in plain text in the Windows Command Shell, this approach allows you to avoid that risk.

STSADM BACKUP/RESTORE VERSUS STSADM EXPORT/IMPORT

There are other STSADM.exe operations that in some circumstances may be considered in backup and restore scenarios besides the backup and restore operations: export and import. These two operations are new to STSADM.exe in WSS v3 and MOSS 2007 and are intended to replace the functionality offered by the Smigrate.exe tool available with WSS v2 and SPS 2003. As their names indicate, the export operation allows an administrator to copy any SharePoint site (not just a Web application or site collection) to one or more local files. The import operation is designed to take the file(s) created by an export operation and import the contents of a previously exported site into a target SharePoint site. These two groups of STSADM.exe operations definitely have some similarities, but the differences between their purposes and features have a definite impact on how you should use them in your environment.

The export operation takes the URL of a SharePoint site as input and creates one to many Windows cabinet files (typically designated by a file extension of .cab, but other extensions can be used) that contains the contents of the target site. Administrators can configure the operation in a variety of ways, such as the maximum site of the storage files created, the use of file compression, and the retention of file and list item version history. The operation creates its cabinet files with whatever name and extension the administrator specifies; the standard practice is to use the .cmp extension for these files, indicating that this is a Content Migration Package (CMP). This is an important distinction to keep in mind when the proper usage of the export and import operations is discussed. If an extension is not supplied when exporting a site with STSADM.exe, the tool automatically generates the files for the package with the .cmp extension. Also, the default size of a .cmp file is 25MB; when an export file reaches that threshold, STSADM.exe automatically creates an additional file as part of the export package.

The import operation restores the contents of a CMP created by the STSADM.exe export operation to a new SharePoint site. The configuration options of the import operation are similar to those of the export operation. To successfully restore an exported site, a site must be available within your SharePoint environment to act as a target for the restore. The target site does not have to be completely empty, but that is recommended. If the target site has content in it, you should use the UpdateVersions parameter to indicate how to integrate the existing files with the migrated content.

One requirement for a successful import operation is that the site template used to create the target site must match the site template used to create the original exported site. If the site templates do not match, STSADM.exe returns an error message to that effect and does not import your exported site.

The big advantage that STSADM.exe's export/import operations have over the backup/restore operations is their ability to be directed at individual subsites within a site collection. With the backup/restore operations, the smallest SharePoint component that can be backed up or restored is a site collection, whereas with the export/import operations, you can target a subsite within a site collection for export.

This allows you to be more specific when selecting SharePoint components that need to be preserved, so that server resources such as CPU resources, RAM, or storage space are not used to back up or restore items within a site collection that do not require preservation. The export/import operations also give you the option to import the exported site back into SharePoint as a top-level site collection if desired or back into the original site collection without having to delete the original site.

> *You can import exported sites back into their original site collections without deleting the site that was the source of the export. This is because SharePoint automatically assigns new GUIDs to the objects within the export, which prevents any conflicts in the content database with the GUIDs of the original objects. One issue to watch for is that this can break any applications or items that reference a list by its GUID, because those applications no longer point at the correct GUID after the import. You can also import exported sites into a path other than their original path, although you should carefully review the output of such an action to confirm that every aspect of the imported site is correctly using and displaying the new path.*

> *The following example outlines what happens when exported sites are imported back to their original site collection for backup purposes and what impact it can have on your site's GUIDs and the custom applications that depend on them. You are preparing to export a site to which you have deployed a custom SharePoint feature, which adds a custom list template and workflow to your site. The list generated by the template has a GUID of 0x010012B0E62B-D58E-4d6e-94A1-E36B3F7807E1, and the workflow is hard-coded to be associated with a list identified by that GUID. You successfully export the site to back it up and then deploy a major update to it. That update fails to gain customer approval, and you're told to roll back those changes, so you import the exported version of the site back into its original site collection, only to find that the workflow now fails to fire when the associated list is modified. This is because the list has now been assigned a new GUID: 5A517C23-8835-4C0E-AAEE-0219B7EF237D. Because the workflow is still looking for the list at its old GUID, it fails to start when the new list is modified.*

Although the advantages offered by the export/import operations are certainly attractive, their drawbacks are numerous and can have serious implications for a comprehensive approach to SharePoint disaster recovery. First of all, although the ability to target individual subsites instead of an entire site collection is good, it really does not provide much more granularity than STSADM.exe's backup/restore operations. Another drawback, as mentioned in the previous note, is that changing all the GUIDs for items within an imported site can break applications or other items that are pointing at the site's original GUIDs. Also, several reports have been made of bugs and instabilities in the SharePoint content deployment APIs leveraged by the export/import operations, but although Microsoft is constantly working to resolve these issues with updates to SharePoint's codebase and has made noticeable progress in this area, it still is not an optimal solution for disaster recovery. In a disaster recovery scenario where you must preserve the exact condition of your content and configuration, the export/import operations are not able to meet that requirement.

The biggest reason that using the export/import operations for STSADM.exe to back up or restore your SharePoint sites is not recommended lies in how Microsoft intends for these tools to be used. The export/import operation involves content migration tools (this is why the explanation of the `.cmp` extension is important) designed to move the contents of your site around your SharePoint environment, not to create exact duplicates of your SharePoint components that can be used to restore your environment in the case of a disaster. If the distinction is difficult to understand, consider it this way: export/import extracts your content from your site, its documents, discussions, calendars, and lists and packages it up to be deployed to a new host site. But backup/restore copies everything from your site, including alerts, the contents of its Recycle Bin, document metadata, custom Data View Web parts, and much more. These items are not included in a site saved via an export operation, but they are with a site preserved through the backup operation.

The export/import operations are great if you want to move a site's content from one environment to another, like a promotion from a site in your quality assurance (QA) environment to a site in your live production environment. If you want to create a new site based on the items within an existing site, using export and import can save you time and ensure that you are accurately reproducing the site. These situations are important, and you are likely to encounter them within your environment, but they do not constitute a disaster. When your database server suffers a catastrophic failure and you need to re-create your entire SharePoint environment exactly as it was before the failure, you cannot do it with the output of an export operation, but you can if you use the backup operation to create a carbon copy of your farm.

CONCLUSION

STSADM.exe can be a powerful tool. One important thing to keep in mind is that although it may appear easy to use, in actuality administrators must know exactly what settings they are specifying when they run the tool. If they fail to get even the smallest detail right, the requested operation displays at best an error and does not make changes to the environment or at worst updates your environment incorrectly.

Now that you have seen the mechanics of backing up and restoring your environment with STSADM.exe, you can focus on the tool's strengths and weaknesses from a disaster recovery perspective.

STSADM.exe and its backup and restore operations are versatile tools. They can cover your entire farm down to units as small as a site collection or its associated databases, and your requests can be tailored to meet your specific requirements. If you are an administrator who prefers using the Windows Command Shell to manage SharePoint over graphical tools, STSADM.exe's backup and restore operations certainly appeal to you. But that does not mean that STSADM.exe, or at least STSADM.exe by itself, is the only tool that you need to preserve and recover your SharePoint environment in the case of a disaster.

On its own, STSADM.exe, like the Central Administration site backup and restore tools, provides you the most benefits when used before you modify your SharePoint environment. The tool only allows you to submit a single administrative operation at a time and runs it immediately, meaning that you have to know when you are going to need it before you run it and you cannot schedule a backup or restore to run in the future at a later date. By itself, STSADM.exe does not provide options to schedule a regularly repeated operation, such as a nightly run of the backup operation, but that does not mean such an activity is not possible.

Since STSADM.exe is a command-line tool, you can create a Windows Scheduled Task on your server that submits a request to run an STSADM.exe backup operation on a defined regular basis. Or you can write a script using a Windows-compatible scripting language such as VBScript or PowerShell that calls STSADM.exe to execute a backup operation, allowing you to incorporate programming logic and additional operations into your request. Both of these approaches can be helpful but still do not give you a complete or fully automated solution to protect your environment in the case of a disaster. Chapter 7 discusses their use in more depth, as well as some additional tools you can implement to reduce their weaknesses and give you better automation.

STSADM.exe's backup and restore operations share some other common drawbacks with the Central Administration's tool. STSADM.exe can only back up the SharePoint configuration settings and contents stored in its databases, so you need to consider other alternatives for backing up and restoring your IIS metabase(s), Windows registry(s), and SharePoint UI files stored on your server(s) file system. As previously mentioned in this chapter, you cannot back up components smaller than a site collection. The export and import operations do allow you to migrate the contents of subsites as needed, but they do not constitute a full-fledged backup option. STSADM.exe does not allow you to manage the backup files it creates, so if you are not careful about monitoring and managing the disk space that your storage location uses, you could run out of room to store your crucial files or end up retaining backups that have gone stale and are no longer relevant.

One challenge specific to STSADM.exe that is important to keep in mind is its rigidity about the switches and input parameter values you use when submitting a call to the tool. This was already touched on earlier, but it is something that you definitely need to keep in mind, especially when restoring a backup file. Mistyping a single character can cause you to back up the wrong resource or restore a backup to the wrong location. The risks when executing a restore operation are especially high because you could end up unintentionally and irrevocably overwriting existing content. Also, unlike the Central Administration tool's multipage process that validates your input at every step before proceeding, STSADM.exe requires you to submit all your requests in a single command and does not perform validation before executing the request. This means that you do not know if there is an issue with your command string until you submit it and STSADM.exe attempts to run it. Review each STSADM.exe command string before you execute it to confirm that all the inputs you are providing are correct, and in a production environment, consider a second review by a peer or supervisor, when possible.

Now that you have seen STSADM.exe's operations related to backing up and restoring your SharePoint environment, you should be able to answer the following questions about their capabilities. You can find the answers to these questions in Appendix B, "Chapter Review Q&A," on the book's Web site at http://www.courseptr.com/downloads.

1. What are the two types of backups that you can create with STSADM.exe's backup operation? What are the differences between the two types?
2. What are the required inputs for the STSADM.exe backup operation when creating a catastrophic backup?
3. If STSADM.exe broke your site collection into multiple files, how do you instruct a STSADM.exe restore operation to use all those files to restore the site collection?
4. What STSADM.exe command can you use to view the components of your SharePoint farm to determine which ones are candidates for backup or restore operations?
5. When are you required to provide database authentication information to restore a catastrophic backup with STSADM.exe's restore operation?
6. What is the primary purpose of the STSADM export and import operations, and why are they ill-suited for disaster recovery?

6

Tips and Tricks for SharePoint's Built-In Backup and Restore Tools

In This Chapter

■ Tips for Backup and Restore Operations
■ Administrative Best Practices

N ow that you know the ins and outs of backing up and restoring your SharePoint environment as an administrator with the Central Administration site and STSADM.exe, you should be ready to go, right? You are now armed with the knowledge and procedures necessary to successfully preserve your business-critical sites in an emergency and can return them to service when the chips are down. But maybe you feel a little overwhelmed by all the information, settings, and requirements that have to be in just the right order for everything to go smoothly. If that's the case, don't worry. Your anxiety is perfectly normal. This stuff isn't easy; if it was, you wouldn't need this book to help you.

One thing you may want to do to become more comfortable with the usage of the backup and restore tools in the Central Administration site and STSADM.exe is to reread, or at least review, Chapters 4, "The Central Administration Site's Backup and Restore Tools," and 5, "STSADM.exe's Backup and Restore Operations." Take some time in a development or testing environment to experiment with the tools to see firsthand how they work. The biggest benefit of this activity is that it gives you an understanding of how you need to configure the tools to meet the specific needs and settings of your SharePoint environment. It also gives you the opportunity to assess what you need to change or add to your environment to make the tools usable, such as shared directories and service account permissions. The advent of virtualization products such as Microsoft's Virtual PC and VMware's Workstation allows you to create a flexible, cost-effective environment to repeatedly test your backup and restore configurations, tools, and processes. With virtualization, you do not need twice the hardware to successfully test; you can use a minimal number of physical hosts to run your virtual servers.

Not to scare you or anything, but you still need to clear some hurdles before you can be considered a master of these backup and restore tools. The purpose of this chapter is to provide you with supplemental information about the backup and restore tools of the Central Administration site and STSADM.exe to help you along that road to mastery. In it are recommended best practices, tips for investigating errors, steps to resolve specific issues, and much more.

TIPS FOR BACKUP AND RESTORE OPERATIONS

The items in this section are related specifically to backup and restore operations executed through the Central Administration site or with STSADM.exe.

BEFORE INITIATING A BACKUP OR RESTORE OPERATION

The backup and restore tools of the Central Administration site and STSADM.exe place a load on your server's CPU and RAM far greater than SharePoint's normal day-to-day processes. It's important to review the available system resources of your server through a tool like the Windows Task Manager (see Figure 6.1) or the Performance Monitor administrative tool (see Figure 6.2) and make sure that the server is not already highly utilized before you initiate a backup or restore operation.

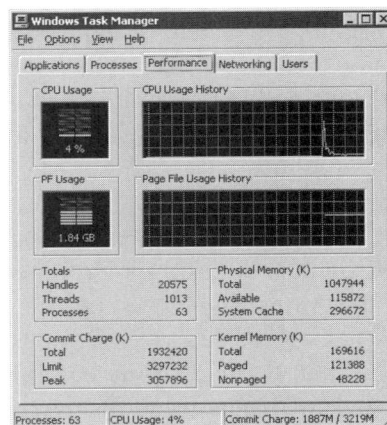

FIGURE 6.1 The Windows Task Manager.

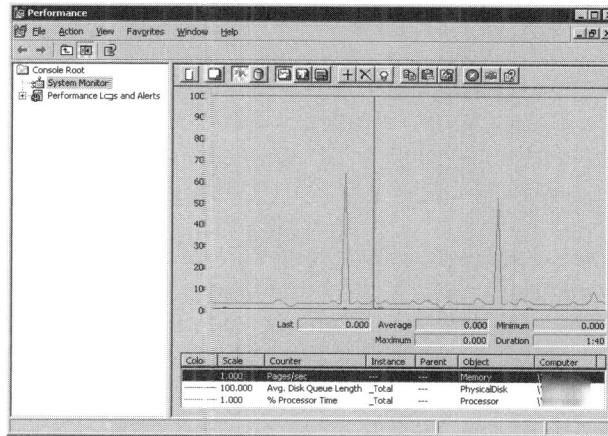

FIGURE 6.2 The Performance Monitor Management Console snap-in.

Establish a baseline for normal performance activity on your server(s) for any comparisons that may become necessary during periods of increased load or usage. In addition, review the server's Scheduled Tasks and SharePoint Timer Jobs to determine if any other planned activities on the server may place a load on it.

TIP

Don't schedule any other administrative activities on servers in your farm, such as the installation of patches or updates, which may require a restart of the servers while a backup job is running. This causes your backup to fail or become corrupted and puts your system at the risk of not being protected in an emergency.

CAUTION

REVIEWING YOUR ENVIRONMENT AFTER A RESTORE

In addition to reviewing SharePoint's logs for errors and status information, you need to review your SharePoint environment's configuration, sites, and content for any possible errors or issues after a restore operation before making it available to your end users. To a lesser extent, you should also check your environment after a backup operation, but beyond the performance impact of generating the backup, your environment should not be affected. Review your Central Administration site to make sure that all your settings for SharePoint have been fully restored, taking special care to review the service accounts associated with the various services necessary to run SharePoint, such as the content access account, search service account, and application pool identities. Examine your sites and their content to confirm that they are in their expected condition. If you have any quality assurance (QA) or integration test scripts in place for your system, execute them against your restored SharePoint environment. If you have customized your SharePoint environment with any updates such as master pages, content pages, Web parts, user controls, site templates, list templates, or others, confirm the presence of these custom components within your SharePoint environment. You may find that some items were not retained by your restore and need to be reinstalled.

This is a situation in which maintaining a detailed record of all configuration settings and changes for your environment proves to be invaluable. That change log gives you the information you need to be able to accurately return your SharePoint environment to its expected state. This change log can be a shared text file, an Excel spreadsheet, or a third-party tool purchased to meet your requirements; it doesn't matter. What matters is that you consistently and accurately record all administrative activities to have a full historical view of your environment's evolution over time. It should go without saying that you need to back up this resource on a regular basis to ensure its availability in a time of need.

TROUBLESHOOTING BACKUP AND RESTORE ERRORS IN GENERAL

Although the error information provided by the Central Administration site or STSADM.exe during a backup or restore operation can be useful in determining the root cause of the error, it may not always give you enough detail to completely diagnose the issue. In these situations, remember that SharePoint still logs data about its activities in other locations on your servers, such as the Windows event logs, SharePoint's Unified Logging Service (ULS) logs (also known as "trace" logs), and IIS's transaction logs. Be sure to examine these sources so that you're getting the full context of what was happening in your system when the error occurred. In addition, SharePoint administrators can set the severity of errors that are written to the Windows event logs and SharePoint trace logs via the Diagnostic Logging page in the Central Administration site. This allows you to increase the verbosity of the errors captured in these logs, reproduce your error, and examine its output. When you've completed your analysis, you can reduce the tolerances for error tracking so that you're not overloading your log files with unnecessary data.

Another valuable tool to consider is SPSReport, a free reporting tool created by Microsoft's support team to create a detailed report of a SharePoint environment's current setup. When it is run on a server in your farm, SPSReport generates a Windows cabinet file (.cab) containing a comprehensive inventory of your SharePoint environment and how it is configured. When you're troubleshooting an issue with Microsoft's support team, running SPSReport is probably going to be one of the first steps the team asks you to take, but you can also run it independently to review its output and look for items or errors that may jump out at you. As an added bonus, SPSReport compiles most of the logs from the server it was run on into its cabinet file output, pulling everything into a single source so you don't have to hunt all over your server for the files you want to view. You can download SPSReport at http://www.codeplex.com/spsreport.

To adjust the severity of the errors tracked in your log files, click the Diagnostic Logging link in the Logging and Reporting section of the Operations page in the Central Administration site. When the Diagnostic Logging page opens as shown in Figure 6.3, the Event Throttling section is displayed, containing description text and three drop-down menus for configuration. Select Backup and Restore from the Select a Category drop-down menu so that the settings you select are specific to events logged that are related to SharePoint's backup and restore operations. If you want your changes to be applied to all logged events, select the All option from the drop-down menu instead of Backup and Restore.

CAUTION

Making changes for All overrides any other logging settings for individual items that may have been previously configured in this page.

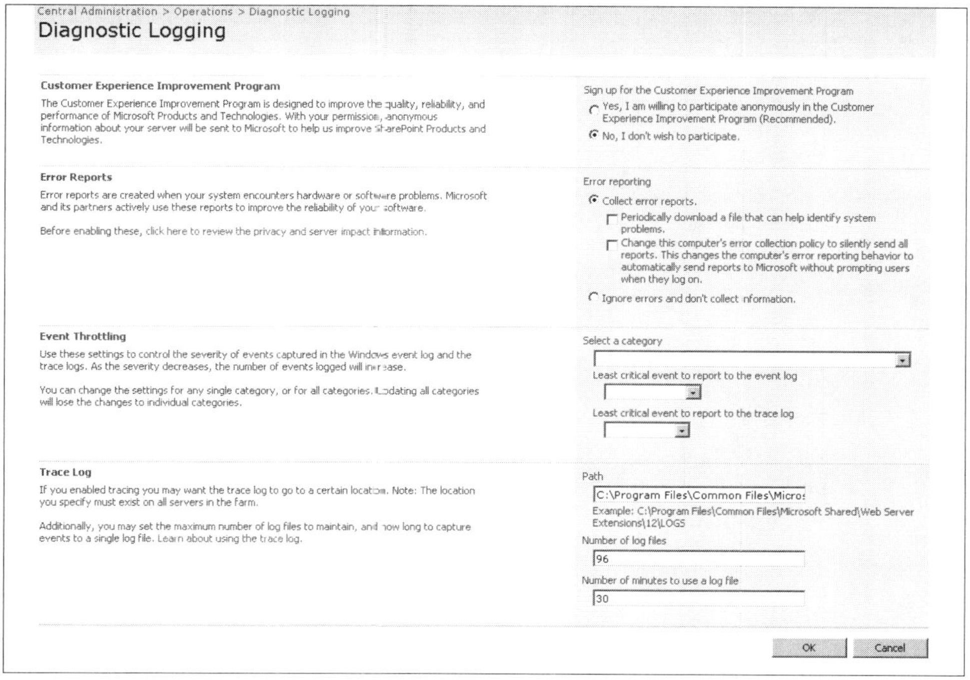

Central Administration > Operations > Diagnostic Logging

Diagnostic Logging

Customer Experience Improvement Program

The Customer Experience Improvement Program is designed to improve the quality, reliability, and performance of Microsoft Products and Technologies. With your permission, anonymous information about your server will be sent to Microsoft to help us improve SharePoint Products and Technologies.

Sign up for the Customer Experience Improvement Program

○ Yes, I am willing to participate anonymously in the Customer Experience Improvement Program (Recommended).

◉ No, I don't wish to participate.

Error Reports

Error reports are created when your system encounters hardware or software problems. Microsoft and its partners actively use these reports to improve the reliability of your software.

Before enabling these, click here to review the privacy and server impact information.

Error reporting

◉ Collect error reports.

☐ Periodically download a file that can help identify system problems.

☐ Change this computer's error collection policy to silently send all reports. This changes the computer's error reporting behavior to automatically send reports to Microsoft without prompting users when they log on.

○ Ignore errors and don't collect information.

Event Throttling

Use these settings to control the severity of events captured in the Windows event log and the trace logs. As the severity decreases, the number of events logged will increase.

You can change the settings for any single category, or for all categories. Updating all categories will lose the changes to individual categories.

Select a category

[▼]

Least critical event to report to the event log

[▼]

Least critical event to report to the trace log

[▼]

Trace Log

If you enabled tracing you may want the trace log to go to a certain location. Note: The location you specify must exist on all servers in the farm.

Additionally, you may set the maximum number of log files to maintain, and how long to capture events to a single log file. Learn about using the trace log.

Path

[C:\Program Files\Common Files\Micros]

Example: C:\Program Files\Common Files\Microsoft Shared\Web Server Extensions\12\LOGS

Number of log files

[96]

Number of minutes to use a log file

[30]

[OK]   [Cancel]

FIGURE 6.3 The Diagnostic Logging page in the Central Administration site.

Selecting a value (None, Error, Warning, Audit Failure, Audit Success, Information) in the Least Critical Event to Report to the Event Log drop-down menu ensures that all events of the selected type and severities greater than it (events are listed in descending order of severity) are written to the Windows Application Event Log on the server hosting the Central Administration site. Selecting a value (None, Unexpected, Monitorable, High, Medium, and Verbose) in the Least Critical Event to Report to the Trace Log drop-down menu ensures that all events of the selected type and severities greater than it (events are listed in descending order of severity) are written to the SharePoint trace log on the server hosting the Central Administration site. Once you have selected the desired logging settings, click the OK button to save your changes. Figure 6.4 depicts an example of a SharePoint ULS log file.

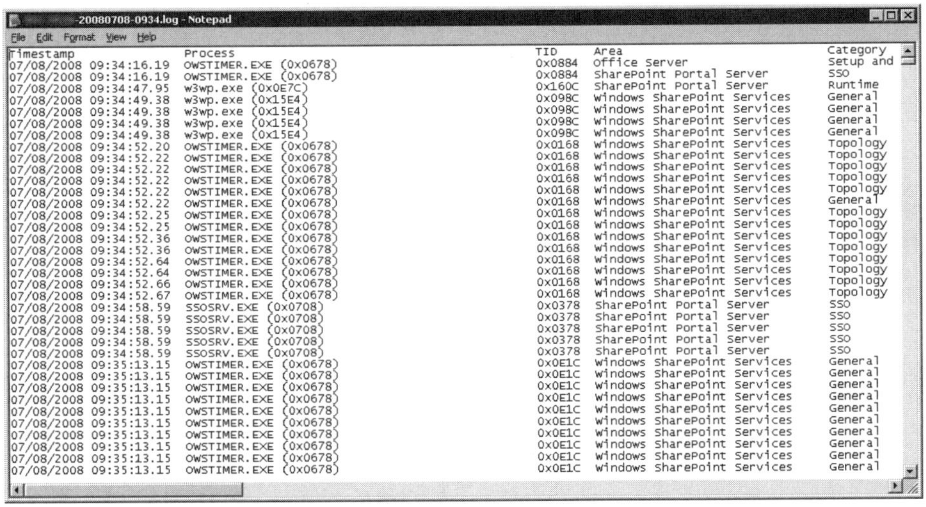

FIGURE 6.4 An example of the SharePoint ULS log file.

MULTIPLE RESTORE OPERATIONS AT THE SAME TIME

This issue may seem pretty clear-cut, but it bears mentioning. It isn't possible to initiate two separate restore operations in parallel using the same backup package as the source. Attempting to run two restore operations with the same backup package results in one of the operations completing successfully (assuming that all other criteria for a successful restore have been met) and the other operation reporting an error. An examination of the sprestore.log file in this situation shows the following error related to the second operation:

```
SqlException: Exclusive access could not be obtained because the
database is in use. RESTORE DATABASE is terminating abnormally
```

In this situation, you may find the `sprestore.log` *file difficult to follow because both operations are writing updates to the file at the same time. Your* `sprestore.log` *file might alternate entries from the failed restoration operation with entries from the successful, which can be confusing if you're not aware of what you're viewing. This is a good example of why you shouldn't attempt to execute multiple administrative activities in SharePoint at the same time. An even better justification for this is SharePoint's dependence on its backend databases; multiple actions can lead to competing updates to the SharePoint configuration database, which can corrupt the data in that crucial database.*

FILE CACHE ERRORS IN FULL RESTORE OF A SHAREPOINT FARM

If you execute a full restore of your SharePoint farm using the Same Configuration option, overwriting your current farm environment with a previous backup, you may encounter errors when modifying the farm's settings via STSADM or the Central Administration site. SharePoint caches configuration data on your Central Administration server's file system, storing data regarding things such as your farm's timer jobs, the number of site collections in your farm, and what content databases are associated with a Web application. Sometimes after a backup operation is completed, SharePoint stores configuration data in this file cache and then reports errors once a farm-level backup has been restored to the environment. This happens because the configuration settings in that cache are out of sync with the contents of your farm's configuration database and can manifest in several ways, such as rendering sites unavailable through a browser with `404 File Not Found` errors or `Null Object Reference` errors when accessing content databases through the Central Administration site.

To resolve this issue, you must clear your server's configuration file cache, which is managed by the Windows SharePoint Services (WSS) Timer service, OWSTIMER.exe. To reset the cache, execute the following steps:

1. Log on to a SharePoint server in your farm running the WSS Timer service.
2. Open the Services management snap-in console and stop the WSS Timer service.
3. In Windows Explorer, navigate to the directory location storing the configuration file cache (see Figure 6.5 for an example). By default, this path is `%ALLUSERSPROFILE%\ApplicationData\Microsoft\SharePoint\Config\<GUID>`.
4. Delete the contents of the configuration file cache directory or move them to another location on the server.

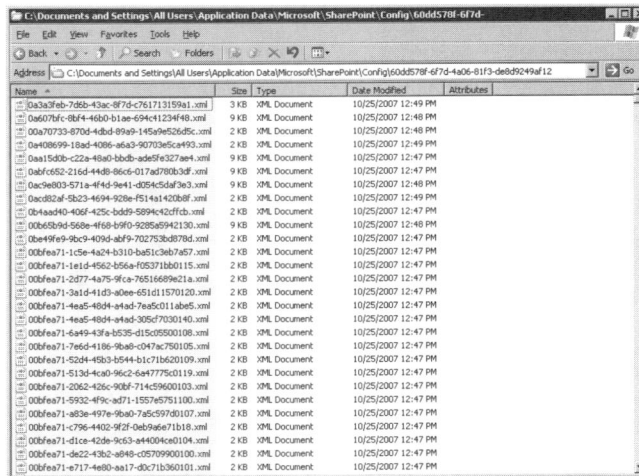

FIGURE 6.5 An example of the SharePoint configuration file cache directory.

5. Restart the WSS Timer service in the Services console.

The WSS Timer service can also be restarted by issuing the following statements in the Windows Command Shell:

```
Net stop sptimerv3
Net start sptimerv3
```

6. Examine the configuration file cache directory to confirm that new files have been successfully written to it. SharePoint repopulates the configuration file cache on the server with information from the restored configuration database for your farm.
7. Repeat steps 1–6 for all other servers in your farm running the WSS Timer service.
8. Review your restored sites and Central Administration site to confirm that your issues have been resolved.

NEW CONFIGURATION RESTORE FAILURES

When reviewing your sprestore.log file after restoring a Web application into a new SharePoint environment via the New Configuration option, you may see an error stating SPException: cannot connect database to Web application.

Use the command line tool or Central Administration pages to attach the database manually to the proper Web Application. In this situation, SharePoint has successfully restored the content database for your Web application to the SQL Server instance for your new environment but was unable to join your new Web application to the content database or create a new IIS Web site for the Web application on the Web server(s) in your environment.

To resolve this issue, execute the following steps:

1. Open the Central Administration site and click on the Applications tab.
2. Select your target Web application and click the Content Databases link in the SharePoint Web Application Management section.
3. In the Manage Content Databases page, click the Add a Content Database link above the list of current content databases.
4. When the Add Content Database page opens (see Figure 6.6), confirm that the desired Web application is listed and enter the appropriate information for the target database server and the target content database hosted on the server. Configure the Database Authentication and Capacity settings as desired, and click the OK button to add the content database.

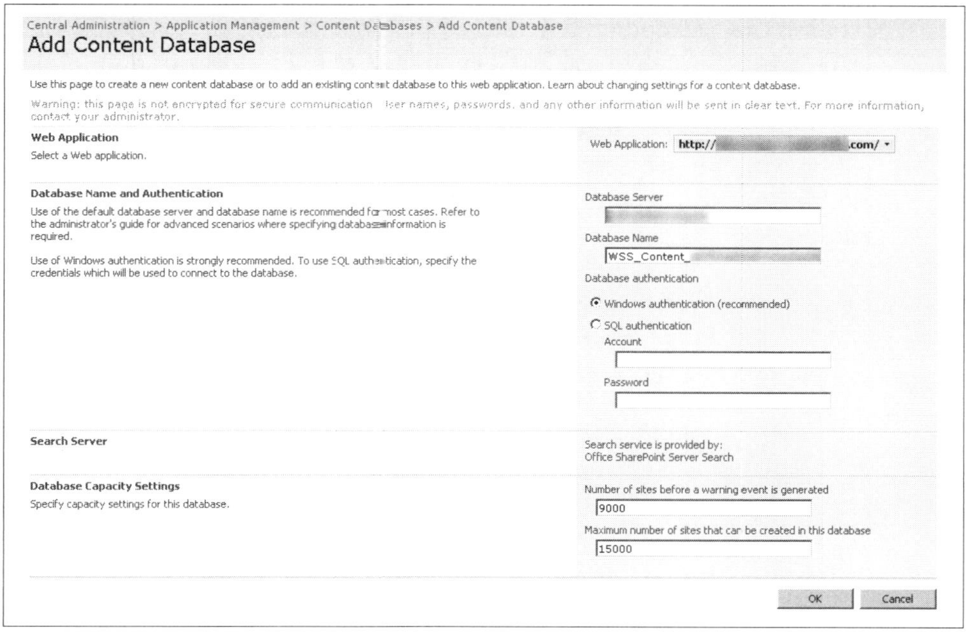

FIGURE 6.6 The Add Content Database page in the Central Administration site.

ISSUE RESTORING TIMER JOBS AFTER A RESTORE

Microsoft Knowledge Base article KB942989 (http://support.microsoft.com/kb/942989) details an issue with timer jobs not being restored in SharePoint when a Web application is backed up and subsequently restored to a new farm. This issue has subsequently been fixed by Microsoft via patches to the SharePoint code, but those updates are not automatically applied, even if you have the Windows Update application enabled and fully automated on your servers. Hotfixes and patches to SharePoint must always be manually applied. Because it is a highly advised best practice to always have your SharePoint environment updated to the latest and greatest patching level available from Microsoft, this is the most certain way to ensure you won't encounter an issue restoring timer jobs. If it isn't possible to apply this hotfix update, the other alternative is to manually create a Web application in your new environment and restore your backup package to this Web application by overwriting it.

RESTORING BACKUPS ACROSS TOOLS

You can use the Central Administration site to restore backup packages created by the catastrophic backup operation of the STSADM.exe command-line tool. STSADM's catastrophic backup operation, like the Central Administration site's, requires the backup files to be stored in a shared UNC path, which you can access by entering the path in the first step of the Central Administration restore process. Simply select the backup package you want to restore and continue the process in the same manner as you would when restoring a backup created by the Central Administration site. Similarly, you can restore backups created through the Central Administration site with STSADM.exe if you treat them as a catastrophic backup package.

> *You can't restore site collection backups created with STSADM.exe in the Central Administration site. For more information on the difference between site collection backups and catastrophic backups created with STSADM.exe, see Chapter 5.*
>
> **NOTE**

ADMINISTRATIVE BEST PRACTICES

This section discusses processes and tips for administrators around the backup and restore process, but not necessarily directly related to those operations. The way you follow these best practices can directly impact the success and effectiveness of your disaster recovery plan when using the Central Administration site's backup and restore tools or STSADM.exe's backup and restore operations.

MANAGING YOUR BACKUP FILE STORAGE LOCATION

Chapter 4 briefly discussed the estimated amount of storage space needed to store a SharePoint backup file, highly recommending that 1.5 times the size of the SharePoint components targeted for backup be made available per backup package created. Rest assured that recommendation has not changed since you digested it two chapters ago. But if you're truly interested in preserving the state of your SharePoint environment and being able to recover it in case of an outage, deletion, or emergency, you need to put more thought into where you're storing your SharePoint backups than just storage space.

First and foremost, it's not enough to allocate enough storage for only a single backup file. Over time you'll be creating multiple backup packages to reflect the changes in your environment. This means that your storage location needs to have enough space to hold those multiple files, not just a single backup package. When your target file location doesn't have enough space for SharePoint to store your package's files, your backup operation errors out and your system becomes at risk because your backups are not up to date.

Are you doing the math right now? Are you calculating how your SharePoint environment is going to expand in the coming years as your users store more and more files, data, and content in it, and then combining those numbers with your desired backup frequency to do some advanced calculus designed to estimate how much backup storage space you'll need in five years? You likely came up with some big, scary numbers. And regardless of how cheap computer storage has become in recent years, it's still not *that* cheap. So how do you keep your storage usage from exploding? Try developing a policy to determine how long a backup file is retained before it's deleted. The policy's criteria can be based on factors such as a period of time (for example, retaining all backup packages less than three weeks old) or the total number of backup packages in the directory (retaining the last 10 backup packages). No specific criteria for your policy will be recommended here, because every organization's configuration, constraints, and budget are different and have a direct impact on how you manage your backup storage space, but you should define such a policy.

One term that effective SharePoint administrators should be familiar with is governance. Establishing governance policies for your environment, such as site quotas, document version management, and the deletion of unused sites/site collections, is not only a good general practice for your SharePoint environment, but it also has specific relevance to your backup and restore practices. When governance is in place to ensure that the content in SharePoint is relevant, concise, and current, you can be confident that you're backing up valuable resources. If your environment is allowed to grow without constraints, you're going to expend those resources, backing up content unnecessarily and putting valuable data at risk when space runs out

NOTE

or backups take too long to complete. Implementing a sound governance plan can pay big dividends for your disaster recovery approach and your overall SharePoint environment.

When determining your storage location, configure it with the proper access settings to grant SharePoint's tools and service accounts the privileges they require to properly create, read, and update the files within it. Chapters 4 and 5 have outlined the accounts that need to be able to access your target location, as well as the rights that need to be granted to them. But it's up to you to prepare your backup storage location with those rights; otherwise, your backup operations will fail. Complete this activity before you start creating backups of your SharePoint environment so that you can test and confirm each account's privileges before you really need them.

Prior to creating backups for your SharePoint environment, you should also consider how you want to organize your backup storage location and the files in it. For a simple SharePoint installation with a single Web application, site collection, and content database serving up content to your users, you may not need to divide your backup packages into multiple directories since your backups regularly include the same hierarchy in a single package. But if you have multiple Web applications and want to differentiate their backup packages, it may be a good idea to consider creating subfolders within your storage location for each Web application. This can add some complexity to your backup strategy, but it allows you and your fellow administrators to easily discern which backup packages are associated with a specific component in your environment. Since SharePoint does not do a good job of descriptively naming the files it creates in its backup operations and you shouldn't really modify your backup files, this approach can help you to order and organize your crucial backup files.

TIP

Develop guidelines for naming the files in your backup packages when SharePoint allows you to name a file it creates. Doing so helps to ensure that all backup files are named consistently and can be identified even by administrators who did not create the files. The exact naming conventions should be specific to the needs of your environment but can include creation date, parent component backed up, backup type, release environment (Development, QA, Production), and much more.

Finally, make sure the location you select to store your backup files is safely protected and backed up in the case of a disaster. This may seem like a no-brainer, but you can easily overlook this when you're completely focused on protecting your SharePoint environment. The safety and accuracy of the files in this location are of the utmost importance to the viability of your environment if disaster strikes.

If your backup files aren't accessible, you can't use them to restore your environment. It's that simple. The good news is that once your SharePoint backup packages are stored in your designated location, they can be preserved and restored just like any other file in Windows, meaning that no SharePoint-specific tools are required to retrieve them. Chapter 10, "Windows Server 2003 Backup and Restore," discusses the various technologies and tools that you can use to back up and restore your file system.

When planning how to store your SharePoint backups, it's important to keep in mind that there's no one-size-fits-all solution out there that you can just plug in and go with. Enterprise solutions such as a storage area network (SAN) offer impressive reliability, capacity, and performance, but they do so at an enterprise-sized price tag. Cutting-edge cloud solutions like Amazon's Simple Storage Service (S3) are affordable and scalable and offer 24×7 support, but they require you to trust a third party to store, protect, and maintain your valued backup files. Network area storage (NAS) devices such as Buffalo's LinkStation are cost effective, securable, and redundant, but they're better suited for smaller organizations than an enterprise IT setting. The great thing about SharePoint backups created with the Central Administration site or STSADM.exe is that they can be stored on any drive or media attached to a Windows server, allowing you to choose the storage option that best fits your needs and budget. The important thing is to remember that the technology's requirements should not drive your decision; backups created with the Central Administration site or STSADM.exe work just as well with a $200 USB 2.0 external hard drive as a $20,000 SAN.

LONG-RUNNING BACKUP OR RESTORE OPERATIONS

One simple rule to remember for the backup and restore of SharePoint is that the larger the target component you select for backup or restore, the longer it takes SharePoint to complete the operation. This is a pretty straightforward rule, but it's especially important to remember if you're using SharePoint's built-in tools to execute the backup or restore. When a backup or restore job requested via the Central Administration site or STSADM.exe runs for more than 17 hours, SharePoint automatically restarts the backup job and provisions an appropriate length of time for the job to run to completion. This allows for any resources reserved by the operation to be released and made available to other SharePoint timer jobs. SharePoint then designates an additional amount of time for the process to continue running until it's completed.

The best way to handle long-running backup or restore operations is to avoid them entirely. The longer a backup operation takes to complete, the greater the risk that the operation may encounter an error. Long-running restore operations pose the same danger of potential errors, but the increased time it takes to return your environment in the case of an outage is often the biggest drawback in that case. Long-running operations are often caused by the amount of data you are attempting to back up or restore. Again, this is an issue that can be mitigated by proper governance policies for your SharePoint environment, as well as effective management of your SharePoint content databases. As your content databases grow, it's important to monitor their growth and manage the site collections that are stored within them. If the database grows to the point where it is too large to back up in a timely manner, it's time to split its site collections into multiple databases. This allows you to back up and restore in a more granular fashion, tackling each content database individually to shorten each operation.

REVIEWING THE SPBACKUP.LOG AND SPRESTORE.LOG FILES

After you've completed a backup or restore operation via SharePoint's built-in administrative tools, review the contents of the operation's associated `spbackup.log` or `sprestore.log` files in your backup package's location regardless of what result SharePoint reports when the operation finishes. Look for any comments or errors that may be relevant to your environment, and confirm that the targeted components were successfully and completely backed up or restored. You need a complete understanding of what impact the operation had on your SharePoint environment and what, if any, further actions you need to take to confirm that it is in a desired state. For more information about the contents and structure of these log files, see Chapter 4.

SHAREPOINT AUTHENTICATION PROVIDERS

One aspect of SharePoint that is not always apparent to new IT professionals is its use of the configuration database to store the majority of its settings and setup information, including security and authentication provider settings. When you back up a SharePoint farm, the environment's users, roles, access rights, and authentication providers are included in the backup package. This means that you must be careful to restore your backup package to a SharePoint environment configured to use the same authentication provider (such as Active Directory or ASP.NET forms-based authentication) as your backup package. Using a target environment with a different authentication provider causes errors when you attempt to restore your backup to the new environment. If you want to use a different authentication provider in your environment, you can add the new provider to it once your restore operation has completed.

When using authentication providers in your SharePoint environment, it's especially important to back up the IIS web.config *files for your SharePoint sites, because they contain the majority of the configuration information about those providers. The data in these files must be accurately restored as part of an overall restore of your SharePoint farm for users to log into the restored SharePoint sites via the authentication provider. For more information on how to back up and restore your* web.config *files and other important files stored in the file system of your SharePoint servers, see Chapter 10.*

CONCLUSION

With the advice and common errors described in this chapter, you should begin to get an idea of the common practices and pitfalls that you may face as you start to use SharePoint's built-in tools to back up and restore you environment. These tools do have their flaws, but with the proper preparation, testing, and planning, they can be used effectively to protect and re-establish your SharePoint environment and the business-critical data stored in it. This chapter outlined some of the things that you need to consider and implement as part of your organization's disaster recovery coverage when using the Central Administration site or STSADM.exe, but keep in mind that you'll encounter your own unique limitations and errors as you use the tools.

The past three chapters have extensively reviewed the ins and outs of backing up and restoring SharePoint with the administrative tools included with the platform out of the box. These tools may not exactly meet your needs or may have some weaknesses that concern you. The tools are not a one-size-fits-all solution; they are not for everyone. The following chapters outline some of the other actions available to reduce or remove these blind spots as well as how you can build your own custom tools to back up and restore your SharePoint environment according to your individual specifications.

After finishing this chapter, you should be able to answer the following questions about issues you may face with SharePoint's built-in backup and restore tools. You can find the answers to these questions in Appendix B, "Chapter Review Q&A," on the book's Web site at http://www.courseptr.com/downloads.

1. What are some of the important items you should be looking for in the spbackup.log and sprestore.log files?
2. What are some of the key items you should examine in your SharePoint environment after completing a restore from backup?
3. How do you manually reattach a content database to your SharePoint environment after a restore operation?
4. Can you restore a backup created with the Central Administration site via STSADM.exe?

7 Custom Development and Scripting for SharePoint Disaster Recovery

In This Chapter

- Who Should Read This Chapter
- The Disclaimer
- Scripting
- Custom Development

In a book that approaches SharePoint disaster recovery with a strong eye toward infrastructure administration and operations, it may seem surprising to find this chapter nestled among discussions on topics such as SQL Server high availability, SharePoint server farm architectures, and the most appropriate backup mechanism to support a given disaster recovery strategy. Furthermore, many are of the opinion that custom development and infrastructure activities mix about as well as oil and water. This book adopts a more holistic view—one that is clearly illustrated in the following quote from Sir Francis Bacon, the famous English author and statesman:

"I have taken all knowledge to be my province."

As far as Web-based platforms go, SharePoint is a behemoth. Much like the Roman Empire in AD 117, SharePoint reaches to all corners of the technological landscape. To leverage SharePoint to greatest effect, you must figuratively wear many hats and have a multidisciplinary understanding of the platform. Cultivating a healthy respect and some degree of skill in a variety of disciplines such as networking, server management, database technologies, and custom development is essential. It is the last of these, custom development, that is one of the primary focuses of this chapter.

Custom development is not the only focus of this chapter, though. Scripting, a distant cousin, is also covered in significant detail as it pertains to SharePoint. This is done because scripting technologies, as a group, ride the line between administration and development. Although developers tend to frown a bit on old-school command prompt batch files, they are still a mainstay for SharePoint administrators seeking to automate all manner of command-line tasks. On the other side of the coin, the object-oriented nature of PowerShell and its ability to leverage the .NET framework make it as much a custom development approach as a scripting technology.

Because scripting technologies are generally more accessible to SharePoint administrators, this chapter begins with scripting and works its way up to custom development topics. Each section builds upon those that were covered before it.

WHO SHOULD READ THIS CHAPTER

If you have read this far into the chapter, please keep going! As indicated earlier, this chapter contains something for nearly everyone in the SharePoint ecosphere.

SharePoint administrators and others whose responsibilities include some aspect of SharePoint farm maintenance should find the "Scripting" section to be of greatest use. The section covers the gamut of scripting options available, examples of how to leverage them, and options for automating their use. A few best practices are also described.

Developers and others who fancy themselves "coders" of a sort can find material of interest in the section "Custom Development." The section explores the various types and namespaces of the SharePoint application programming interface (API) that are of greatest relevance in the development of software to address disaster recovery and related needs. An analysis of out of the box versus custom development is also undertaken, and a handful of common custom development scenarios are presented.

Finally, architects and others who have governance and guidance responsibilities should pay attention to the end of the "Custom Development" section. Under "Designing Applications for Disaster Recovery Readiness," a number of best practices for the development of software with an eye toward disaster recovery are discussed. Knowledge of such practices can mean the difference between an application that operates equally well within both normal production environments and disaster recovery networks/data centers and one that crashes and burns when removed or relocated from its expected "home" environment.

THE DISCLAIMER

As the cover states, this is a book about SharePoint disaster recovery. It is not a book that is dedicated to covering the many facets of SharePoint development.

Much as other books cover the topic of disaster recovery in a section or chapter, so too does this book cover custom development and related areas/disciplines.

There is a limit to the amount of information and guidance that can be presented in one chapter, so a conscious decision was made to stay "out of the weeds" and instead stay focused on those aspects of SharePoint custom coding, scripting, and the overall development process that are most applicable to the topic of disaster recovery. Source code and scripts are provided only insofar as is needed to illustrate a concept or point. General best practices for SharePoint development, such as the use of Features to deploy code, the packaging of components into SharePoint Solution Packages (also known by their file extension as .wsp files), and which objects should and should not be explicitly disposed of, are absent from this chapter. These practices still apply; they simply aren't discussed. Many good books cover these topics in detail. If you're serious about SharePoint development, buy one.

SCRIPTING

For as long as the Windows operating system has been around (and IBM's PC Disk Operating System [DOS] before it), the ability to script a series of actions or commands has been present in the Microsoft world in some form. Scripting addresses a basic system need: the ability to carry out a discrete series of tasks or operations in a predictable, consistent, and reproducible manner. Scripts can perform nearly any manual operation that a user or administrator can perform, and they do so in a reproducible and more efficient fashion.

Given these facts, it is easy to understand why scripting remains the tool of choice for performing many administrative operations, particularly those operations that are complex or lengthy. The power of scripting is well known; it is one of the reasons why every version of Windows that has ever been released has supported one or more forms of scripting or batch file execution.

This section explores the range of scripting options that are commonly available to administrators and those with operational responsibilities. Following that is a discussion of how scripting can be used to address common SharePoint tasks.

This section contains a number of script samples, their associated outputs following execution, and references to the operating system upon which they were developed. Because the scripts and their outputs depend on the environment in which they are executed to varying extents, the following platforms, components, and applications were used in the generation of the examples that follow:

- **Operating system.** Microsoft Windows Server 2003 R2 Standard Edition Service Pack (SP) 2
- **Microsoft .NET Framework.** Versions 1.1, 2.0 SP1, 3.0 SP1, and 3.5 SP1

- **Database.** Microsoft SQL Server 2005 Enterprise Edition SP2 Version 9.00.3042.00 (X64)
- **Web server.** Microsoft Internet Information Services (IIS) 6.0
- **SharePoint.** MOSS 2007 Enterprise Edition Version 12.0.0.6318

In addition to this list, specific sections and technologies (such as PowerShell) have further dependencies that are mentioned within their appropriate sections.

Scripting Options

Although scripting began with the humble DOS batch file, the technology continued to evolve with each release of Windows. Nowadays, scripting within the Windows environment has become so powerful that it's capable of executing logic and carrying out actions that were previously the purview of custom compiled solutions only.

As a general rule, scripts are easier to write, easier to maintain, and relatively easy to understand when compared to custom developed solutions. Also, the cost of entry to writing scripts is minimal; it requires much less in terms of supplemental software/equipment, knowledge, and time than most full-fledged programming approaches. This flexibility does not come without a cost or trade-off, though. On the whole, scripts tend to be measurably less efficient when executing and are limited in the types of activities that they can perform relative to custom developed solutions.

What follows is a discussion of the three most commonly found and supported scripting technologies a SharePoint administrator has at his disposal: command prompt batch files, VBScript, and PowerShell.

Command Prompt Batch Files

Like the invention of the wheel, the command prompt and associated batch files proved so useful and versatile when created that they simply never went out of style. This is no small statement when you consider that the command prompt was introduced with the release of IBM's original DOS back in 1981. You would be hard pressed to identify another computer-based technology that has survived almost three decades—and in nearly the same form as it was introduced.

In a modern Windows environment, accessing the command prompt is straightforward. You can either navigate to the Windows Start menu and select Command Prompt from the Accessories menu (as shown in Figure 7.1), or you can select Run from the Start menu and type cmd in the Run dialog box before pressing the OK button (Figure 7.2).

A command prompt batch file (or simply *batch file*) typically manifests within the file system of a machine as a file possessing a .bat extension. Batch files are generally small (several kilobytes or less), contain no special formatting or encoding, and can easily be opened within Windows Notepad or another text-editing application. Each line in the batch file can contain a command that accepts one or more options; these commands are normally processed in sequential order from the top of the file to the bottom by the Windows command interpreter (cmd.exe).

Complex batch files can contain conditional processing directives (`if` and `choice` statements), jumps (`goto` statements), and other commands that may result in nonsequential processing or an execution path that is not entirely obvious through simple review of the script.

FIGURE 7.1 Opening the command prompt from the Accessories menu.

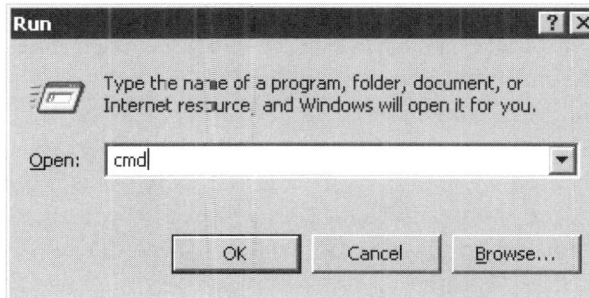

FIGURE 7.2 Accessing the command prompt from the Run dialog box.

A simple batch file example appears in Figure 7.3. The batch file shown recycles the SharePoint Timer Service by issuing two commands. The first command stops the service using the versatile `net` command. When the timer service has stopped and the control returns to the script, the second command starts the service. The batch file also uses `echo` commands to write a description of each step that is being performed to the console window.

The file shown in Figure 7.3 was created in just a couple of minutes by opening Windows Notepad, typing the text in the figure, and saving the file as `TimerRecycle.bat`.

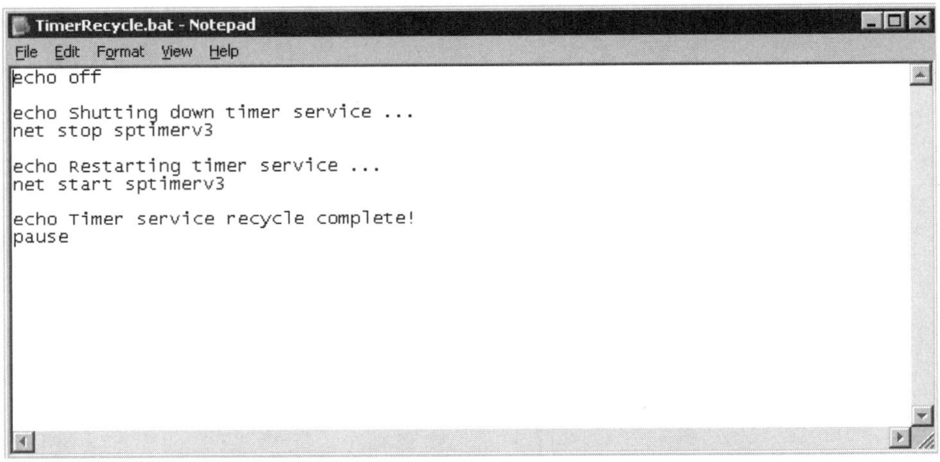

FIGURE 7.3 A batch file to recycle the SharePoint Timer Service.

Running the batch file is as simple as double-clicking it from within Windows Explorer. Because files possessing a `.bat` extension are associated with the Windows command interpreter by default, an instance of the command interpreter is loaded and executes each line in the batch file when the file is double-clicked. You can see the execution results in Figure 7.4.

Batch files like the one shown in Figure 7.3 are normally employed to carry out relatively basic tasks that are highly repetitive, cryptic in their syntax, or prone to errors when typed manually. This makes batch files ideal tools for the low-level, recurring, and monotonous tasks that typically bore an administrator to tears.

Another extremely significant strength of batch files is the simplicity with which they are created, edited, and executed. As described and demonstrated earlier, a batch file can go from concept to implementation in a matter of minutes. All that is required to create a batch file is a good command prompt reference (or particularly good recall from the early days of DOS) and a text editor—nothing more.

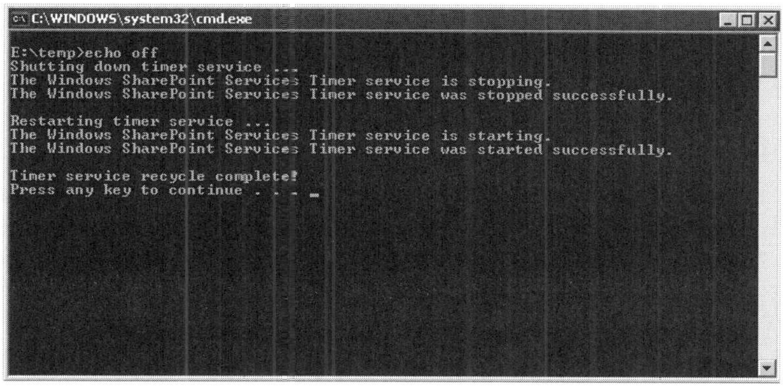

FIGURE 7.4 The result of executing the `TimerRecycle.bat` batch file.

Finally, support for batch files is ubiquitous across Microsoft operating systems and products. As mentioned earlier, Windows inherently knows how to treat files that have a `.bat` extension, and many applications that are written to run on the Windows platform have command prompt support built in; that is, they can be executed from a command prompt or from within a batch file. In fact, STSADM.exe (discussed at length in Chapter 5, "STSADM.exe's Backup and Restore Operations") is basically a command prompt extension to those areas of the SharePoint API that provide operational and administrative support.

Unfortunately, batch files are bound by a handful of constraints that make them an inappropriate choice in many cases. Command-line batch files have evolved very little since their inception in 1981, so they still maintain one foot in the pre-Windows world. Their lack of awareness regarding component object model (COM) and .NET technologies, as well as their dearth of support for anything but the simplest of decision logic, leaves them ill equipped to address anything but the simplest of administrative tasks. In addition, batch files lack the ability to present commonly accepted user interface (UI) elements such as dialog boxes and forms, making them a weak choice for interactive tasks.

VBScript

The limitations of command prompt batch files were well known in the lead-up to the release of Windows 98. It was at that point, though, that Microsoft decided to enhance the resources available for scripting and batch execution on the Windows platform. As part of the Windows 98 platform, Microsoft released the Windows Script Host (WSH). At roughly the same time, Microsoft also released free downloads of the WSH add-on to support WSH-based scripting on Windows 95 and Windows NT 4.0. Windows 2000 was still in beta at the time but subsequently included the WSH at release.

The WSH is composed of two functional parts:

- **The script environment host executable.** This is actually one of two applications that are available within the Windows system directory: cscript.exe and wscript.exe. Although not strictly enforced or specifically required, cscript.exe is intended for launch from within the command prompt shell, whereas wscript.exe is intended to establish a hosting environment when launched directly from within Windows. Regardless of their intended launch environments, both employ the same underlying scripting engine. These executables are directly responsible for processing scripts, and they supply two critical classes for use by scripts: the `WScript` and `WshArguments` classes.
- **The script host object model.** The WSH exposes numerous classes for use by scripts executing within the environment it supplies. The majority of these (save for the aforementioned `WScript` and `WshArguments` classes) are contained within the Windows Script Host runtime library (`wshom.ocx`) that exists within the Windows system directory.

At this point, you might be asking yourself, "What exactly does the WSH have to do with VBScript?" The answer to that question is straightforward. The WSH, as the "host" portion of its name implies, is an application that hosts a scripting engine. Currently, Microsoft supplies and supports two scripting engines for use within the WSH environment: the Visual Basic Scripting Edition (VBScript) engine and the JScript engine. JScript, for those who may not be familiar with it, is Microsoft's implementation of the ECMA 262 language specification and is similar to JavaScript.

In the time since the release of the WSH, use of VBScript by administrators has eclipsed that of JScript. Microsoft has also leaned toward using VBScript for operational scripting. Evidence to this effect can be found by examining the number of administrative VBScripts that Microsoft supplies with the Windows operating system and Windows Resource Kit. For these reasons, the rest of this section examines the use of VBScript only. If JScript is more to your liking, though, the bulk of the principles and information that follows applies to JScript, as well.

Microsoft left the WSH environment open to extension for any scripting engine that implements the Windows Script specification, and some developers have taken advantage of this fact. If C# is your language of choice and you want to leverage it within the WSH, you might find the CS-Script engine (http://csscript.net/) worth investigating.

VBScript is a lightweight subset and direct descendent of Visual Basic for Applications (VBA), the language that gained popularity as the engine behind the custom development capabilities within the Microsoft Office family of applications. VBA, in turn, is derived from Microsoft's fully featured Visual Basic language. Those who are familiar with Visual Basic quickly become comfortable when working with VBScript.

Semantically speaking, saying "running a VBScript" is equivalent to saying "running a VBScript through WSH." The rest of this chapter mentions VBScript only, but be aware that the WSH supplies the environment in which a VBScript is interpreted. The WSH also supplies some of the classes and types that are typically employed for use within VBScripts.

VBScript files can be identified within the file system as basic text files that have a .vbs extension. As with command prompt batch files, VBScript files can be easily opened, edited, and saved from within any text-editing application (such as Windows Notepad). The .vbs extension is also registered within the Windows operating system, so double-clicking a VBScript file immediately launches the appropriate WSH executable (wscript.exe) and begins execution of the script.

TIP *Although you can edit VBScript with nothing but a basic text editor, approaching script development in this fashion can be rather error prone and more than a little frustrating. You can find various applications across the Internet that simplify the process of working with VBScripts. Some of these applications include features such as color-coding keywords, line numbering, and predictive lookup for object types (IntelliSense). Some even offer full virtual sandbox environments with support for debugging for the testing of scripts. Some of the applications are free, whereas others are not. At a minimum, it's recommended that you employ a text editor that color-codes VBScript keywords (such as Notepad++, http://notepad-plus. sourceforge.net) to help catch potential syntax errors and mistypes before you attempt to run a script.*

VBScripts, as a general rule, have a greater range of functionality and logic support available to them than batch files that are run through the command interpreter. Probably the single greatest improvement that VBScripts offer over batch files is their ability to interact with and leverage COM components that are automation objects. (That is, they support late-binding via the IDispatch interface.) This means that VBScripts are "object aware" and can leverage an entire range of component building blocks that batch files can't.

Support for COM Automation components is not the only thing VBScript offers that batch files don't. Many of the core elements of the Visual Basic programming language exist within VBScript, as well, so VBScript contains much greater support for conditional branching, complex decision logic, error handling, and more.

Functionality that VBScript internally lacks can often be "bolted in" through the use of one or more COM components.

To illustrate some of the power and depth that a VBScript can bring to the automation of administrative functions, examine the `DumpOssErrorInfo.vbs` script shown in Figure 7.5.

```
DumpOssErrorInfo.vbs
1    'Establish the strings that identify the WMI service and query that will be used.
2    wmiService = "winmgmts:\\.\root\cimv2"
3    wmiQuery =   "Select * from Win32_NTLogEvent Where " & _
4                 "Logfile = 'Application' and " & _
5                 "SourceName = 'Office Server Search' and " & _
6                 "EventType = '1'"
7
8    'STEP 1: Attach to WMI and execute the query that will retrieve the OSS error events.
9    Set objWMI = GetObject(wmiService)
10   Set ossErrors = objWMI.ExecQuery(wmiQuery)
11
12   'Establish some variables for reporting in the final step
13   errorCount = 0
14   lastError = 0
15
16   'STEP 2: Iterate through each error, increment the error counter, and see if the error is newer than the last "newest" one.
17   For Each errorEvent In ossErrors
18       errorCount = errorCount + 1
19       If errorEvent.TimeWritten > lastError Then lastError = errorEvent.TimeWritten
20   Next
21
22   'STEP 3: Create a DateTime helper that will convert the error event's WMI date/time to readable format.
23   Set dtHelper = CreateObject("WbemScripting.SWbemDateTime")
24   dtHelper.Value = lastError
25
26   'STEP 4: Display the results by echoing them to a dialog box for the administrator.
27   WScript.Echo "The Application Event Log contains " & errorCount & " OSS errors, " & _
28                "the last of which was encountered at " & dtHelper.GetVarDate
29
```

FIGURE 7.5 The contents of the `DumpOssErrorInfo.vbs` script.

The `DumpOssErrorInfo.vbs` script carries out the following series of actions (viewable as comments on lines 8, 16, 22, and 26 in Figure 7.5's example script):

1. The script attaches to the local Windows Management Instrumentation (WMI) service and executes a query that returns a collection of all the event log entries for the Office SharePoint Search (OSS) service.

2. Each of the error events in the collection is processed one at time. As each event is processed, a counter is incremented, and the event is examined to see if it is the newest event gathered. If the event is the newest, its date and time are recorded.

3. Because the date and time information for the most recent event is not in a form that would be recognized as such by a human, a helper object is created to convert the information to an understandable format.

4. The total count of Office SharePoint Search service errors present in the event log, along with the date and time of the most recent error, are displayed to the administrator. You can see an example of how this information is displayed in Figure 7.6.

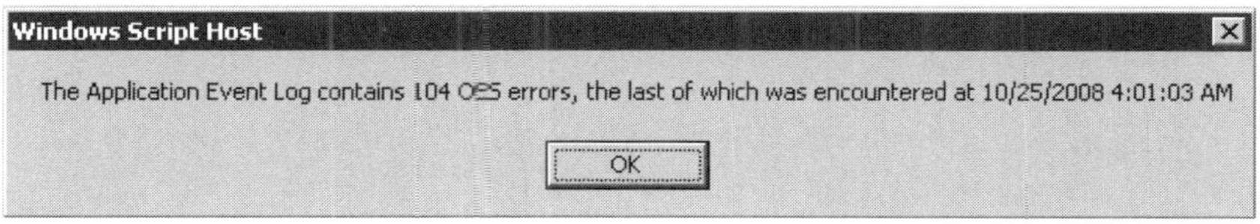

Windows Script Host ☒

The Application Event Log contains 104 OES errors, the last of which was encountered at 10/25/2008 4:01:03 AM

OK

FIGURE 7.6 The dialog box that is displayed upon execution of the DumpOssErrorInfo.vbs script.

Of course, the additional power that is available through VBScript is not without some additional cost or consequence. A review of the batch file example (Figure 7.3) and the VBScript example (Figure 7.5) should make it clear that VBScript is more complex and exacting in its syntax. This fact means that script development typically requires a greater number of iterations to write, test, debug, and repeat. This, in turn, means that VBScripts generally take longer to develop and mature than their batch file counterparts.

Another limitation of VBScript comes in the type of components it can utilize —that is, COM Automation components. As a technology, COM has been on a steady decline for many years. The original release of Microsoft's .NET Framework (or simply .NET) in 2002 signaled that the end of COM was coming. Since that time, the bulk of new development has been within .NET. Without significant assistance and workarounds (such as the use of COM-callable wrappers, or CCWs), the .NET framework and components built upon it cannot be utilized by VBScript. This new emphasis and the rising popularity of .NET programming basically means that VBScript's days are numbered.

PowerShell

If COM was "old and busted" in 2002, then .NET was the "new hotness." In releasing the .NET framework, Microsoft made a dramatic shift away from the limitations and operational model of COM and toward a new programming paradigm that featured a fully developed framework class library (FCL), a new common language runtime (CLR) environment that behaved much like a virtual machine, improved memory management that supported garbage collection (versus COM's deterministic finalized reference counting approach), and much more. Since its introduction, .NET has become a cornerstone upon which both developers and Microsoft's own products and platforms have come to rely. In its latest release, SharePoint leverages and depends on the functionality of the 2.0 and 3.0 releases of the .NET framework.

The 3.0 release of the .NET Framework is really more of a supplement to the 2.0 release than an update. .NET's core feature, the CLR, is not updated with 3.0; instead, the release adds several new libraries to the platform, focusing on user interfaces (Windows Presentation Foundation, or WPF), communications (Windows Communication Foundation, or WCF), workflow (Windows Workflow Foundation, or WF), and security (Windows CardSpace). The current releases of SharePoint, Windows SharePoint Services v3 (WSS) and Microsoft Office SharePoint Server 2007 (MOSS), require both the 2.0 and 3.0 releases of the .NET Framework for installation.

As .NET gained mindshare, the rift between existing scripting technologies and .NET-based products grew more pronounced. Command prompt batch files, although still useful, took an antiquated approach to driving automation. Object orientation simply did not exist when batch file technology originated, so batch files were left without a means to address .NET in much the same way that they were unable to interact with COM. VBScript, although capable of leveraging and interacting with COM Automation components, simply was not able to take advantage of .NET in a meaningful way. With the noted limitations in existing scripting technologies and the base of .NET applications growing week after week, Microsoft realized that it had to do something to give those who wrote scripts the tools they needed to continue operating.

At the Barcelona IT Forum in November 2006, Microsoft officially announced the availability of Windows PowerShell 1.0. Aimed squarely at administrators and those possessing operational responsibilities, PowerShell was Microsoft's answer to the question, "What comes after command prompts and VBScript?"

Much like the move from COM to .NET, the shift from VBScript to PowerShell is a dramatic one. PowerShell seeks to approximate the look and feel of the command prompt environment that came before it, but under the hood, PowerShell is radically different in several ways. Here are just a few examples:

- **At its core, PowerShell is object oriented.** This is the single biggest difference between PowerShell and the other scripting technologies discussed thus far. Rather than processing standard text, PowerShell works with object instances. It does this natively, not via automation as VBScript does.
- **PowerShell leverages the full power of the .NET framework.** PowerShell is built upon Microsoft's .NET Framework 2.0, and it can natively instantiate and manipulate types that exist within the framework class libraries. By extension, it can also leverage other .NET assemblies (such as the SharePoint API types), not just the base FCL assemblies.

- **PowerShell has its own language.** Because PowerShell natively works with objects and has some requirements similar to those of a full-blown programming language, a new language was needed to support a variety of complex functions and tasks without making simple tasks unnecessarily cryptic or difficult to execute.
- **PowerShell users can navigate nearly anywhere.** The file system (both local and remote) can be navigated just as with the command prompt and VBScript, but PowerShell extends the concept of a "drive" to include other stores, such as the Windows certificate store, the Registry, environment variables, and more. This functionality is also extensible and customizable.
- **PowerShell is secure.** Understanding that scripts can be used to wreak havoc and cause widespread damage, by default PowerShell prevents the execution of script files. Without changes, only scripts that are digitally signed and trusted can be run. This restriction does not impact the execution of PowerShell commands in an interactive fashion, though.

NOTE

You can run scripts without their being signed by altering the PowerShell execution policy (that is, Set-ExecutionPolicy -Unrestricted). However, don't make such a change without carefully considering its potential security impact.

Although PowerShell is included within Windows Server 2008, it is available as a separate download for Windows XP SP2, Windows Server 2003 SP1, and Windows Vista. Because PowerShell depends on the Microsoft .NET Framework 2.0, you must install .NET 2.0 before you install PowerShell.

You can recognize PowerShell scripts within the file system by their extension of .ps1. Unlike batch files and VBScript files, however, PowerShell scripts cannot be run simply by double-clicking them. Double-clicking a PowerShell script actually opens the script within Windows Notepad for editing. This behavior is by design and is implemented for reasons of security.

TIP

It probably comes as no surprise that you can edit PowerShell scripts, like batch files and VBScripts, with a simple text editor. As with VBScripts, though, the PowerShell syntax is rather involved, and scripts can become complex quickly. Products exist to simplify the process of writing, editing, and debugging PowerShell scripts; an excellent tool that also happens to be free is PowerShell Analyzer. You can find it at http://www.powershellanalyzer.com/.

You can only run PowerShell scripts from within the PowerShell environment, which you can typically access by launching PowerShell from the Start menu's Run dialog box, shown in Figure 7.7.

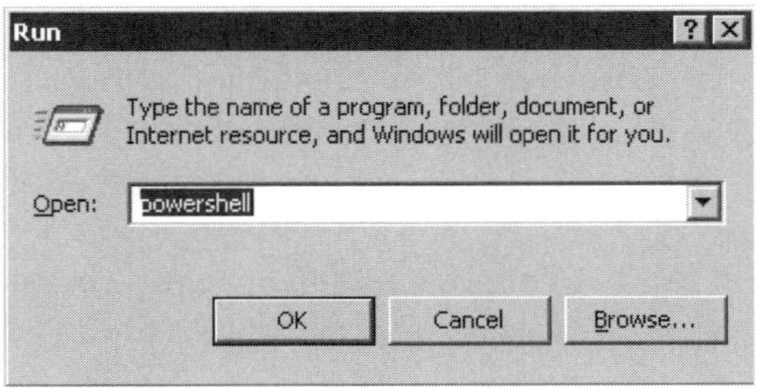

FIGURE 7.7 Launch PowerShell from the Run dialog box.

For a sample of what you can accomplish with PowerShell, examine the GetSpServicesStatus.ps1 script that appears in Figure 7.8. This simple script is actually a single line command sequence that supplies the current operational state of the various Windows services that MOSS supplies or employs. The script carries out the following actions:

1. The get-service cmdlet (pronounced *commandlet*) on line 1 retrieves one ServiceController object for each of the named services.
2. The retrieved ServiceController objects are piped (that is, supplied as input) to the format-table cmdlet on line 3.
3. The format-table cmdlet creates a text-based table and displays the values for each of the named properties on the ServiceController objects supplied. Each ServiceController's set of property values is placed on a different line.

You can see the result of executing the GetSpServicesStatus.ps1 script in Figure 7.9. Note each of the selected services, their descriptions, and their states.

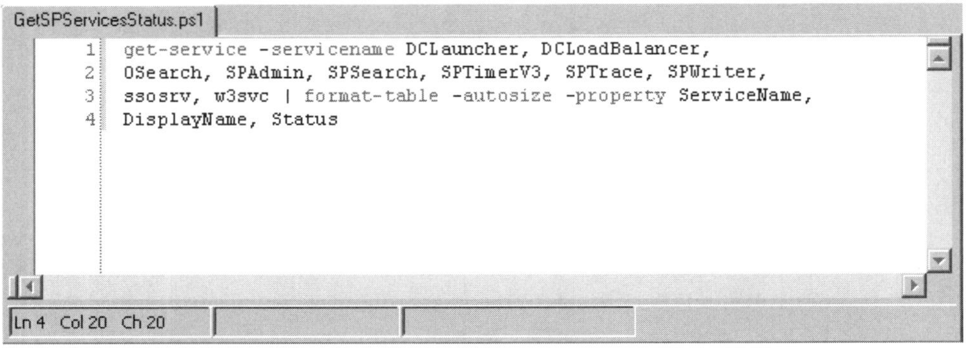

```
GetSPServicesStatus.ps1
    1   get-service -servicename DCLauncher, DCLoadBalancer,
    2   OSearch, SPAdmin, SPSearch, SPTimerV3, SPTrace, SPWriter,
    3   ssosrv, w3svc | format-table -autosize -property ServiceName,
    4   DisplayName, Status
```

Ln 4   Col 20   Ch 20

FIGURE 7.8 The GetSpServicesStatus.ps1 PowerShell script.

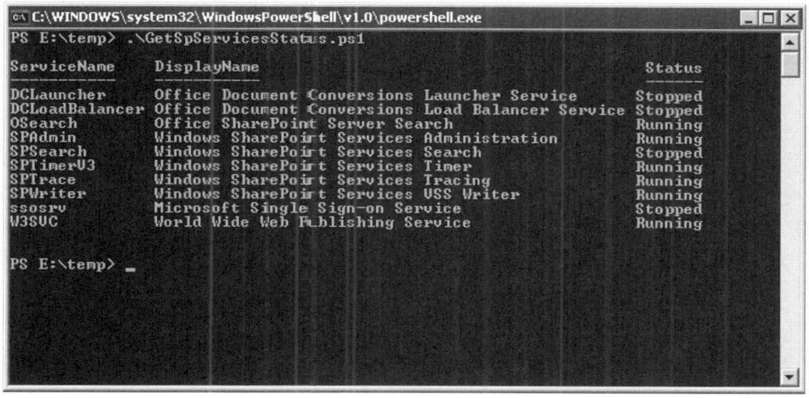

FIGURE 7.9 Results of executing the `GetSpServicesStatus.ps1` PowerShell script.

The `GetSpServicesStatus.ps1` script is simple in its structure and operation, but it hints at what is possible with PowerShell. You can use PowerShell for far more powerful tasks and operations than demonstrated here. In fact, a number of Microsoft products, such as Microsoft Exchange Server and Microsoft System Center Virtual Machine Manager (SCVMM), rely upon administrative tools that consist of a graphical user interface (GUI) built on top of a PowerShell foundation. When an administrator clicks a button or initiates some form of action through the administrative GUI, the tool translates the desired actions into PowerShell commands that are then executed.

Microsoft is pouring quite a bit of time and effort into PowerShell, and it is truly intended to be "the new command prompt" going forward. If scripts must be written against .NET, PowerShell is the only game in town.

As Peter Parker (aka Spider-Man) learned, "With great power comes great responsibility." In the case of PowerShell, it can also be said that with great power comes a rather steep learning curve. It could be argued that PowerShell is as much a custom development tool as it is a scripting language, and you must become familiar with .NET's framework class libraries to fully leverage PowerShell's most powerful capabilities. Much has been done to ease the transition from older technologies like the command prompt and VBScript (for example, aliases), but at its core PowerShell takes a fundamentally different, object-oriented approach to scripting. Those intending to adopt PowerShell should allot plenty of time for learning in their schedules because learning PowerShell is only half the battle. Those intending to use PowerShell with SharePoint must familiarize themselves with the SharePoint object model (discussed later in this chapter).

PowerShell's approach to security, although perfectly understandable in today's computing environment, does create some challenges that do not exist with batch files and VBScripts. Although developers who have had to distribute software via the Internet may be familiar with Authenticode and code-signing certificates, these are certain to be new concepts for most administrators and operations personnel. As is often the case, the complexities associated with signing scripts for general use typically lead administrators to simply downgrade the execution policy on servers running PowerShell to permit unsigned script execution. As mentioned earlier, changing the PowerShell execution policy reduces the overall security of the PowerShell environment and may introduce security risks. The decision to make such a change should not be made without considering (and accepting) the risks associated with it.

LEVERAGING SCRIPTS AND SCRIPTING ENVIRONMENTS

The previous pages presented the common forms of scripting available to administrators, as well as their relative strengths and weaknesses. The next pages briefly focus on a few facets of scripting environments and their interactive experience. You'll learn some of the common ways to use scripts to carry out operations within the SharePoint environment. In addition, you'll read some consideration points when developing custom scripts, including some practices that make scripts more robust and maintainable.

Although a variety of third-party scripting options and technologies are available for use with SharePoint and on the Windows platform in general, this section focuses exclusively on the technologies presented thus far in this chapter: command batch files, VBScript, and PowerShell.

Interactive Use of the Command Prompt

The DOS-based command prompt offers a command-line experience that nearly all administrators and operations personnel are familiar with. This is especially true for those who manage SharePoint environments, as the STSADM.exe application is SharePoint's Swiss Army Knife of the command prompt environment.

Interactive use of STSADM.exe for both backup/restore and export/import operations is covered in detail in Chapter 5; refer to it for tips and information on the interactive use of this powerful administrative tool for SharePoint.

STSADM.exe is not the only command prompt application specifically targeted for use in SharePoint operations. An oft-overlooked yet exceptionally useful command prompt application comes in the form of PSCONFIG.exe.

PSCONFIG.exe offers command prompt access to the functions available through the GUI of the SharePoint Products and Technologies Configuration Wizard. Figure 7.10 demonstrates the application's usage and command options.

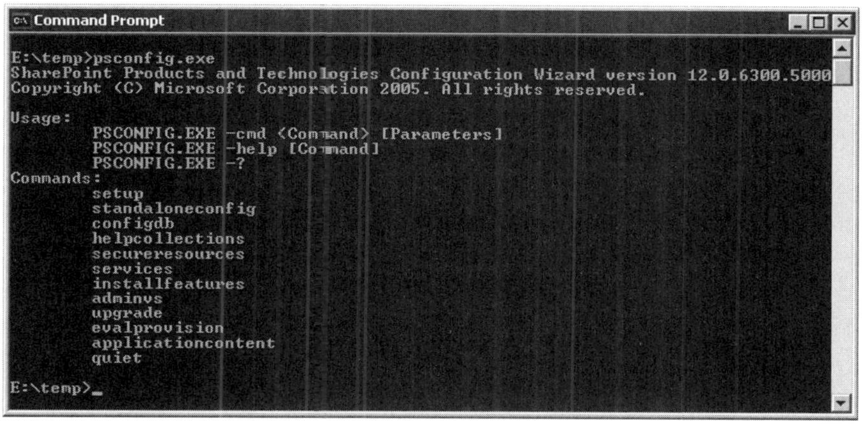

FIGURE 7.10 PSCONFIG.exe's usage and command options.

Just as STSADM.exe offers the same functionality found in the SharePoint Central Administration site and expands on it, PSCONFIG.exe permits the execution of some operations and the assignment of some properties that are not possible through the use of the window-based SharePoint Products and Technologies Configuration Wizard. PSCONFIG.exe is most commonly used in the creation of a specifically named farm configuration database prior to the establishment of a new SharePoint farm. With PSCONFIG.exe, you can create a farm configuration database that possesses a name of your choosing rather than one that takes the default form of `SharePoint_Config_<guid>`, where `<guid>` is a system-generated globally unique identifier. This is accomplished through the use of PSCONFIG.exe's `configdb` command.

Interactive Use of PowerShell

In truth, the script that was shown in Figure 7.8 was actually an interactive use of PowerShell; the "script" itself was nothing more than a single line command.

PowerShell offers enormous opportunities for SharePoint administrators and operations personnel. Its object-oriented nature and ability to leverage .NET types makes it an ideal match for SharePoint. SharePoint itself is, after all, a .NET-based application platform.

Without modifications to its environment, PowerShell knows nothing about SharePoint. Although you can modify the command prompt environment path setting to simplify access to the STSADM.exe application (see the section titled "Accessing STSADM.exe" in Chapter 5), it is recommended that if you're seeking to use PowerShell for scripting and operations with SharePoint, you create or modify the default PowerShell profile on servers hosting SharePoint.

The PowerShell base profile is itself a PowerShell script that is loaded and run each time an instance of the PowerShell environment is launched interactively (for any user) or noninteractively. This makes the profile an excellent place to put commands that set up variables and establish references commonly needed in each environment. In the case of SharePoint, for instance, the base profile is an excellent location to reference and load the assemblies that are required for PowerShell to interact with the SharePoint object model.

To load the SharePoint assemblies on a machine-wide basis each time the PowerShell environment is started, carry out the following steps:

1. Navigate to the profile location that applies to all users and all instances of PowerShell. By default, this location is the `\system32\WindowsPowerShell\v1.0` folder within the `Windows` directory.

2. Open the `profile.ps1` script if it exists, or create it if it doesn't. This file contains PowerShell directives that are loaded or executed whenever an instance of PowerShell is started. If the file is being created from scratch (fairly common for a new PowerShell installation), be sure that the file is simply a text-based file that you can open from Windows Notepad.

3. Add the lines seen in Figure 7.11 to the file and save it. These lines ensure that common SharePoint types are made available for use within the PowerShell environment. The commands shown load the common SharePoint assemblies using their fully qualified names. If your administrative requirements or the design of your planned application dictate that additional assemblies be loaded, you can add the required assemblies to the list shown in Figure 7.11 by using the same format and syntax. To load assemblies using this syntax, the specified assemblies must be present in the global assembly cache (GAC) of the hosting machine. The GAC is located on the local file system of the hosting machine in the `Assembly` folder within the `Windows` directory.

Once you've carried out this series of steps, the assemblies housing common SharePoint types are readily available from within the PowerShell environment. One way to verify that these types are available is to execute the command seen in Figure 7.12. The command shown retrieves the assemblies that have been loaded for the current application domain (in this case, the current PowerShell environment) and lists them as seen in Figure 7.13. Note the presence of the `Microsoft.SharePoint.dll`, `Microsoft.SharePoint.Search.dll`, and `Microsoft.SharePoint.Security.dll` entries in roughly the middle of the list.

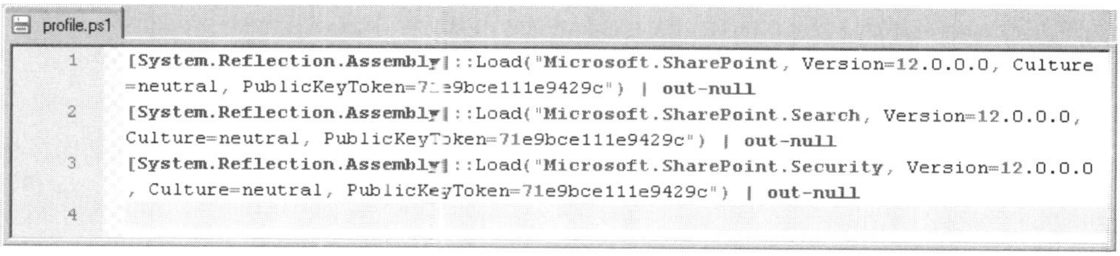

```
profile.ps1
1   [System.Reflection.Assembly]::Load("Microsoft.SharePoint, Version=12.0.0.0, Culture
    =neutral, PublicKeyToken=71e9bce111e9429c") | out-null
2   [System.Reflection.Assembly]::Load("Microsoft.SharePoint.Search, Version=12.0.0.0,
    Culture=neutral, PublicKeyToken=71e9bce111e9429c") | out-null
3   [System.Reflection.Assembly]::Load("Microsoft.SharePoint.Security, Version=12.0.0.0
    , Culture=neutral, PublicKeyToken=71e9bce111e9429c") | out-null
4
```

FIGURE 7.11 Assembly references for common SharePoint types.

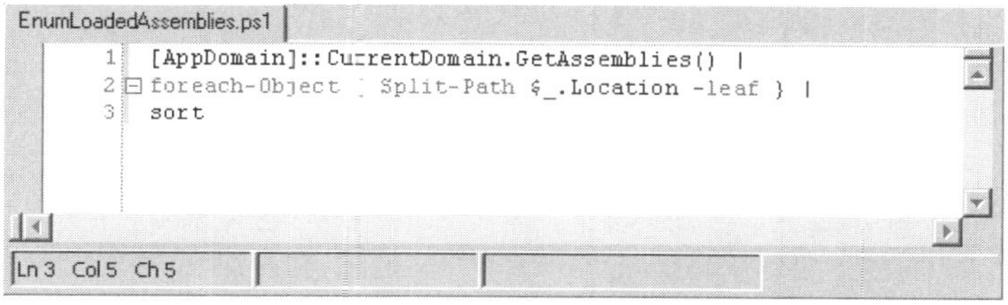

```
EnumLoadedAssemblies.ps1
1   [AppDomain]::CurrentDomain.GetAssemblies() |
2   foreach-Object { Split-Path $_.Location -leaf } |
3   sort
```

Ln 3 Col 5 Ch 5

FIGURE 7.12 PowerShell command to list loaded assemblies.

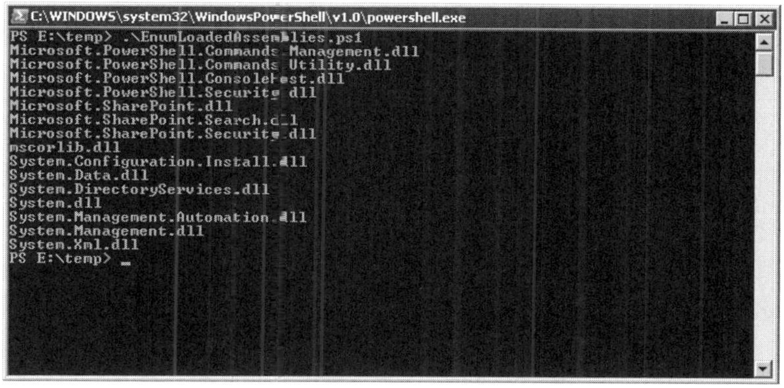

```
C:\WINDOWS\system32\WindowsPowerShell\v1.0\powershell.exe
PS E:\temp> .\EnumLoadedAssemblies.ps1
Microsoft.PowerShell.Commands.Management.dll
Microsoft.PowerShell.Commands.Utility.dll
Microsoft.PowerShell.ConsoleHost.dll
Microsoft.PowerShell.Security.dll
Microsoft.SharePoint.dll
Microsoft.SharePoint.Search.dll
Microsoft.SharePoint.Security.dll
mscorlib.dll
System.Configuration.Install.dll
System.Data.dll
System.DirectoryServices.dll
System.dll
System.Management.Automation.dll
System.Management.dll
System.Xml.dll
PS E:\temp> _
```

FIGURE 7.13 The loaded assemblies for the PowerShell environment.

> **NOTE**
> If the `profile.ps1` script is not signed, by default the PowerShell environment rejects it for security reasons. The script either needs to be signed or the execution policy for the PowerShell environment needs to be modified through the use of the `set-executionpolicy` command to allow the execution of local, unsigned scripts.

Once the assemblies housing SharePoint have been loaded into the PowerShell environment, an administrator has the ability via the SharePoint object model to interrogate and manipulate site collections, services, lists, and other common SharePoint types with ease. This makes PowerShell particularly attractive as a replacement for custom console applications that are developed solely for the purpose of performing a one-time manipulation of the farm, a Web application, or some other SharePoint object.

For example, many organizations using SharePoint have a desire to change the page that is returned to users if they supply a URL for a page that does not exist. By default, SharePoint returns the page shown in Figure 7.14 whenever an HTTP 404 error (page not found) is encountered.

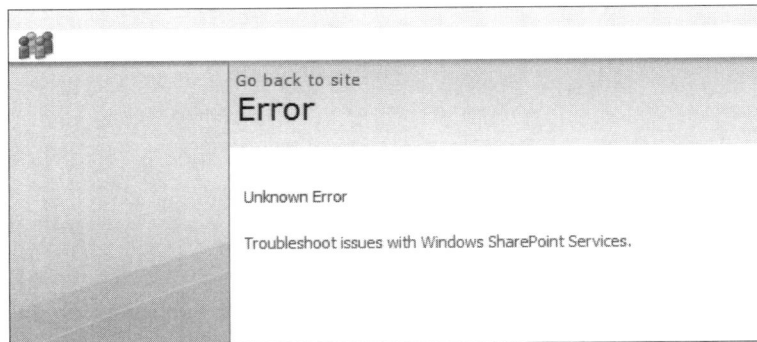

FIGURE 7.14 SharePoint's default "page not found."

There are many reasons why an organization would want to alter the contents of this page. Perhaps the information presented falls short of what many corporate communication policies intend to convey, the page does not carry branding elements over from the originating site, and more.

Microsoft has published a knowledge base (KB) article on how to change the page that is used for HTTP 404 errors (http://support.microsoft.com/kb/941329), but the process described within the article is convoluted at best. Amidst the page creation and copy steps described is the need to write a console application that does nothing but manipulate the `FileNotFoundPage` property on the hosting Web application. Although console application development is not exceptionally difficult for rank-and-file developers, it can represent a genuine barrier to those without the development knowledge and tools.

It is in exactly this type of scenario that PowerShell truly shines. Instead of writing the console application referenced in the KB article, the PowerShell shown in Figure 7.15 can be executed.

```
1  $webAppToModify = [Microsoft.SharePoint.Administration.SPWebApplication]::Lookup("http://your-site-here")
2  $webAppToModify.FileNotFoundPage = "MyCustomError.htm"
3  $webAppToModify.Update()
```

FIGURE 7.15 PowerShell script to assign the `FileNotFoundPage` property.

Assuming a page called `MyCustomError.htm` had been created and placed in the appropriate location in the file system of the SharePoint Web frontend machine(s), something similar to Figure 7.16 would be shown when attempting to retrieve nonexistent pages from the sites hosted in the Web application that had been modified.

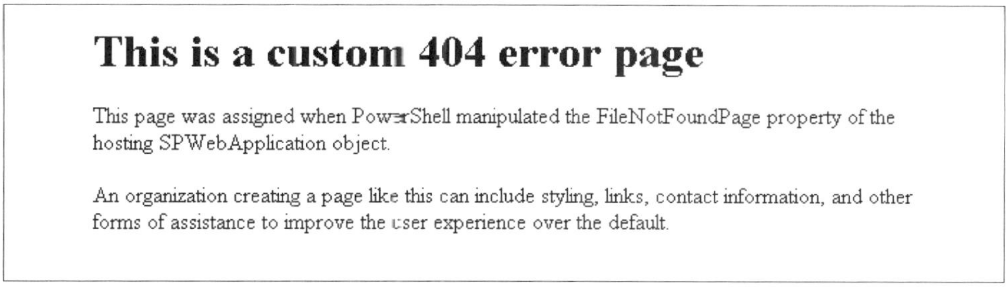

This is a custom 404 error page

This page was assigned when PowerShell manipulated the FileNotFoundPage property of the hosting SPWebApplication object.

An organization creating a page like this can include styling, links, contact information, and other forms of assistance to improve the user experience over the default.

FIGURE 7.16 A basic custom error page.

Executing the three lines of PowerShell shown in Figure 7.15 is dramatically faster and more efficient than pulling out the heavy guns of Visual Studio to write, compile, test, and finally execute the console application described in the KB article.

Finally, it is worth mentioning that PowerShell is essentially backward-compatible with the DOS-based command prompt. This means that STSADM.exe, PSCONFIG.exe, and other common command prompt applications and utilities are available directly from within the PowerShell environment.

Noninteractive Script Execution

Interactive access to the command prompt and PowerShell is obviously important for carrying out one-off tasks and querying the SharePoint environment on-demand. When most administrators think of the command prompt, VBScript, and PowerShell, though, their larger interest lies in the development of scripts that can be run in a noninteractive or unattended fashion. This is arguably the greatest benefit that scripting technologies bring to the table.

As you may have concluded by the absence of an associated interactive use section in this chapter, VBScript does not offer an interactive execution environment. You can execute DOS commands by typing them at a command prompt and PowerShell commands by typing them at a PowerShell prompt, but no "VBScript prompt" exists for an administrator to type a VBScript command and have it immediately execute. The WSH can only execute VBScript commands in unattended fashion through the use of script files.

The primary out-of-the-box mechanism through which the execution of scripts is carried out on the Windows platform is the Windows Task Scheduler, an administrative tool available in all current Windows operating systems. The Task Scheduler possesses a number of characteristics that make it ideal for the automated and unattended execution of scripts:

- **It runs as a service.** The Task Scheduler service is started by Windows under the Local System account context when the operating system is started, so no user needs to be interactively logged onto the server for the Task Scheduler to operate.
- **It impersonates a user.** Many administrative scripts require elevated privileges to properly execute. A user account and password is assigned to a task in the Task Scheduler when it is created to permit scripts to execute within the security context of a desired user.
- **It provides flexible scheduling.** A variety of scheduling options are available from within the Task Scheduler. For example, tasks can be run daily, weekly, or monthly. They can also be run at times not defined by dates, such as interactive logon, when the computer starts, and much more. More complex scheduling (for example, task repetition and shutdown for excessive run time) is possible through advanced options.
- **It's easy to use.** By default, the Task Scheduler utilizes a multistep wizard for the establishment and configuration of new tasks, walking a user through all facets of the task creation process.

One of the most common uses of the Task Scheduler in a SharePoint environment is to perform a catastrophic backup of a farm. The following steps illustrate the creation and scheduling of such a backup.

1. To schedule a task for execution, you need a batch file, script, or PowerShell cmdlet. For this example, open a text editor, such as Windows Notepad, to create a script for the task to execute. Notepad is accessible from the Windows Start menu and is located at All Programs, Accessories, Notepad. See Figure 7.17.

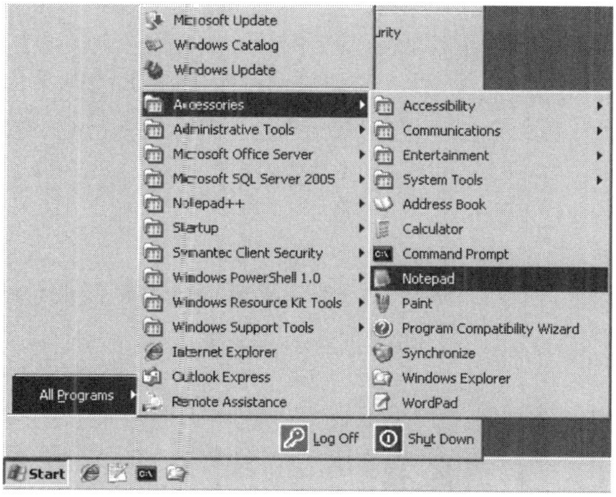

FIGURE 7.17 Launching Windows Notepad.

2. When Notepad opens, enter the single STSADM.exe command shown in Figure 7.18, replacing the path specified (\\ss-nas3\BACKUPS\ SHAREPOINT_FARM) with a valid Universal Naming Convention (UNC) path in your environment. Most backup scripts include additional commands and comments (which are discussed at the end of this section), but the command specified in Figure 7.18 is the bare minimum needed for a full farm catastrophic backup. For additional switches and an expanded discussion of STSADM.exe-based backups, refer to Chapter 5.

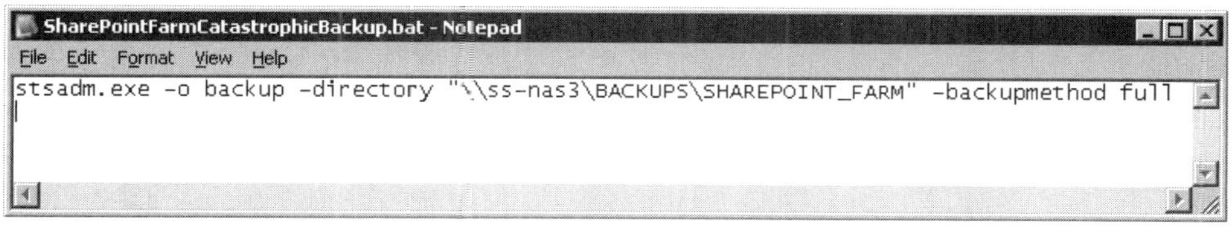

```
stsadm.exe -o backup -directory "\\ss-nas3\BACKUPS\SHAREPOINT_FARM" -backupmethod full
```

FIGURE 7.18 A simple script designed to create a full farm backup.

3. Save the script just entered by selecting Save As from Notepad's File menu. When the Save As dialog box appears, navigate to a location within the local file system and save the script with a descriptive name. In Figure 7.19, the backup script is saved with the name SharePointFarm Catastrophic Backup.bat. Make a note of the location where the file is saved, because you'll need it when you establish the scheduled task.

CAUTION

Regardless of the name chosen, be sure that the file possesses a `.bat` *extension. A straightforward way to do this is to ensure that the Save as Type drop-down box is set to All Files and that a* `.bat` *extension is specified at the end of the file name, as shown in Figure 7.19. Without the explicit assignment of this extension, the cmd.exe command interpreter is not launched once Task Scheduler executes the task. This results in no backup being performed.*

FIGURE 7.19 The Save As dialog box for Notepad.

4. Once you've created and saved the backup script, test it. An error in the script (in this case, a malformed STSADM.exe command) typically results in full failure. By first running the script interactively, you can confirm that it functions as intended. An example of a successful catastrophic backup in mid-operation is shown in Figure 7.20.

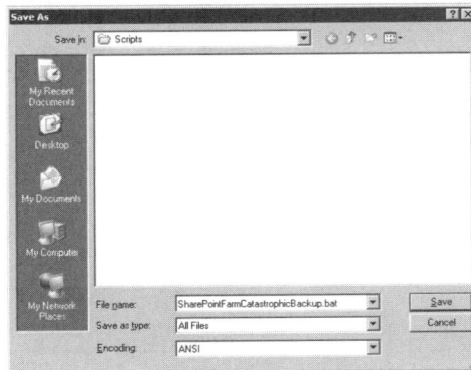

FIGURE 7.20 A catastrophic SharePoint farm backup during execution.

5. After you've verified the script, schedule it through the Windows Task Scheduler. To launch the task scheduling wizard, open the Windows Start menu and navigate to Control Panel, Scheduled Tasks, Add Scheduled Task, as shown in Figure 7.21. If the Add Scheduled Task option is not displayed in your Windows Start menu, simply click on the Scheduled Tasks item to open it and then double-click the Add Scheduled Task item to open the wizard. Note that an alternative way to access the Scheduled Tasks area (shown in Figure 7.21) is to open Windows Explorer and navigate to the Tasks folder in the Windows directory.

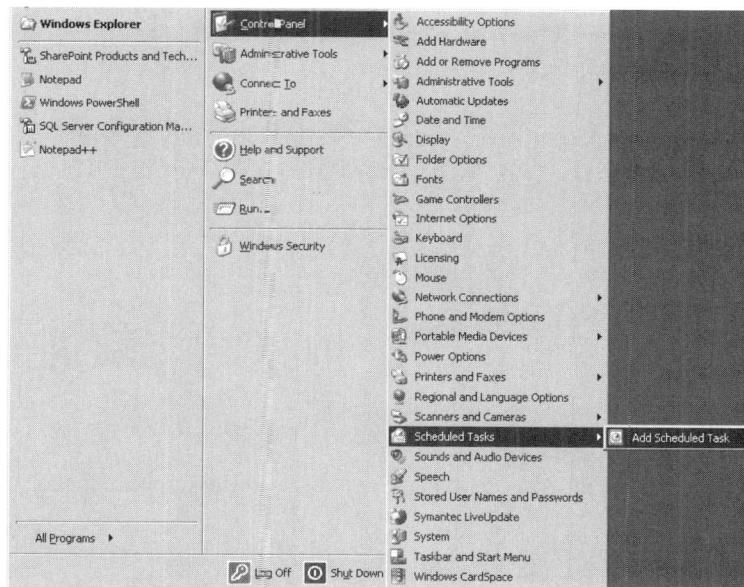

FIGURE 7.21 Opening the Windows Task Scheduler wizard.

6. The Scheduled Task Wizard appears, as seen in Figure 7.22. After you click the Next button, the wizard presents a list of applications for selection as the target in the scheduling process (see Figure 7.23). The backup script that was saved in step 3 is not present in the list shown, so you need to manually specify the script to be scheduled by pressing the Browse button.

7. The Select Program to Schedule dialog box appears. Navigate to where you stored the backup script file in step 3, select the batch file by clicking on it, and then click the Open button to return to the Scheduled Task Wizard, as shown in Figure 7.24.

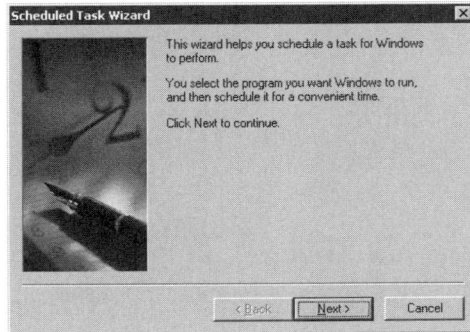

FIGURE 7.22 The first page of the Scheduled Task Wizard.

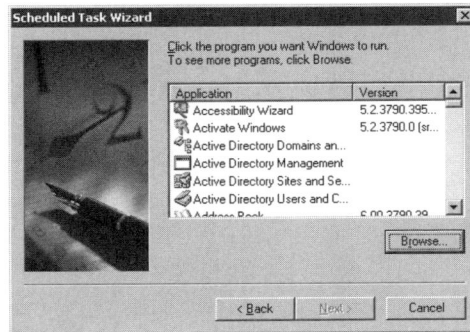

FIGURE 7.23 Scheduled Task Wizard with applications for selection.

FIGURE 7.24 The Select Program to Schedule dialog box showing the selected backup script file.

8. Upon returning to the Scheduled Task Wizard, a new wizard page appears prompting for both the name of the task to be scheduled and the frequency with which to perform it. By default, the name of the task is the same as the script file name minus its file extension. It is recommended that you modify the task name so that it reflects both the task being carried out and the interval at which the task is being scheduled for execution. In Figure 7.25, the name of the task was modified to reflect its weekly interval of execution. The Next button was then pressed to advance the wizard.

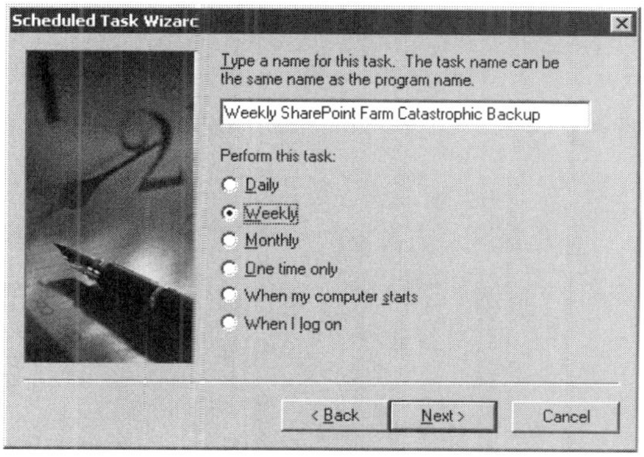

FIGURE 7.25 Setting the name and interval of the scheduled task.

9. The options that are tied to the scheduling interval appear for modification. Figure 7.26 displays the options that are specific to a weekly scheduling interval. By default, the start time that is displayed is the current time on the hosting system's clock. More often than not, the time shown is not an appropriate time at which to start a full farm backup during normal operations. Given the resource-intensive nature of backups, it's recommended that you run them during nonbusiness hours and in consideration of other SharePoint operations (such as search index crawls or other backups) that are scheduled for execution. Once a viable set of options has been supplied for the Task Scheduler, the Next button becomes enabled. Click the Next button to continue.

10. The wizard prompts for the username and password of the account under which the scheduled task should run. It is under the context of the account specified here that the scheduled task executes, so it's imperative that the supplied account be granted the necessary rights and privileges on the local server, within the database(s), and at the destination file share to carry out the backup operation from end to end. When credentials have been supplied as seen in Figure 7.27, click the Next button to continue.

FIGURE 7.26 Weekly scheduling options for the Task Scheduler.

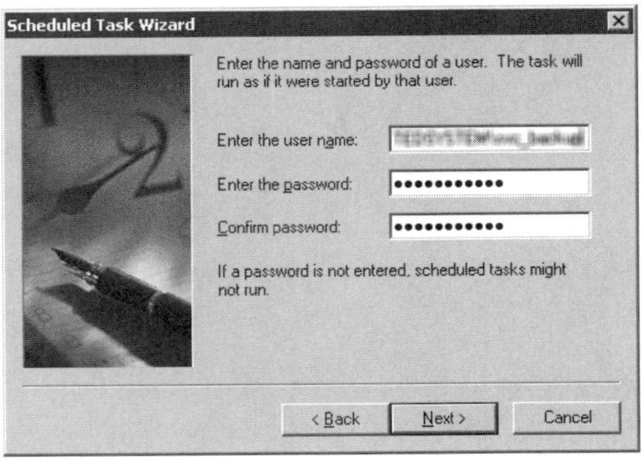

FIGURE 7.27 Specifying the account context under which the scheduled task executes.

The bulk of SharePoint production backup operations originate on a SharePoint member server and target a file share, network-attached storage (NAS) device, or some other backup destination on the network. In a Windows environment, it is recommended that a domain account be created for the purpose of scheduled backup operations and be granted only the rights it needs to complete its specific task. This least-privileged mode of operation is considered a best practice. Using one account specifically for backup purposes affords greater control and easier assignment of the privileges that the account requires at the backup source and destination.

11. With all basic parameters set for the scheduled task, the wizard's summary page is displayed as seen in Figure 7.28. Clicking the Finish button closes the wizard and enables the scheduled task. You can specify additional advanced properties by placing a check mark in the Open Advanced Properties for This Task When I Click Finish check box. Doing so results in the Advanced dialog (seen in Figure 7.29) appearing after the wizard closes.

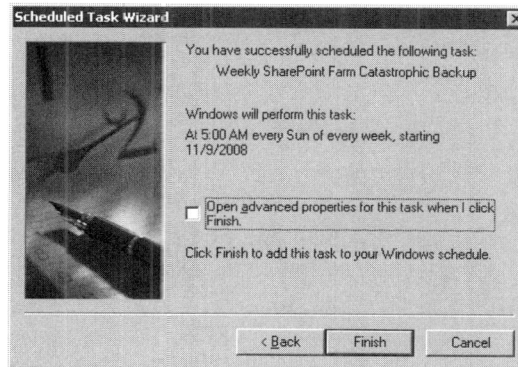

FIGURE 7.28 Scheduled Task Wizard summary page.

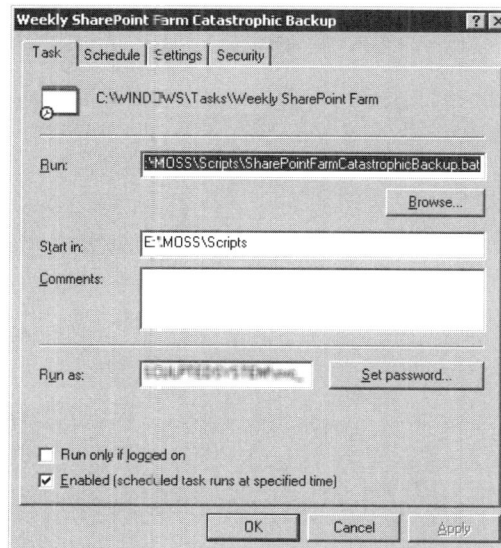

FIGURE 7.29 Advanced settings for the scheduled backup task.

If changes to the scheduled task are necessary later, you can access the advanced settings dialog for a scheduled task from the same area of the Start menu seen in Figure 7.21. Simply navigate to Control Panel, Scheduled Tasks, and right-click on the scheduled task requiring modification. Selecting Properties from the context-sensitive menu that pops up (as seen in Figure 7.30) launches the advanced settings dialog shown in Figure 7.29.

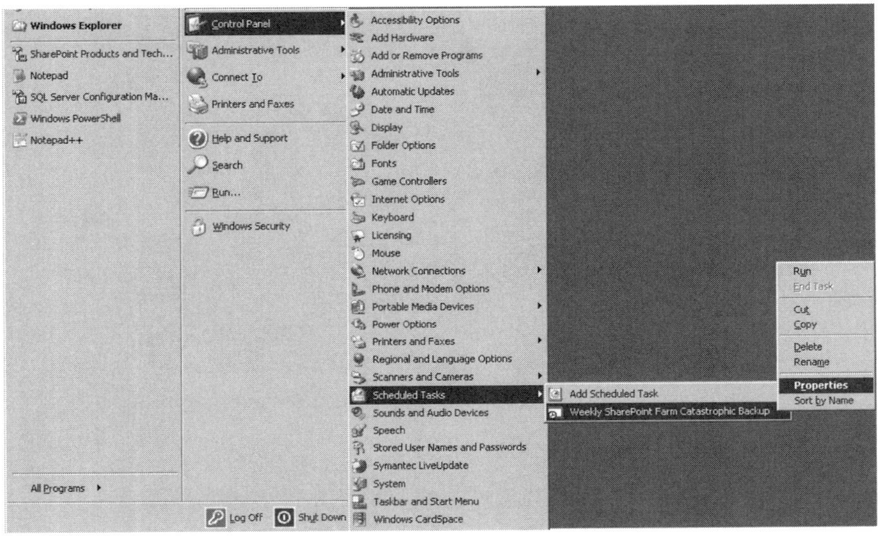

FIGURE 7.30 Launching the advanced settings dialog for a scheduled task.

Although you can launch command prompt batch files and VBScripts by specifying their fully qualified file names (for example, `E:\temp\TimerRecycle.bat` or `E:\temp\DumpOssErrorInfo.vbs`), this is not true with PowerShell scripts. As mentioned earlier in this chapter, you can only launch PowerShell scripts from within the PowerShell environment. This means that setting up a PowerShell script for execution by the Windows Task Scheduler requires an additional step: prepending the `powershell.exe` executable name to the script file name that appears in the Run text box of the advanced properties dialog for the scheduled task. An example of this appears in Figure 7.31. The full path to the PowerShell script is `E:\temp\PSBackupScript.ps1`, so to execute the script within Windows Task Scheduler, type the Run command `powershell.exe "E:\temp\PSBackupScript.ps1"`.

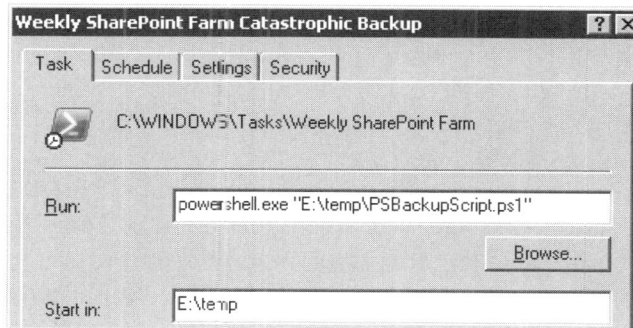

FIGURE 7.31 Adjusting the Run command for PowerShell scripts.

When the configuration of any scheduled task is completed, it is recommended that you test the scheduled task by manually selecting the Run option from the menu shown in Figure 7.30. Be aware that selecting Run has no immediately perceivable effect because the script is being executed through the Task Scheduler service in a separate process. If a scheduled task encounters an error, it does not display an error message via a dialog box or pop-up window, which is why it's so important to test your batch files, scripts, and PowerShell cmdlets on their own prior to creating a Scheduled Task for them. Determining if the script is running successfully requires some detective work. The following are a few areas and items that can be checked as indicators of success or failure of script execution:

■ **Scheduled task menu.** While the scheduled task is executing, the context-sensitive pop-up menu for the scheduled task changes from what is seen in Figure 7.30 to what appears in Figure 7.32. As the task is executing, the Run menu option is grayed out, and the End Task menu option becomes selectable. When the task completes or fails, the reverse is true.

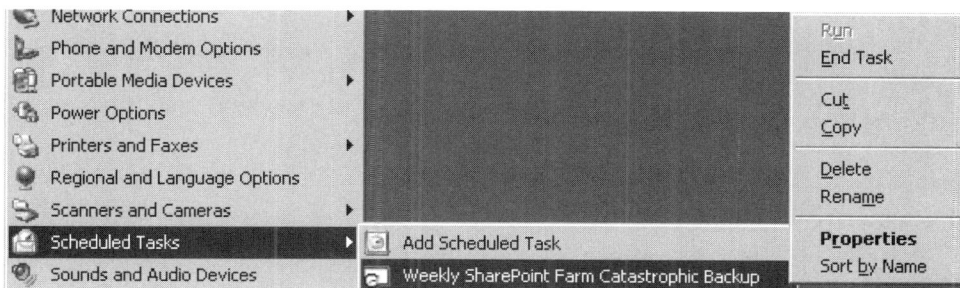

FIGURE 7.32 Scheduled task context-sensitive menu while task is executing.

- **Target file system location.** The backup destination specified within the script shows file activity while the scheduled task is executing. You can obtain the specific state of the backup job by opening the spbackup.log file that appears within the most recent backup folder (spbr0001).
- **Windows Event Log.** If the scheduled task appears to have failed, the Windows Event Log (accessible by typing eventvwr at the Start, Run dialog box as shown in Figure 7.33) can help in troubleshooting. Failed login attempts for the account specified, for example, can be found in the Security log. Additional task failures may appear in the Application log. Figure 7.34 shows a sample Application log and highlights the way an error appears within the log.

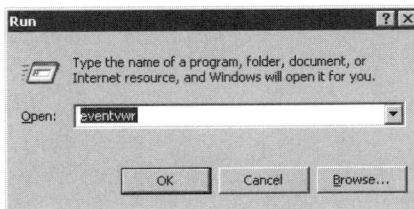

FIGURE 7.33 Launching the Windows Event Viewer from the Run dialog box.

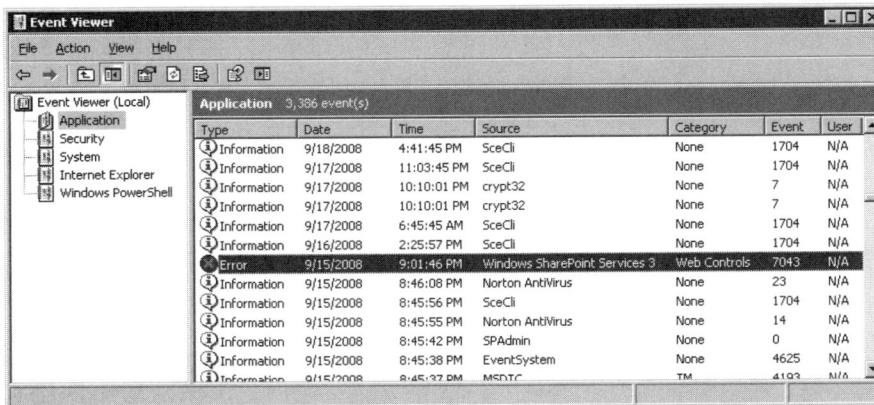

FIGURE 7.34 The Application log in Windows Event Viewer.

Although the Windows Task Scheduler is by far the most common manner in which scripts are executed noninteractively, other lesser-known avenues to execution do exist. For example, custom applications and services exist that launch, or "shell out," to scripts in much the same way that the Task Scheduler does. Prior to .NET, for example, VBScript was the underlying scripting language that powered "classic" Active Server Pages (ASP).

One of the more interesting developments regarding non-interactive script execution is the growing popularity of PowerShell as a sort of administrative go-between. It was mentioned earlier that PowerShell is being used as a sort of glue between interactive administrative user interfaces and certain Microsoft server products. At the same time, PowerShell is beginning to see use in some novel areas for unattended command execution. Microsoft SQL Server 2008, for instance, fully embraces PowerShell. With SQL Server 2008, the SQL Server Agent service can leverage PowerShell to carry out PowerShell tasks and scripts, run new SQL Server-specific cmdlets, and more.

Given the amount of time and effort behind Microsoft's push for PowerShell, as well as its alignment with .NET, it is fully expected that PowerShell will play an ever-growing role in future SharePoint versions.

TIPS FOR DEVELOPING YOUR OWN SCRIPTS

Whether you are an administrator, a developer, or some other professional tasked with adding value to SharePoint, it's hard to beat a good script. Nothing is more laborious than having to execute the same set of commands over and over again without end. By the same token, certain commands and sequences are particularly painful to type out even once. In each of these cases, a well-written script can keep you efficient, productive, and sane. Operations that are commonly scripted within the SharePoint environment include

- **Backup and restore operations.** As demonstrated, backup and restore operations are excellent candidates for scripting. Advanced scripts can ensure that the size of all backups stored do not consume more storage than desired, archive old backups, notify on failed backup attempts, and so on.
- **Site import and export operations.** A variation on the preceding backup and restore item, import and export operations tend to see more use in site duplication and the movement of sites from one location or farm to another. MOSS's content deployment functionality is an excellent example of precisely this type of automated operation.
- **Site provisioning and creation operations.** In organizations with mature governance policies, the creation of Web applications, site collections, and subsites is typically performed through automated mechanisms instead of by hand. This ensures consistency and adherence to prescribed organizational standards.
- **New farm configurations.** Although SharePoint farm creation is not a regular task in most environments, it's a task that most organizations want to get right the first time. Scripting the installation and setup of SharePoint ensures that the resultant farm is configured to the desired specifications.

■ **General maintenance and clean-up operations.** As experienced administrators often (reluctantly) admit, SharePoint 2007 does not always operate like a well-oiled machine. To keep things running at peak performance, you often need to recycle services, export logs, reclaim disk space, truncate files, and more. Scripting makes these processes robust and consistent.

Developing your own scripts is not difficult. This section alone demonstrated several simple scripts to carry out tasks, such as service recycling, error reporting, and automated farm backups. Probably the easiest way to get started with custom script development is to become familiar with what has been done and is readily available. Searching the Internet for "SharePoint scripting" returns a wealth of scripting articles and sources. Existing scripts can often be used as is with only slight changes. Even scripts that cannot be reused can provide ideas and suggest possibilities for your own scripts.

One particularly noteworthy source for scripting help and support is Microsoft's own TechNet Script Center (http://www.microsoft.com/technet/scriptcenter). The site contains articles, samples, tools, references, and many other resources that can be used without the need for alteration or in the creation of new scripts. Each of the scripting technologies that were covered in this section (command prompt, VBScript, and PowerShell) is addressed on the site, as well as several others. New material is added each week, making the site a must-visit destination.

Some Scripting Best Practices

As you begin to develop your own scripts, you should keep a handful of best practices in mind. Adhering to these suggestions ultimately makes your scripts more consistent, more robust, and easier to support by you and others.

■ **Naming.** If variables are used within your scripts (as is commonly the case with VBScript and PowerShell), adopt a naming scheme. The actual scheme used is less important than its consistent application across all scripts that you write. Ideally, your choice of scheme makes your scripts easier to read rather than more difficult. For some variable naming suggestions, refer to Microsoft's scripting guide (http://www.microsoft.com/technet/scriptcenter/guide/sas_sbp _xmzd.mspx).

■ **Location in the file system.** Once you've written a script, odds are favorable that you're going to write more. Before your script army grows too large, establish a script home location within the file system of the servers on which scripts are run. This should be in the same place on each server, and it should be located on a data drive (as opposed to `C:`, which is generally the default system drive) to make the management and backups of your scripts a straightforward affair.

- **Documentation.** Every script technology can embed comments and other documentation within written scripts. Use that ability. Whether it's a DOS-based batch file's REM command, VBScript's apostrophe ('), or PowerShell's pound sign (#), the result is the same: scripts that are easier to follow and easier to learn for those unfamiliar with them. More than a few administrators have adopted more favorable views on in-line commenting after struggling with uncommented scripts they had written (and forgotten) months or years earlier.

- **Error and exception handling.** Scripting technologies approach error handling in different ways. DOS-based batch files have a relatively primitive ERRORLEVEL check that can be used. VBScript is markedly better with its ON ERROR GOTO, ON ERROR RESUME, and ERR objects. PowerShell's TRAP and THROW error-handling facilities bring even more potential to the table. The point being made, though, is that good scripts anticipate and handle problems that occur during execution. Maybe a desired network share is not available. Perhaps a local drive has run out of space. It could be that the executing process does not have rights to the target object. Each of these conditions can be anticipated, so it's recommended that you leverage the error- and exception-handling capabilities of your chosen scripting platform to recover (or at least gracefully degrade) when possible problems occur.

- **Event logging.** As was illustrated in the Windows Task Scheduler example, it can be difficult to determine what a script is actually doing and whether it's successfully executing when it's being run noninteractively. The value of descriptive Windows Event Log entries can't be overstated in such circumstances. Although Event Log interaction is not generally possible with command prompt batch files, facilities exist within VBScript (through WMI) and PowerShell (using .NET's System.Diagnostics.EventLog type) to write messages to the Windows Event Log. When used in combination with the error- and exception-handling techniques described in the previous point, it becomes possible to build scripts that are robust and for which an execution path can be easily traced.

- **Testing and observation.** Nothing beats "trying it out" before scheduling a script for execution. It's all too common an error for an administrator or operations person to create a script, schedule it for execution, and then forget about it until a real problem (such as database failure) makes itself known. If a script wasn't tested before it was scheduled for execution, though, there's a reasonable chance that the script never ran as desired in the first place. No one ever wants to learn that his backups failed at precisely the time when he needs them for a restoration. When you write a script, test it interactively. If it passes, test it as a scheduled task. If it passes again, examine system resource utilization when it is run yet again. A trend should be making itself apparent: know your scripts, know how long they run, and know what they consume in terms of system resources. Such knowledge can give you confidence; it can also give you what you need to go back and improve a script if you discover problems along the way.

CUSTOM DEVELOPMENT

Custom development is a large topic, but it's one that deserves some attention. SharePoint is exceptionally extensible in most areas, and this is certainly true regarding disaster recovery.

The first part of this section discusses common disaster recovery extension points offered through the SharePoint API. Then it presents the broader topic of application development behaviors that can lead to software that is engineered specifically with an eye toward error-free and efficient disaster recovery operation.

EXTENDING SHAREPOINT THROUGH THE API

Despite SharePoint's wealth of tools and capabilities, there is still more that you can do to enhance and extend its feature set. Luckily, SharePoint 2007 is nothing if not extensible. Although both WSS v3 and MOSS 2007 offer ample features and capabilities, it's fairly common to work with the platform and after a while wish that it did "just this one thing" differently or that it took certain capabilities a bit further than it does. If your disaster recovery needs are not met by SharePoint's out-of-the-box feature set and you're in the realm of thinking about how a particular feature could be made better, custom development options are probably worth exploring.

This section explores the most logical disaster recovery extension points for the SharePoint platform and how you might utilize them. This chapter employs numerous domain-specific concepts and a significant degree of development terminology, so an average fluency with .NET development, object model hierarchies, and object-oriented programming is assumed.

Before getting too far into this section, spend a little bit of time familiarizing yourself with the MOSS software development kit (SDK). This is available in online form at http://msdn.microsoft.com/en-us/library/ms550992.aspx, and you can download it for local installation at http://www.microsoft.com/downloads/details.aspx?familyid=6d94e307-67d9-41ac-b2d6-0074d6286fa9&displaylang=en. The MOSS SDK contains references for both the WSS v3 and MOSS object models. Both references are invaluable resources for custom SharePoint development that you can use to further research the material covered in this section.

Several code samples appear in this chapter. Because the source code and its output depend on the environment in which they were written and executed, it should be noted that the following platform, components, and applications were used in the generation of the examples that follow:

- **Operating system.** Microsoft Windows Server 2008 Enterprise Edition 64-bit with Service Pack (SP) 1 running on VMware Workstation 6.5.0 build-118166
- **Microsoft .NET Framework.** Versions 3.0 SP1 and 3.5 SP1

- **Database.** Microsoft SQL Server 2005 Enterprise Edition SP2 Version 9.00.3073.00 (X64)
- **Web server.** Microsoft Internet Information Services (IIS) 7.0
- **Development.** Microsoft Visual Studio Team System 2008 Development Edition with Service Pack (SP) 1
- **SharePoint.** MOSS 2007 SP1 Enterprise Edition Version 12.0.6318.5000

As stated, the topic of custom development and SharePoint is an extremely broad one, so this section is relatively constrained in its focus. Attention is paid only to those logical extension points for SharePoint's built-in capabilities as they pertain to disaster recovery. Particular focus is given to enhancements surrounding the backup and restoration of content, and familiarity with development in the Visual Studio .NET 2005 or 2008 environment is assumed. COM-based technologies such as the Windows Volume Shadow Copy Service (VSS), although relevant to the topic of disaster recovery, are not addressed due to the relative complexities associated with implementing them through .NET.

SPBackupRestoreConsole and Related Types

When SharePoint backups are configured and executed, whether through STSADM.exe or the SharePoint Central Administration site, they leverage the `SPBackupRestoreConsole` class within the SharePoint object model and the types with which it is associated. Custom applications seeking to orchestrate backup and restore operations for SharePoint direct most of their calls through the `SPBackupRestoreConsole` class in some fashion.

Although not a true static class, `SPBackupRestoreConsole` largely behaves like one. Only one instance of the class exists at any given time within the scope of the SharePoint farm, and the bulk of its members and properties are static. Backup and restore operations, job history operations, and informational requests such as the amount of disk space a particular backup operation may consume all begin with calls to the `SPBackupRestoreConsole`.

The `SPBackupRestoreConsole` and primary related types can be found in the `Microsoft.SharePoint.Administration.Backup` namespace within the `Microsoft.SharePoint.dll` assembly. The relationship of these types to one another is represented by the Unified Modeling Language (UML) diagram shown in Figure 7.35.

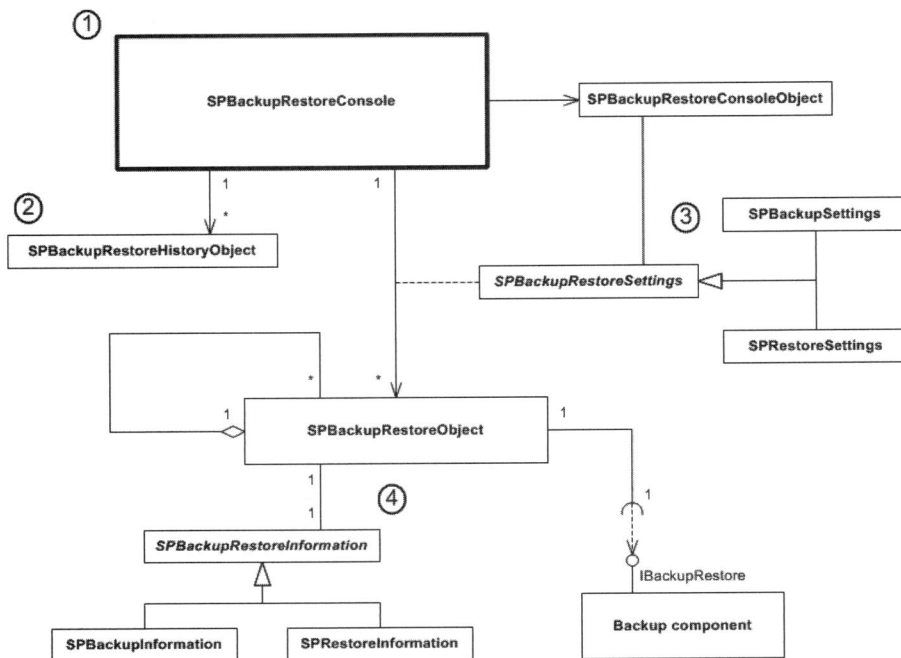

FIGURE 7.35 Relationships between the SPBackupRestoreConsole and associated types.

The circled numbers within the diagram represent several types, patterns, and interactions worthy of mention:

1. As mentioned, the SPBackupRestoreConsole type is the entry point into most standard backup and restore operations originating at the SharePoint farm level. With methods such as CreateBackupRestore, DiskSize Required, GetHistory, and Run, SPBackupRestoreConsole is capable of queuing, monitoring, and directing all farm and component-level backup and restore activities.

2. One or more SPBackupRestoryHistoryObject instances can be retrieved via a call to the GetHistory method on the SPBackupRestoreConsole. Objects of this type provide all the information needed to determine if a backup succeeded or failed, when it was attempted, who initiated it, and more.

3. The preparation for actual backup or restore operations typically employs a derived type from the SPBackupRestoreSettings abstract class (SPBackupSettings and SPRestoreSettings for a backup or restore,

respectively) and an `SPBackupRestoreConsoleObject` instance. Generally speaking, you prepare an instance of the appropriate `SPBackupRestore Settings` subclass that identifies the location and type of backup or restore to be performed. Execution of the `CreateBackup Restore` method on the `SPBackupRestoreConsole` returns a globally unique identifier (GUID) that can be used for the bulk of the remaining backup, restore, querying, and related operations. The GUID can also be used to obtain additional information about the requested backup or restore operation in the form of an `SPBackupRestoreConsoleObject` instance.

4. Instances of `SPBackupRestoreObject` are composite objects that identify a particular item for backup or restore (such as a Web application or a site collection) and possibly reference children (also `SPBackupRestoreObject` types) that are below them within the backup/restore hierarchy. One root `SPBackupRestoreObject` exists representing the entire farm, and a number of subordinate `SPBackupRestoreObjects` represent the Web applications, shared services providers (SSP)s, and so on. Additional `SPBackupRestoreObjects` exist below these representing their children (for example, content databases are children of Web applications), and so on.

An example demonstrating the basics of how you might orchestrate a farm backup using the types and techniques described appears in Figure 7.36. Although functional, the example is just a starting point. Rather than hard-coding `backupSettings.BackupDevice` and `backupSettings.BackupMethod` as shown in the example, you should parameterize such inputs. Also, clean up the backup GUID after the job has completed.

The code shown in Figure 7.36 assumes that the `Microsoft.SharePoint.dll` *assembly is referenced and that the* `Microsoft.SharePoint.Administration.` `Backup` *namespace has been imported for use by the* `ExecuteFarmBackup` *method.*

One potential application that leverages this portion of the SharePoint object model jumps out immediately. Although the Central Administration site and STSADM.exe provide mechanisms for full farm backups and restores, they are limited in both their user interface (UI) and reporting. You could develop an application with a rich user experience that does significantly more monitoring and reporting. Such an application could also offer greater control and access to reports regarding previous backup and restore attempts. In addition, the hypothetical application could interface with scheduling systems such as Windows Task Scheduler to manage farm backup scheduled tasks that operate outside the realm of SharePoint. In essence, you could create a more robust, more interactive experience for farm-level SharePoint backups and restores.

```
private void ExecuteFarmBackup()
{
    // Prepare an SPBackupSettings object that will identify the location of the
    // backup, as well as what is targeted for backup.
    SPBackupRestoreSettings backupSettings = new SPBackupSettings();
    backupSettings.BackupDevice = @"\\nas-backup\MOSS\SharePoint_Farm_Backups";
    backupSettings.BackupMethod = SPBackupMethodType.Full;

    // Use the CreateBackupRestore method to process the backup settings and
    // return a GUID that can be used to identify the desired job.
    Guid backupGuid = SPBackupRestoreConsole.CreateBackupRestore(backupSettings);

    // Set the currently defined backup to run actively; if this doesn't return
    // a true, then another backup is already in-progress and the code must fail.
    if (!SPBackupRestoreConsole.SetActive(backupGuid))
    {
        throw new Exception("Backup or restore already in progress");
    }

    // The SetupActive operation succeeded.  Execute a run operation to carry
    // out the backup.  The GUID identifies the particular operation (a backup) to
    // execute.  Specifying a null for the second parameter (for the
    // SPBackupRestoreObject) instructs SharePoint to use the entire farm for the
    // specified backup operation.
    SPBackupRestoreConsole.Run(backupGuid, null);

    // Once the backup has finished, the Remove() method should be used to clean
    // up the SharePoint environment.  The GUID of the operation is passed to the
    // method (as shown below).  This is typically handled later in monitoring.
    //
    // SPBackupRestoreConsole.Remove(backupGuid);
}
```

FIGURE 7.36 Sample code showing how to perform a full SharePoint farm backup.

Content Components and IBackupRestore Implementation

By default, SharePoint is capable of backing up and restoring four different types of objects: entire farms, content publishing Web services, Web applications, and content databases. Each of these objects is known as a content component and is represented by an `SPBackupRestoreObject` instance, as shown in Figure 7.35.

As is also shown in Figure 7.35, a content component contains two additional objects that drive its backup and restore behaviors: an object that derives from the abstract `SPBackupRestoreInformation` class (either `SPBackupInformation` or `SPRestoreInformation`), and a backup component that implements the `IBackupRestore` interface. Under normal operations, a one-to-one mapping exists between a derived type of the `SPBackupRestoreInformation` class and an associated `IBackupRestore` implementation for any given `SPBackupRestoreObject`.

Because both `SPBackupInformation` and `SPRestoreInformation` are sealed types, and the `SPBackupRestoreObject` itself is a sealed type, your ability to customize and extend the backup and restore capabilities of SharePoint to include custom objects lies with the `IBackupRestore` interface and types that implement it.

To understand how this could be useful, consider a couple of examples:

- **`Web.config` files.** As discussed in Chapter 10, "Windows Server 2003 Backup and Restore," a strategy for the backup and restore of critical system files must be implemented alongside SharePoint's own backup and restore mechanisms to ensure complete coverage of all critical and dependent SharePoint farm targets. `Web.config` files are so closely tied to SharePoint Web applications that many would prefer a mechanism that couples `web.config` files to their Web applications when SharePoint backup and restore operations are performed.
- **Associated databases.** In some environments, it is not uncommon to find additional SQL Server databases that are both used by SharePoint and housed in the SQL Server instances supporting SharePoint. Such databases could be a critical facet of farm operations, but custom databases (that is, those that are not SharePoint content databases) are not included within SharePoint's backup and restore operations by default.

In both of the examples just cited, creation of a content component that implements `IBackupRestore` can be an avenue to the inclusion of the desired items (`web.config` files and custom databases) in SharePoint's backup and restore operations.

Creation of types that implement `IBackupRestore` is an involved process and goes significantly deeper than this chapter is able to cover in a step-by-step fashion.

Although the `IBackupRestore` interface holds significant promise as an extension point for SharePoint's backup and restore infrastructure, information and examples illustrating its use are difficult to find. The Microsoft SharePoint Developer Documentation Team Blog approached the topic in an article that is recommended reading for all seeking to learn more about `IBackupRestore`. You can find the article at http://blogs.msdn.com/sharepointdeveloperdocs/archive/2008/02/07/ how-to-create-a-content-class-that-can-be-backed-up-and-restored.aspx.

SPSiteCollection Backup/Restore

Thus far, the custom development options that have been discussed have been based on types that exist in the `Microsoft.SharePoint.Administration.Backup` namespace. These types encompass the bulk of the formal, farm-level backup and restore options that most administrators are familiar with. They are not the only avenue by which to execute backup and restore operations, though.

A more lightweight approach to the backup and restoration of site collections specifically exists with the `SPSiteCollection` type. This type has both a `Backup` and a `Restore` method, and operation of both methods is exceptionally straightforward. Figure 7.37 demonstrates a site collection backup using this type.

```
private void ExecuteSiteCollectionBackup()
{
    // Prepare some key variables that will drive what is backed up and the location
    // to which it is saved.  The values shown here assume a site collection whose
    // root is http://samplesite and a destination for the backup file of
    // \\nas-backup\MOSS\Backups\SampleSiteBackup.bak.  If a file with the same name
    // already exists, it is overwritten.
    String backupFilename = @"\\nas-backup\MOSS\Backups\SampleSiteBackup.bak";
    String siteCollectionUrl = @"http://samplesite";
    Boolean overwriteExistingBackup = true;

    // Grab a reference to the Web application that serves up the site collection using
    // the known URL, and work from there to grab the SPSiteCollection object needed.
    SPWebApplication hostingWebApp = SPWebApplication.Lookup(new Uri(siteCollectionUrl));
    SPSiteCollection targetSiteCollection = hostingWebApp.Sites;

    // The Backup operation is a simple method call.
    targetSiteCollection.Backup(siteCollectionUrl, backupFilename, overwriteExistingBackup);
}
```

FIGURE 7.37 A site collection backup performed through the `SPSiteCollection` type.

The code shown in Figure 7.37 assumes that the `Microsoft.SharePoint.dll` *assembly is referenced and that the* `Microsoft.SharePoint` *and* `Microsoft.SharePoint.Administration` *namespaces have been imported for use by the* `ExecuteSiteCollectionBackup` *method.*

Restoring a site collection backed up in this fashion is as simple as changing the `Backup` method call to a `Restore` method call. Even the method parameters and their ordering remain the same between calls.

Backups created in this fashion are written out as a single file, which hints at one of the major differences between backups performed in this fashion and those that are performed through the `Microsoft.SharePoint.Administration.Backup` namespace; specifically, no backup and restore history is maintained for operations carried out through the `SPSiteCollection` type. Logging of backup and restore operations is not performed, either, making use of the `SPSiteCollection` type a lightweight approach to site collection backup and restore operations.

Use of the SPSiteCollection.Backup method results in the same type of file output as that which is generated when running the STSADM.exe command for a site collection backup (that is, STSADM.exe —o backup —url <url> -filename <filename>). This makes SPSiteCollection backups and STSADM.exe site collection backups interoperable. You could, for instance, back up a site collection through the SPSiteCollection type and use the resultant file with a restore operation using STSADM.exe —o restore —url <url> -filename <filename>.

As an example of where the SPSiteCollection type could be leveraged particularly effectively, consider the following scenario. Out of the box, SharePoint backups can only be executed by farm administrators or those who possess administrative-level access to the servers that SharePoint runs on. Because site collection backups can easily be executed from within a SharePoint site through custom code leveraging the SPSiteCollection type, you could develop a solution to give site administrators the capability to execute on-demand backups for site collections for which they have some responsibility. Such a solution could take the form of a custom administrative action, user control, or WebPart, and it could be enabled or disabled for specific groups and individuals as governance policies demand.

Content Deployment API

SharePoint's Content Deployment API, also known as the PRIME API (internally at Microsoft), offers another set of tools and approaches for preserving and migrating SharePoint content and structure. The bulk of the Content Deployment API types live in the Microsoft.SharePoint.Deployment namespace. The UML shown in Figure 7.38 represents the key types within the namespace.

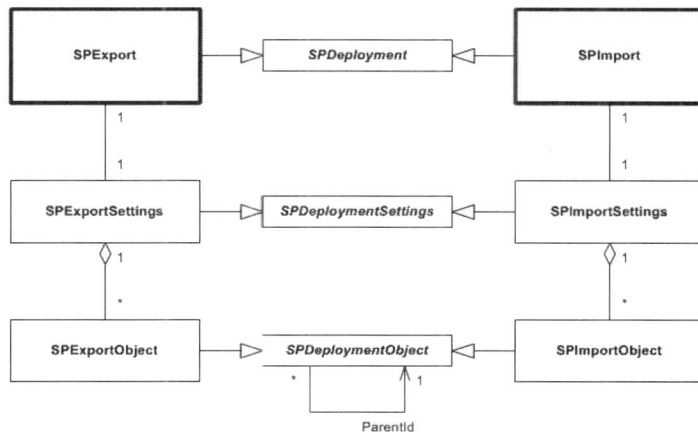

FIGURE 7.38 Relationships between key types within the Microsoft.SharePoint.Deployment namespace.

Out of the box, the SharePoint platform and some associated tools leverage the Content Deployment API in a number of ways. Here are just a few:

- **STSADM.exe.** Both the `STSADM.exe -o export` and `STSADM.exe -o import` commands leverage the Content Deployment API to carry out export and import operations.
- **MOSS Content Deployment.** Available as a feature within MOSS (not WSS), Content Deployment permits administrators to define content paths (sources and destinations) and jobs (scheduled executions) for the movement of site content from one location to another. This is commonly used in publishing scenarios to push content from an authoring farm to a production farm.
- **SharePoint Designer 2007.** As mentioned in Chapter 3, "SharePoint Designer's Backup and Restore Tools," SharePoint Designer relies upon the Content Deployment API to generate content migration packages (CMPs) and Personal Web Packages (FWPs).

As implied by the descriptions thus far, the Content Deployment API does not operate from the classic perspective of backup and restore; rather, the content deployment classes approach site persistence with the goal of copying from one site and importing into (or merging with) another. It is easier to think of backup and restore as a cloning process: that which is restored matches that which was backed up. Depending on how an export and import are run, how associated dependencies are handled, whether or not content already exists in the destination site, and so on, the results on the import side of an export/import operation set may differ significantly from the exported source. This tends to make the Content Deployment API less suited to full-fidelity backups and more useful for exporting portions of a site, merging content on import, and more.

For basic export and import functionality, though, the Content Deployment API is relatively easy to use. An example demonstrating the export of a site is shown in Figure 7.39.

The code shown in Figure 7.39 assumes that the `Microsoft.SharePoint.dll` assembly is referenced and that the `Microsoft.SharePoint.Deployment` namespace has been imported for use by the `ExecuteSiteExport` method.

The result of running the code shown in Figure 7.39 is a single `SampleSite Export.cmp` file at the selected export location. This particular example is shown because it segues nicely into the solution to a particular problem that was discussed a bit earlier in this book.

```
private void ExecuteSiteExport()
{
    // Set up some key variables that will form the basis for the export operation.
    // These settings are all self-explanatory, save for perhaps the fileNameBase.  When
    // exporting a site, the Content Deployment API will create one or more export files;
    // the number of files created depends on both the amount of content being exported and
    // the FileMaxSize property of the assigned SPExportSettings object.  The fileNameBase
    // property below simply identifies how naming of exported files will proceed.  The first
    // file will be named SampleSiteExport.cmp, the second will be SampleSiteExport1.cmp,
    // the third will be SampleSiteExport2.cmp, etc.
    Uri siteToExport = new Uri("http://samplesite");
    String exportLocation = @"\\nas-backup\MOSS\Backups";
    String fileNameBase = "SampleSiteExport";

    // Supply the assigned parameters to the constructor to build the SPExportSettings object
    // that will hold the definition and configuration of the export operation.
    SPExportSettings baseSettings = new SPExportSettings(siteToExport, exportLocation, fileNameBase);

    // Set a number of additional SPExportSettings.  The FileMaxSize property is of particular
    // note and will be discussed later in the text.
    baseSettings.ExportMethod = SPExportMethodType.ExportAll;
    baseSettings.FileCompression = true;
    baseSettings.FileMaxSize = 256;                         // default is 24 (for 24MB)
    baseSettings.IncludeSecurity = SPIncludeSecurity.All;
    baseSettings.IncludeVersions = SPIncludeVersions.All;

    // Instantiate a new SPExport object, supply our configuration, and execute the Run method
    // to launch the export operation.
    SPExport exporter = new SPExport(baseSettings);
    exporter.Run();

    // Proper clean-up practices dictate that the Dispose method be called on objects that implement
    // IDisposable and are explicitly instantiated within this code block.
    exporter.Dispose();
}
```

FIGURE 7.39 Exporting a site using the Content Deployment API.

Chapter 3 mentioned that SharePoint Designer 2007 has an inherent limitation with regard to the general size of a site collection backup it can create with its Backup Web Site function. As already mentioned, SharePoint Designer's Backup Web Site capability leverages the Content Migration API behind the scenes. Due to the default value of the SPExportSettings.FileMaxSize property, SharePoint Designer is limited to a default single file size of 24MB for backups. Many site collections are larger than this, so SharePoint Designer's Backup Web Site ability tends to fall short.

As is seen in Figure 7.39, though, it's a relatively straightforward matter to write some code that performs site exports with file sizes that are much larger than 24MB. The example illustrated in Figure 7.39 sets the FileMaxSize to 256MB. The file that is generated as a result of the operation has a .cmp extension and is compatible with SharePoint Designer. This means that the file that is exported via the previous code can be used to restore a site through SharePoint Designer's Restore Web Site function.

The Content Deployment API can be leveraged in other ways, as well. It can execute incremental exports, provide for path updating on imports, export with compression, and more. In the right situation, it may be of greater use and application than the standard backup and restore types.

DESIGNING APPLICATIONS FOR DISASTER RECOVERY READINESS

Thus far this chapter has discussed scripting, best practices relating to scripting, and ways to develop against the SharePoint object model to provide functionality that is not present within the out-of-the-box platform. All of this information is highly relevant to the topic of disaster recovery, but there is another area that is often overlooked in a discussion of disaster recovery and custom application development. That area can best be summarized with the following question: how do you engineer an application for maximum supportability in a disaster recovery situation or scenario?

Although conventional best practices relating to .NET programming call for the implementation of certain code patterns, some of these patterns can actually run counter to the "bigger picture" (which includes disaster recovery) if it is taken into account. What's best for performance, for instance, can actually operate counter to a strategy that maintains maximum supportability and location portability at its core.

This section approaches SharePoint development (and .NET code development in general) from a disaster recovery mindset and makes a handful of suggestions that are consistent with maximum recoverability, redundancy, and supportability for most custom applications in the event of a disaster.

Storage of Application Configuration Data

Nearly all applications, regardless of origin or intent, depend on some form of configuration data for proper operation. *Configuration data*, in this case, is defined as data that (a) is required for proper application operation, and (b) can vary based on the environment in which the application is installed and executed. This data can take many forms and be stored in many locations, including the following:

- Paths to file system–based configuration data
- Database sources and their associated connection strings
- Resources describing internal error codes and their associated descriptions
- Application credentials (encrypted or not) to access local and remote resources
- Locale-specific settings and assemblies
- References to assemblies that contain shared components
- Logging settings and associated reporting information
- If capable of unattended execution, schedules for noninteractive processing

- E-mail recipients, templates, and conditions under which e-mail should be sent
- Product IDs, registrations, and other codes
- Version information

When it comes to disaster recovery, the rule of thumb regarding the storage of configuration data is this: if the data can be externalized, every reasonable attempt should be made to do so. Configuration and operational data should also be separated from actual application logic whenever possible. Practices such as embedding string literals within application code are not recommended. Custom code that demonstrates a reddish-brown color within the Visual Studio environment (indicative of the use of string literals) should be rethought under these guidelines.

Development within the .NET environment is made substantially easier (from a disaster recovery perspective) with the use of `web.config` files for Web-based applications and `app.config` files for Windows forms applications. These files, which are tied to an application, can abstract the storage of application-specific settings, database connections strings, external type registrations, and more in a way that readily supports disaster recovery. If you're leveraging these configuration files, though, you must realize that the configuration files are typically tied to the installation location of their associated application. If the application is not installed to a directory or drive that is supported by backup operations, the configuration data present in the externalized file or files is typically lost with the application in the event of a disaster.

In addition to the use of `web.config` and `app.config` files, storage of application configuration data can be externalized either through the use of a database or a separate custom settings file (such as an XML configuration file). Each option offers a different set of strengths and weaknesses, so the decision regarding which to use depends on the acceptable trade-offs. Storage of configuration data in a database is attractive from a supportability and abstraction standpoint since the database itself is likely stand-alone and backed up, but use of a database in this fashion can result in a poorly performing solution. The use of an XML file tends to be better performing, but it also tends to encourage a custom storage scheme that is less supportable across an enterprise unless schemas are standardized.

When you're storing application configuration data for custom SharePoint solutions, both `web.config` storage and database storage are feasible options and should be considered for use based on application needs and governance requirements. Because a SharePoint site is an ASP.NET site, it's easy to store and retrieve settings data from `web.config` files. The SharePoint object model also includes some specialized types (such as the `SPWebConfigModification` type) that make it easy to integrate configuration data changes during installation or activation of custom code. At the same time, many SharePoint object types representing easily recognized entities (such as `SPFarm`, `SPService`, and `SPWeb`) have a Properties collection that can be used to persist custom data to the associated SharePoint databases. This means that use of the `Properties` collection to store configuration data for the aforementioned types results in that data being included in any backup approach that covers the SharePoint databases.

The only proscribed options for configuration storage have been mentioned. Placing string literals in-line with application code greatly reduces supportability and location portability. One notable addition to the list is the Windows Registry. In the days of COM, storage of settings in the Windows Registry was considered a step forward; from a disaster recovery perspective, storage of application settings in such a fashion is not recommended if it can be avoided. Though current backup mechanisms often capture the Registry and its settings, accessing and modifying the settings contained within the Registry is much more involved and less friendly than working with external settings files. It would be a challenge to identify circumstances under which the storage of SharePoint settings in the Registry would be preferable to the use of the `SPFarm.Properties` collection.

Storage of Transient and Persistent Application Business Data

Configuration data may be responsible for getting an application running and identifying how it should interact within its runtime environment, but it is an application's business data that is tied to the real value that the application brings to an organization. Business data takes many forms; the list that follows contains just a few of the multitude of file and data types that fall into this category:

- Spreadsheets
- Written documents, including e-mail messages
- Presentations, multimedia files, and other audio/visual assets

Whereas configuration data is required for an application to simply execute, business data can generally be thought of as the data that is produced or consumed in the day-to-day operations of an application. Business data can be persistent and live beyond the scope of execution of the application; it can also be transient or temporary data that is used by an application during computations, auto-saves, and so on.

The question of where business data should be stored by an application is not a new one. The following are some recommendations and points for consideration:

- **Clearly separate business data from other data.** On both servers and client workstations, a best practice is to format two separate logical disks for local storage requirements. One logical drive contains the Windows system and program files (typically `C:\`), whereas the other (oftentimes `E:\`) contains application and business data. The use of two separate logical drives in this fashion makes the creation, maintenance, and targeting of backup operations much easier.

- **Leverage environment variables.** Environmental portability and disaster recovery are aided significantly when assumptions are avoided regarding the structure of the file system hosting an application. This is particularly true when it comes to the storage of transient application data. Many applications need to use the hosting system's file system for activities such as compression/decompression, encryption/decryption, and other stream-related operations. In these instances, environment variables that are supplied by the hosting operating system can be used to ensure that proper file system locations are employed. In the case of temporary or working files, for instance, the %TEMP% environment variable defines the default temporary files location for users who are currently logged onto the operating system.

- **Make business data storage locations configurable.** This is an extension to the point that was made with the previous item. When the storage of persistent data is a requirement, some mechanism must be provided to permit the configuration of the storage location. This could be something as common as the Save As dialog box seen throughout the Windows world, or it could be an application configuration file setting that drives all data to a single location. Regardless of the mechanism selected, avoid assumptions about the hosting system's file system structure at all costs.

- **Employ network-available services when possible.** Disaster recovery operations are significantly aided when critical business data can be centralized for backup and restore purposes. Traditional file shares represent one example of how such centralization can be achieved, but they are by no means the only mechanism. Databases, custom business services, and even SharePoint (through WebDAV and the WebClient service) can be utilized for this purpose.

With SharePoint custom solutions, the storage of transient data should obey the points just described. The storage of persistent business data, however, is largely a nonissue. Simply storing business data in SharePoint lists and document libraries ensures that the business data is covered in the event of a disaster through standard farm backup procedures.

Accessing Network Resources

In today's highly interconnected computing environments, network resources are a common reality and storage location for much of the data leveraged by applications. The following are common examples of network resources:

- File shares (that is, file system storage locations not resident on local disks)
- E-mail stores (POP3, IMAP) for e-mail-enabled applications
- Databases
- FTP sites
- Any HTTP-enabled sites and services (overlaid file shares, Web services, and so on)

The best support for disaster recovery scenarios for network resources comes when those resources are accessed through indirection or some form of abstraction layer. Although the abstraction of such resources can be an application-specific exercise, several mechanisms are built into common operating systems and network stacks to decouple the naming of such resources and services from their actual implementations:

- **Domain Name Service (DNS).** DNS is perhaps the most common approach to separating uniform resource locators (URLs) and namespaces from actual resource implementations. DNS is the standard for Internet naming. If a user supplies a common English name (such as www.amazon.com) to a DNS server, the DNS server resolves the hostname to an IP address (72.21.203.1). DNS decouples names from IP addresses, but it comes with a cost in the form of DNS servers, increased management overhead, and some need to update names and their associated IP addresses.
- **DFS (Distributed File System/Services) for Windows and Novell networks.** Practically speaking, DFS can be regarded as a "file system switchboard" service. Enterprise wide, DFS supports the practice of specifying, mapping, and redirecting network file paths. This approach decouples file path references from their underlying implementations, but it carries with it the need for additional maintenance that is operating system specific.
- **Mapped network drives.** Mapped network drives are a common approach to identifying network resources using local path specifications. Nearly all applications and platforms support the notion of mapped drives in some sense, making them a solid backward-compatible approach to separating identifier from implementation. Unfortunately, mapped drives tend to be established on a per-user or per-session basis. This limits their potential usefulness in many cases, particularly regarding activities that are carried out within the context of a noninteractive account.

Given these options, the only methods that are proscribed wholesale for use in accessing network resources are those involving direct IP address access and the use of NetBIOS names. Both of these methods fail to leverage an abstraction layer of some sort, so their viable use within a functional disaster recovery environment is questionable. After all, most "live" data centers (or failover targets) have servers and naming schemes that differ from those being used in the standard production environments that are being protected by the disaster recovery implementation.

When it comes to custom SharePoint applications, developers are advised to simply use DNS whenever possible if calls to other sites or network resources are required. SharePoint's alternate access mappings (AAM) capability simplifies the process of extending any SharePoint site that may have an IP address in its URL to make it addressable by DNS name, so SharePoint is exceptionally DNS friendly for applications attempting to access its sites and Web services. Because SharePoint's AAM capabilities and zone mappings are also accessible through the SharePoint object model (such as `SPWebApplication.AlternateUrls`), it's easy to ensure that custom SharePoint applications can cope with environmental changes and gracefully fall back to alternate access points to a site if needed.

Application Logging and Monitoring

The previous design readiness suggestions focused primarily on ways in which addressing and usage of application resources and data could be decoupled. The final set of recommendations offered in this section focus on providing insight and understanding into how an application is operating.

Logging and monitoring are fairly common application requirements, but these areas are often inadequately addressed or supported when development is undertaken. Many times, they are seen as a "nice to have," rather than a critical facet of a fully functional and well-architected application.

In a disaster recovery scenario, logging and monitoring take on additional importance. This is especially true when a custom application may have a recovery time objective (RTO) that is measured in hours or maybe even minutes. You simply don't have the luxury of taking any measurable amount of time in such circumstances to focus on troubleshooting a problematic application. If an application has issues coming online when recovered, the reasons for those issues need to be clearly spelled out.

At a minimum, applications should communicate not only errors, but critical informational items regarding where data is being accessed and utilized, security checks that pass and fail, anytime an application is falling back to a default value, and so on. A common mechanism for the communication of this information is the Windows Event Log, but items that are more "informational" in nature are often better supported and controlled through the use of trace switches and flags.

Being built upon ASP.NET, SharePoint has access to ASP.NET's full array of event tracing and notification capabilities. Errors, warnings, and other informational items can be written to the ASP.NET trace log. Critical application errors can be added to the `AllErrors` collection of the `SPHttpContext` for further processing and analysis downstream in the ASP.NET pipeline. In addition to these capabilities, SharePoint has its own unified logging service (ULS) to which developers can write messages of any sort. These capabilities greatly simplify the problem of pinpointing issues that arise with custom SharePoint code and applications.

Supporting Windows performance counters is another step forward that can promote greater supportability and troubleshooting with mission-critical applications. This is particularly true for applications that operate as services or lack any form of interface. Thoughtfully chosen and implemented counters can mean the difference between befuddled head scratching and insight when attempting to identify the source of a problem during recovery.

Both SharePoint and ASP.NET come with a variety of performance counters that can be leveraged out of the box to troubleshoot application and performance problems. In addition, developers have the standard abilities offered by .NET to create performance counters of their own for their SharePoint applications.

CONCLUSION

Although SharePoint disaster recovery operations are typically the province of farm administrators and operations personnel, knowledge of the ways in which you might customize, extend, and automate the SharePoint platform can prove very useful. Possession of custom development and scripting knowledge can help you avoid repetitive tasks that commonly lead to errors, permit the development of tailored solutions that solve novel or business-specific technology problems, and generally save countless hours and many headaches in the long run.

Scripting is the primary mechanism through which administrators and operations personnel automate repetitive and difficult tasks, and several options are available for use. The command prompt batch file has been around since the days of DOS and will likely be around for years to come, but it is somewhat limited in its ability to carry out operations on the SharePoint platform. VBScript represents an evolutionary step forward over batch files, but its basis in COM means that, as a technology, it is heading into the sunset. Finally, the fully object-oriented nature of PowerShell and the rapid growth of support for it make it an excellent resource for nearly any form of scripting task involving the SharePoint platform.

All of the scripting technologies discussed permit the noninteractive execution of scripts, and all but one permits some form of interactive execution, as well. Interactive and noninteractive execution modes and concerns differ from technology to technology, but the Windows operating system comes equipped with a mechanism that can be leveraged with all discussed scripting technologies: the Windows Task Scheduler. Configuration of the Task Scheduler is interactive and wizard based, and it makes the scheduling of noninteractive script executions a simple affair.

Regardless of the scripting technology chosen, a number of best practices should be observed to make scripts as maintainable and robust as possible. Although specifics vary from platform to platform, script writers should familiarize themselves with error-handling mechanisms and logging support. Prior to writing scripts, important topics such as standards for documentation, naming conventions, and location of scripts within the file system should be discussed and decided. Scripts should be thoroughly tested as they are written, after they are complete, and once they have been scheduled for noninteractive execution.

When the SharePoint platform lacks the facilities to adequately address disaster recovery needs, custom development using the SharePoint API can be used in situations and scenarios that are either inappropriate or simply too complex for scripting alone. SharePoint makes a number of options available for custom backup and restore operations, including the types of the `Microsoft.SharePoint.Administration.Backup` namespace and the relatively lightweight `SPSite Collection` type. SharePoint also offers a Content Deployment API that is exposed through the `Microsoft.SharePoint.Deployment` namespace, and the types found within can be leveraged to extend export and import operations.

Finally, you should factor a number of techniques and considerations into the design of any application that is a candidate for location and operation in multiple environments, because this often happens in a disaster recovery scenario when multiple data centers and workstation environments are in play. Certain practices such as indirect access to network resources, clear segregation between applications and their associated configuration data and business data, and the centralization of business data can significantly aid in the recoverability of an application and greatly reduce downtime in the event of a disaster. Architecting applications to adequately support logging and performance monitoring can also greatly improve troubleshooting efforts when an application does encounter problems in both disaster and nondisaster scenarios.

Having completed this chapter, you should now be able to answer the following questions. As with the other chapters, answers to the following questions appear in Appendix B, "Chapter Review Q&A," on the book's Web site at http://www.courseptr.com/downloads.

1. What are the three most commonly utilized scripting technologies that are available for use? Which represents the most capable and overall best choice for the SharePoint platform? Why?

2. What four benefits and capabilities does the Windows Task Scheduler offer for noninteractive script execution?

3. Which three areas or locations can be examined to ascertain the state of a script that is executing noninteractively?

4. What critical modification must be made to scheduled tasks that involve PowerShell scripts to get the scripts to execute?

5. Through what object are all operations involving farm-level backup and restore operations conducted?

6. Which two object types hold the information and implementation of an `SPBackupRestoreObject` content component?

7. How do backups performed through the `SPSiteCollection` type differ from standard farm-level backups?

8. True or false: The Content Deployment API is leveraged by both the STSADM.exe –o backup command and SharePoint Designer 2007 for its backup-related operations?

9. What are the differences between application configuration data and business data?

8

SQL Server 2005 Backup and Restore

In This Chapter

- SharePoint's Database Options
- How to Back Up a SQL Server 2005 Database
- SharePoint and Backing Up SQL Server 2005
- How to Restore a SQL Server 2005 Database Backup
- SharePoint and Restoring a SQL Server 2005 Backup

It seems these days that the majority of applications, whether they are used by the largest of corporations or the average Joe User, rely heavily on backend databases to retain the information associated with the applications. Tools like Lotus Notes and Microsoft BizTalk, as well as Web sites such as Amazon.com, Yahoo.com, and Microsoft.com, store large quantities of data in databases that they could not function without. In SharePoint, you have yet another excellent example of an application platform built on top of backend databases, using those databases to store content, user profile data, configuration settings, and much more.

But SharePoint is also somewhat unique in how much it depends on its backend databases. An overwhelming majority of the data and settings associated with SharePoint are actually stored in SharePoint's databases, not the file system of the SharePoint servers in a farm. It can be quite a surprise to a first-time SharePoint administrator to learn that the documents in a library are actually stored in SharePoint's backend database; this is not a fact easily explained or grasped until you really start to examine the platform. In fact, by default SharePoint does not save content on a server's file system. It inserts all content into a row in a SharePoint content database in SQL Server and retrieves it as requested to be displayed to the user in a Web browser. Whenever SharePoint loads a page for a user, it makes a call to its databases to determine what goes on the page and how it is displayed.

Granted, SharePoint also uses the template files and application code stored on its servers when rendering a page, but it's a good bet that if you have unique content on a SharePoint site, it's being retrieved from a database.

The same goes for the configuration settings and details for your SharePoint environment. That information is not saved in a configuration file or the Windows Registry on your SharePoint servers. Instead, SharePoint has a specific configuration database designed to house the configuration settings for your environment, as well as details on every server, Web application, and site collection in it. Saying that SharePoint is somewhat dependent on its databases to operate is like saying that you somewhat need oxygen to live; if SharePoint's databases go down, it cannot display documents, content, or even the simplest of pages without an error message. That means that if you want your SharePoint environment to be up and running 24 hours a day, 7 days a week, 365 days a year, you had better take a close look at your SQL Server installation and how to keep it up and running, because if it goes down, it makes no difference what SharePoint's status is.

This chapter covers the basics of how to back up and restore your SQL Server databases and then dive into some of the other things that you need to consider when preparing to build a stable and reliable database environment for your SharePoint farm. Be warned, this chapter does not go into great detail about the specifics of how to architect, configure, and administer Microsoft's SQL Server product to survive a catastrophic event. It's a good idea for you to discuss and review the concepts and practices in this chapter with your database architects or administrators (DBAs) so they can be integrated with the DR activities of the parties responsible for your databases. If you are also responsible for the administration of the SQL Server environment used by your SharePoint farm, you may want to consider obtaining an additional resource on SQL Server DR to further supplement the information in this chapter.

SHAREPOINT'S DATABASE OPTIONS

As you have hopefully already encountered by this point in your journey with SharePoint, SQL Server in some shape or form is required to successfully install the platform. Windows SharePoint Services version 3 (WSS v3) and Microsoft Office SharePoint Server 2007 (MOSS) can both run with several variations of SQL Server as their backed database but cannot use other non-SQL server database platforms such as Oracle, MySQL, or even Microsoft's Access in that role. This requirement can be frustrating and limiting if your organization favors a database platform other than SQL Server, but it is not something that can be worked around or hacked to use a different type of database. If you implement SharePoint, you are also going to be installing some incarnation of SQL Server; it is just that simple.

As absolute as that constraint is, you are not without some options in exactly what flavor of SQL Server you choose to use as your SharePoint database provider. The list that follows outlines the five most common SQL Server variants that can host WSS v3 and MOSS's backend databases:

- **SQL Server 2000.** You must have Service Pack (SP) 3 or greater installed for SQL Server 2000 for supported compatibility with the latest versions of SharePoint. Any of the available SQL Server 2000 editions (Developer, Workgroup, Standard, and Enterprise) can be used with SharePoint, although how you are able to use SQL Server 2000 is limited by the constraints imposed by the edition you choose to use. SQL Server 2000 is no longer available for purchase, but you can use it if your organization still has valid licenses for it. Although it isn't the latest and greatest database product available, SQL Server 2000 provides a stable database platform for SharePoint, analysis services, graphical and command-line management tools, and much more.
- **SQL Server 2000 Desktop Engine (also referred to as the MSDE).** The MSDE is a free edition of SQL Server 2000 distributed by Microsoft for use in small applications or environments. Although it offers many of the same features as SQL Server 2000, the MSDE is limited by the fact that it can only run on a single CPU, can only address up to 1 gigabyte (GB) of RAM, and has a maximum storage limit on its databases of 4GB. The MSDE download from Microsoft also lacks a graphical management tool, but there are separate tools available if needed, and it can be managed from the command line.
- **SQL Server 2005.** Microsoft supports SharePoint on SQL Server 2005 SP1, but the SP2 upgrade is strongly recommended. Again, any available edition of SQL Server 2005 is supported with SharePoint, subject to the edition's limitations. SQL Server 2005 offers substantial performance gains when serving as SharePoint's backend database over SQL Server 2000, as well as additional memory management and business intelligence functionality.
- **SQL Server 2005 Embedded Edition (also referred to as the Windows Internal Database).** SQL Server 2005 Embedded Edition is a special version of SQL Server 2005 included with the installation package for WSS v3. If you chose the all-in-one installation option for WSS v3, the setup program installs Embedded Edition by default as the backend database provider for WSS v3. Embedded Edition can only be used if you are using the single server installation option for WSS, but it has no documented limits on database size. The management tools provided by Microsoft for Embedded Edition can only be accessed via the command line.
- **SQL Server 2005 Express.** Much like the MSDE, SQL Server 2005 Express is a free edition of SQL Server 2005 distributed by Microsoft for use in small applications or environments. Express is constrained by three major limitations: the size of its databases (limited to 4 gigabytes of storage), its ability to use only a

single CPU, and its ability to only address up to 1GB of RAM. Express can be managed via an available graphical management tool or the command line. If you choose the all-in-one, or Basic, installation option for MOSS, the setup program installs Express by default as the backend database provider for MOSS. Express can also be used as a database solution for WSS v3 if you manually install it on the server designated as your database host prior to installing WSS.

Since the release of SQL Server 2005, Microsoft has made a large amount of information and data available regarding its benefits over the previous SQL Server 2000 release, both in general terms and specifically with regards to SharePoint. Use of SQL Server 2005 can increase performance in search times, page loads, and much more. In addition to these benefits, SQL Server 2005 is a mature product that has been available for several years and has been updated by Microsoft with a range of hotfixes and updates, as well as two major service packs. In an enterprise environment, SQL Server 2005 should without a doubt be your database platform of choice for your SharePoint environment, although there are factors that may require you to use SQL Server 2000 instead. Please don't misunderstand the point here: the latest versions of SharePoint run without error on SQL Server 2000, and your users aren't going to be denied any of the core functionality of SharePoint, but there are quite a few strong reasons why you should seriously consider upgrading to SQL Server 2005. The material covered in this chapter primarily discusses the use of SQL Server 2005 in a SharePoint environment. Much of the content also applies to SQL Server 2000, but there are cases where it doesn't.

Recently, Microsoft released the next version of its SQL Server product line: SQL Server 2008. Although SharePoint (with SP1 applied) is supported on SQL Server 2008, this has only been the case for a short period, and the SharePoint community is just beginning to understand how the two platforms can work together. SQL Server 2008 offers a wide range of new features and impressive improvements that definitely make it worth consideration for your SharePoint environment, but the fact of the matter is that most enterprises are not quick to embrace a major platform release such as SQL Server 2008 in a production environment without extensive testing of functionality and stability. Due to this fact, SQL Server 2008 is not included in this book.

The visual examples provided in this chapter were generated in a testing environment using the following platforms and components listed next. Depending on how your environment is configured, your experiences may vary slightly.

■ **Operating System.** Microsoft Windows Server 2003 R2 Enterprise Edition Service Pack (SP) 2

- **Microsoft .NET Framework.** Versions 1.1, 2.0 SP1, 3.0 SP1, and 3.5
- **Database.** Microsoft SQL Server 2005 Developer Edition SP2
- **Web server.** Microsoft Internet Information Services (IIS) 6.0
- **SharePoint.** MOSS 2007 Enterprise Edition

HOW TO BACK UP A SQL SERVER 2005 DATABASE

The following steps walk you through the process necessary to back up a database in SQL Server 2005 through the SQL Server Management Studio GUI tool. These steps are designed to give you an idea of what you need to consider when backing up your own databases and how you could go about the process. As covered later in this section, this is not the only way to back up your SharePoint databases through SQL Server, and it may not be the best option for you to choose, but it is a starting point from which you can better understand how SQL Server handles database backups.

NOTE

The user executing the backup must, at a minimum, be granted the db_backup operator *security role within the target database server in order to backup a database.*

1. Open SQL Server Management Studio and connect to the SQL Server database instance hosting the database you want to back up. Figure 8.1 depicts the connection dialog box shown when opening SQL Server Management Studio.

FIGURE 8.1 Enter the connection information for the target SQL Server database instance to connect to it via SQL Server Management Studio.

NOTE

SQL Server Management Studio is the GUI client management tool provided with SQL Server 2005 to administrate database instances and databases running on the platform. It is installed by default on all servers hosting SQL Server 2005 and can be individually installed on client computers to allow for connections to remote SQL Server hosts.

2. Once SQL Server Management Studio connects to the target database instance and opens, the contents of the instance are displayed in the tree view of the Object Explorer pane (which, by default, opens on the left side of the window). Expand the Databases entry in the Object Explorer, and find the name of the database targeted for backup. See Figure 8.2 for an example.

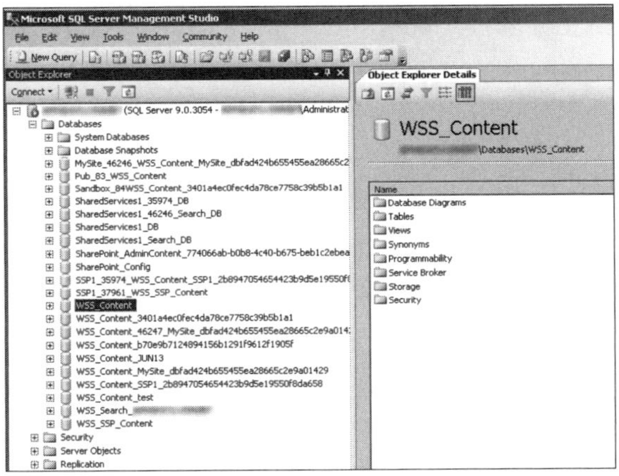

FIGURE 8.2 SQL Server Management Studio with a database selected for backup.

3. Right-click on the name of the database, select the Tasks option when the menu opens, and then click on the Back Up option (as shown in Figure 8.3) to open the Back Up Database dialog box.

4. The Back Up Database dialog box opens, allowing you to customize the backup operation to meet your needs. On the General page (see Figure 8.4), you can configure the target database for the backup and determine the backup type, components to be backed up, the backup set associated with the backup, and the destination for the file(s) created by the backup operation. The Options page (see Figure 8.5) allows you to configure settings for overwriting existing backup files, backup reliability testing, and how transaction logs and tape drives are handled by the backup operation. After you have configured the backup according to your requirements, click the OK button to start the backup operation.

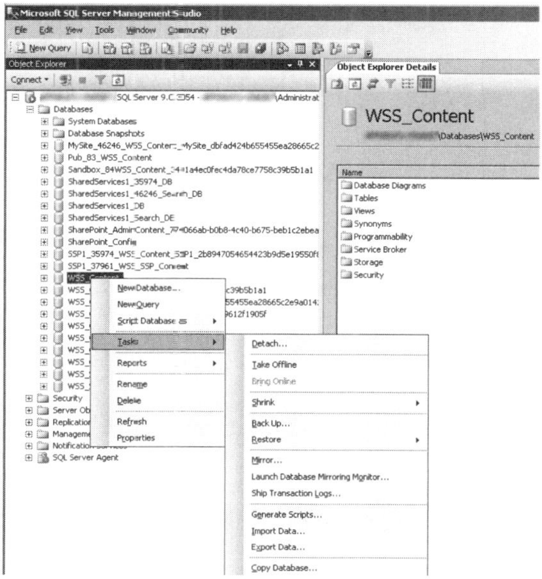

FIGURE 8.3 The Tasks Back Up menu option in SQL Server Management Studio.

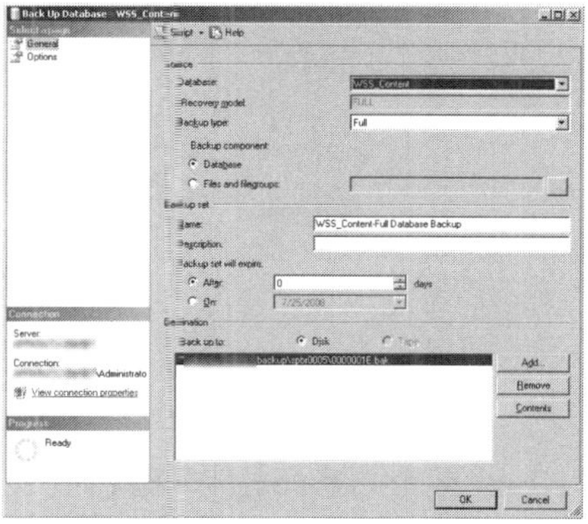

FIGURE 8.4 The General page of the Back Up Database dialog box.

The Script drop-down menu (see Figure 8.6) at the top of the Back Up Database dialog box allows you to create a Transact-SQL (T-SQL) script that can be executed to back up your database without the GUI interface described in these steps. The script created by this process uses the same configuration settings that you selected in the dialog box, allowing you to determine how to back up your database the way you want it done in a user-friendly tool and turn those settings into a format that an experienced database administrator can use to back up your database repeatedly.

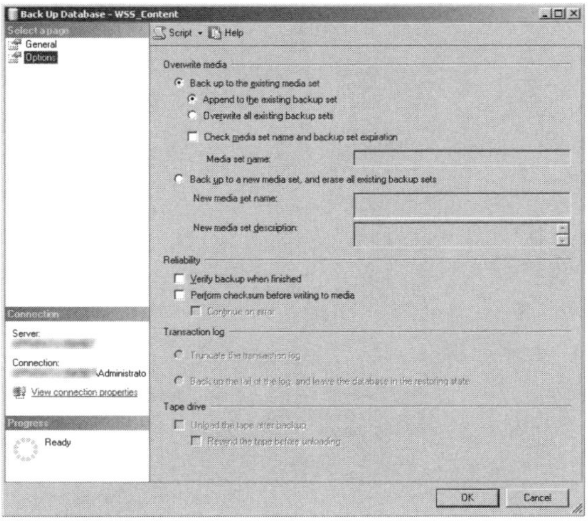

FIGURE 8.5 The Options page of the Back Up Database dialog box.

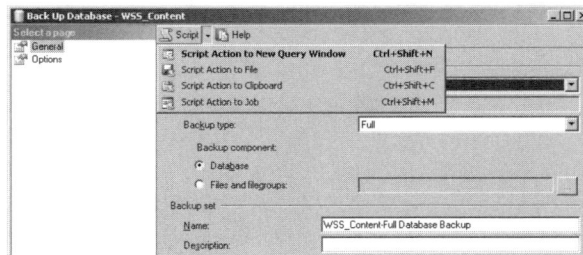

FIGURE 8.6 The Scripts drop-down menu of the Back Up Database dialog box.

5. As the backup runs, the Progress box in the lower-left corner of the dialog box (see Figure 8.7) displays a percentage indicating how much of the backup operation has been completed. There is also a link displayed below the Progress indicator allowing you to cancel the operation.

6. After the backup is finished, a message box stating The backup of database <your database's name> completed successfully is displayed (see Figure 8.8). Click the OK button to return to the SQL Server Management Studio main window.

Before moving on to how to restore the target database from the backup file you just created, take a moment to review the configuration options available for your SQL Server backups. As noted in step 4, there are quite a few options available for configuring your database backup to meet your specific needs. If possible, it's a good idea to discuss these options with your database administrator before implementing them, to confirm the correct course of action to take for your system.

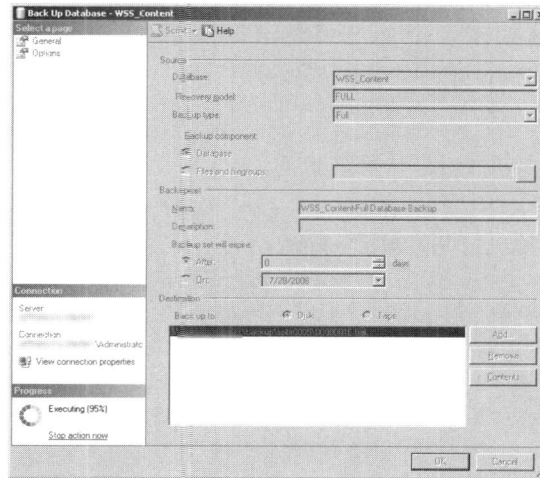

FIGURE 8.7 The Progress indicator shows the status of the backup operation as it runs.

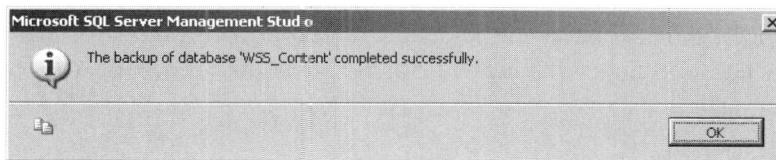

FIGURE 8.8 When the backup operation is completed, SQL Server Management Studio displays the dialog box listed earlier.

DATABASE RECOVERY MODELS

SQL Server offers three types of recovery models for each database it hosts: Full, Simple, and Bulk-Logged. SQL Server uses these recovery models to determine how much data about a database is retained when it creates a backup of the database. The main differentiating factor between the three recovery models is how the transaction logs for a database are managed and backed up depending on the model selected. By default, a database uses the same recovery model as the SQL Server system-level "model" database, which should be Full if the setting is not changed after installation. A database's recovery model can be modified in the SQL Server Management Studio via the database's properties or via a T-SQL command.

Full Recovery Model

As its name implies, the Full recovery model records every transaction made in the database. The Full recovery model is the only model that allows for a database to be restored to a specific time in its history. You should use the Full recovery model if your data is mission critical and you need the ability to restore backups to a specific point in time. For the Full recovery model to be completely effective, you must make regular data and log backups of your database.

Simple Recovery Model

The Simple recovery model retains the least amount of information about the database being backed up. No transaction logs are retained, meaning that the database can only be restored to the most recent full or differential database backup, not to a specific point in the database's history. The Simple recovery model is ideal when your data is not critical (such as a development environment), is not subject to frequent change (not a likelihood for a SharePoint database), or is not a requirement to recover all transactions since the last backup.

Bulk-Logged Recovery Model

The Bulk-Logged recovery model represents a middle ground option between the Full and Simple recovery models. Like the Full recovery model, the Bulk-Logged recovery model tracks transactions made in the database, but it's designed to reduce the logging of bulk operations such as data imports and index management actions to a minimum, providing some of the performance benefits of the Simple recovery model.

When evaluating recovery models, it is important to keep in mind the storage implications of choosing one model over another, in addition to what backup and restore data is being retained. Because the Full recovery model records every transaction executed in a database, it requires a great deal more space to store that data within the database's transaction logs. You may find that you are prevented from using the Full recovery mode due to a lack of available storage, in which case you must keep in mind the impact that has on how you can restore your databases.

CAUTION

DATABASE BACKUP TYPES

SQL Server 2005 offers several types of backups that can be made for the databases hosted in an instance, which in two cases are similar to the types of backups available for SharePoint components that were discussed in Chapters 4, "The Central Administration Site's Backup and Restore Tools," and 5, "STSADM.exe's Backup and Restore Operations." After reading those chapters, you should be acquainted with full and differential backups, but SQL Server also allows administrators to back up a database's Transaction logs, whereby SQL Server records a history of every action and update made to the database and its contents.

NOTE *SQL Server 2005 stores a database in the file system of a host server across a set of files. Each database must have at least one data file and one log file, although they can also have more than one. Filegroups are collections of files that are used to help with data placement and administrative tasks such as disk storage management.*

The list that follows defines each backup type within the context of SQL Server and discusses their common use cases.

- **Full.** A full database backup backs up the entire database, including its full data files and the transaction log components necessary to allow the whole database to be recovered. Because a full backup encompasses everything associated with a database, its output requires the most storage space. Additionally, a full backup of a database is required before any other type of backup can be made for a database.
- **Differential.** A differential backup of a SQL Server database only includes the data in the database that has changed since the last full backup was made of the database. Differential backups can be requested for a database or one of its files or filegroups. The biggest advantage to a differential backup is that it doesn't take up as much space as a full backup and can be completed more quickly. As noted in the previous bullet, you must first perform a full backup of a database for the differential option to be available.

NOTE *To restore a differential backup, you must first restore its associated full backup set or include that full backup set in the requested restore operation.*

- **Partial.** Partial backups, a new option introduced with the release of SQL Server 2005, are designed to provide a smaller and faster backup alternative for large databases with multiple filegroups. Partial backups always include the database's primary filegroup and any other filegroups set as writeable. If a database is set to be read-only, a partial backup of that database only includes the primary filegroup. The partial backup option was originally designed for read-only databases using the Simple recovery model, but it can also be used with read-write databases and the Full and Bulk-Logged recovery models.
- **Transaction log.** A transaction log backup creates a backup copy of the log files detailing all the modifications that have been made to a database over time. Transaction log backups are only available with the Full and Bulk-Logged recovery models; because the Simple recovery model does not offer the ability

to recover to a specific point in time, there is no need to track changes that have been made to a database. Transaction logs are also important to preserve because of the role they can play in other SQL Server HA functionality such as database mirroring and log shipping.

> *SQL Server writes all its actions to a database's transaction logs immediately after the actions are requested, before changes to the database are actually completed. This ensures that the requested changes to the database are recorded and preserved in the transaction logs should a system failure or data corruption occur during execution.*

BACKUP EXPIRATION SETTINGS

In the Backup Set section of the General page in the Back Up Database dialog box, you can configure specific expiration settings for your database backup. Depending on the radio button you select, your backup can expire after a specified number of days or on a specific date. The option button for the After option is selected by default in the Back Up Database dialog box, and the Days field value is set to 0. You can modify this default value by configuring the "media retention" setting within SQL Server's configuration options. If you are backing up your database via a maintenance plan or regularly scheduled backup, specifying a value for this setting prevents SQL Server from overwriting your backup file until the number of days or date threshold has been met.

> *Setting an expiration value for your backup does not prevent it from being overwritten by applications or users outside of SQL Server. The files can still be deleted through the file system or overwritten in their storage location.*

BACKUP DESTINATIONS

Unlike SharePoint, SQL Server has the ability to back up its databases directly to a tape storage location, in addition to a server's hard disk. In the Destination section of the General page in the Back Up Database dialog box, you may enter up to 64 paths by clicking the Add button and navigating to the desired storage location. This allows you to simultaneously create multiple copies of your backup files without manual intervention. You can also remove a backup path from the list by selecting it and clicking the Remove button. Selecting a path and clicking the Contents button displays summary information for the backup and a list of the backup sets associated with it.

The location you select for your backup media set must be associated with or available from the server hosting the SQL Server instance that you are connected to. So if you are running SQL Server Management Studio on your workstation and connecting to a remote database instance, you are only able to save the backup to a file system directory or attached tape drive on the database host server, not on your local workstation. Once the backup is created, you can copy it down to your local workstation if you desire, but you cannot create backup files on your local workstation through the backup operation.

OVERWRITE EXISTING BACKUP MEDIA

The Overwrite Media section of the Options page in the Back Up Database dialog box allows you to determine how SQL Server handles any existing files in the backup storage location that were created by a previous backup operation (see Figure 8.5 for an example of the Options page). You have the option to add your current backup's data to the existing backup media set or create a new backup media set and have SQL Server erase the previous files. If you chose to use the current media set, you still can decide whether to append your data to the existing files in the media set or to overwrite them. You are also given the option to have SQL Server look for potential naming and expiration date conflicts between the media sets by selecting the Check Media Set Name and Backup Set Expiration check box and entering a media set name in the text field. If you chose to create a new media set, you must enter a new name for the media set in the associated text field.

RELIABILITY CHECKS

Another backup and restore feature introduced with SQL Server 2005 is the ability to check a backup media set when the operation is finished to confirm that the output of the operation is viable. In the Reliability section of the Options page in the Back Up Database dialog box, you have the option to require SQL Server to verify the backup files when the operation is completed as well as to request a checksum verification of the backup before it is written to its storage media. The backup file verification confirms that the media set has been written to its storage media without error. The checksum verification confirms that the data within the backup media set is consistent with any checksums associated with the database to ensure that valid data is being written to the storage media and has not become corrupted.

As with almost every decision an IT Professional must make throughout the course of a day, there are potential drawbacks to performing reliability checks that must be taken into account. Specifically, these checks can have a significant negative impact on the database's throughput while they are being performed and utilize a great deal of the host server's available CPU processing power, both of which can cause a serious degradation of the database's performance. It is important to determine how necessary it is to perform reliability checks on your database's backup and when these activities are occurring if requested, so that conflicts with periods of high user activity can be avoided.

SHAREPOINT AND BACKING UP SQL SERVER 2005

The steps at the beginning of the previous section show you one method by which you can create a backup of a database in SQL Server 2005; you can use them to back up pretty much any database hosted in a SQL Server 2005 database instance. There are other, more complex ways to create database backups in SQL Server 2005, such as T-SQL scripting and maintenance plans, but as mentioned earlier, it is best to leave those more involved approaches to the experts. Because you now have a starting point for backing up your SharePoint environment via SQL Server, it is important to start thinking about the issues and restrictions specific to SharePoint that you need to address when moving forward with the process.

TIP

For the best results when backing up your SharePoint databases, you should plan on executing the backup operations during periods of reduced user activity in your SharePoint environment, such as after normal business hours or during planned maintenance periods. This ensures that a minimal number of changes are being made to your databases while the backups are being created; it also prevents your end users from experiencing any performance issues when attempting to access SharePoint. SQL Server backup operations can be resource intensive for their host instances, and you should try to avoid impacting SQL Server's ability to serve its data to SharePoint as much as possible.

If you need to back up a SharePoint database during normal business hours or when there is regular or elevated user activity in the sites within that database, you should consider applying a "No Access" site lock for affected sites in the SharePoint Central Administration site prior to executing the backup. This action can ensure that your users do not encounter degraded performance when accessing the site during a backup operation, as well as prevent them from tying up the database when the operation is also trying to use it. This is not required for a backup operation but can reduce the time a backup takes to complete and the number of support calls that may be made regarding poor performance.

WHAT CAN BE BACKED UP

Above all else, the most important aspect of your SharePoint environment, the reason why it is so important to your business, is what your end users put into it. The contents of your SharePoint sites, whether they are documents, lists, forms, or some other form of knowledge capital, are most likely to be the first and foremost item that your organization needs replaced should disaster strike its SharePoint environment. Happily, SharePoint's content databases can be easily backed up and restored at a later date using SQL Server's tools, using either the steps described above or the other options offered by SQL Server. There is an exception to this rule, which is covered in the next section.

In addition to content databases, the databases associated with your environment's shared services providers (SSPs) can be backed via SQL Server's backup tools. These databases hold data specific to the service being provided by the SSP, such as security information, user profiles, or stored search queries. Although this data is not quite as mission critical as the contents of your SharePoint sites, it is also likely to be unique to your environment and not easily re-created by means other than a restore of the database hosting the information.

SharePoint also creates another type of database whenever an SSP is created in a farm: the search database. This database contains information used by the SharePoint search engine to customize your environment's search experience, such as keywords, best bets, search history, and search metadata, and it can be backed up and restored through SQL Server. By breaking the search database from its SSP database, Microsoft has allowed you as a SharePoint administrator to manage these resources more efficiently according to the needs of your organization. So if search is a much more crucial resource to your business than your portal's user profiles, you have the option to back up your SSP's search database on a much more frequent schedule than its own database.

WHAT CANNOT BE BACKED UP

Much like the out-of-the-box backup tools provided with SharePoint, SQL Server cannot back up your SharePoint environment's IIS Web server settings, custom code or site templates, the SharePoint 12 hive, or any other items located in the file system of your SharePoint servers. Because these items are not stored in a SharePoint database in SQL Server, it stands to reason that they cannot be backed up. Nonetheless, it is important to keep this fact in mind when developing your comprehensive disaster recovery plan so that you are aware of what holes you need to fill with alternative tools or approaches.

Another facet of SharePoint that you need to keep in mind when evaluating components that cannot be covered by a SQL backup is search. Although an SSP's search database does contain a great deal of information about your environment's search application and how it is used, it does not include its most vital aspect: the search index. The search index contains everything that you see displayed as results after entering a query; it is the main repository that SharePoint's search engine builds based on your content sources to provide its search results. Because SharePoint stores its search indices on the file system of your environment's index server(s) and not in the database, they cannot be backed up through SQL Server.

From a technical standpoint, it is most certainly possible for you to back up the SharePoint content database for your environment's Central Administration Web application as well as the configuration database for your environment using SQL Server's backup tools. You can create backups of these databases just like you can any other database, but the important thing to understand is that there are limited situations where you can and should do it. Because changes are constantly being made to a farm's Central Administration and configuration databases and the data in those databases is crucial to the consistency and viability of the farm, it is not possible to back up these databases through SQL Server's tools while your farm is in operation. Restoring a farm from database backups of the Central Admin and configuration databases taken from a running farm is in no way supported by Microsoft. The recommended best practice when using SQL Server to back up and restore your SharePoint environment is to restore your content and SSP databases to a new SharePoint farm built from the ground up, which is described for you later in this chapter.

DATABASE SIZING

As with any SQL Server backup operation, the size of the SharePoint database you are backing up directly affects the amount of time that the operation takes to complete: the larger the database, the longer it takes to finish. As your databases grow larger and larger, you need to continually evaluate the timing and approach you take when backing them up so you can minimize the impact of your backup operations on your SharePoint environment's ability to serve its users. You may find that after a certain point you are no longer able to take full backups quickly enough on a frequent basis and need to consider using differential backups or moving some site collections to new content databases to shorten your backup periods. Monitoring and managing the size and usage of your SharePoint databases should already be a part of your operational SharePoint maintenance plan, but doing so regularly is even more important when you start considering disaster recovery as well.

Microsoft IT does not recommend using SQL Server's backup tools for environments smaller than 100GB (based on the total size of all databases in the environment). In this case, Microsoft's opinion is that SharePoint's built-in tools such as STSADM.exe are more than sufficient to meet the disaster recovery needs of most organizations.

When the environment becomes larger than 100GB, SQL Server's tools make more sense to use, because they are better suited to handle large amounts of data such as that. Of course, every organization's needs and requirements are different, and you may find that this recommendation does not hold true for you. For more information on Microsoft's recommendations, see http://technet.microsoft.com/en-us/library/cc901593.aspx.

It is also important to keep in mind that this discussion does not take into account third-party tools and their ability to back up and restore large SharePoint environments over 100GB. Appendix A, "Third-Party Backup and Restore Tools," is on the book's Web site at http://www.courseptr.com/downloads. It discusses in more detail some of the third-party tools available in the market today to provide you with an introduction to their functionality and potential for use in your SharePoint environment.

There is no hard, fast limit on how large a SharePoint site collection should be. In plenty of cases, SharePoint site collections and their associated SQL Server content databases have grown to be hundreds of terabytes (TB) large and still been viable for end users. But just because this is possible does not make it feasible, especially from a disaster recovery perspective. Microsoft recommends limiting your content databases to 100GB, or 200GB in extreme cases. Discuss this topic with your organization's SQL Server DBA, as they often have their own preferences for general database size limits that need to be observed.

The good news is that SharePoint can be quite flexible when it comes to its content databases, allowing you to associate one to many of them with a single Web application. The main limitation is that you cannot divide a site collection across content databases, which means that if a single site collection grows beyond your size restrictions, it must be split into two collections or have content removed to comply. SharePoint administrators also have several commands available, such as STSADM.exe's `mergecontentdbs` *operation, to help them move site collections from one content database to another.*

For extremely large environments, there is more to consider than just the maximum size of your content databases when planning your SharePoint farm design and database architecture. You should not have more than two SQL Server database instances for content databases associated with your entire SharePoint farm. (Additional instances can be used to host your configuration database, as well as SSP databases.) Each instance should host no more than 10–12TB of data in those content databases. Although these numbers may appear to be mind-bogglingly large, they are certainly possible. As storage becomes cheaper and organizations move more and more documentation to electronic formats, platforms such as SharePoint become ever more important thanks to their ability to make those documents discoverable, shareable, and maintainable.

Another less obvious item to consider is how utilized the site collections are within your SharePoint databases. If numerous users access the site, collaborate on documents, or update content at the same time, it can have a direct impact on your backup and restore planning. These activities lead to SharePoint reading and writing to its databases with increased frequency, which in turn means SQL Server is writing large amounts of data to the transaction logs associated with these databases. Because a full backup of a SQL Server database includes the database's active transaction logs, heavy usage of your sites adds to the time it takes to back up (and restore) the databases associated with them. If you find that this is having a negative impact on your ability to preserve your SharePoint farm's databases, you may need to reevaluate your farm and site hierarchies to better distribute use traffic across databases.

NOTE

The previous database sizing issues have a similar impact on SQL Server restore operations. One reason why it is important to test both your backup and restore strategies is so that you have an accurate estimate of how long each activity should take in expected conditions. If your restore operations are taking hours to execute due to the size of your databases and your system needs to be available as soon as possible, you are better served by finding that out through testing rather than the first time you do a live execute of your disaster recovery plan and an outage is costing you real money every second.

HOW TO RESTORE A SQL SERVER 2005 DATABASE BACKUP

As with the previous walkthrough of how to back up a database in SQL Server 2005, the following steps give you a general idea of what is involved in restoring a backup of an existing database through the SQL Server Management Studio. This is not the only way you can restore a database in SQL Server and is not necessarily going to be the best approach for you to take with your SharePoint environment and its specific needs. These steps are intended to get you thinking about the needs and requirements for your environment and what information you need to have on hand before you execute a SharePoint database restore in it through SQL Server.

CAUTION

If the database being restored is not currently hosted in the target database instance, the user must have `CREATE  DATABASE` *permissions in the instance to restore the database. If the database already exists in the target database instance, the user must be assigned the* `sysadmin` *and* `dbcreator` *server roles in the instance or be the owner (also known as the "dbo" role) of the database. If a password has been assigned to the backup media set being used in the restore operation, that value must be provided for SQL Server to execute the restore.*

1. Open SQL Server Management Studio and connect to the SQL Server database instance to which you want to restore the database backup.

2. When SQL Server Management Studio connects to the target database instance and opens, the contents of the instance are displayed in the tree view of the Object Explorer pane (which by default opens on the left side of the window). Expand the Databases entry in the Object Explorer and find the name of the database targeted to be overwritten with a previously created backup.

3. Right-click on the name of the database, select the Tasks option when the menu opens, select the Restore option, and then click on the Database option to open the Restore Database dialog box. See Figure 8.9 for an example.

This action automatically takes the target database offline and prevents other applications or processes from accessing it. Whenever possible, attempt to undertake a restore operation during a period of advertised or regular downtime for your SharePoint environment.

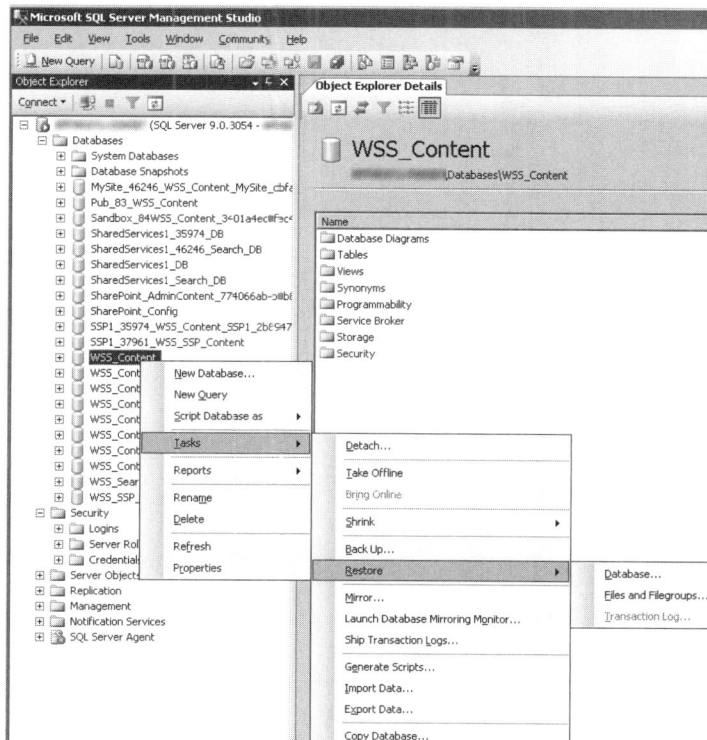

FIGURE 8.9 Select the Restore, Databases option from the Task menu.

4. The Restore Database dialog box opens, allowing you to customize the restore operation to meet your needs. On the General page (see Figure 8.10), you can configure the database to be restored, determine the source of the backup set used in the restore operation, and select the specific backup set used to restore the database. The Options page (see Figure 8.11) allows you to configure settings for overwriting the existing database; preserve replication settings; prompt before each restore activity; restrict access to the database once it is restored; configure where the database's files are restored on the server's file system; and determine the type of recovery state the database is placed in when the restore operation is completed. After you have configured the restore according to your requirements, click the OK button to start the restore operation.

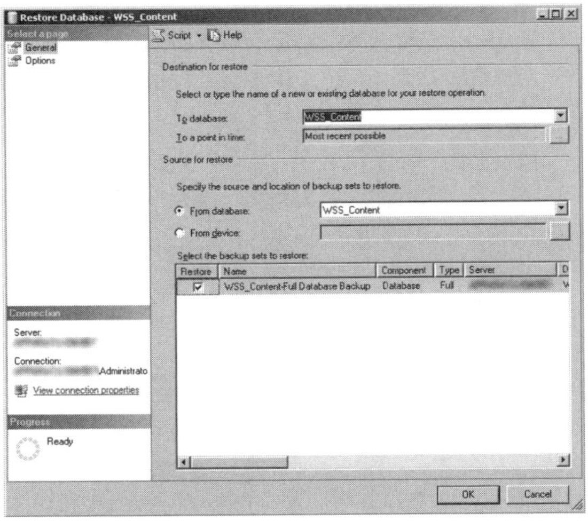

FIGURE 8.10 The General page of the Restore Database dialog box.

As with the Back Up Database dialog box, the Script drop-down menu at the top of the Restore Database dialog box allows you to create a T-SQL script that can be executed to restore your database without the GUI interface described in these steps.

5. As the restore operation executes, the Progress box in the lower left corner of the dialog box displays a percentage indicating how much of it has been completed. There is also a link displayed below the progress indicator allowing you to cancel the operation.

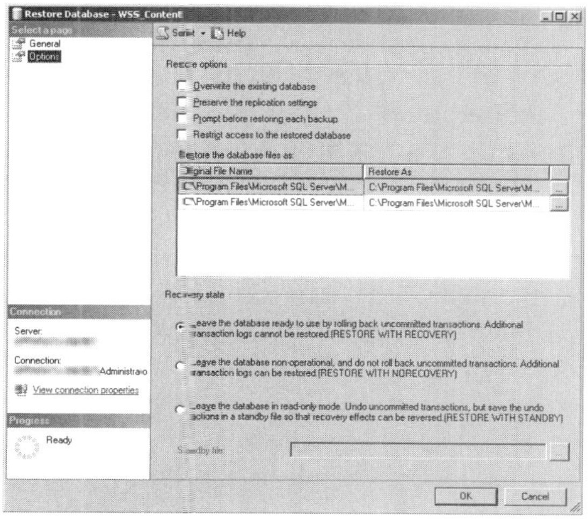

FIGURE 8.11 The Options page of the Restore Database dialog box.

6. Once the restore is finished, a message box stating `The restore of database <your database's name> completed successfully` is displayed (see Figure 8.12). Click the OK button to return to the SQL Server Management Studio main window.

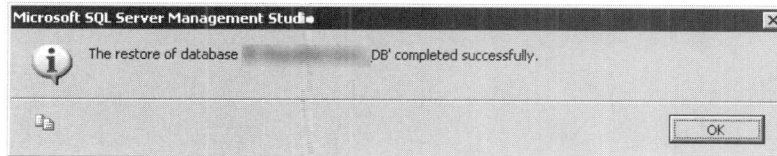

FIGURE 8.12 When the restore operation is completed, SQL Server Management Studio displays the dialog box shown above.

Similar to database backups through SQL Server Management Studio, several configuration options are available in the Restore Database dialog. You can use these options to set what backup set is used for the restore, where the backup is restored to, what state the database is placed in when the restore is finished, and much more. Again, discussing these options with your database administrator is highly recommended so that you can determine the best configuration to use with your environment.

RESTORE DESTINATION OPTIONS

The first section of the Restore Database window's General tab, titled Destination for Restore, not only allows you to select where the backup is restored within the target database instance, but it allows you to choose a specific point in time where you want the database restored. In the To Database field, you can select a database from the drop-down menu to be overwritten by the backup, or you can type the name of an existing or new database as the restore target. By default, the database displayed in the field is the database you right-clicked on to open the Restore Database window. The drop-down menu is populated with all the databases hosted by the database instance.

The next field, To a Point in Time, is grayed out (disabled) by default and contains the text `Most recent possible`, indicating that the database will be restored to its condition when the backup set was created. To change this setting, click the ellipses (...) button to the right of the disabled text field, which opens the Point in Time Restore dialog box (see Figure 8.13).

The Point in Time Restore option is not available for databases configured to the Simple recovery model.

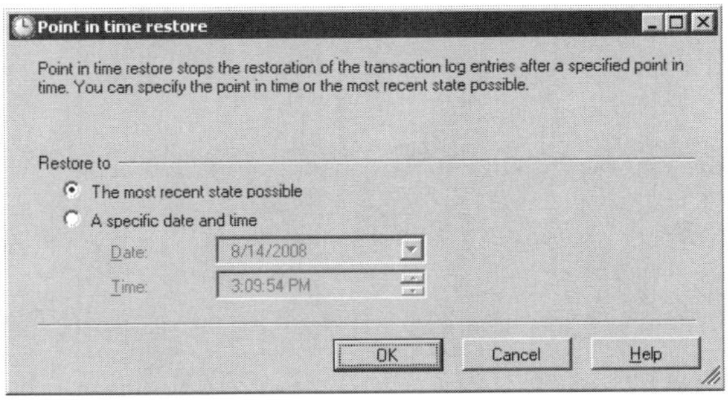

FIGURE 8.13 The Point in Time Restore dialog box.

In this window, the option The Most Recent State Possible is initially selected, and the Date and Time fields are disabled. To select a specific point in time for the database to be restored to, select the A Specific Date and Time option button, which enables the Date and Time fields. Clicking the Date drop-down menu displays a calendar control (see Figure 8.14) where you can navigate to the specific date desired. You can update the Time field by either typing the desired value for each digit of the time or using the Up and Down arrows to the right of the text field to select the correct numerical value.

Selecting a date more recent than the date the target backup set was created or in the future results in the database being restored to the most recent possible state.

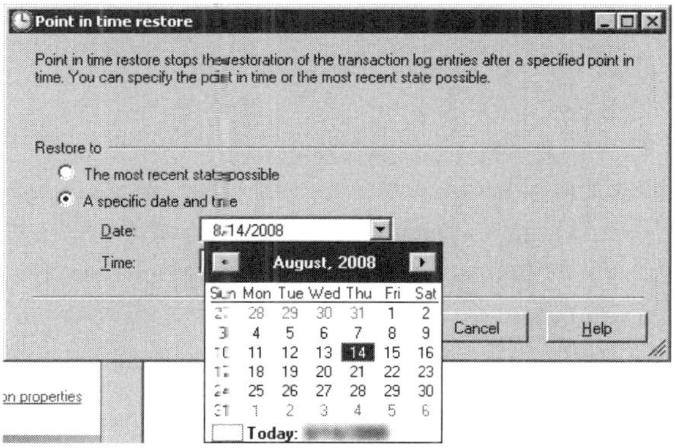

NOTE

FIGURE 8.14 The Date drop-down menu of the Point in Time Restore dialog box.

RESTORE SOURCE OPTIONS

In the Source to Restore section, you can specify which backup set is used to restore your database. By default, the From Database option button is selected, and the drop-down menu next to it is populated with the name of the database you right-clicked on to open the Restore Database window. This menu is populated with the databases hosted in the instance that have previously had backup sets created for them; if a database has not been backed up, it does not appear in this list. If the target database has not been backed up with SQL Server before, this field is blank. Selecting a different database in the From Database drop-down menu results in the Select the Backup Set to Restore list box being updated to show the backup sets associated with the selected database. If the Select the Backup Set to Restore list box displays more than one backup set, you can select the desired backup set by clicking its check box.

Selecting the From Device option button disables the From Database drop-down menu and the Select the Backup Set to Restore list box. To select a device as the source of the backup, click the ellipses (...) button to the right of the disabled From Device text field. This opens the Specify Backup dialog box, where you can select a file, tape, or device to be used as a backup source for the restore operation. You select your type of device from the Backup Media drop-down menu (File, Tape, or Backup Device, depending on what types of devices are attached to your system) and then click the Add button to add an instance of the selected device type. The Locate Backup File dialog box opens, allowing you to select the desired backup from a list. After selecting a backup, click the OK button to close the window, to return to the Specify Backup window with your selected backup displayed in the Backup Location field. You can remove that backup by clicking the Remove Button or view the items in the backup by clicking the Contents button. Clicking the OK button saves your configuration and returns you to the Restore Backup window, where your selected backup is now shown in the Select the Backup Set to Restore list box.

> *Keep in mind that the backup files to be used in the restore operation must be stored in a location that can be accessed from the server hosting the target database instance. If the files are stored on an unconnected device, such as your local workstation, you must either copy the files to the server or map a connection on the host server to your local workstation.*

RESTORE OPTIONS

The first section on the Options tab of the Restore Backup window, Restore Options, contains four check boxes that can be selected to configure different aspects of the requested restore operation. By default, all four check boxes are unchecked.

- **Overwrite the Existing Database.** When you select this option, the restore operation completely overwrites, using the data from the selected backup set, any existing database and its associated files if its name matches the database listed in the To Database field on the General tab.
- **Preserve the Replication Settings.** This option allows you to keep the original replication settings of the database in the backup set when restoring it to a server different from the server the database was backed up on. If the new server hosting the database has different replication settings than the original host, selecting this option prevents the server from overwriting the restored database with its local settings. It can be used only when the Leave the Database Ready for Use by Rolling Back the Uncommitted Transactions option is selected in the Recovery State section.

> *Microsoft does not support the use of SQL Server 2005's replication functionality with SharePoint. Therefore, this setting may seem irrelevant, but it can still be handy. If replication is configured in the new server hosting the restored database, selecting this option ensures that replication is not enabled for the restored database.*

- **Prompt before Restoring Each Backup.** This option prompts the user for confirmation prior to restoring each backup set requested by the restore operation, which can be helpful when you need to pause the restore operation for activities such as swapping backup tapes.
- **Restrict Access to the Restored Database.** Selecting this option limits access to the database when the restore operation has completed to the following SQL Server security roles: db_owner, dbcreator, or sysadmin.

Below the four check boxes is the Restore the Database Files As list box. This list box displays each of the database files associated with the database in the backup set, showing the full path and name of the file as it existed when the backup was created and the full path and name that it has when the restore operation is completed. You can modify the storage location and name of any file in the list box by clicking the ellipses (...) button to the right of the Restore As column for the file you want to change. This action opens a window titled Locate Database Files, which is similar in appearance to Figure 8.16's Locate Backup File window. Navigate to the desired location in the window's tree directory and click the OK button to return to the Restore Database window.

RECOVERY STATE

The Recovery State section of the Options tab contains three radio button options that are used to determine what condition the database is in once the restore operation is completed.

- **Leave the Database Ready for Use by Rolling Back the Uncommitted Transactions.** This option is selected by default and allows for the restored database to be immediately used once the restore operation has completed. This option is also known as Restore with Recovery.
- **Leave the Database Non-Operational and Do Not Roll Back Uncommitted Transactions.** This option keeps the database in a restoring state after the requested restore operation has completed, which is useful when restoring a database with multiple transaction logs or when restoring a sequence of backups to a database (such as a full backup followed by a differential backup). The database cannot be used until a subsequent restore operation using the first option in this list has been completed. This option is also known as Restore with No Recovery.
- **Leave the Database in Read-Only Mode.** This option allows a database to remain in a restoring state but makes read-only access to the database available when the requested restore operation is completed. This option creates a standby file on the local file system of the server hosting the database instance to allow for the actions of the restore operation to be undone; the option is also known as Restore with Standby.

Below the three option buttons is the Standby File text field, which is only enabled if the Leave the Database in Read-Only Mode option button is selected. To change the location of the standby file, modify the text in the text field or click the ellipses (...) button to the right of the Standby File text field, which opens a window titled Locate Rollback Undo File. Navigate to the desired location for the standby file in the window's tree directory, and click the OK button to return to the Restore Database window.

NOTE

If there is not enough storage space for the standby file (which is simply a copy of the existing database), in the file system at the location specified, the restore operation will fail. If the filegroup for the target database is 20GB, the standby file will require an additional 20GB of available space.

SHAREPOINT AND RESTORING A SQL SERVER 2005 BACKUP

Unfortunately, restoring a SharePoint database is not as simple as executing the previous steps to restore your environment. Because SharePoint is constantly accessing, reading from, and updating its databases, you must take certain precautions to avoid inconsistent or corrupted data. The following sections detail the steps that must be taken, depending on the restore situation, as well as some other considerations that you should take into account when planning your restore strategy for your SharePoint databases.

RESTORING A SQL BACKUP TO AN EXISTING SHAREPOINT ENVIRONMENT

Although not many additional steps are required to restore a SharePoint database in SQL Server for an existing and operational SharePoint farm, the following steps are important to ensure the integrity and stability of the data in your system:

1. If the WSS Timer service on the SharePoint server hosting your farm's Central Administration site is running, stop it via the Services management console snap-in on the server, and wait for approximately five minutes to allow any running jobs to complete before proceeding with the database restore. Don't restart the timer service until the database has been fully restored.
2. Open SQL Server Management Studio and the Restore Database window for the target SharePoint database to be restored in SQL Server.
3. When the Restore Database window opens, confirm or modify the destination and source data, and then select the Options tab to open it.

4. Unless you have specific requirements or needs for your SharePoint environment, the Overwrite the Existing Database check box is the only Restore option that you should select.

5. In the Recovery State section, select the Restore with Recovery radio button if you are including all the database's transaction logs in the current restore operation. If you need to restore additional transaction logs after this operation, select the Restore with No Recovery option button. You should not use the Restore with Standby option when restoring a SharePoint database.

6. Click the OK button to initiate the restore operation for this database.

7. If there are additional databases in your SharePoint environment that need to be restored, repeat steps 2 through 6 as needed.

8. Finally, restart the WSS Timer service on your farm's Central Administration site host server.

RESTORING A SQL BACKUP TO A NEW SHAREPOINT ENVIRONMENT

One of the great things about SharePoint's reliance on its databases is that it makes the data in your SharePoint farm much more manageable and portable. For instance, using the later steps, you can move or copy a content database full of sites from one SharePoint farm to another without losing content or configurations within a site. This is especially useful if you want to move a site collection from a quality assurance (QA) environment to a production environment, or you want to create a copy of a given site collection in a new farm without having to re-create all its contents from scratch.

There are some prerequisites to consider when planning to restore a backup of a SharePoint content database via SQL Server to a new environment:

■ Prepare the database for migration. If your environment is using MOSS (WSS does not offer the profile and membership functionality affected by this situation) and the database is targeted to be restored to another farm, you must run STSADM.exe's preparetomove operation against the database prior to backing it up. If the operation is not used before the backup is created, the database's connection to its SSP is broken, causing SharePoint profile and membership synchronizations to error out and fail once the database is restored to a completely new farm. When the backup is complete, you can restore the original database to service via the preparetomove operation's undo switch. For more information on the preparetomove operation, see http://technet.microsoft.com/en-us/library/cc262122.aspx. If you didn't run the preparetomove operation against the database prior to backing it up, and you didn't prep it in this fashion, there will be some clean-up work after the fact—usually only after you notice the various synchronization errors being thrown in the event log. If an admin fails to prepare the database prior to backing it up or detaching it, there's a good chance that sync errors will begin to show up in the event log. You can remedy these after the fact through a separate switch combination of STSADM.exe's `preparetomove` and `sync` operations. For more information on the sync operation, see http://technet.microsoft.com/en-us/library/cc263196.aspx.

- **Do not attempt to restore the database to the same SharePoint environment that it originated from without overwriting the original.** It is not possible to use this process to clone a database back into its original SharePoint farm. This causes data integrity issues and GUID conflicts throughout your farm.
- **The new SharePoint farm must already be built.** The restore steps in this section assume that a new SharePoint farm has already been installed and configured and is ready to receive the restored content database.
- **Patch levels and versions must be equivalent.** The new SharePoint farm must be running the same version and patch level of SharePoint as the farm that the database backup was created in.
- **All installed custom code and files in the original farm must be present in the new farm.** The new SharePoint farm must have all the same solutions, features, site definitions, workflows, and any other custom code or files installed and configured as the original farm.
- **Only restore content databases.** This process cannot be used to restore a configuration database to a new farm; only content databases for one or more site collections can be restored into a new farm using this process.

To restore a SQL Server database backup of a SharePoint content database to a new farm, execute the following steps:

1. Restore the database in the SQL Server database instance for the new farm. If the database does not previously exist in the instance, you can create an empty database in the instance and overwrite it with the backup or type the name of the new content database into the To Database field in the Restore Database window. Don't overwrite existing content databases for the new farm.

2. After you've restored the database, ensure that the target farm's database access service account, SSP service account, and (IIS) application pool service account for the Web application hosting the content database's sites have been placed in the `db_owner` role for the restored database. You can check this via the User Mapping option of each login in SQL Management Studio by right-clicking on the account and selecting the Security, Logins

option from the menu. If these accounts have not been granted the db_owner role, you must do so to be able to add the restored account to the farm.

3. If there is not already a Web application in your farm that you want to associate the site collection(s) in the restored database with, create it. Open the new farm's Central Administration site in a browser and click the Application Management tab.

4. When the Application Management page opens, click the Create or Extend Web Application link in the SharePoint Web Application Management section.

5. In the Create or Extend Web Application page (see Figure 8.15), click the Create a New Web Application link.

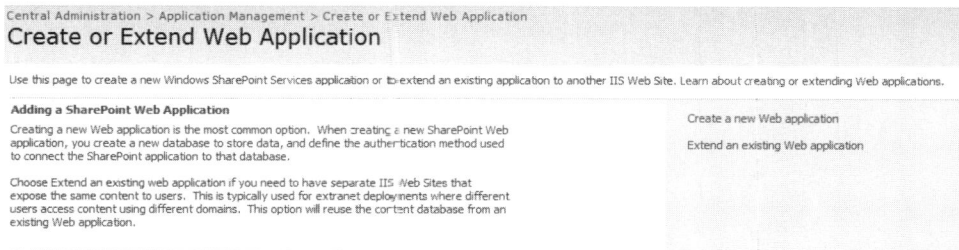

Central Administration > Application Management > Create or Extend Web Application

Create or Extend Web Application

Use this page to create a new Windows SharePoint Services application or to extend an existing application to another IIS Web Site. Learn about creating or extending Web applications.

Adding a SharePoint Web Application

Creating a new Web application is the most common option. When creating a new SharePoint Web application, you create a new database to store data, and define the authentication method used to connect the SharePoint application to that database.

Choose Extend an existing web application if you need to have separate IIS Web Sites that expose the same content to users. This is typically used for extranet deployments where different users access content using different domains. This option will reuse the content database from an existing Web application.

Create a new Web application

Extend an existing Web application

FIGURE 8.15 The SharePoint Central Administration site's Create or Extend Web Application page.

6. When the Create New Web Application page opens (see Figure 8.16), select the desired configuration settings for the new Web application and click the OK button to create it.

7. When the new target Web application has been created to receive the restored content database, its initial content database can be deleted because the site content you are interested in resides in the restored content database. Return to the Application Management page in the Central Administration site and click the Content Databases link in the SharePoint Web Application Management section.

8. When the Manage Content Databases page opens (see Figure 8.17), if any content databases exist for the Web application, click the linked name of the content database for the Web application to open its Settings page. If there are no content databases currently for the Web application, proceed to step 9.

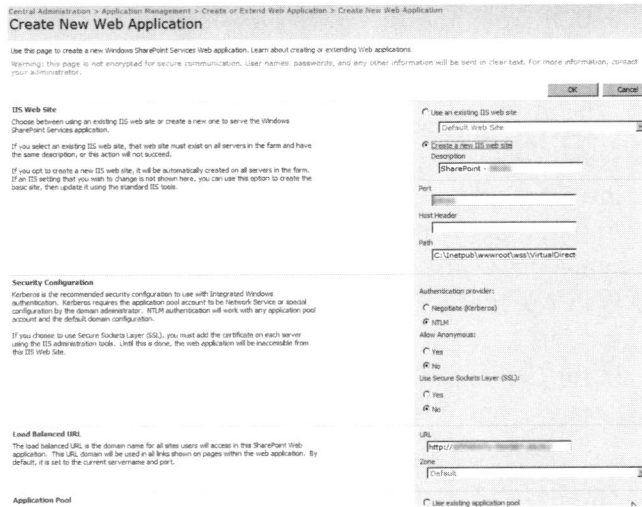

FIGURE 8.16 The SharePoint Central Administration site's Create New Web Application page.

Take care to confirm that the correct Web application is listed in the drop-down menu in the upper-right corner of the page. If it is not, click the arrow for the drop-down menu and select the Change Web Application option. When the dialog box opens, navigate to the correct Web application and select it.

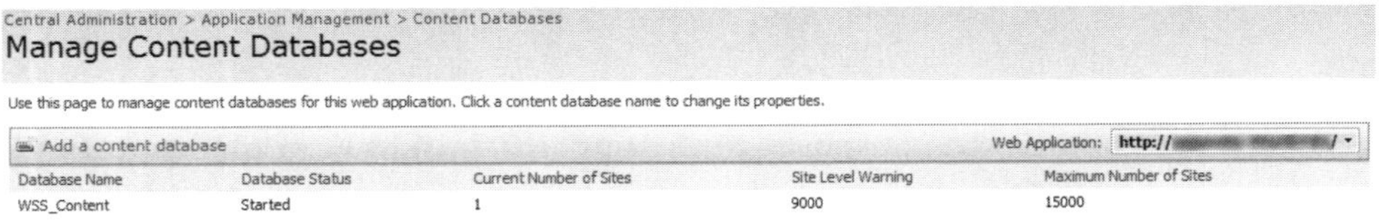

CAUTION

FIGURE 8.17 The Manage Content Databases page.

9. When the Manage Content Database Settings page opens (see Figure 8.18), check the Remove Content Database check box, which causes a confirmation window to be displayed (see Figure 8.19) if the content database contains existing site collections. If the confirmation window is displayed, determine whether the content database can be deleted. If it can, click the OK button in the confirmation window and click the OK button to remove the content database.

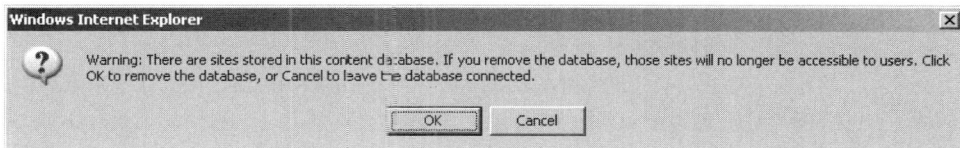

FIGURE 8.18 The Manage Content Database Settings page.

FIGURE 8.19 The confirmation window displayed when a user clicks the Remove Content Database check box warning them of the implications of the action.

10. After all content databases have been removed from the Web application, return to the Manage Content Databases page for the target Web application and click the Add Content Database button in the upper-left corner of the page.

11. In the Add Content Database page (see Figure 8.20), enter the name of the database instance hosting the restored content database in the Database Server field and the name of the restored content database in the Database Name field. Confirm the other settings for the content database and click the OK button to add the database.

If you are more comfortable using the command line STSADM.exe application, you can replace steps 10 and 11 with the following command to add the restored content database to your new farm:

```
stsadm.exe -o addcontentdb -url <new web application's URL> -
databasename <name of the restored content database> -databaseserver
<name of database instance hosting the restored database>
```

FIGURE 8.20 Add Content Database page.

12. After the content database has been added to the Web application, review the contents of the database through SharePoint to confirm that the addition of the database was successful. View the Web application's new site collection(s) through the Central Administration site to confirm that they are properly listed, and open them directly through a browser to verify that all their contents and settings were correctly restored into the new environment.

A reset of the IIS Web servers hosting your new farm may be required for these changes to be visible to end users.

TIP

CONCLUSION

Like SharePoint, Microsoft provides several options for backing up and restoring your SQL Server databases to meet the specific needs of your organization. The procedures discussed in this chapter merely scratch the surface of what is possible with SQL Server's backup and restore options, and the advent of a new version of

SQL Server brings with it even more opportunities for ensuring the security and long-term viability of your business-critical data. And none of this even takes into account the third-party tools available to enhance, extend, or replace SQL Server's backup and restore tools. (For an introduction to some of these tools, see Appendix A on the book's Web site at http://www.courseptr.com/downloads.) With the information in this chapter, you should be able to start compiling a backup and restore strategy for your databases, selecting the configuration and procedures that best suit the needs of your organization and infrastructure.

Keep in mind that although simply backing up your SharePoint databases is a good start on preparing your SharePoint farm for the possibility of a catastrophic event, that is all it is: a start. How SharePoint relies on and uses its databases is far from normal and, as you have seen, this means that special considerations and plans must be made when backing up and restoring those databases. Again, like SharePoint, using SQL Server's tools to back up and restore your SharePoint database is unlikely to be a complete disaster recovery solution for your organization. Making that assumption leaves you vulnerable and most likely unable to quickly recover your system in the event of a disaster, if at all. Restoring a backup can be a time-intensive process and can cost your enterprise countless man-hours of lost productivity as your users wait for SharePoint to be brought back online.

Thankfully, backup and restore is not the only method available with SQL Server for restoring and, just as importantly, maintaining service to your farm's databases. Chapter 9, "SQL Server 2005 High Availability," introduces you to the concept of high availability (HA) and some of the paths you can take to help your SQL Server environment withstand an outage or disaster. These practices are invaluable to your business, because they are intended to minimize the duration of an outage as much as possible so your SharePoint farm can remain available to your end users.

SQL Server backup and restore can be a powerful asset in your SharePoint disaster recovery toolkit, but as has been shown with so many of the other tools you have at your disposal, it does not necessarily stand well on its own for SharePoint. As you continue through this guide, you should start to think about how you want to put together all this information to construct your own SharePoint disaster recovery solution. You are not quite done learning the various tools and platforms you need to consider, but you are getting there.

After finishing this chapter, you should be able to confidently answer the following questions about SQL Server's backup and restore tools. You can find the answers to these questions in Appendix B, "Chapter Review Q&A," on the book's Web site at http://www.courseptr.com/downloads.

1. What is the difference between a database backed up using the Full recovery model and one backed up with the Simple recovery model?
2. What types of storage media can be used to store SQL Server database backups?

3. What SharePoint databases should not be backed up with SQL Server? Why?

4. What are the performance implications for your SharePoint farm when backing up and restoring large SharePoint databases?

5. What state can a database be placed in when it is stored to a SQL Server database instance?

6. What is the correct process for restoring a database to an existing SharePoint farm?

9

SQL Server 2005 High Availability

In This Chapter

- Log Shipping
- Database Mirroring
- Database Clustering

igh availability (HA) is not a term that this book has discussed in great detail yet, but it's an integral part of a good disaster recovery system and specifically relevant to SQL Server. HA refers to the ability of a technology platform, system, or environment to remain online and available in the face of outages or failures by one or more of its constituent subsystems.

It is pretty much physically impossible and all too often financially unrealistic for a system such as your SharePoint environment to be 100 percent available all day, 365 days a year. Designing and engineering for HA means that the system is built to be fully available for a given percentage of time, such as 95 percent, 99 percent, or 99.999 percent (also referred to as having *five nines* of uptime) and withstand unplanned situations such as a hard drive failure, a network outage, or a disaster such as the data center being washed away in a flood.

Because SharePoint is so dependent on the availability of its databases to serve content to its users, your SQL Server database instance(s) should be the first area of your farm that you review when planning for HA. Microsoft has wisely recognized the importance of making SQL Server HA and provides several options and tools to assist in that endeavor. In addition, several third-party tools are available that you can use to support your HA configuration and execution.

You must also review several other components of your SharePoint environment when considering HA, such as your frontend SharePoint servers, search indices, server hard drives, network connections, and even the data centers that host your servers. These items are covered in more detail in Chapter 10, "Windows Server 2003 Backup and Restore" and Chapter 11, "Windows Server 2003 High Availability."

The first step you must take in planning and designing your SQL Server HA architecture is to evaluate your environment's HA requirements and available budget. SQL Server HA can have a high cost associated with it, which you must consider when determining exactly how to implement it and establish what amount of uptime you are expected to provide for your SharePoint environment.

Three built-in options are available for SQL Server HA (depending on the type of SQL Server license in use): log shipping, database mirroring, and clustering. Each of these options can be a viable solution for your SharePoint environment, but determining which one best fits the needs and limitations of your organization and environment is an important activity that you need to be sure to include early in your SharePoint design process. After all, your decision has lasting implications and is not easily changed without affecting SharePoint. This is yet another item for discussion that you should cover with your database administrator. Your administrator's insights and expertise are invaluable for not only selecting an HA solution but also implementing it and supporting it over time.

Each of these HA solutions may require the purchase of additional Windows Server, SharePoint, and SQL Server licenses and hardware to implement, adding definitive costs to your environment, regardless of what licenses or hardware approach you decide to take. Microsoft states that passive SQL Server installations configured for HA do not require additional licenses, as long as they do not process queries. You should contact your Microsoft licensing or sales resources for specific information about how to properly license your HA resources. You may also be able to leverage virtualization products from Microsoft or VMware to reduce hardware costs by creating multiple virtual servers on a single physical host, but you must carefully evaluate the performance and support implications of this option. Furthermore, these solutions can involve the use of separate data centers to host the servers used to make SQL Server highly available, allowing your SharePoint databases to keep serving content because they can fail over to servers in a completely different geographic location. Although this can be valuable, it also adds another factor to infrastructure costs and can introduce the potential for latency as data is transferred between the data centers.

The visual examples provided in this chapter were generated in a testing environment using the following platforms and components. Depending on how your environment is configured, your experiences may vary slightly.

- **Operating System.** Microsoft Windows Server 2003 R2 Enterprise Edition Service Pack (SP) 2
- **Microsoft .NET Framework.** Versions 1.1, 2.0 SP1, 3.0 SP1, and 3.5
- **Database.** Microsoft SQL Server 2005 Developer Edition SP2
- **Web server.** Microsoft Internet Information Services (IIS) 6.0
- **SharePoint.** MOSS 2007 Enterprise Edition

LOG SHIPPING

Although it was possible but not supported in SQL Server 2000 (except in the Enterprise Edition of the platform), log shipping has been added as a key component of SQL Server 2005. Log shipping takes advantage of the platform's backup functionality that was covered in Chapter 8, "SQL Server 2005 Backup and Restore" and uses it to create a second iteration of the target (or primary) database in a separate database instance. It creates a secondary copy of the primary database by taking a transaction log backup from the primary database and copying it to a secondary database. The transaction log copy process needs to occur on a regular basis to keep the secondary database synchronized with its primary source in case a disaster occurs and it is needed. One advantage of log shipping is that once the backup of the transaction log is created in the primary database instance, the remainder of the process occurs in the secondary database instance, allowing the primary instance to return to normal activities.

THE SERVER COMPONENTS OF LOG SHIPPING

Log shipping requires at least two servers—a primary and a secondary—and allows the use of an optional third server to monitor the log shipping operation.

- **Primary.** This is the database you want to back up to a SQL Server instance on a separate server. All configuration of the log shipping process must occur on this server. You must back up the primary database using the Full or Bulk-logged recovery models for the backups to be used with log shipping; log shipping is not available when the target database uses the Simple recovery model. There can be only one primary server for a target database, but its logs can be shipped to multiple secondary servers for redundancy.

- **Secondary.** This is the database that functions as a separate backup copy of your primary database. You must initially restore the secondary database from a full backup of the primary database using either the Restore with No Recovery or Restore with Standby options before you can update it with transaction logs via log shipping. A single secondary server can host multiple databases backed up via log shipping.
- **Monitor.** This server lives up to its name by tracking all the activities of the log shipping process, such as transaction log backup dates, secondary server transaction log copy and restore dates, and information on any failures or errors that may occur. A monitor server is not required to use log shipping, but if you do decide to use it, it should be hosted somewhere other than your primary or secondary server. A single monitor server can track multiple log shipping configurations.

LOG SHIPPING JOBS

SQL Server executes four distinct SQL Server Agent jobs as part of the log shipping process:

- **Backup.** The SQL Server Agent executes this job on the primary server to back up the target database, log the action to the local server (as well as the monitor server), and clean up any old backup files or logs created by previous iterations of the job. This job kicks off the log shipping process; when it is finished, SQL Server initiates a Copy job on the secondary server and returns the target database to normal processing. By default, Backup is configured to run every two minutes, but you can configure it to run more or less frequently based on your requirements.
- **Copy.** The SQL Server Agent executes this job on the secondary server to copy the transaction log backup from the primary server to the secondary server. Its actions are logged on the secondary server and reported to the monitor server, and then it deletes any old backup files or logs.

Be careful to monitor the size of any database and its transaction logs if you are using log shipping. As these files grow, so does the amount of data that you need to send over the network from your primary server to the secondary server. The larger the transaction log, the longer it takes for it to be copied from the primary to the secondary and the more bandwidth that is being tied up over your network.

- **Restore.** The SQL Server Agent executes this job to restore the copied transaction log to the secondary database and bring it in line with the content of the primary target database. Its actions are logged on the secondary server and reported to the monitor server; then it deletes any old files or logs associated with the job.

- **Alert.** If a monitor server is configured for the log shipping process, this job is created on the monitor server and shared by all servers using the monitor server. The SQL Server Agent executes this job to raise alerts when any job within the log shipping process fails to run successfully to completion. Additional configuration must be completed for SQL Server to deliver these alerts to an operator. If a monitor is not configured, alert jobs must individually be configured on the primary and secondary servers to report the result of the jobs run on each server.

HOW TO CONFIGURE LOG SHIPPING

Your environment must meet the following requirements to enable log shipping for one or more of your SQL Server databases:

- **Servers.** In addition to the server hosting your primary SQL Server database instance, you must have a second database instance hosting on a separate server to function as the secondary server. A monitor server is optional.
- **File share.** A network file share must be available to store the backed up transaction logs. Microsoft recommends, but does not require, that this file share be located somewhere other than your primary or secondary server in the interest of enhanced availability for your data.
- **SQL Server license.** All servers participating in the log shipping process must be running one of the following versions of SQL Server: SQL Server 2005 Standard Edition, SQL Server 2005 Workgroup Edition, or SQL Server 2005 Enterprise Edition. Log shipping is not available with SQL Server Embedded Edition or SQL Server Express Edition.
- **Case sensitivity.** All servers participating in the log shipping process must have the same SQL Server case sensitivity configuration.
- **Recovery model.** You must back up the database targeted for log shipping using the Full or Bulk-logged recovery models.
- **SQL Server Agent.** The SQL Server agent service must be running on each server for the associated jobs to execute. In most cases this service is active by default, but if it is not running, the log shipping process is not fully functional.

The following steps provide an example of how to enable and configure SQL Server log shipping with a primary and secondary server:

1. Open SQL Server Management Studio and right-click on the target database for log shipping. Select the Properties item from the menu.
2. When the Database Properties dialog box opens (see Figure 9.1), click the Transaction Log Shipping link in the left pane.

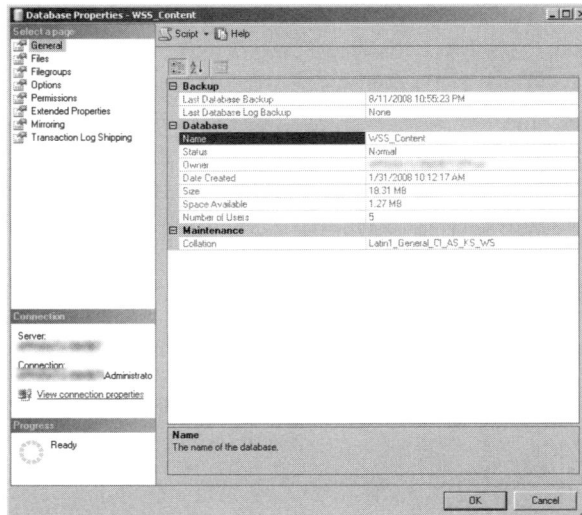

FIGURE 9.1 The General page of the Database Properties dialog box for a selected database in SQL Server Management Studio.

3. This action opens the Transaction Log Shipping page (see Figure 9.2) with most of its options disabled. Click the Enable This as a Primary Database in a Log Shipping Configuration check box to enable the other fields, buttons, and items in the page.

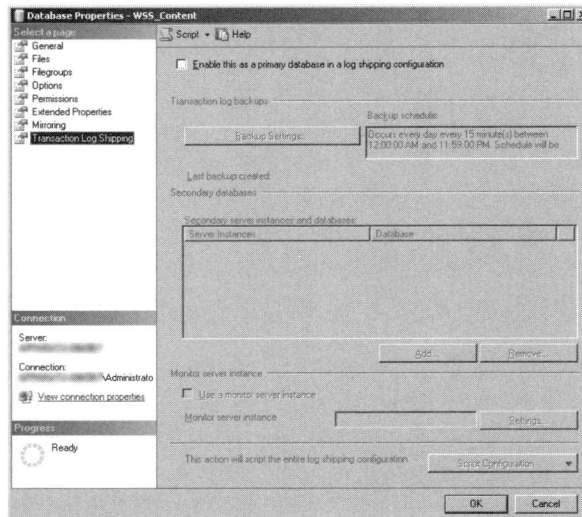

FIGURE 9.2 The Transaction Log Shipping page of the Database Properties dialog box.

4. To open the Transaction Log Backup Settings dialog box (see Figure 9.3), click the now enabled Backup Settings button.

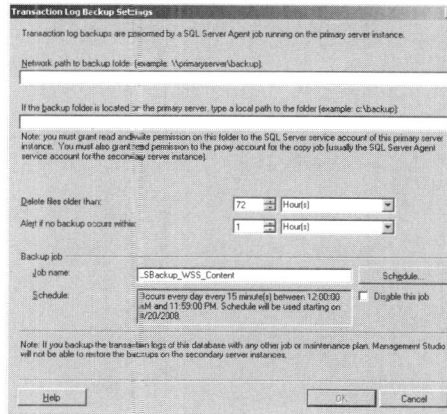

FIGURE 9.3 The Transaction Log Backup Settings window allows you to set the storage location of the transaction log backups, manage the deletion schedule for those backups, and set operator alerts in the case of errors.

5. In the Network Path to Backup Folder text box, enter the Universal Naming Convention (UNC) path for the network share you have designated as the storage location for the backed up transaction logs. If you have chosen to use a local folder on the primary server, leave this field blank and enter the path to that directory in the If the Backup Folder Is Located on the Primary Server, Type a Local Path to the Folder text box.

Regardless of its location, the primary server's SQL Server service account must have read and write privileges for the directory provided. Additionally, the secondary server's SQL Server Agent service account must have read privileges in the directory.

6. Configure the Delete Files Older Than and Alert if No Backup Occurs Within fields according to the needs and requirements of your system. The first field helps to keep your transaction log backups from overwhelming your storage system, whereas the second warns your database's operators if its transaction logs are not being backed up on a regular basis.

Be careful not to set too small of an interval on the deletion of your backup files, or they may be deleted before the log shipping Copy job can create a copy of the files on the secondary server.

7. In the Backup Job section, you have the option of renaming the job used to back up the target database if the default name provided is not sufficiently descriptive. More importantly, clicking the Schedule button opens the Job Schedule Properties dialog box (see Figure 9.4), allowing you to configure how frequently the database's transaction logs are backed up and sent to the secondary server. You can modify the various schedule settings for the backup in this window; be sure to closely review the Summary text field to confirm that the settings match your preferred schedule before clicking the OK button to save your changes.

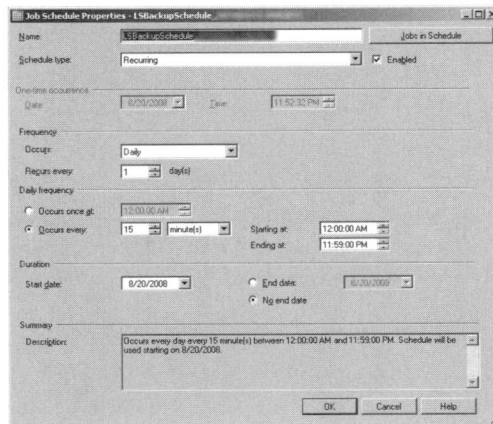

FIGURE 9.4 The Job Schedule Properties window.

8. To save your changes to the Transaction Logs Backup Settings, click the OK button. This returns you to the Transaction Log Shipping page of the database's Properties window.

9. Now that you have configured the backup of the primary database's transaction logs, click the Add button in the Secondary Databases section to select a secondary server to receive the backed up logs.

You must enter a storage location for the transaction log's backups in step 5 for the Add button to be enabled.

TIP

10. This opens the Secondary Database Settings dialog box (see Figure 9.5). By default, most of the items are disabled when this dialog box first opens; you must connect to the secondary server to be able to modify them. Click the Connect button to open a SQL Server login screen, and enter the connection data for the secondary server's database instance to proceed.

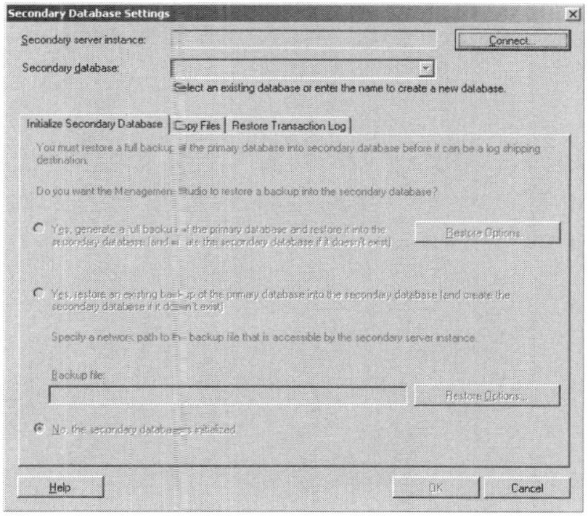

FIGURE 9.5 The Secondary Database Settings dialog box prior to the establishment of a connection to the secondary server.

11. The Initialize Secondary Database tab is now enabled, allowing you to select whether you want the secondary database initialized by a fresh full database created by the log shipping process, by an existing full backup that has already been taken, or to inform SQL Server that the database has already been initialized. Select the option button next to the correct option for your system, configure any necessary Restore Options, and then click the Copy Files tab.

12. In the Copy Files tab (see Figure 9.6), you must provide a destination directory on the secondary server for the transaction log backup files copied from the primary server. (The window's OK button is not enabled until you enter a value in this field.) You may also configure how long these log files are retained for, when operators should be alerted in case of an outage, and the schedule by which the log files are copied from the primary server to the secondary server. After you have completed the Copy Files configuration, click the Restore Transaction Log tab to continue.

The schedule for copying files to the secondary server should match the schedule for transaction log backups as closely as possible. Copying the files with a greater frequency can result in the same data being copied multiple times, while a lesser frequency can result in the loss of transaction data if backups are overwritten or deleted before they can be copied.

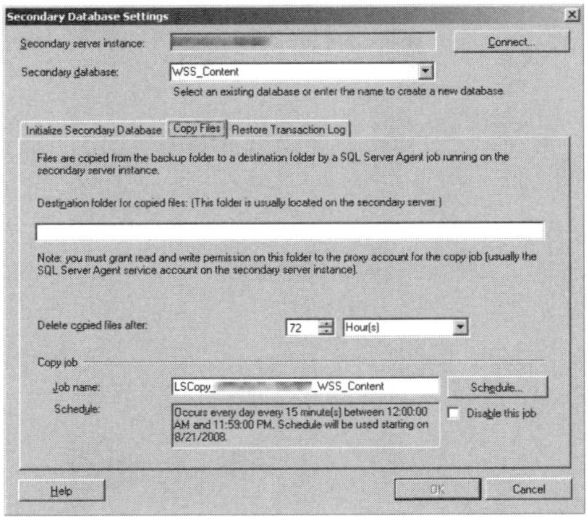

FIGURE 9.6 The Copy Files tab of the Secondary Database Settings dialog box.

13. In the Restore Transaction Log tab (see Figure 9.7), you must select the state that the database is in while restoring backups. The No Recovery Mode option is selected by default, but you can also opt to place the database in Standby Mode. The tab also offers the ability to delay a restore, alert an operator if a restore cannot be run, and change the schedule for restore operations.

14. After you have completed your Secondary Database Settings configurations, click the OK button to return to the Database Properties dialog box.

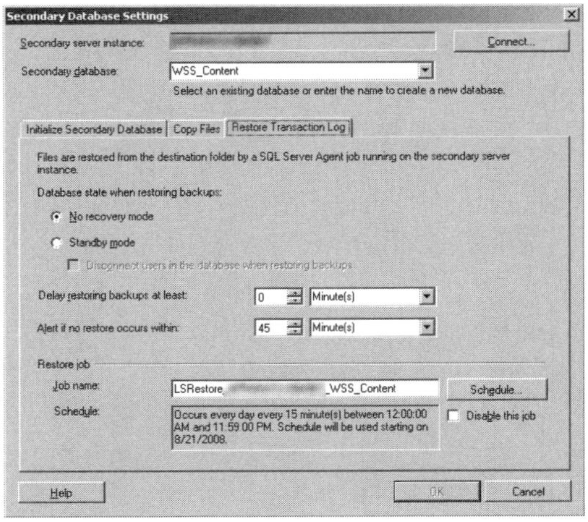

FIGURE 9.7 The Restore Transaction Log tab of the Secondary Database Settings window.

15. If you want to configure a monitor server for the log shipping process, select the Use a Monitor Server Instance check box in the Monitor Server Instance section. This enables the Settings button in that section; click it to open the Log Shipping Monitor Settings dialog box (see Figure 9.8).

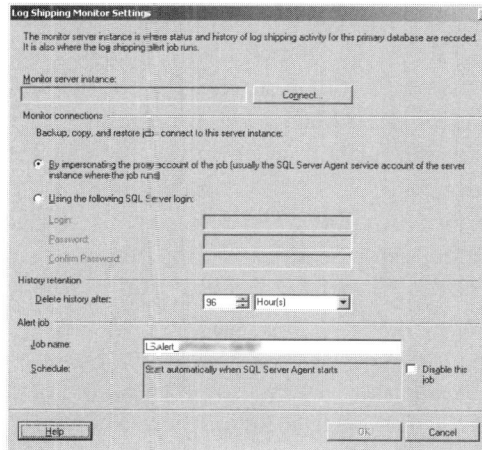

FIGURE 9.8 The Log Shipping Monitor Settings dialog box.

16. When the Log Shipping Monitor Settings dialog box opens, click the Connect button to open a SQL Server login screen and enter the connection data for the secondary server's database instance to proceed. In this dialog box, you can also configure the account used to connect to the monitor server, how long the monitor server retains history data, and when alert jobs are scheduled to run. After you have completed your configuration, click the OK button to return to the Database Properties dialog box.

17. After you have completed the log shipping configuration for the database, click the OK button in the Database Properties dialog box to commit your changes.

SHAREPOINT AND LOG SHIPPING

As with SQL Server database backups in general, several types of SharePoint databases cannot be preserved via SQL Server log shipping. The following list addresses each type of database and whether it can be made highly available via transaction log shipping.

- **Configuration database.** You should not log-ship SharePoint configuration databases, due to their integration with the content database of the Central Administration site and how data about the server instance hosting the database is written directly into the database.
- **Search database.** Because search databases are tightly integrated with the index files stored on the file system of a SharePoint index server, you should not log-ship them. The time it takes to transfer log files between primary and secondary servers results in inconsistencies between the database and the indices. In the case of a disaster, it is likely a better option to re-create the indices from scratch or back them up using the Central Administration site or STSADM.exe than a SQL Server backup.
- **Shared service provider (SSP) database.** You can log-ship SSP databases, as long as the SSP does not host Search, but they do require special care when being connected back into a farm. See the "Restore a Shared Services Provider via the Central Administration Site" section in Chapter 4, "The Central Administration Site's Backup and Restore Tools," for more information on this process.
- **Content databases.** You can log-ship SharePoint content databases to a secondary server. You can also attach them to a standby SharePoint farm for limited read-only viewing, if you restore them in Restore in Standby mode. Depending on how the standby farm is set up, some functions such as search, user profiles, and people search may not be available without some extra configuration efforts.

As you can see in the list, not every type of SharePoint database can be highly available through SQL Server log shipping. This directly impacts how you should use log shipping to implement HA for your SharePoint farm's databases, because you are not able to simply switch over to your secondary log-shipped databases if your primary databases are lost. You can take two approaches when using SQL Server log shipping with SharePoint: creating standalone secondary clones of your SSP and content databases or creating a full standby SharePoint farm based on your log-shipped SSP and content databases. Because you cannot make your configuration and search databases highly available via log shipping, you must build a new farm to host the log-shipped SSP and content databases to restore your environment to its users.

It is worth noting that even if the reasons above weren't enough to dissuade you from log shipping SharePoint databases other than content databases, it simply is not possible from a technical standpoint. Other than the content databases, every database within SharePoint is configured to use the Simple recovery model, which means that log shipping cannot be used with those databases. This is configured by the SharePoint installation process when it creates the databases in SQL Server and should not be modified manually. Poking around in SharePoint's databases without properly leveraging the SharePoint API is akin to sticking your hand into a bag full of badgers: you're eventually going to come into contact with something that you'll end up regretting. Manually modifying SharePoint's databases is completely unsupported by Microsoft. (Their stance on bags of badgers is at this point undefined.)

The first option means that you are not going to build a new farm until a disaster occurs, but it does reduce your startup time because the content is preserved and ready to be reintroduced back into the farm. If an outage hits a single database, it gives you a running resource to add back into your farm. The second option allows you to have a full, up-to-date replacement available for your farm in the case of a catastrophic event, shortening the time that your environment is unavailable to your users. While the specifics of implementing the first option have already been covered in the chapter, you need to take additional steps to create a full standby SharePoint farm using log-shipped databases.

There are two key disaster recovery terms that are key in helping you to determine which log shipping option is best for your environment: recovery time objective (RTO) and recovery point objective (RPO). An RTO defines the maximum amount of time that a restoration of your SharePoint environment can take following a disaster. An RPO defines the maximum window of data loss (in the time leading up to an outage) that can be tolerated in the event of a disaster. Understanding your organization's RTO and RPO targets gives you a better idea of how quickly your SharePoint databases need to be recovered so that you can choose the right log shipping option (or SQL Server HA option in general) to meet those objectives. RTO and RPO are discussed at further length and detail in Chapter 12, "SharePoint Disaster Recovery Planning and Key Concepts."

Building a standby SharePoint farm provides a system for the log-shipped SSP and content databases to be integrated into and gives you a fallback option if a disastrous event should befall your primary production SharePoint farm. It also gives you a read-only environment where users can view data or run reports without impacting the performance of your production farm. (Keep in mind that this may influence how the platforms in your standby farm are licensed.) You can use the following steps as a guide to build your own standby SharePoint farm.

1. Configure log shipping for each database selected to be replicated into the standby farm using the Restore to Standby mode.
2. Install SharePoint in the farm, using the SQL Server database instance hosting the log-shipped databases as the database host for the standby farm.

NOTE

Take special care to apply the same patches, hotfixes, or updates to the standby farm as have been applied to your production farm. You must build the standby farm to the same SharePoint version as your production farm. If your production farm has any custom code or language packs installed, make sure to install them to the standby farm.

3. Configure the standby farm to match the setup of the production farm. If you have an SSP configured in your production farm, you must either create a new SSP to match it or restore a backup of the SSP from the production farm into the standby farm so you can be certain that the configuration matches exactly. Although you should conduct a search in the standby farm, make sure to disable any search crawls unless you specifically need them. Confirm that the standby farm's MySite configuration in the SSP matches that of the production farm's SSP.

4. To build the new standby Web applications for each Web application in your production farm, execute steps 2 through 11 from the list in the "Restoring a SQL Backup to a New SharePoint Environment" section in Chapter 8, adding the log-shipped content databases to each new Web application.

5. In the standby farm, configure an Alternate Access Mapping (AAM) that points to the URL of your production farm; see Figure 9.9 for an example.

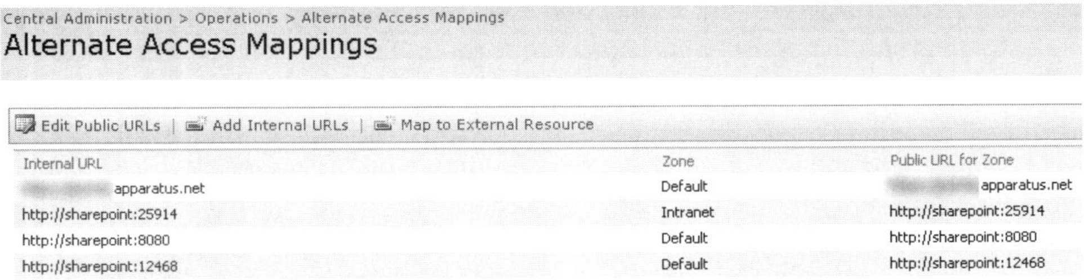

Central Administration > Operations > Alternate Access Mappings
Alternate Access Mappings

Edit Public URLs | Add Internal URLs | Map to External Resource

Internal URL	Zone	Public URL for Zone
apparatus.net	Default	apparatus.net
http://sharepoint:25914	Intranet	http://sharepoint:25914
http://sharepoint:8080	Default	http://sharepoint:8080
http://sharepoint:12468	Default	http://sharepoint:12468

FIGURE 9.9 The Alternate Access Mappings page in the SharePoint Central Administration site.

6. On the file system of all the Web front end servers in the standby farm, open the server's Hosts file (typically located at %WINDIR%\system32\drivers\etc\, see Figure 9.10 for an example) and add an entry pointing the production farm's URL at the server's local loopback IP address, 127.0.0.1. This ensures that any requests for the production farm that originate on the local server are directed back to the local server, not a server in your production farm.

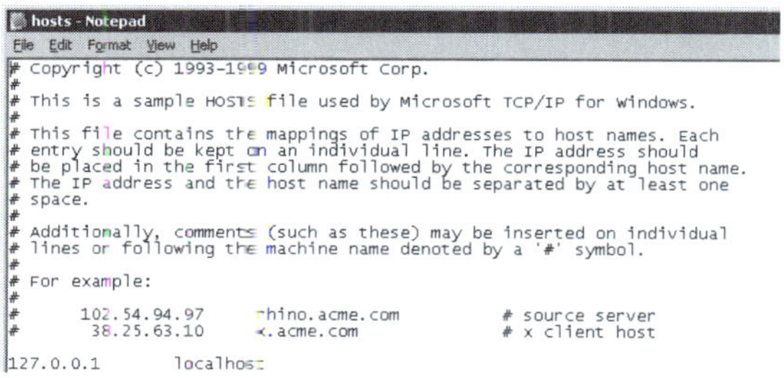

```
hosts - Notepad
File Edit Format View Help
# Copyright (c) 1993-1999 Microsoft Corp.
#
# This is a sample HOSTS file used by Microsoft TCP/IP for Windows.
#
# This file contains the mappings of IP addresses to host names. Each
# entry should be kept on an individual line. The IP address should
# be placed in the first column followed by the corresponding host name.
# The IP address and the host name should be separated by at least one
# space.
#
# Additionally, comments (such as these) may be inserted on individual
# lines or following the machine name denoted by a '#' symbol.
#
# For example:
#
#      102.54.94.97     rhino.acme.com          # source server
#       38.25.63.10     x.acme.com              # x client host

127.0.0.1       localhost
```

FIGURE 9.10 An example of the Hosts file on a Windows Server.

7. In the SSP of the standby farm, open the search content source named "Local Office Server SharePoint Sites" for editing (Figure 9.11 depicts an example of the content source). Remove any URLs that refer to local servers in the standby farm or the URL of the standby farm and replace them with the URL of the production farm.

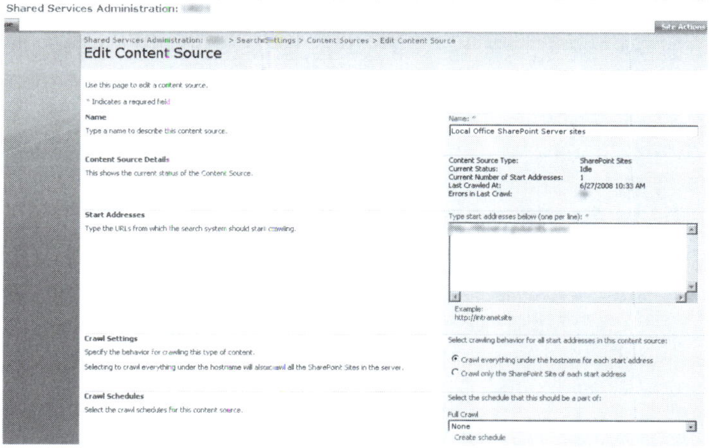

FIGURE 9.11 The "Local Office Server SharePoint Sites" content source for SharePoint search.

8. Your standby farm is now ready to be used as a read-only copy of your production farm that can be failed over to in case of an outage or disaster.

CAUTION

Once your standby farm is created, you must be careful to mirror every configuration change and/or update that you make to your primary SharePoint farm to your standby farm. If the two environments are not kept in sync, you risk displaying inconsistent content to your users or worse, breaking your standby farm entirely when it attempts to use your modified SSP and content databases that are log shipped into it.

Although there are several benefits to using SQL Server log shipping as your HA solution, there are also quite a few drawbacks that you must take into consideration when evaluating the approach. This is not to say that log shipping is or is not a good solution, our main caution is that you should pay close attention to the items below and determine how they relate to your environment, needs, and limitations. You may find that log shipping fits you like a glove, or you may find that one of the other HA solutions in this chapter are what you need to bring long-term stability to your database environment.

LOG SHIPPING PROS

Log shipping may be the right HA solution for your environment for a variety of reasons. The following list outlines its positive attributes. Take a look to see if it meets your needs.

- **Independence.** The jobs used to log ship a database are not tied to SharePoint in any way, nor are they impacted by any other processes in the SQL Server database instance. This means that changes to your SharePoint configuration or its databases do not directly impact or harm your log shipping procedures.
- **Cost-Effective.** Unlike some other HA solutions (such as clustering) log shipping does not require high-priced components and (as noted earlier) can be implemented for the costs that may or may not be associated with provisioning and licensing an additional SQL Server instance.
- **Highly Configurable.** As described earlier, there are a large number of options and configurations to be set for log shipping to allow it to meet the needs of your environment.
- **Easily Configurable.** Again, the information earlier in this chapter shows that the settings for a database's log shipping configuration are easy to access and modify as needed.
- **Read-Only Availability.** If you wish so, a read-only version of your SharePoint environment can be created using its log shipped content databases for research or reporting purposes to reduce the load placed on your primary farm.
- **Low Impact on Performance.** Once the transaction logs of your SharePoint database are backed up, the log shipping process is executed on the server(s) hosting the secondary database and has no impact on the performance of your primary database server.
- **Unlimited Use.** You can log ship as many databases in an instance as you want, there is no hard limit imposed by the platform.
- **Uses Backups.** The transaction log backups used by the log shipping process to update the secondary database can also be used to restore the primary database to a previous point in time as necessary. This means that you are able to make your database highly available and implement a backup/restore solution for it at the same time, an option not available with SQL Server's other HA solutions.

- **Captures Everything.** Because SQL Server records information about a database update to the database's transaction log before it even writes it to the database, all the requested database modifications received by SQL Server leading up to the moment of an outage are copied over to the secondary server and written to that database.
- **Distributed and Redundant.** By requiring a secondary database instance to host your secondary database, log shipping makes your system more HA by providing fallback options for your primary database server. Additionally, the ability to ship database logs to multiple secondary database instances means that you can further limit your risk by increasing the number of fallback options you have available.

Log Shipping Cons

As with most technology solutions, log shipping in SQL Server 2005 is not a perfect solution. Review the following list to see where it falls short and how that might impact your SharePoint environment.

- **Manual Failover.** Out of the box, SQL Server does not automatically fail a system over to the log-shipped secondary database if the primary database goes down. It is possible to do additional configuration in order to automate this process, but by default you must manually switch over to the log-shipped databases. This can impact the amount of time it takes in order to restore your system after an outage, depending on how quickly your IT staff is notified of the outage and what availability they have to restore the system to the log-shipped databases.
- **Latency.** Updates are not automatically copied to the secondary database when they are made in the primary database, and several factors can affect the amount of time it takes for them to make it over to the secondary database. First and foremost amongst is how frequently you set the transaction logs of the primary to be backed up (the shortest amount of time allowed between backups is one minute), but the size of your logs and available bandwidth between the primary and secondary database instances also have an impact on latency. This means that the data in your secondary database is not going to be up to date until the transaction logs are copied to it, which can impact the content of a standby farm. Additionally, the more frequently you take backups of your database's transaction logs, the greater the performance strain you are placing on your database instance's host server. Because of its latency, log shipping does not provide the ability to restore a database to the point in time immediately prior to its failure. That means if your organization's RPO and RTO requirements for SharePoint mandate instantaneous failover with no lost transactions or data, log shipping is not a viable HA solution for your SQL Server environment.

- **Poor Status Visibility.** Although the log shipping process does generate status reports for all of its actions and does allow for the configuration of a monitoring server, this information is not going to be easily available. These reports can only be accessed by logging on to the server where they are stored and only raises alerts to operators of the associated SQL Server instances when they log into the instances. Additional custom measures or the use of a monitoring platform such as the Operations Manager platform from Microsoft are going to be required in order to make this information available to your SharePoint administrators or to automatically deliver the alerts as they occur without requiring administrators to log into a system.
- **Not a Complete Solution.** As previously mentioned, you are not able to log ship all of your SharePoint databases, requiring additional steps such as building a whole new farm or creating a standby farm in order to use the log-shipped databases in the case of a disaster.
- **Errors and Data Loss.** Any errors that are written to your primary databases are also going to be transferred to your secondary databases via log shipping. Log shipping is not to prevent the loss of data due to accidental deletion; if it is deleted in the primary database it is also deleted in the secondary database once the transaction is log shipped over.

If the features and functionality of log shipping in SQL Server 2005 seem appealing but you still have concerns about some or all of the drawbacks to the process, have no fear. There are, however, other alternatives when it comes to HA for SQL Server, and the next one on the list, database mirroring, offers several enhancements to log shipping's feature set while also improving on its weaknesses. While the two options are similar, there are definitely some differences between the two, especially when it comes to the increased cost of implementing database mirroring. In addition, it is possible to implement both log shipping and database mirroring for your SharePoint environment, giving you the best of both worlds.

DATABASE MIRRORING

SQL Server's database mirroring functionality is very similar to log shipping in how it maintains a copy of the primary database for HA purposes, in that both approaches copy transaction log data from the primary over to the secondary database. While the similarities between the two HA solutions for SQL Server may be striking, the differences between them are even more so. Database mirroring differs from log shipping in several areas, the three most apparent being when the transaction log data is copied to the secondary server, how that data is transferred from one server to another, and how the databases behave when the primary server suffers an outage.

Database mirroring's most appealing advantage over log shipping is that transactions committed to the primary database are copied over to the secondary database instance at once after they are written to the database. This gives database mirroring a distinct advantage over log shipping by reducing latency and ensuring that the contents of the secondary database are completely current. When the transactions are sent to the secondary database the individual transaction records themselves are sent to the secondary database via TCP, not transaction log backups via a file system copy. But the most desirable aspect of database mirroring is the fact that it can be configured to automatically failover to the secondary server should the primary server suffer an outage, a big change from log shipping's reliance on a manual failover.

TIP

If the network being used to send the transaction records is not secure, you should take precautions to secure and encrypt the database mirroring traffic as it is sent. For specific information on this subject, Microsoft has published an article on Database Mirroring Transport Security at http://msdn.microsoft.com/en-us/library/ ms186360(SQL.90).aspx.

CAUTION

Microsoft only supports the use of database mirroring in a production environment if you are running SQL Server 2005 with a version of SP1 or greater. If you are not running at or greater than this version, you should seriously consider updating or upgrading your SQL Server environment before implementing database mirroring in production.

THE SERVER COMPONENTS OF DATABASE MIRRORING

Database mirroring requires at least two servers, a principal and a mirror, and allows the use of an optional third server, a witness, to automate failovers from the principal to the mirror in the case of an outage on the principal.

- **Principal.** This is the database you wish to mirror to a SQL Server instance on a separate server. Backups of the principal database must be taken using the Full recovery model in order for the database to use database mirroring, it is not available when using the Simple or Bulk-logged recovery models. There can be only one principal server for a target database and it can have only one mirror server as a partner in the mirroring session. This role can be implemented on servers using the Enterprise or Standard licenses for SQL Server.
- **Mirror.** This is the database that functions as the mirroring partner for your principal database. The mirror database must be initially restored from a full backup of the principal database using the Restore with No Recovery option

(and then any transaction log backups required to make the database up to date) before it can be updated with transactions via database mirroring. See Figure 9.12 for an example of where this setting is selected. See the "How to Restore a SQL Server 2005 Database Backup" section of Chapter 8, "SQL Server 2005 Backup and Restore," for more information on how to restore a database in the SQL Server Management Studio. A single secondary server can host multiple databases acting as mirrors to principal databases on other servers. Databases hosted on the mirror instance not acting as a mirror can also be principal databases in database mirroring with other database instances. This role can be implemented on servers using the Enterprise or Standard licenses for SQL Server.

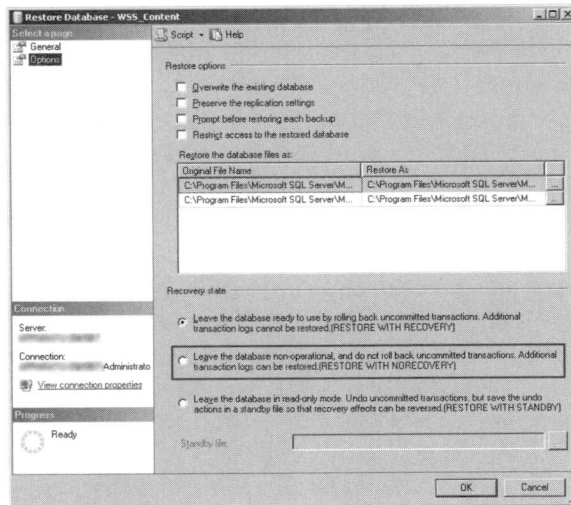

FIGURE 9.12 The Options page of the Restore Database dialog box with the Restore with No Recovery radio button highlighted.

■ **Witness.** This server is optional and is needed only if you require SQL Server to automatically failover to the mirror database if a failure or outage occurs on the principal database. The witness server does not perform resource-intensive activities or host content as part of the database mirroring process; its only role is to detect a failure in the principal database and enable automatic failover to the mirror. You can implement this role on servers using the Enterprise, Standard, Workgroup, or Express Edition licenses for SQL Server.

Microsoft does not support mirroring configurations where databases from the same principal database instance are copied to mirrors in separate database instances. Whenever possible, you should strive to mirror all the databases in a principal instance to a single mirror instance.

CAUTION

How to Configure Database Mirroring

Your environment must meet the following requirements to enable database mirroring for one or more of your SQL Server databases:

- **Servers.** In addition to the server hosting your principal SQL Server database instance, you must have a second database instance hosting on a separate server to function as the mirror server. A witness server is optional but is required if you want to have automatic failover.
- **SQL Server License.** The principal and mirror servers must be running one of the following versions of SQL Server: SQL Server 2005 Standard Edition or SQL Server 2005 Enterprise Edition. The witness server must be running one of the following versions of SQL Server: SQL Server Express Edition, SQL Server 2005 Standard Edition, SQL Server 2005 Workgroup Edition, or SQL Server 2005 Enterprise Edition. Database mirroring is not available with SQL Server Embedded Edition.
- **Service Pack.** All servers in the mirroring configuration must be updated to SQL Server 2005's SP1 update or greater.
- **Permissions.** Your mirror database instance must provide the same permissions and roles that are granted to your principal database instance.
- **Recovery Model.** The database targeted for database mirroring must be backed up using the Full recovery model.

The following steps provide an example of how to enable and configure SQL Server database mirroring with a principal, mirror, and witness server.

1. Open SQL Server Management Studio and right-click on the target database for database mirroring. Select the Properties item from the menu.
2. When the Database Properties dialog box opens (see Figure 9.1), click the Mirroring page link in the left pane.
3. This action opens the Mirroring page (see Figure 9.13) with most of its options disabled. Click the Configure Security button to configure the database mirroring security settings.
4. This opens the Configure Database Mirroring Security Wizard, as shown in Figure 9.14; click the Next button to continue.
5. The wizard next prompts you for witness server configuration information (see Figure 9.15). If you want to set up a witness server and enable automatic failover for this database mirroring configuration, select the Yes option and click the Next button. If not, select the No button and click the Next button. In this example, select the Yes option button to configure a witness server.

FIGURE 9.13 The Mirroring page of the Database Properties dialog box; most of its fields are disabled until database mirroring has been configured through the Configure Security button.

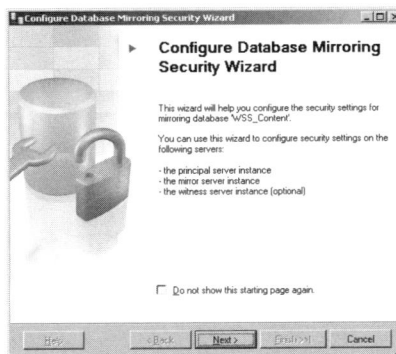

FIGURE 9.14 The opening screen of the Configure Database Mirroring Security Wizard.

6. The wizard's Choose Servers to Configure screen opens (see Figure 9.16), displaying the three database mirroring server roles that can have the database mirroring security configuration saved on them, with check boxes to the left of them. The check boxes for the principal and mirror server instances are checked by default and disabled to prevent the selection from being modified. The witness server instance check box is checked by default but can be unchecked. Ensure that all three server instances are checked, and click the Next button to continue.

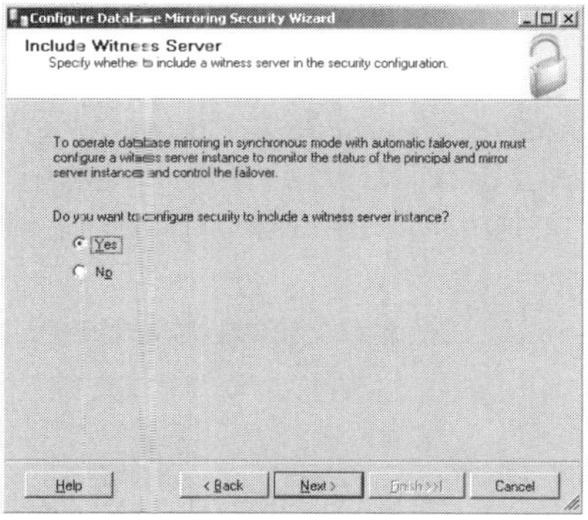

FIGURE 9.15 The Include Witness Server screen of the Configure Database Mirroring Security Wizard.

If you choose not to configure a witness server, the third server role is not displayed in the screen.

NOTE

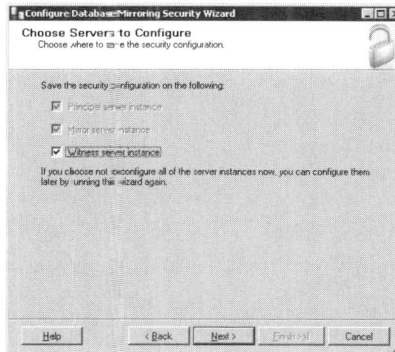

FIGURE 9.16 The Choose Servers to Configure screen in the Configure Database Mirroring Security Wizard.

7. This opens the wizard's Principal Server Instance screen (see Figure 9.17). In this screen, you are shown the current database instance hosting the principal database for the mirroring process in a disabled drop-down menu. In this window, you can opt to have SQL Server encrypt each transaction as it is sent from the principal server by selecting the associated check box, specify the networking port that the principal server uses to communicate with the mirror and witness server, and rename the endpoint for transactions sent from the principal server. When you have entered the information and configuration data for your principal database instance, click the Next button to continue.

If you have previously established a database mirroring endpoint for the target database, the Encrypt Data check box, as well as the Listener Port and Endpoint Name text fields, are disabled, preventing you from modifying the configured endpoint. To change the current mirroring endpoint, you must execute Transact-SQL commands to DROP *or* ALTER *the mirroring endpoint.*

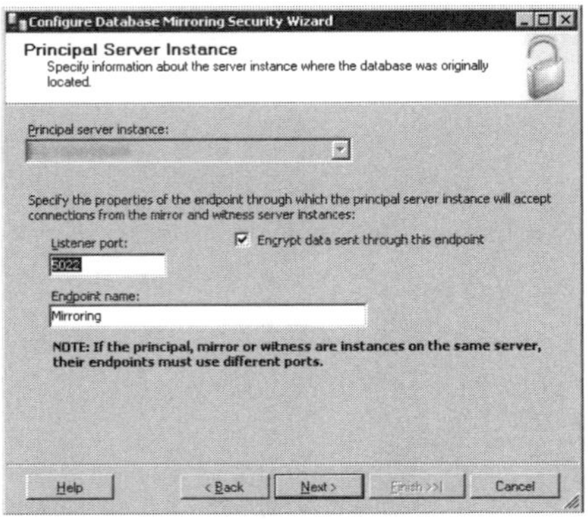

FIGURE 9.17 The Principal Server Instance screen in the Configure Database Mirroring Security Wizard.

8. The wizard proceeds to the Mirror Server Instance screen (see Figure 9.18), which looks similar to the Principal Server Instance screen in Figure 9.17, except that the database selection drop-down menu is now enabled. In this screen, you are able to select the database instance hosting the mirror database for the mirroring process from the drop-down menu. If the desired database instance is not available in the drop-down menu, click the Connect button to open a dialog box to log into the database instance or select the Browse for More option from the drop-down menu. After selecting the current database instance, you can opt to have SQL Server encrypt each transaction as it is sent from the mirror server by selecting the associated check box, specify the networking port that the principal server uses to communicate with the mirror and witness server, and rename the endpoint for transactions sent from the principal server. If you attempt to select the same database instance as the one you established as the principal server, SQL Server displays an error message instructing you to select another instance, and the Next button is disabled (see Figure 9.18). After you have entered valid information and configuration data for your mirror database instance, click the Next button to continue.

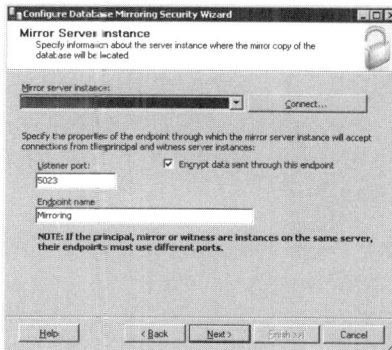

FIGURE 9.18 The Mirror Server Instance screen in the Configure Database Mirroring Security Wizard.

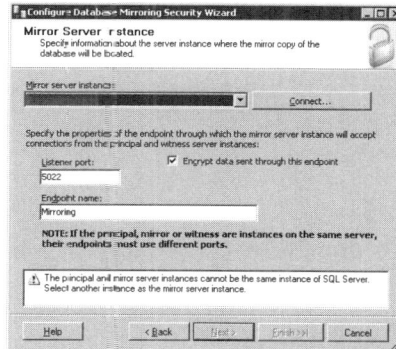

FIGURE 9.19 The Mirror Server Instance screen in the Configure Database Mirroring Security Wizard displaying an error when the principal database instance is also submitted as the mirror instance.

9. The wizard again opens a screen similar to the Principal Server Instance screen in Figure 9.17—the Witness Server Instance screen (see Figure 9.20)—and it has the database selection drop-down menu enabled. In this screen, you are able to select the database instance hosting the witness database for the mirroring process from the drop-down menu. If the desired database instance is not available in the drop-down menu, click the Connect button to open a dialog box to log into the database instance or select the Browse for More option from the drop-down menu. After selecting the current database instance, you can opt to have SQL Server encrypt each transaction as it is sent from the witness server by selecting the associated check box, specify the networking port that the principal server uses to communicate with the mirror and witness server, and rename the endpoint for transactions sent from the principal server. Like the mirror server

screen, if you attempt to select the same database instance as the one you established as the principal or mirror server, SQL Server displays an error message similar to Figure 9.19 instructing you to select another instance, and the Next button is disabled. After you have entered valid information and configuration data for your witness database instance, click the Next button to continue.

NOTE

If you opt not to include a witness server in step 5 or not configure its security in step 6, this screen is not displayed.

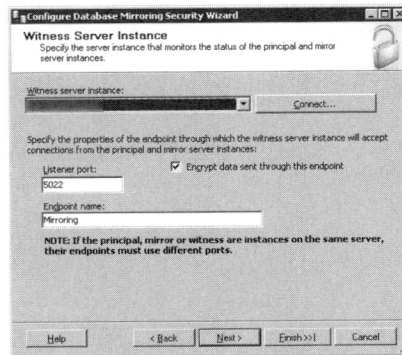

FIGURE 9.20 The Witness Server Instance screen in the Configure Database Mirroring Security Wizard.

10. The Service Accounts screen opens, allowing you to specify a service account in DOMAIN\ACCOUNT format for each of the servers in the database mirroring configuration. As Figure 9.21 shows, the screen provides instructions regarding when accounts should and should not be specified, as well as what actions SQL Server takes if the accounts listed do not currently have SQL Server logins. Once the account information has been configured, click the Next button to continue.

NOTE

If you opt not to include a witness server in step 5, the text field for the Witness service account is not displayed.

11. The last screen of the wizard is now displayed (see Figure 9.22), allowing you to review what you have configured before clicking the Finish button to finalize the security configuration process. If you see any items that need to be modified, click the Back button to navigate to them and make your changes. When you are ready, click the Finish button to complete the wizard and have SQL Server begin to configure the database monitoring configuration's security.

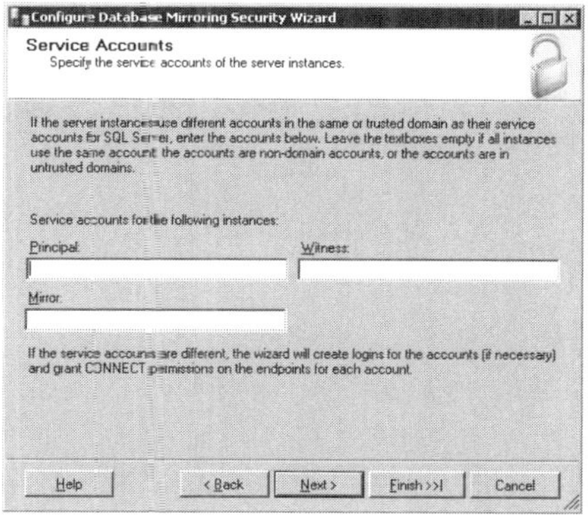

FIGURE 9.21 The Service Account screen in the Configure Database Mirroring Security Wizard.

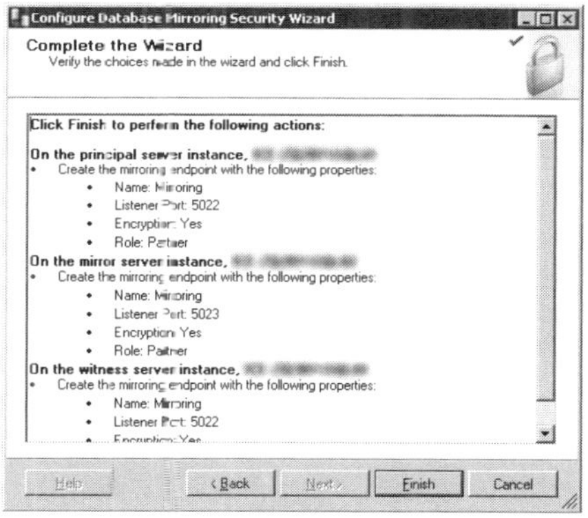

FIGURE 9.22 The Complete the Wizard screen in the Configure Database Mirroring Security Wizard.

12. The Configuring Endpoints screen (see Figure 9.23) displays the progress of the security configuration as it executes. Once the tool is finished, ensure that all tasks have completed with a status of Success, review the status messages and reports as needed, and click the Close button to return to the Mirroring page of the database's Properties window.

13. After SQL Server has completed the endpoint configuration process, the wizard closes and you are prompted with a window asking if you want to start database mirroring for the target database using the configuration that just completed, as shown in Figure 9.24. Click the Start Mirroring button if you are ready to enable the process, or click the Do Not Start Mirroring button if you are not. In this example, the Do Not Start Mirroring button was clicked.

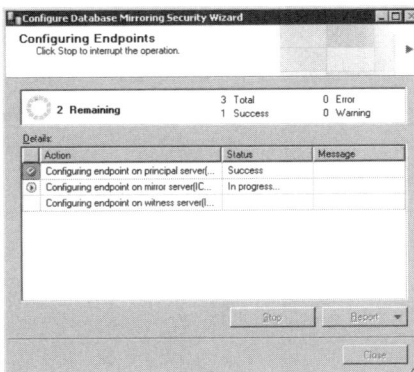

FIGURE 9.23 The Configuring Endpoints screen in the Configure Database Mirroring Security Wizard.

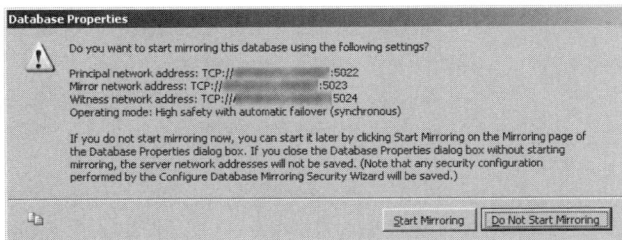

FIGURE 9.24 The Database Mirroring Database Properties dialog box prompts the user to either start or not start database mirroring using the provided configuration.

14. Regardless of whether you choose to start the mirroring process, when you return to the Mirroring page, it is apparent that many more fields are now enabled after security was configured, as shown by Figure 9.25. In the Server Network Address section, the text fields for the Principal, Mirror, and Witness servers are now enabled and populated with the network connection string used to contact each of these servers. If you did not start mirroring in step 13, only the Start Mirroring button is enabled. If you did start monitoring in step 13, the Pause, Remove Mirroring, and Failover buttons are enabled. In the Operating Mode section, the High Performance (Asynchronous) and High Safety with Automatic Failover (Synchronous) option buttons are enabled if you chose to include a witness server in step 5. If you did not include a witness server in step 5, the High Performance (Asynchronous) and High Safety without Automatic Failover (Synchronous) option buttons are enabled. In both cases, the latter radio button is selected by default. The Status section contains a text box displaying the

database mirroring status for the database and a Refresh button, which is disabled if mirroring has not been started. If the Status field indicates that the database has not been configured for mirroring, click the Start Mirroring button to initiate the process.

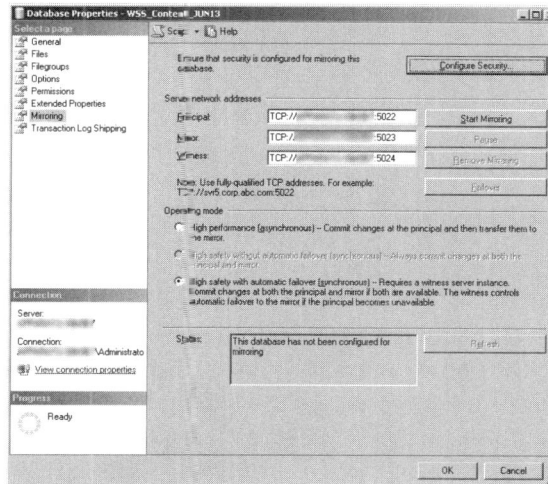

FIGURE 9.25 The Mirroring page of the Database Properties dialog box after the Configure Database Mirroring Security Wizard has completed without error.

15. After mirroring has been started for the database, you are able to suspend the process by clicking the Pause button. A dialog box is displayed asking you to confirm your request, and you are then returned to the Mirroring page. The former Pause button is now marked as the Resume button and can be clicked to resume the mirroring process for the database.

Pausing the mirroring process places the mirrored database in a suspended status and results in transactions not being transferred from the principal database to the mirrored database until mirroring is resumed. You can use the Pause option as a short-term solution to improve performance on the principal database instance, but you should not use it for extended periods. The transaction log of the principal database is not truncated while mirroring is paused so that all logged transactions can be sent to the mirrored database once the process is resumed. If mirroring is not resumed in a timely fashion, the transaction log can grow too large and use all of its available disk space, ultimately causing an outage of the principal database if it cannot write to its transaction logs.

16. To completely stop the database from being mirrored, click the Remove Mirroring button. A dialog box is displayed asking you to confirm your request, and you are then returned to the Mirroring page. To restart mirroring for this database, you must manually re-create all the configured mirroring settings. This action permanently removes the mirroring associations and security settings between the principal, mirror, and witness servers, but the copy of the mirrored database is not deleted from the mirror database instance.

> *If you chose to keep the mirrored database, you must perform a Restore with Recovery action against it to make it available, since it was originally created using Restore with No Recovery. You should consider renaming the mirrored database to avoid confusion between it and the principal database.*

17. To manually fail a database over from its principal to its mirror, click the Failover button. A dialog box is displayed asking you to confirm your request, and you are then returned to the Mirroring page. After completing the failover, the mirroring server roles of the two databases have been swapped, so the original principal now has the mirror role and the original mirror is now the principal database.

> *Keep in mind that this change of roles has only occurred in SQL Server from a mirroring perspective; it does not communicate this update to the applications or services that use the database and may impact their ability to access the database.*

18. If you want to change the operating mode of the mirroring process, simply select the button next to the option you desire and click OK, closing the database's Properties window and saving your changes.

Step 14 briefly discussed a crucial component of SQL Server's database mirroring functionality: the operating mode. The option you select for this section directly impacts how SQL Server handles your mirrored database in the case of an outage. The three options available are described next:

- **High Performance (Asynchronous).** This operating mode commits changes to the principal database, sends them to the mirror, and then proceeds with normal processing without waiting for confirmation by the mirror server that the transfer was successful. High Performance mode offers improved performance because the principal server is not waiting on the mirror server to execute operations, but there is also an increased risk of error due to the lack of confirmation. This database mirroring mode is better suited when the operational performance of the database is more important to your organization and a zero-loss RPO isn't a strict requirement.

- **High Safety without Automatic Failover (Synchronous).** This operating mode does not mark a transaction as completed until it has been written to the transaction log of both servers. Because it does not require a witness server, the database must be manually failed over to the mirror in the case of an outage. If your organization requires that a mirrored database meet a zero-loss RPO target, High Safety without Automatic Failover is the best database mirroring choice available.

- **High Safety with Automatic Failover (Synchronous).** This operating mode does not mark a transaction as completed until it has been written to the transaction log of both servers, but it does provide automatic failover because it requires a witness server. High Safety with Automatic Failover mode is best suited if your organization places a high priority on real-time RTO targets for databases; the availability of automatic failover means that the database's downtime is limited to the time it takes to bring the mirror online.

As previously stated, one of the most attractive features for database mirroring is its ability to provide automatic failover capabilities for your SharePoint databases in the event of an outage on your principal database instances. But it should not be the only option that you consider when evaluating database mirroring, because the high-performance operating mode for database monitoring can be a potential HA solution for your SharePoint environment. Take some time to carefully consider the requirements and implications of each of these options prior to implementing database mirroring in your environment. The choice you make directly impacts your database architecture, the performance of your system, and your disaster recovery and HA planning.

SHAREPOINT AND DATABASE MIRRORING

Although you have to make some tough decisions when configuring database mirroring for use with SharePoint's databases, a good portion of your configuration choices are driven by other factors, mainly how your infrastructure is or can be implemented to meet your needs. For some enterprises, it may not be cost effective to implement multiple farms in geographically diverse locations, whereas for others it may be a business-critical requirement, and each option (plus all those in between) has an impact on how you can use database mirroring and what can be mirrored.

For a single farm environment entirely hosted within a single data center where only your SharePoint databases are mirrored, you can use all three operating modes without issue. In this situation it is assumed that your SharePoint servers either remain online through an outage of your principal databases or that you have an HA solution outside of SQL Server to ensure that they are able to serve content to your end users. All the SharePoint databases for your farm can be made highly available via database mirroring: Configuration, Content, SSP, Central Administration Content, Search, and so on.

> *Regardless of how your mirrored databases are failed over in the case of an outage on your principal database instances, with a single farm environment, you must still update your SharePoint environment to recognize the mirror instances as the new hosts for its databases. SQL Server does not communicate this change to SharePoint, so the onus is on you to manually update your farm's configuration information to reflect this change. You can accomplish this manually via the STSADM.exe* renameserver *operation, and you can automate or use SQL Server aliases to obscure this switch from your SharePoint farm's perspective, but you should consult your network and database administrators for the optimal way to achieve this in your enterprise.*

For a single farm environment with components hosted in multiple data centers, again you can use all three operating modes, but in this case you need to address sticking points as part of the architecture. In this type of environment, the mirrored database instance is hosted in a separate data center from the principal instance, providing geographical redundancy in the case of an outage. Regardless of the operating mode used, Microsoft states that the network within and between the data centers must provide bandwidth capacity of at least 1 gigabyte and the average latency for traffic on the network must be less than 1 millisecond between the environment's SharePoint servers and all the database instances in the environment (in both directions). These constraints mean that the data centers must be capable of providing large, fast connections to the servers they host and that, in most cases, these data centers must be closely located to reduce latency (at the cost of increasing risk to localized catastrophes).

> *If a witness server is configured for automatic failover, Microsoft recommends placing it in a third data center to ensure that it can initiate the failover process in the case of an outage on the principal server. Because this may not always be a feasible configuration, it is still possible to host the witness server in one of the two data centers, but you must understand that it is exposed to the same risks as the other servers hosted with it and a manual failover is required if the witness server is impacted by an outage. The recommendation is to host the witness server in the same data center as the mirrored instance so that a potential outage on the principal has a reduced chance of impacting the witness server as well. It is also strongly recommended to include the witness server in any monitoring solutions you may establish, not only to track the status of the mirroring process but to confirm that the witness server is healthy and able to execute the failover when needed.*

If you have multiple farms in separate data centers, the synchronous operating modes for database mirroring really are not an option because of the amount of time it would take for a transaction to be sent across the network, written to each database, and the results to be sent back across the network. These activities are directly impacted by network latency—something that is unavoidable over a WAN connection between data centers that do not share large, fast connections. Database mirroring can still be used with the asynchronous operating modes to provide mirrored copies of your crucial SharePoint data. The other drawback to using mirroring for multiple farms is that, like log shipping, it can only be used to mirror your content databases or SSP databases as long as their associated SSP is not hosting SharePoint's search functionality.

If you need a synchronous solution for your SharePoint databases, the most likely solution available is database clustering, covered later in this chapter. But if the hardware requirements for clustering are too high for your budget, you may be able to achieve similar results at a lower cost by combining SQL Server's log shipping and database mirroring processes into a single solution for your SharePoint environment.

TIP

LOG SHIPPING AND DATABASE MIRRORING WITH SHAREPOINT

By combining log shipping and database mirroring, you can create a geographically distributed solution that offers the best attributes of each approach and take advantage of those attributes to cover each other's deficiencies. On its own, database mirroring fails as a solution for geographic redundancy because it cannot send transactions requested for a SharePoint content database over a WAN connection quickly enough in a synchronous manner to avoid impacting end user performance, but the use of an asynchronous approach raises the risk of data inconsistencies between the principal and mirror databases. Likewise, log shipping by itself is not effective as a zero-loss, real-time disaster recovery solution because it does not necessarily allow for small enough snapshots to be taken of transactions and can impact the performance of the primary server as backups are being made.

The idea here is to create a solution using log shipping and database mirroring where transactions in a production SharePoint database can be made highly available in a separate data center without incurring performance loss while writing those transactions to the constituent databases as accurately as possible. This approach combines the best aspects of each approach to offset their drawbacks to provide a failover solution with geographic redundancy for your SharePoint databases. Figure 9.26 depicts an example of this configuration, involving four distinct SQL Server database instances across two geographically dispersed locations.

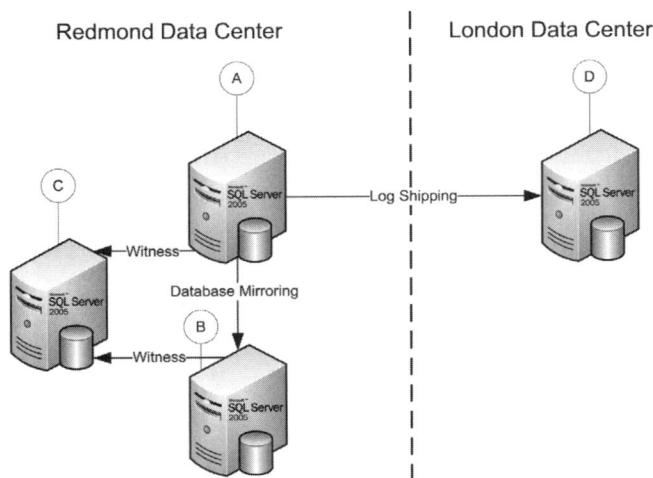

FIGURE 9.26 A hypothetical mockup of a SQL Server disaster recovery configuration using both database mirroring and log shipping.

The first step in this process is to mirror the target database (labeled as server A in Figure 9.26) using the high safety (synchronous) with automatic failover operating mode, meaning that you must configure a witness server in addition to the principal and mirror servers. The mirror (labeled as server B) and witness (labeled as server C) servers should be located in the same data center as the principal server; using local servers avoids latency issues when transactions are sent from the principal to the mirror. This allows your database to automatically failover to the mirror if an outage occurs on the principal server, but the database could still be lost if the entire data center suffers an outage.

To address this risk, configure log shipping on the principal server so that it is acting as a primary to send its backups to a secondary database instance located in a separate data center (labeled as server D). You should not use this secondary instance to host the mirror or witness servers. After log shipping from the principal has been configured, failover the database to its mirror. When the original mirror server becomes the primary, configure it as a primary server to ship its logs to the same secondary server as the original principal and fail the mirror back so that the original principal is now back in that role.

> *It is not possible to configure log shipping for the mirror server in SQL Server Management Studio; you must create a T-SQL script and run it to set up log shipping for the mirror server. You can configure log shipping for the principal server via either SQL Server Management Studio or a T-SQL script.*
>
> **NOTE**

When configuring log shipping for both the principal and mirror servers in this manner, SQL Server should report an error stating that the transaction log backup could not be generated because the database is in Restore with No Recovery or Restore with Standby mode. This is perfectly normal and does not impact the outcome of this process.

CAUTION

When the configuration is complete, the principal server generates transaction log backups that are copied to the secondary server, giving you a geographically dispersed copy of your SharePoint database that can be restored should tragedy strike your principal database or its host data center. The mirror database is configured to generate transaction log backups as well, but they are not created unless a failover is executed to make it the principal database in the configuration. You now have an HA database solution that provides automatic failover, is not based in a single geographic location, reduces performance impacts on your environment, and does not require expensive storage replication hardware.

DATABASE MIRRORING PROS

Are you still unsure if database mirroring is the best HA solution for your SQL Server 2005 instances? The following list describes the strong points of database mirroring and their benefits for SharePoint to help you with your decision.

- **Independent.** Like log shipping, database mirroring's functionality is not tied to SharePoint, nor is it impacted by any other processes in the SQL Server database instance. This means that changes to your SharePoint configuration or its databases do not directly impact or harm your database mirroring procedures.
- **Highly configurable.** There are several options and configurations to be set to allow database mirroring to meet the needs of your environment.
- **Easily configurable.** Not only is database mirroring straightforward for an administrator to configure, but the infrastructure to host it does not require specific hardware to implement it.
- **Immediate.** When a change is made to a principal database, it is also immediately sent to the mirror.
- **Automated.** If a witness server is configured along with the principal and mirror servers, when an outage occurs, a failover from the principal to the mirror can be automatically executed without administrator intervention.
- **Responsive.** Failovers are executed quickly, regardless of whether they are manually or automatically requested.
- **Distributed and redundant.** As previously explained, you can use database mirroring in various ways, both on its own and with log shipping, to ensure the long-term stability of your SQL Server environment and the SharePoint farm that depends on it.

Database Mirroring Cons

Database mirroring also comes with its own set of drawbacks that you must consider before deciding to implement it, as described here.

- **Limit on number of mirrored databases.** Microsoft IT states that database mirroring is supported on up to 50 SharePoint databases in a SQL Server instance. You should view this number as an absolute ceiling in this area, because your infrastructure configurations may lower the number based on their performance capabilities and drawbacks. As always, thoroughly test your system to confirm that it can support your planned configuration and usage.
- **One mirror per database.** A database cannot be mirrored more than once, creating a single point of failure for your HA solution. You should regularly test and confirm your database mirroring configuration to ensure that it continues to function as expected.
- **No easy read-only option.** Mirrored databases cannot be made available for read-only querying without the creation of an additional snapshot based on the mirror.
- **Relatively new technology.** Database mirroring functionality was introduced to the SQL Server platform with the release of SQL Server 2005. Although database mirroring has had time to gain acceptance and usage as a valuable HA tool, your database administrator may have greater familiarity with other approaches and solutions.
- **Failover options do not include full environment.** Although the automatic failover option for database mirroring is attractive, it does not provide a complete failover solution to ensure continuity of service for your SharePoint environment. You must either manually update your farm to point at the new primary database instance after a failover or configure your own solution to respond to a failover when it happens, adding more dependencies and points of failure to your system.
- **Performance impact.** Although database mirroring's performance footprint on its host server, in most cases, is much smaller than log shipping, it can still negatively affect the host and its overall performance.
- **Dependent on networking.** Attempting to do synchronous database mirroring in a network with suboptimal bandwidth or latency leads to performance issues for your principal database and the SharePoint environment that uses it.

Database mirroring is certainly a viable HA solution for SQL Server worth serious consideration. It lets you automatically failover to a fallback database instance should your production database fail. It also gives you the confidence of knowing that the data in your fallback instance is an exact copy of your production database.

It is flexible and can be used with various hardware and software configurations. But you may find that it is not a good fit for the needs of an organization and its HA requirements. What if you need your databases to always be online and cannot suffer an outage of even an hour while you update your SharePoint farm to point at your mirrored database instance? What if you need more than one fallback instance to add additional redundancy to your environment but the performance implications of log shipping rule it out as an option? These are just two examples of when configuring a cluster of servers running SQL Server may be the best solution to your problems.

DATABASE CLUSTERING

Clustering is not unique to SQL Server or even to database platforms in general. A server cluster consists of one or more servers, each configured identically, that are designed to consistently serve up an application or platform even if an error or outage occurs on one of the members of the cluster. Although this section focuses on how to use clustering with SQL Server, you can use it to provide HA capabilities for various platforms, such as Microsoft Exchange, Microsoft Internet Security and Acceleration (ISA) Server, Microsoft Identity Integration Server (MIIS), and many more.

This section puts the spotlight on the Microsoft Cluster Service (MSCS) solution included in Windows Server 2003, but it is by no means the only clustering platform available to you for your SharePoint and SQL Server environment. Other clustering solutions are available in the marketplace to provide a viable HA solution for your database environment, each offering unique functionality, options, and challenges to give you some flexibility toward how you cluster your SharePoint database. Although some products may be specific to the UNIX or Linux platforms, others, such as Symantec's Veritas Cluster Server, are completely compatible with SharePoint and SQL Server and have been successfully implemented as enterprise clustering solutions in the most demanding of situations.

The decision to highlight MSCS in this section is not meant to endorse it as a clustering product or indict its competitors. The goal is to show you how to implement a widely used clustering product for your SharePoint and SQL Server environment, not laud one product over another. It is up to you to evaluate the products in this space and determine which one is the best solution for your enterprise, infrastructure, and their requirements. Like so many other aspects of SharePoint, this is not a one-size-fits-all kind of situation.

NOTE

THE SERVER COMPONENTS OF MICROSOFT CLUSTER SERVICE

One advantage of clustering as the HA solution for your SQL Server environment is the flexibility it gives you in designing the architecture of your solution. To create a cluster, you need at least two servers; that way you can create two separate nodes within the cluster. Clustering's flexibility lies in that you can place more than one server in a node (MSCS allows up to eight servers in a node, depending on the edition of Windows Server 2003 being used) and that you are not required to have the same number of servers in each node. So if you want to create a node with one server and a node with two servers, that option is available to you. You can also have more than two nodes in your cluster. (MSCS allows up to 32 nodes in a cluster.) Each node is expected to be able to serve as the primary provider of database services for the cluster, so that if a node is taken down or suffers an outage, another node in the cluster can be brought online to continue that service with no or little downtime.

MSCS is available as an included component of Windows Server 2003's Enterprise and Datacenter editions. Microsoft is careful to state that MSCS is intended to be used as an HA solution but is not completely fault tolerant. *Fault tolerant* describes systems and solutions designed with an extremely high degree of redundancy and the ability to provide nearly instantaneous recovery times; the downside is that these systems often come with a prohibitively high price tag to match. MSCS was designed to enable systems to be highly available while using standardized, cost-effective hardware and software, rather than the specialized systems leveraged by a fault-tolerant solution. This is not to say that MSCS is necessarily a low-cost solution, but it can implement an effective HA solution MSCS at a much lower cost than a fully tricked-out solution designed to be fault tolerant.

Some aspects of clustering with MSCS are inflexible—specifically the hardware required for the servers in the cluster and how that hardware must be configured. The following list outlines the hardware and networking needs you are likely to encounter for MSCS:

- **Servers.** As mentioned previously, at least two servers must be available in order to create a database cluster with MSCS. Unlike log shipping and database mirroring, these servers cannot host databases that exist outside of the cluster. Take special care to evaluate the needs of your database environment and confirm that the hardware configuration you select can meet those needs in a clustered configuration.

With MSCS, you must also verify that your planned hardware is on the Windows Hardware Compatibility List (HCL) and approved for use in a cluster configuration. To view the HCL for Windows Server 2003, see http://www.windowsserver catalog.com/.

NOTE

- **Identical configurations.** Each server within the cluster must have an identical configuration for its RAM, CPU, system disk, and so on.
- **Redundant network hardware.** Each server within the cluster must have at least two network interface cards (NICs): one for communication with the clients accessing the database server, and one to connect to its cluster node for heartbeat and status updates.
- **Specialized network hardware.** Each server within the cluster must be able to establish fast and reliable communications with the other members of the cluster, usually via hardware such as a peripheral component interconnect (PCI) cluster interconnect.
- **Specialized storage.** Each server within the cluster must be able to access a centralized storage area network (SAN) to access the data created, stored, and updated by a cluster, such as database files. MSCS follows the "shared-nothing" model in its use of storage within a cluster, meaning that all the servers in a cluster can access the cluster's storage repository, but it is updated and managed by only one server at a time: the primary server or node in the cluster.

The maximum amount of shared storage space that a SQL Server database can use when hosted in an MSCS cluster is 2 terabytes (TB).

- **High-speed connection to SAN.** Each server must have a high-speed connection to the SAN, such as Small Computer System Interface (SCSI), Fibre Channel (FC), or Internet SCSI (iSCSI).
- **Network resources.** At a minimum, you must provide a Network Basic Input/Output System (NetBIOS) name and a unique static Internet Protocol (IP) address for the cluster, as well as static IP addresses for all the NICs used by servers within the cluster.

For more detailed information from Microsoft on the hardware requirements of MSCS, see http://support.microsoft.com/kb/259267.

CONFIGURING MICROSOFT CLUSTER SERVICE

After you have procured, installed, and configured your hardware and network solution, you are ready to start configuring a database failover cluster using SQL Server 2005 and MSCS. When you have built your servers and installed the Windows Server 2003 operating system on them, you must complete some prerequisite steps in the operating system of each server:

- **Enable Windows Cryptographic Service Provider (CSP) service.** If this service is stopped or disabled on any servers in the cluster, SQL Server's setup application reports an error.
- **Enable Task Scheduler service.** If this service is stopped or disabled on any servers in the cluster, SQL Server's setup application reports an error.
- **Install and configure Microsoft Distributed Transaction Coordinator (MSDTC).** If the database instance to be clustered is expected to run SQL Server Integration Services (SSIS), Notification Services, or Workstation Components in addition to the Database Engine, you must install and configure the MSDTC and its components on every server node in the cluster. If the SQL Server Database Engine is the only component being installed in the database instance, the MSDTC is not required.
- **Do not install antivirus.** Microsoft recommends *not* installing antivirus software on the server nodes in your cluster, because it can cause conflicts or problems with MSCS.
- **Do not compress hard drives.** The hard drive on each server node where SQL Server is to be installed must be uncompressed.
- **Mount SAN storage.** Windows Server allows additional drives or storage volumes to be mounted, including those presented via SAN storage, and requires that a drive letter be assigned to each drive when it is mounted, which limits a server to 25 mount points. You can avoid this limitation by mounting a local physical drive to a letter, such as D, and then mounting SAN volumes as directories under the D volume as directories.

Your system should now be ready for MSCS to be configured and a cluster to be created with at least two servers functioning as nodes within the cluster. Unfortunately, this chapter cannot provide a walkthrough on how to configure an MSCS cluster; the SAN storage required by the cluster is not a resource that you can easily acquire, and the available technical resources for creating the scenarios and walkthroughs in this book do not include SAN storage. The following list highlights several issues to consider as part of planning and configuring your server cluster with MSCS for it to host a SQL Server database instance.

- **Cluster service account.** Microsoft recommends the creation of a service account to be used as the identity of the MSCS service running on each server node in the cluster. This account must be a domain account granted Local Administrator rights on every server in the cluster. This account must also be able to log into your clustered SQL Server database instance with public rights to monitor its status. By default, the server's Local Administrators group has this right, but in some cases database administrators remove that access as a security measure.

■ **SQL Server service accounts.** The service accounts to be used as the identity of SQL Server's various services running on each server node in the cluster must be domain accounts, not local accounts on each server node.

■ **Turning on and off server nodes and storage.** Review Microsoft's instructions for configuring MSCS, because they contain specific information regarding when the various server nodes and storage resources should be turned on and off during a cluster's configuration.

■ **Quorum disk.** MSCS stores the cluster's configuration data and log files on a dedicated volume that must be created and configured as the cluster's quorum drive. This drive must be configured and available before the cluster is created. The quorum drive should not be used for purposes other than storing the cluster's configuration data.

■ **Cluster administrator application.** If your installed version of Windows Server 2003 includes MSCS, you can find this application in the Start menu's Administrative Tools directory. This is the tool you must use to create and manage your server clusters.

■ **Cluster name.** The name of your cluster should follow Domain Name System (DNS) naming rules. Upper- and lowercase letters, numbers, and dashes can be used in the name, which must be between 1 and 63 characters in length. The name should also be unique within its parent domain.

■ **Storage configuration options.** When running the New Server Cluster Wizard through the Cluster Administrator tool, in its Select Computer page, you are prompted to enter the name of the first computer to be added as a node in the new cluster. This page also includes an Advanced button that, when clicked, opens a dialog box where you can allow the wizard to automatically configure the cluster's SAN storage (called the Typical configuration) or to manually do it yourself (Advanced configuration). With the Typical configuration, the wizard selects all of the disks in the mounted SAN source as disks available to the cluster and creates resources within the cluster for these disks. If you select the Advanced configuration, you must use the `cluster.exe` executable to configure the cluster's SAN storage.

■ **Quorum model.** The Proposed Cluster Configuration page of the New Server Cluster Wizard includes a Quorum button that, when clicked, allows you to specify the type of quorum model that the cluster uses: Standard or Majority Node Set (MNS). The Standard, or Single Device, quorum model uses a single disk accessible by all servers in the cluster, whereas MNS creates a copy of the quorum data on each server in the cluster. The Standard model is the one you are most likely to use when clustering your SQL Server databases. MNS is intended for independent software vendors (ISVs) or independent hardware vendors (IHVs) who may want to abstract their quorum storage from the cluster service.

NOTE

MSCS also offers a Local quorum model, but it can only be used in clusters with a single server node.

- **Heartbeat.** After the cluster has been created and additional server nodes have been added to it, make sure to configure the heartbeats that the cluster uses to confirm that the network interfaces for each node are functioning properly. Without this configuration, the cluster has no way to know if a server node is available within a cluster.
- **Configuration review and testing.** Just because you have successfully created and configured your cluster does not mean your work is done. You should immediately test your cluster and confirm that it functions without error and is able to successfully failover from one node to another when the primary node is unavailable. Review all server logs to confirm that no errors are being reported within the cluster. You should establish regular tests of this process, and any other cluster functions that you find mission critical, to verify that the cluster continues to function as designed.

Now that you have created your MSCS cluster, complete with at least two server nodes within it, you are ready to install SQL Server and create your database instance in the failover cluster. As with the creation of the server cluster, due to resource limitations, it's not possible to provide you with a detailed description of the steps necessary to create your database instance successfully. However, the following is a checklist of items that you should review and evaluate while completing the process.

- **Follow SQL Server security best practices.** Configure your new instance with the same security settings and measures as nonclustered instances, while taking into account the special requirements of the cluster service account and the fact that your SQL Server service accounts must be domain accounts.
- **Speed up SQL Server install.** If you want to reduce the time it takes for the SQL Server installer to finish, preinstall the 2.0 version of the Microsoft .NET Framework on each server node in the cluster.
- **Install SQL Server on a cluster.** To install SQL Server on each server node in the cluster, simply log on to the cluster at its shared address (rather than the address of the server acting as the active node in the cluster) and run the SQL Server installer. SQL Server is built to be aware of and work in a clustered environment. The installer is able to detect the cluster environment and installs the software to each server node in the cluster you select through the wizard.
- **Validate the components to install.** If you are installing SQL Server via the GUI wizard, make sure to check the Create a SQL Server Failover Cluster check box in the Components to Install page. It appears as an indented item underneath the SQL Server Database Services check box and is not checked by

default. You must check it for the installer to install SQL Server to all the nodes within the cluster.

■ **Determine how to name your instances.** You can create MSCS failover clusters using either the default instance for the cluster or a named instance. The choice is up to you.

■ **Review your failover configuration.** Installing a single database instance in the cluster is referred to as an Active/Passive failover configuration. You can also configure multiple instances to be hosted within a single cluster, referred to as an Active/Active failover configuration. In an Active/Active configuration, you must assign each instance a different primary server within the cluster. This configuration allows for SharePoint's databases to be separated between the instances for scalability purposes.

■ **Correctly name the virtual server.** The value provided in the Virtual Server Name page of the installation wizard should be the name of the cluster, not the name of the current active node within the cluster.

■ **Install SQL Server on every node in the cluster.** In the Cluster Node Configuration page, select every server node in the cluster so that SQL Server is installed to all of them.

■ **Test your system.** When the installation wizard completes, completely test your system to confirm that the database instance is available to client connections, is not reporting any errors, and can be successfully failed over from one node to another. Establish regular tests of this process, and any other cluster functions that you find mission critical, to verify that the cluster continues to function as designed.

SharePoint and Database Clustering

Now that you have successfully created a failover cluster for a SQL Server database instance, you can consider the implications of using that instance to host SharePoint databases. One major advantage to the use of a failover cluster for your SharePoint database instance(s) is that you can use it to host all types of SharePoint databases without a special configuration (beyond what it takes to create and configure the cluster). The only step requiring specific attention is how you identity the address of the database instance when creating the SharePoint farm; you must submit the name of the cluster, not the name of the active server node for the cluster.

SharePoint views the clustered instance as it does any other database instance and during installation of your farm creates all its needed databases without error. The configuration, Central Administration content, and Search databases can be hosted in the clustered instance because the name of the cluster is used and written to these databases instead of the name of the active server node in the cluster. So in the case of an outage on the active server node, when the cluster fails over to another server node, you can still use these databases. The only outage that SharePoint experiences is during the failover itself; when the new active node comes online in the cluster, service is returned to normal without requiring updates to the SharePoint farm.

DATABASE CLUSTERING PROS

Database clustering is a powerful HA tool for SQL Server 2005 and offers several reasons why it is a viable option for your SharePoint databases. The following list covers the most compelling reasons for its use.

■ **True automatic failover.** When an active node within a cluster suffers an outage or failure, the cluster automatically fails over to another node within the cluster. Since SharePoint references the identity of the cluster and not a specific node within it, it does not need to be updated to recognize the change in database hosts.
■ **Rapid failover.** Clustering your database means that in the case of an outage your system has a drastically shorter time to return to normal service. It only takes the amount of time required for the cluster administration process to switch over to another server in the node, no manual intervention or configuration is required to implement the failover in any way.
■ **Scalable.** Since Windows Server 2003 and MSCS support up to eight server nodes within a cluster and use flexible SAN technology for storage, your clustering solution can be configured in a variety of ways to meet the needs of your system and easily expanded to grow with your system.
■ **Compatible with log shipping.** Like database mirroring, databases hosted with a cluster can be log shipping to another instance to provide even more redundancy for your data.
■ **Choice of SQL Server backup model.** Unlike in database mirroring, you can back up databases in a cluster using any backup model.

DATABASE CLUSTERING CONS

Unfortunately, database clustering also comes with some disadvantages that can prove to be a stumbling block to its implementation. Following are those disadvantages.

■ **Network requirements.** Although server nodes within a cluster can be located in separate data centers, the bandwidth requirements for heartbeats and SAN connectivity mean that most times nodes cannot be more than a few miles from one another.

- **SAN storage requirements.** The technology required to implement shared SAN storage, from both a hardware and software perspective, requires special expertise to implement, operate, and maintain. This also adds a dependency on yet another system for your SharePoint environment's overall health and well-being.
- **Costs.** In addition to the effort required to implement SAN storage, the hardware and software for the technology come at a high price. Various providers and configurations are available in the marketplace, but even the low end of the cost spectrum may prove prohibitive for your budget.
- **Fault tolerance.** Log shipping and database mirroring provide a certain level of fault tolerance because the redundant data they preserve is stored on a storage medium completely separate from that of its source. Since clustering uses a shared SAN to store the data files for your databases, an outage to that SAN configuration impacts your entire cluster and the applications that use it.

CONCLUSION

There is at least one blanket statement that can be made when it comes to SQL Server and HA: no one ever wants a database to crash or become unavailable. Unfortunately, even with the improvements that have been made in the quality, speed, and capacity of modern IT infrastructure and the software that runs on it, such events are inevitable. Hard drives fail, network connections get yanked, and lightning strikes, no matter what you do to try to prevent it. Your responsibility as an administrator is not to prevent the impossible; it is to design your system so that when disaster strikes it has minimum impact on the least number of users possible. Microsoft recognizes this, and the solutions available to enable HA for SQL Server 2005 show the effort the company has put into helping you succeed in your role.

As a SharePoint administrator, you must be even more cognizant of your system's dependency on its database provider. An outage of your company's intranet, for even an hour, can result in a drastic loss of productivity and revenue. As SharePoint evolves as an application platform, organizations are finding more and more creative uses and ways to stretch it to its limits. You need your environment and its backend databases to be as stable as possible, and SQL Server HA plays a large role in creating that stability.

Log shipping, database mirroring, and clustering offer attractive HA solutions for your database instances, but they also come with drawbacks that you need to carefully weigh and test. It is somewhat frustrating that there is no cut-and-dried solution to specific HA circumstances, but this is not an entirely bad thing. The wide range of approaches available to you and your database administrator gives you a great deal of flexibility when implementing SQL Server HA for your

SharePoint environment, not only in how you configure a specific procedure but also because you have the ability to combine procedures to overcome their individual deficiencies.

Regardless of how you make your SQL Server databases highly available, you should seriously reflect on the possibility of implementing them in your environment. If the content in your SharePoint farm is business critical, irreplaceable, or unique, you should do everything you can to protect it. If your users depend on your SharePoint sites to always be available and cannot perform their work without SharePoint, you need to make sure it is online when they need it.

Now that you have SQL Server HA under your belt, see if you can confidently answer the following questions about SQL Server HA. You can find the answers to these questions in Appendix B, "Chapter Review Q&A," on the book's Web site at http://www.courseptr.com/downloads.

1. How many servers can receive a single database's transaction logs via log shipping?
2. What steps do you need to take to configure a read-only SharePoint farm based on log-shipped databases?
3. What are the hardware requirements of database mirroring?
4. What resources must you configure to enable automatic failover of a mirrored database?
5. Can you name the editions of Windows Server 2003 that include MSCS?
6. What SharePoint components can you include in a database instance hosted on a failover cluster?

10 Windows Server 2003 Backup and Restore

In This Chapter

- What to Back Up
- How to Back Up Windows Server 2003 and Its Components
- How to Restore Windows Server 2003 and Its Components

By now you should be comfortable with the idea of backing up and restoring your SharePoint and SQL Server 2005 platforms and have an understanding of the tools and techniques that you can use to complete those operations. While these items probably make up some of the most important information you need to get from this reference guide, they are not the only things that you need for a complete backup and restore strategy. There is something just as crucial to the long-term well-being of your SharePoint farm as SharePoint and the SQL Server databases its content resides in: the operating system that SharePoint runs upon and the files stored in a server running it—specifically Windows Server 2003.

Every server in your SharePoint farm, regardless of whether it is a Web frontend, indexer, or database host, shares one base attribute: its operating system must be an edition of Windows Server. SharePoint and SQL Server cannot be installed on UNIX, any of the many Linux distributions available, Mac OS, or any other non-Microsoft operating system. SharePoint is not supported on Microsoft's client operating systems, Windows XP or Vista, and on the database side of things only the Express Edition of SQL Server 2005 is supported. Microsoft supports SharePoint when it is installed on editions of Windows Server 2003 Service Pack (SP) 1 or later.

It is supported on Windows Server 2008 as long as SharePoint's SP1 updates have been applied. SQL Server 2005 is supported on editions of Windows Server 2000 SP4, Windows Server 2003 SP1 or later, and Windows Server 2008 if SQL Server's SP2 updates have been applied.

Thanks to the rise in popularity and functionality of virtualization products such as Microsoft's Virtual PC and VMware's Workstation, it is possible to install SharePoint on a Windows Server 2003 virtual machine (VM) hosted within Windows XP or Vista. This is a configuration commonly used by SharePoint developers so they can access SharePoint's DLL files within Visual Studio to use within their SharePoint Web parts and applications. VMs like this are also useful for administrators to test updates, configurations, and installs. Hybrid solutions have also been developed to enable the installation of Windows SharePoint Services v3 (WSS) on client Windows operating systems, but Microsoft does not support these solutions, and you should carefully research them before implementing them.

This chapter focuses specifically on the SharePoint-specific elements of your farm in the Windows Server operating system that are not covered by SharePoint or SQL Server's built-in backup and restore tool sets. Even if you are backing up your farm in the Central Administration site or your content databases through SQL Server, if you experience a catastrophic event, you must be prepared to recover or re-create several items outside of these tools. In the coming pages, you will see what elements outside of SharePoint you must back up, examine some of the tools available for backing them up, and learn how to restore them as needed.

Although SQL Server 2005 also has a strong dependency on its operating system and stores crucial configuration data and files in it, the information in this chapter focuses specifically on items and elements within Windows Server 2003 as they relate to SharePoint. To understand the similar types of items that may need to be backed up to fully restore a SQL Server database instance, you should consult your organization's database administrators (DBAs) or a resource similar to this book geared toward SQL Server 2005.

The visual examples provided in this chapter were generated in a testing environment using the following platforms and components. Depending on how your environment is configured, your experiences may vary slightly.

- **Operating system.** Microsoft Windows Server 2003 R2 Enterprise Edition SP2
- **Microsoft .NET Framework.** Versions 1.1, 2.0 SP1, 3.0 SP1, and 3.5
- **Database.** Microsoft SQL Server 2005 Developer Edition SP2
- **Web server.** Microsoft Internet Information Services (IIS) 6.0
- **SharePoint.** Microsoft Office SharePoint Server (MOSS) 2007 Enterprise Edition

In February 2008, Microsoft released its latest edition of the Windows Server operating system: Windows Server 2008. Although SharePoint (with SP1 applied) is supported on Windows Server 2008, this has only been the case since the release of that service pack update and, like SQL Server 2008, the SharePoint community is just beginning to understand how the two platforms can work together. Windows Server 2008 offers a range of new features and impressive improvements, such as IIS 7, that definitely make it worth consideration for your SharePoint environment, but the fact of the matter is that most enterprises are not quick to embrace a major operating system release such as Windows Server 2008 in a production environment without extensive testing of functionality and stability. Due to this fact, Windows Server 2008 is not included in this book.

WHAT TO BACK UP

Like any other application that you can install on a server running Windows Server 2003, SharePoint places numerous files and data crucial to its operation in the file system of each server that hosts it. As Chapter 8, "SQL Server 2005 Backup and Restore," mentions, SharePoint is a unique application in that it depends on so many systems and applications to function properly. Beyond its heavy reliance on its SQL Server databases, SharePoint stores key items throughout a server that you need to be able to restore if your server suffers an outage.

The difficult thing about this need is that these key items reside in a variety of locations and states inside the Windows Server 2003 operating system. Some of them are files in SharePoint's key folder within the server's file system. Another example is the configuration data for the various Web sites created to host SharePoint content in the Web server provided with Windows Server 2003, IIS, which is stored in a repository referred to as the IIS metabase. Even the Windows Registry, one of the most important elements of any Windows Server 2003 installation, contains important SharePoint data that you may need to preserve in case of a disaster.

SHAREPOINT'S "12 HIVE"

Most applications, when installed in Windows Server 2003, create a directory for the application within the Program Files directory (this directory is the location pointed at by the %PROGRAMFILES%PATH variable) in the server's system drive (typically the C: drive). See Figure 10.1 for an example. This directory usually contains the executables, libraries, and configuration files necessary for the application to run on the server. SharePoint follows this convention, but only to a point. After you install SharePoint, you should see a directory named Microsoft Office Servers within the Program Files directory. An examination of its contents reveals several files necessary to run SharePoint. Interestingly, in most cases you don't need to specifically back up this directory; the best way to restore this directory is either by doing a a full server backup or by completely reinstalling SharePoint from scratch.

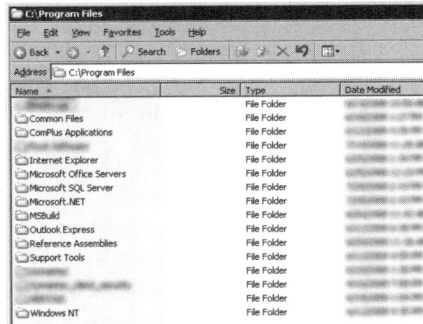

FIGURE 10.1 The Program Files directory in a Windows Server 2003 installation hosting MOSS.

Where SharePoint strays from the conventional approach to the Program Files directory is in its use of a directory commonly referred to as the *12 Hive*. The 12 Hive is also located within the Program Files directory, but it is nested within several other folders that are sometimes leveraged by other Microsoft applications. You can find it at the following path (see Figure 10.2):

```
%COMMONPROGRAMFILES%\Microsoft Shared\Web Server Extensions\12\
```

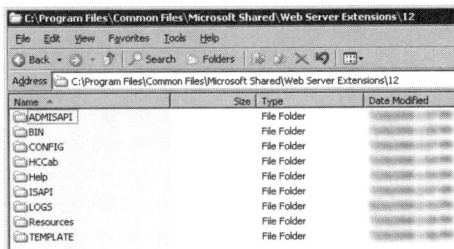

FIGURE 10.2 The SharePoint 12 Hive directory in a Windows Server 2003 installation.

So what is in the 12 Hive? The short answer is "Quite a bit." The directory contains several more applications and libraries crucial to SharePoint's operation: administrative tools like STSADM.exe, configuration data, diagnostic logs, and all the files that are used to create a consistent user interface (UI) and user experience

(UX) for the content served by SharePoint. This last item is the most important item to remember from a disaster recovery perspective, because the templates, images, and styles are the most likely targets for customization in your SharePoint environment, and you must be able to restore these customizations when you restore your farm. You have the same need when it comes to any custom applications, Web parts, or other pieces of code that you may deploy to enhance, extend, or modify the functionality of your SharePoint environment. In most cases, when you implement any of these types of changes, you are updating a file or directory within the 12 Hive, making its stability and availability a priority for you so you can restore your environment to its previous state in the case of a disaster.

The 12 Hive has not always been known as such. In Windows SharePoint Services (WSS) v2 and SharePoint Portal Server (SPS) 2003, the directory was labeled as 6.0 rather than 12.0 and was referred to as the 6 Hive or the 60 Hive. With WSS v3 and MOSS 2007, the folder was updated to 12.0 in reference to SharePoint's latest release being included as part of the overall Office platform, which was in its twelfth release even though it was labeled as Office 2007. The next release of SharePoint is tentatively also included in the next revision of the Office platform, Office 14. (The number 13 is considered to be unlucky in the United State, so it was skipped.)

It isn't necessary to back up the entire 12 Hive directory, but you may find that it is the easiest route to take. If you want to narrow the scope of your backup activities for the 12 Hive, it is vital that you maintain accurate records of what items have been deployed to this directory, such as master pages, site definitions, style sheets, language packs, SharePoint Features, or any other updates that may have been applied via a SharePoint solution package. Many of these updates may reside in the TEMPLATE directory within the 12 Hive, but it can depend on how they have been configured to modify the 12 Hive. In general, you should make every effort to understand how each update you make to your SharePoint farm impacts your servers and the 12 Hive specifically, but this is especially important if you are backing up individual items or directories within the 12 Hive.

Before backing up the 12 Hive, make sure to check how much space it is using on the server's file system, and confirm that you have adequate space available to store its backup. This is important to do in general, but the 12 Hive uses more space on the hard drive of your server than you might expect. Testing shows that the directory can use over 700MB of space with a fresh install of MOSS 2007 in Windows Server 2003, and this number only goes up as you add master pages, features, site definitions, and other custom components to the directory over time. SharePoint also, by default, stores log files in this directory, which can contribute to the space it uses over time.

TIP

By default, SharePoint's installation and configuration applications tend to set up storage locations throughout your server's file system for a variety of logs, search indices, and other configuration files. An easy way to improve the scope and accuracy of your Windows Server file backups is to configure SharePoint to store all these files in similar and/or nearby locations to one another. By configuring SharePoint to store your environment's Unified Logging Service (ULS) logs, usage analysis logs, search indices, content deployment files, etc., within unique folders under a single umbrella directory, all of your files are stored in a single location that can be specifically targeted for backup.

IIS

WSS v2 and SPS 2003, the editions of SharePoint's previous release, stored all the configuration information about a SharePoint site's Web server configurations in the IIS 6 metabase of the servers hosting the site. That situation has changed somewhat in WSS v3 and MOSS 2007. SharePoint now inserts data about a site's configuration in IIS into its configuration database, such as its host headers, enabled port numbers, and authentication settings. This allows SharePoint to retain that data, in case a Web server is lost to an outage, but it is important to understand that this does not encompass all the data needed to re-create your Web site in IIS. Some items, such as Secure Socket Layer (SSL) certificates and Internet Protocol (IP) bindings, are stored outside of the SharePoint configuration database, and you need to take specific steps to ensure that they are backed up properly.

NOTE

IIS version 6.0 is the Web server included by default with Windows Server 2003. IIS 7.0 was introduced as part of Windows Server 2008 and offers several enhancements over version 6.0, including how the metabase is configured and stored. Keep in mind that this chapter only covers IIS 6; the practices and procedures discussed here may not be directly relevant to how IIS 7 uses and manages its metabase.

The Metabase

The IIS 6 metabase is a database designed to store Web site configuration data for IIS, using two XML files: `MetaBase.xml` and `MBSchema.xml`. It is stored at the following path within Windows Server 2003:

```
%SystemRoot%\system32\inetsrv\
```

These two files are used to store configuration data for each site hosted by IIS on the server, regardless of whether or not it is hosting a SharePoint site. They can be modified manually via a text editor, such as Notepad.exe, but Microsoft does not recommend that practice. Approved methods for modifying the configuration of a Web site in the IIS metabase include the IIS Manager snap-in for the Microsoft Management Console, IIS's optional Web-based administration console, and several Application Programming Interfaces (APIs) that expose the metabase to custom code.

It is not possible to directly edit the IIS metabase while IIS is running unless the Enable Direct Metabase Edit check box has been checked within the Web server's Properties dialog in the IIS Manager application.

Webroots

Most Web sites that IIS hosts install all their static content and application code within a site-specific directory in an area in the server's file system known as the IIS Webroot. The default location for the IIS Webroot is `C:\inetpub\wwwroot`, but it may be different in your environment depending on your configuration. SharePoint is somewhat different from most .NET Web sites in its usage of the IIS site directory: the content files and application code used to generate its sites are found in the 12 Hive instead. But several files important to your SharePoint environment are still stored in the directory associated with your SharePoint site in IIS, such as `web.config` files, Web part `.dwp` and `.webpart` files, dynamic link library (DLL) files, and much more. These files are not backed up by SharePoint or SQL Server's backup tools and need to be preserved in case of a disaster.

Secure Socket Layer Certificates

IIS uses SSL certificates to allow the client browser to verify that the Web server is who it says it is. Certificates are used to confirm the identity of the Web server as transmissions travel between the server and the client and can be used to encrypt those transmissions so they cannot be intercepted and used by someone other than their intended recipient. SSL certificates are often issued by certificate providers, who validate that the certificate is being issued to an entity associated with the Web site. Organizations can also issue self-signed certificates, which are not validated by a neutral third party and require client browsers to take additional steps to accept them, as well as configure a Domain Certificate Authority to authorize and validate self-signed certificates throughout the enterprise. If your environment is using SSL to encrypt and secure its SharePoint sites, these certificates are stored on the file system of your Web servers. If the server is lost, these files must either be restored from a backup or regenerated by the certificate's provider to re-enable SSL encryption for your SharePoint site.

THE GLOBAL ASSEMBLY CACHE

In every server running Windows Server 2003, there is a repository for DLLs known as the global assembly cache (GAC). DLLs are a collection of code functions, processes, and methods that have been compiled into a library file and can be accessed by applications to run the functionality provided by its contents without duplicating it inside the applications. Microsoft also provides a framework for implementing code access security (CAS), where applications and DLLs can be limited to access only certain functionality and resources in a host server, so that critical operations on the server are not affected by malicious code. The GAC provides a way to work around the restrictions that CAS imposes; all DLLs placed in the server's GAC are trusted by applications and code throughout the server, including SharePoint. SharePoint applications throughout your server trust any DLLs installed in the GAC that are accompanied by `<SafeControls>` entries in the application's `web.config` file. Use of the GAC also allows DLLs to be easily reused by multiple applications and provides version management and control features not found in ASP.NET's `bin`. Microsoft recommends following a CAS policy whenever possible, but sometimes limitations imposed by the resources that an application must access make that untenable. Regardless of the reason, if any Web parts or other components within your SharePoint farm install DLLs into your server's GAC, you must back them up.

CUSTOM CODE

Two common locations for custom code to be installed—the IIS Webroot directory of your SharePoint site and the GAC—have already been covered, but it is completely possible to install custom code, SharePoint components, and third-party tools anywhere in your server's file system that you or the developer of these items may see fit. Because these items are not likely to be included in SharePoint or SQL Server backups, you must back them up on your own. It is important to note the installation location of any application or component that you install on your SharePoint server and make sure that you are able to either back up it and its configuration data or reinstall it as needed as a part of your disaster recovery process.

AUTHENTICATION PROVIDERS

With the release of WSS v3 and MOSS 2007, Microsoft expanded the security model of SharePoint beyond its previous dependency on Active Directory so that a variety of systems can now be used to authenticate and authorize users when they access your SharePoint system. One drawback to this new authentication provider model is the fact that it introduces an additional dependency to your system, often on a component that exists outside of SharePoint. It is possible to use providers such as ASP.NET's Forms-Based Authentication (FBA), Windows CardSpace, Lightweight

Directory Access Protocol (LDAP), and many other options to allow users to log in and access your SharePoint server. But if your SharePoint environment goes down and you have to restore it from backup, your users are not going to be able to access it unless you also restore your authentication provider and its supporting infrastructure. When you configure your farm's authentication provider(s), make sure to note its configuration and what parts of it need to be backed up.

WINDOWS REGISTRY

The Windows Registry is a repository used to store configuration data for Windows Server 2003, its hardware, and the software installed on it. For example, any changes made to a server's networking configuration via the Control Panel are stored in the Registry. SharePoint uses several entries within the Registry, and often any custom components installed to extend, enhance, or modify SharePoint's functionality create entries in the Registry. You need to preserve these values to restore the server's configuration to its previous state.

SharePoint development and deployment best practices strongly recommend that when deploying custom updates to your SharePoint environment, it is best to use SharePoint Solution Packages (.wsp files) or MSI installer packages. Several of the items in this section, such as custom entries in IIS's web.config *files, DLLs in the GAC or ASP.NET's bin directories, custom code, authentication providers, and registry updates, can, and mostly likely should, be deployed via* .wsp *or* .msi *packages. This puts all the package's updates into a single file that can be backed up and redeployed as needed, rather than trying to locate and restore each piece of your package on its own.*

HOW TO BACK UP WINDOWS SERVER 2003 AND ITS COMPONENTS

If you or your organization already has a strategy, procedures, or tools in place to back up your servers running Windows Server 2003, you probably don't need the information in this section. You already have the means with which you can back up the important elements of your SharePoint farm that reside outside the reach of SharePoint's backup tools. It's important to confirm that your backup strategy includes the items listed in the previous pages and to verify via testing that it works as it should, but you shouldn't need to consider another backup solution unless you aren't happy with your current solution.

It's important to recognize the need for backing up your Windows Server 2003 servers; if you don't currently have a backup plan, you should seriously consider implementing one for your entire organization's servers, not just your SharePoint resources. The following pages outline how to create a server backup using some of the tools included with Windows Server 2003, as well as how to individually back up some of the components previously mentioned that SharePoint depends on for key functionality. As you will see, a wide variety of options are available to you to back up these components. You need to examine your system's needs and requirements and find the solution that is right for you. If you're interested in considering third-party backup and restore tools for Windows Server 2003, be sure to look at Appendix A, "Third-Party Backup and Restore Tools," on the book's Web site at http://www.courseptr.com/downloads.

BUILT-IN TOOLS

The Windows Server 2003 operating system includes several tools that you can use to back up a server, two of which are covered in this chapter: the Windows Backup Utility and compressed folders. The first, Windows Backup Utility, allows you to back up large sections of your server, such as a drive, volume, or the entire server, while compressed folders allow you back up smaller groups of files or data, such as an IIS Webroot.

The Windows Backup Utility

The following steps walk you through the process necessary to back up an item in Windows Server 2003 through the Windows Backup Utility tool. They are designed to give you an idea of what you need to consider when backing up items in your server (or the entire server) and how to go about the process.

1. Log on to the server containing the items you want to back up via a Remote Desktop Connection (RDC) as an administrator.
2. Click the Start button and navigate to Programs, Accessories, System Tools, Backup.
3. This opens the Backup or Restore Wizard, as shown in Figure 10.3. To open the Backup Utility tool, click the Advanced Mode link. You can also back up your server by following the steps of the wizard without opening the Advanced Mode. The outcome is similar to what is described here, but Advanced Mode offers more configuration tools and options for your backup.
4. The Backup Utility opens, displaying a Welcome tab (see Figure 10.4) next to three other tabs for Backup, Restore and Manage Media, and Schedule Jobs. The Welcome tab contains three buttons: Backup Wizard (Advanced), Restore Wizard (Advanced), and Automated System Recovery Wizard. Click the Backup tab to proceed with the backup.

FIGURE 10.3 The Welcome screen of the Backup or Restore Wizard.

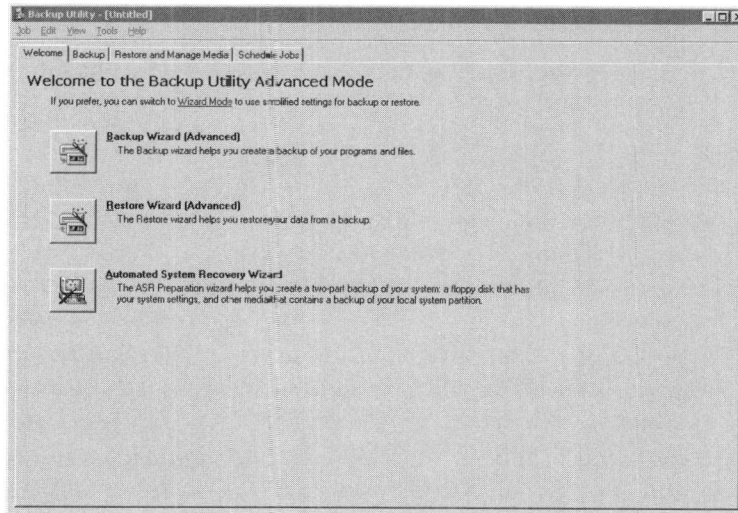

FIGURE 10.4 The Welcome tab of the Windows Backup Utility.

5. The Backup tab opens, with the contents of your server's file system displayed in tree view in the left pane, as shown in Figure 10.5. The right pane contains icons for your server's My Computer and My Network Places items, and the lower section of the tab has an area where you can set the destination for the backup file and a Start Backup button. Navigate through the left tree view to find the drive, folder, or file you want to back up, and then click the check box to the left of its name to select it.

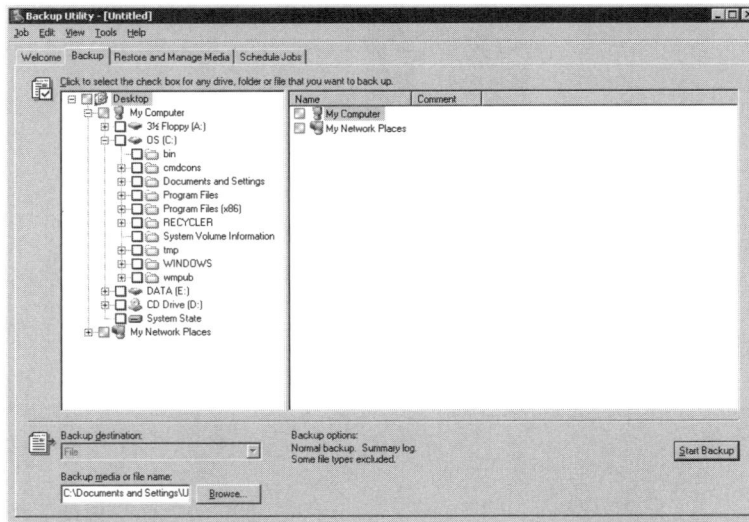

FIGURE 10.5 The Backup tab of the Windows Backup Utility.

System State data within Windows Server 2003 contains, among other things, the Windows Registry, the Active Directory service database, the IIS metabase, and system files that are protected by Windows File Protection. The actual files that make up the System State on your server depend on the version of the operating system that is installed and how it has been configured. Selecting to back up a server's System State selects all the items within it; you cannot pick and chose which items within the System State you want included. Likewise, when restoring System State from a backup, the entire System State is updated from the backup. Unfortunately, System State does not usually encompass every configuration item you need backed up within your server, Microsoft actually recommends that you back up all boot and system disk volumes in addition to the server's System State.

6. After you have selected the item (or items) that you want to back up, review the location displayed in the Backup Media or File Name text field at the bottom of the window. If the location listed there is not where you want the backup file for this operation stored, either update the path in the field or click the Browse button to open a window where you can select the proper storage location. If your server has a tape storage device attached to it, the Backup Destination drop-down menu is enabled, and you can select the Tape option from the menu. If you don't have a tape device attached to your server, the Backup Destination menu is disabled, and the File option is your only choice.

If possible, you should strive to store your backups on storage media physically separate from your server, which is one reason why tape and Network-Attached Storage (NAS) solutions are so commonly used as backup media. If your server suffers an outage, there's a good chance that its hard drives could be affected by the outage, and if your backups are stored on those hard drives, they may not be accessible, which completely defeats the purpose of making the backups in the first place. Storing your backups separately from your server increases the odds that you can use them to restore your system successfully in case of a disaster.

7. After choosing the storage location for the backup file, click the Start Backup button to initiate the backup process.

8. The tool opens the Backup Job Information window (see Figure 10.6), where you can start the backup operation or further configure its options before proceeding. You may enter a description for the backup in the Backup Description field, determine if the backup file to be created overwrites any existing backup files in the target storage location or appends its updates to the end of existing files in the If the Media Already Contains Backups section, or update the If the Media Is Overwritten, Use This Label to Identity the Media text field with a desired value. Click the Start Backup button to begin the backup operation.

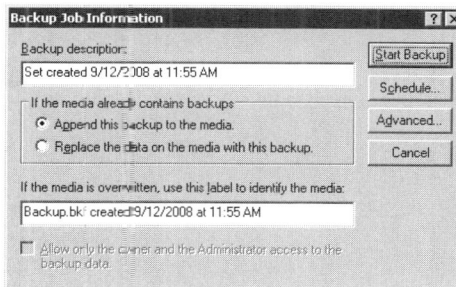

FIGURE 10.6 The Backup Job Information dialog box.

9. After the backup operation starts, the tool displays the Backup Progress window with an initial status message stating `Preparing to backup using shadow copy`, as Figure 10.7 shows. Prior to kicking off the backup, the Windows Backup Utility performs a crawl of the items selected for backup to determine how much data is to be included and how long the backup should take. The tool then proceeds to back up your selected target. Clicking the Cancel button rolls back the operation and does not create a backup file in the target storage directory.

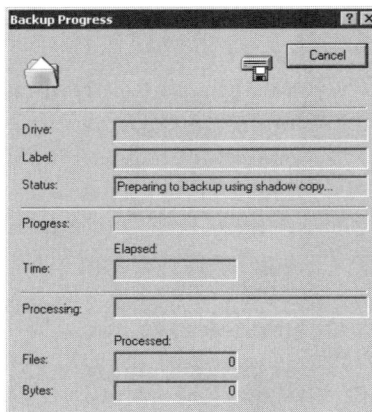

FIGURE 10.7 The Backup Progress window at the start of a backup operation.

10. When the operation completes, the Backup Progress window is updated with a Status of Completed, the Cancel button is now the Close button, and a Report button is displayed below the Close button (see Figure 10.8). Click the Report button to open the log for the backup operation.

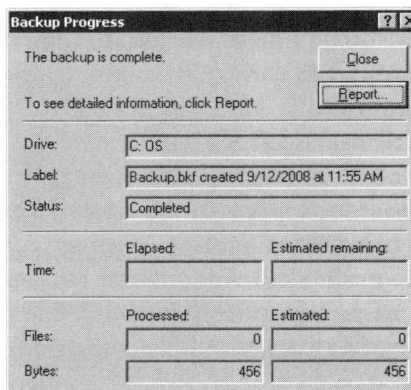

FIGURE 10.8 The Backup Progress window after a successfully completed backup operation.

11. Clicking the Report button causes a new Notepad.exe window to be opened, displaying the backup operation's log file, shown in Figure 10.9. If you wish, you can review the contents of the log file and then close the Notepad.exe window to return to the Backup Progress window. Click the Close button to complete the backup operation and return to the Backup Utility window.

FIGURE 10.9 A backup operation's log file displayed in Notepad.exe.

As you may have noticed, the Backup Job Information dialog box (see Figure 10.6) also has two buttons that weren't mentioned while creating that backup: Schedule and Advanced These buttons provide additional options for configuring your backup, so it's a good idea to take a quick look at them before moving on.

If you click the Schedule button from the Backup Job Information window, the Backup Utility first displays a message box stating that you must save your backup selections before scheduling the backup and then asks if you want to do so (see Figure 10.10). Click the Yes button to open a dialog box to save the backup's settings to the server's file system.

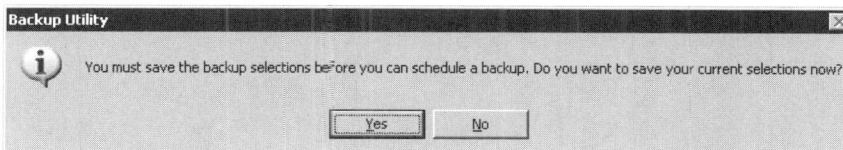

FIGURE 10.10 If you haven't saved the settings for your requested backup operation prior to scheduling it, you're prompted by the tool to do so.

After you save the settings, the tool opens the Scheduled Job Options dialog box (see Figure 10.11). In the Schedule Data tab, enter a name for the scheduled backup job in the Job Name text box, and click the Properties button to configure a schedule for the job.

This opens the Schedule Job dialog box (as shown in Figure 10.12), allowing you to schedule the job to run at a date and time somewhere in the future. The options, selections, and settings in this window are identical to those of the Windows Scheduled Task utility also available from the Start menu at Programs, Accessories, System Tools, Backup. Configure the backup operation to run according to your requirements, and click OK to save your configuration settings.

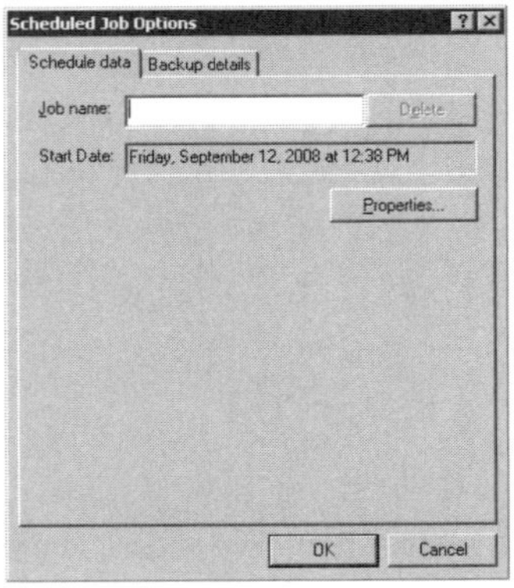

FIGURE 10.11 The Scheduled Job Options dialog box.

As part of the Scheduled Task configuration process, you are required to provide an account identity that is used to run the task. Although this can be a local account, you should seriously consider using a domain service account specifically tasked with backup operations like this, so that you can assign it common rights across multiple servers and centralize access and privileges for this and other backup operations.

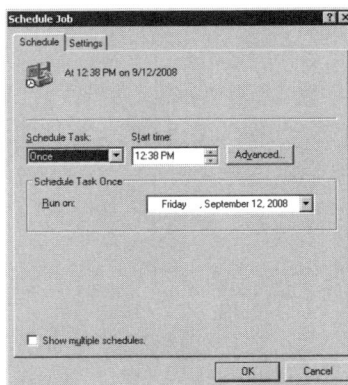

FIGURE 10.12 The Schedule Job dialog box.

After you have returned to the Backup Job Information window, the other way you can continue to configure your backup operation is via the Advanced button. Clicking the Advanced button opens the Advanced Backup Options dialog box, shown in Figure 10.13. Here you can opt to have the operation back up items stored in remote storage devices (such as tape drives), verify the backed up data after the operation has finished, compress the backup file, or back up system-protected files with System State information.

In the Backup Type drop-down menu, you can select one of the following options:

- **Normal.** This option backs up all selected files, folders, or drives and marks them as backed up for future reference.
- **Copy.** This option backs up all selected files, folders, or drives but does not mark them as backed up.
- **Incremental.** The Incremental option only backs up the selected items if they were created or modified since their last backup and marks them as backed up for future reference.
- **Differential.** The Differential option only backs up the selected items if they were created or modified since their last backup but does not mark them as backed up.
- **Daily.** The Daily option only backs up the selected items if they were created or modified on the current date.

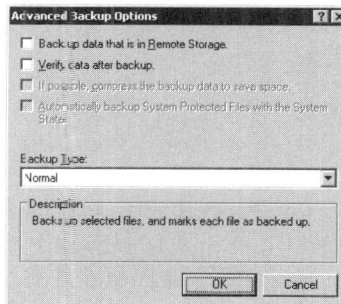

FIGURE 10.13 The Advanced Backup Options window.

Compressed Folders

Compressed folders, often referred to as *zipped* folders, allow users to create an archival file with a .zip extension based on the contents of a target folder. Compressed files contain compressed copies of the original files in the target folder; those original files are not modified or affected by the act of creating a compressed folder. This functionality is built into Windows Server 2003 and is similar to that of third-party tools such as WinZip or PKZIP. Compressed folders are normally created manually by users, but they can also be generated automatically through the use of the Scheduled Task Utility.

To create a compressed folder, right-click in the folder you want to create the compressed folder in and select the New, Compressed (zipped) Folder option from the menu. This action creates an empty compressed folder that you can now drag or copy items into to be compressed. The target items are not moved into the compressed folder; instead, Windows creates a copy of that file and compresses it.

You can also right-click on a file or folder that you want to compress and select the Send To, Compressed (zipped) Folder option from the menu, which creates a compressed folder prepopulated with the contents of the target file or folder. If you seeded the new compressed folder with a folder, it has the same name as the original folder but an extension of .zip to differentiate it from the original folder.

Although compressed folders offer benefits such as ease of use and creation of smaller backup packages, they are not really a viable long-term solution for backing up your Windows Server 2003 servers or their contents. Compressed folders were intended to be a way to quickly shrink files and folders to a manageable size and structure for transport, not a long-term disaster recovery option. They don't offer any built-in scheduling tools, meaning that custom scripting is required to properly use the tool with the Scheduled Jobs utility. They also don't recognize specialized tape backup devices, meaning that additional tools or scripts must be used to transfer them to tape so they're stored remotely from the item that they back up. Compressed folders provide great flexibility and are a good short-term solution for backing up crucial files, but they aren't necessarily a good long-term piece of a comprehensive disaster recovery approach.

IIS

Both the Windows Backup Utility and compressed folders can be used to back up the Webroot folders for the Web sites hosted within the IIS Web server on your Windows Server, but it may not make sense to use those tools for other crucial elements of IIS, like the metabase and SSL Certificates. If you're backing up the entire file system of your Windows Server 2003 installation, there's no need to take additional steps to back up these items, but if you're only preserving select items in the server, the better approach is to take advantage of the specialized tools available to back up the IIS metabase and SSL certificates.

The IIS Metabase

You can back up the IIS metabase in two different ways: via the IIS Manager snap-in for the Microsoft Management Console or the iisback.vbs script file included with IIS 6.

The following steps outline how to back up the metabase via IIS Manager.

1. Open the IIS Manager management snap-in on the target server and right-click on the local computer object in the left pane of the console.
2. From the All Tasks menu option, select the Backup/Restore Configuration option.
3. This opens the Configuration Backup/Restore dialog box (see Figure 10.14). Click the Create Backup button to open the Configuration Backup dialog box.

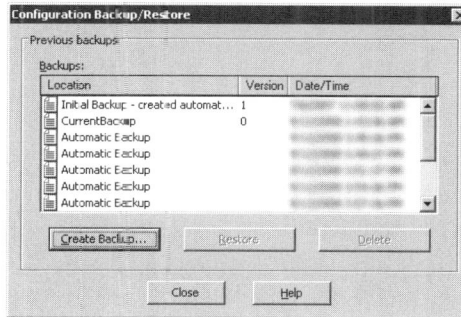

FIGURE 10.14 IIS Manager's tool to back up and restore the metabase: the Backup/Restore Configuration dialog box.

4. In the Configuration Backup dialog box (see Figure 10.15), enter the name of the file to be used as the IIS metabase backup in the Configuration Backup Name text field. If you want to encrypt the backup, click the Encrypt Backup Using Password check box and enter twice the password used to secure the backup in the associated text fields. Click OK to create the backup for the IIS metabase.

FIGURE 10.15 In the Configuration Backup window, enter a name for the backup, which you can encrypt with a password if desired.

Don't specify a file path or extension for the backup of the IIS metabase through the IIS Manager console. The tool reports an error stating that an invalid character is being used in the backup's name if you attempt this. Backups are automatically stored in the \WINDOWS\system32\inetsrv\MetaBack *directory on your server's system drive. The tool actually creates two backup files in this directory using the supplied name: one with an extension of* .md0 *(the metabase itself) and one with an extension of* .sc0 *(the metabase's schema).*

The following steps outline how to back up the metabase via the IISback.vbs script.

1. Open a Windows Command Shell window on the server hosting the IIS metabase you want to back up.
2. Change your directory to the \WINDOWS\system32 directory on your server's system drive.
3. Enter the following command and press Enter. (See Figure 10.16 for an example.)

```
Cscript iisback.vbs /backup /b <BackupName>
```

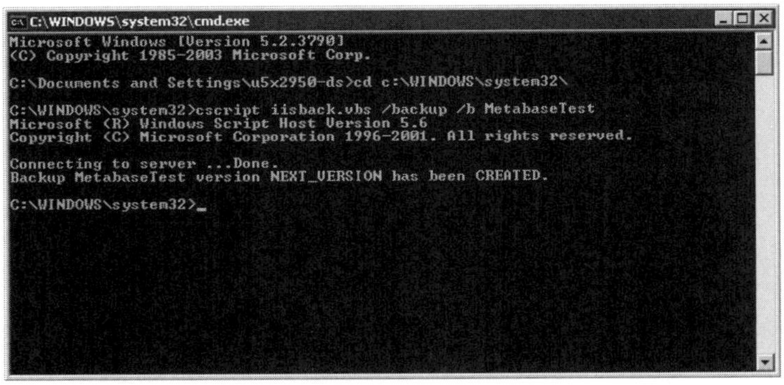

FIGURE 10.16 An example showing the use of the IISback.vbs script to back up the IIS metabase.

IISback.vbs is an administrative script included with IIS. Written in VBScript, it was specifically intended to back up and restore the IIS metabase. The preceding cscript command is required in the Windows Command Shell to be able to execute the script. The script also offers several other parameters, allowing it to be configured to apply a password to the backup or against a remote server. To view all the options for the script, run the following command in the Windows Command Shell:

```
Cscript iisback.vbs /?
```

Like the IIS Manager console, it isn't possible to specify the location of the backup file created by the script; it is also created in the \WINDOWS\system32\ inetsrv\MetaBack directory on your server's system drive.

SSL Certificates

To back up an SSL certificate that's installed on your server, you can export it with one of two approaches: via the Certificate Manager snap-in for the Microsoft Management console or through the IIS Manager. Follow these steps to export an SSL certificate through the IIS manager:

1. On the server hosting the Web site using the target SSL certificate, open IIS Manager and right-click on the Web site using the SSL certificate you want to back up. Select the Properties option from the menu to continue.
2. When the Properties window opens, click the Directory Security tab (see Figure 10.17). When the tab is displayed, click the Server Certificate button in the Secure Communications section to open the Web Server Certificate Wizard.

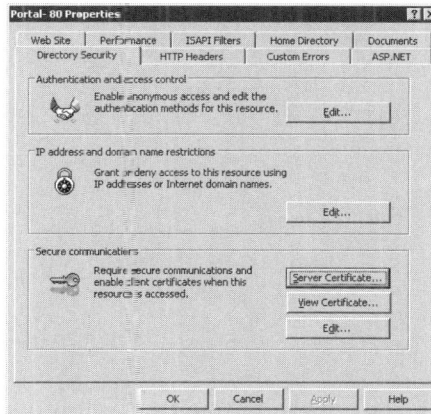

FIGURE 10.17 The Directory Security tab of a Web site's Properties in IIS Manager.

3. Click the Next button in the Welcome page of the Web Server Certificate Wizard (see Figure 10.18) to proceed.
4. Select the option button next to Export the Current Certificate to a .PFX File in the Modify the Current Certificate Assignment page (see Figure 10.19), and click the Next button to continue.
5. Enter a name for the exported certificate file in the Path and File Name text field of the Export Certificate page (see Figure 10.20), and click the Next button to continue. To change the storage location of the file, click the Browse button to select the new target location.

FIGURE 10.18 The Welcome page of the Web Server Certificate Wizard.

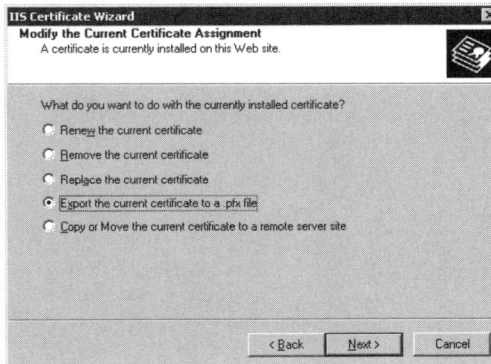

FIGURE 10.19 The Modify the Current Certificate Assignment page of the Web Server Certificate Wizard.

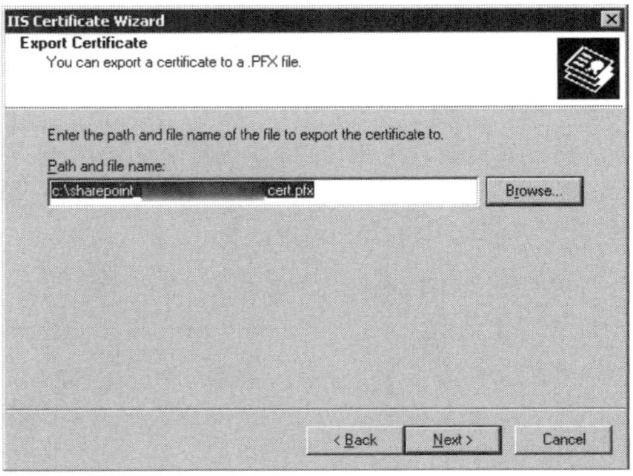

FIGURE 10.20 The Export Certificate page of the Web Server Certificate Wizard.

6. Enter a password and confirm it in the Certificate Password page (see Figure 10.21). This password is used to encrypt the exported certificate file. Make sure to record the password in a secure and safe location that is accessible to anyone who may need to import this certificate in the future. Click the Next button to continue.

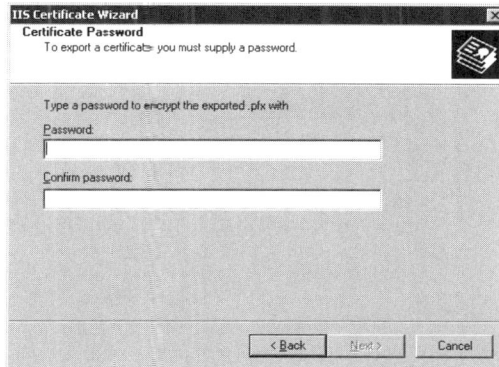

FIGURE 10.21 The Certificate Password page of the Web Server Certificate Wizard.

7. Review the information in the Certificate Summary page (see Figure 10.22) and click the Next button to export the certificate.

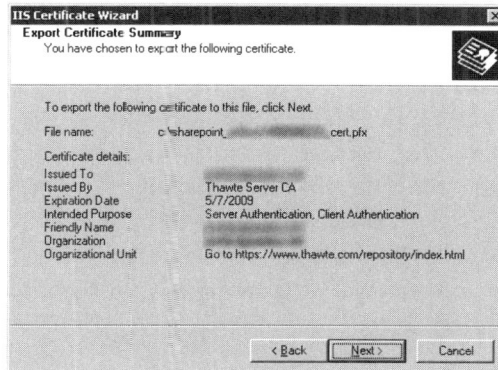

FIGURE 10.22 The Certificate Summary page of the Web Server Certificate Wizard.

8. If the certificate was successfully exported, the wizard displays a dialog box to report its status (see Figure 10.23). Click the OK button to return to the Web site's Properties window.

FIGURE 10.23 The Web Server Certificate Wizard reporting a successful export of the SSL certificate.

BACKING UP THE WINDOWS REGISTRY

You can back up the Windows Registry via the Windows Backup Utility. You can also back up the Registry via the Registry Editor provided with Windows Server 2003, REGEDIT.exe. You can save the full Registry or individual subkeys, keys, or whole subtrees by saving the selected components as files on your computer, backup media, or shared network drives. Simply open REGEDIT.exe, select the Registry components you want to back up, and select the Export option from the File menu. The Export Registry File dialog box opens to allow you to select the location you want to export the components into and provide a name for the export file. Click the Save button to save the exported Registry components to the target location and complete the export process.

As an alternative, backing up a server's System State with the Windows Backup Utility, as described earlier in this chapter, automatically includes the Windows Registry in the backup. The main drawback to this approach is that the backup is required to also then include the other configuration pieces of the System State, which you may not want to overwrite in the event the backup is used to restore the Windows Registry.

HOW TO RESTORE WINDOWS SERVER 2003 AND ITS COMPONENTS

As you have by now noticed in previous chapters, it is not enough to know how to back up a resource in your SharePoint environment or to actually back it up. You also have to know how to put that backup to use and be able to restore it into your environment when necessary.

BUILT-IN TOOLS

The following sections outline how to restore backups for your key Windows Server 2003 resources using the backup tools mentioned earlier in this chapter.

The Windows Backup Utility

The following steps walk you through the process necessary to restore a backup created with the Windows Backup Utility tool. They are intended to give you an idea of what you need to consider when restoring items in your server (or the entire server) and how to complete the process.

1. Log on to the server that you want to restore a backup to via a Remote Desktop Connection (RDC) as an administrator.
2. Click the Start button and navigate to Programs, Accessories, System Tools, Backup.
3. This opens the Backup or Restore Wizard, as shown in Figure 10.3. To open the Backup Utility tool, click the Advanced Mode link.
4. The Backup Utility opens, displaying a Welcome tab (see Figure 10.4) next to three other tabs for Backup, Restore and Manage Media, and Schedule Jobs. The Welcome tab contains three buttons: Backup Wizard (Advanced), Restore Wizard (Advanced), and Automated System Recovery Wizard. Click the Restore and Manage Media tab to proceed with the backup.
5. The Restore and Manage Media tab opens, displaying the backups stored on the server's hard drive and attached storage media in the left pane, as shown in Figure 10.24. The right pane contains information about each backup package, and the lower section of the tab has an area where you can set the target destination for the backup file to be restored to and a Start Restore button. Navigate through the left tree view to find the backup package you want to restore, and then click the check box to the left of its name to select it.

As mentioned earlier, if you choose to include a System State backup in the items to restore, this is an all-or-nothing proposition. Restoring the System State overwrites all the items within it; you can't pick and choose the components you want to restore. Consider this fact carefully so that you don't inadvertently overwrite crucial configuration data on your server during a restore operation.

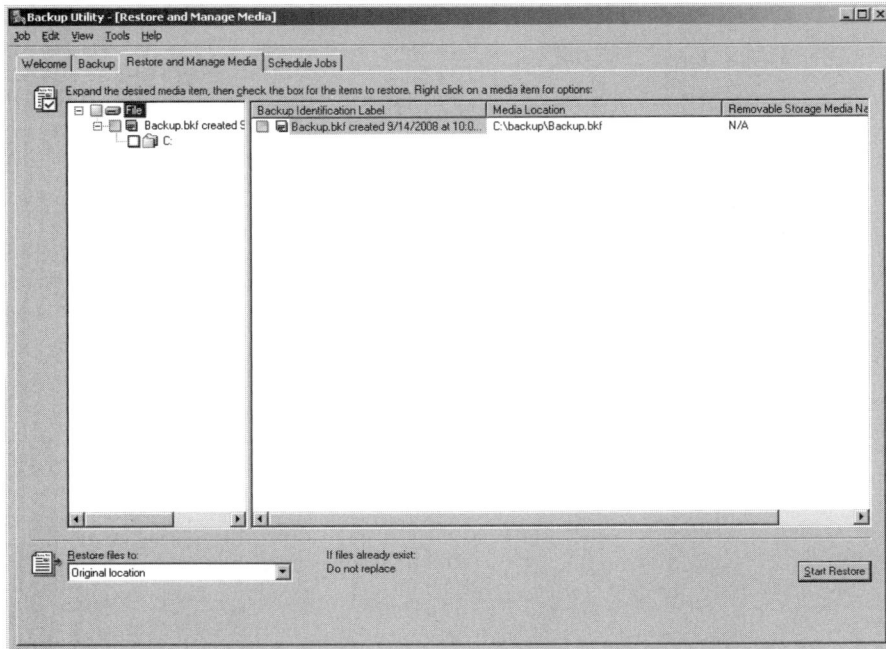

FIGURE 10.24 The Restore and Manage Media tab of the Windows Backup Utility.

6. After you've selected the item you want to restore, review the location displayed in the Restore Files To drop-down menu at the bottom of the window. If the location listed there is not where you want the backup file for this operation restored to, click on the drop-down menu and select either the Alternate Location or Single Folder options. Choosing either selection displays an Alternate Location text box and a Browse button; you can either enter the desired path for the restore target in the text box or click the Browse button to navigate to the target location on the server in a dialog box.

The Original Location option restores the folders and files in the backup to the same location on the server where they originally resided. The Alternate Location option restores the backed up folders and files to a location different from the one they originated in, but it maintains the directory structure that existed for the files when they were backed up. The Single Folder option restored all the files and folders in the backup package to a single folder on the server, without retaining any of the folder structure that existed in the original backed up files.

7. After choosing the backup file to be used and the restore location for the backup file, click the Start Restore button to initiate the restore process.

8. The tool opens the Confirm Restore dialog box (see Figure 10.25), containing three buttons: OK, Cancel, and Advanced. To initiate the restore operation, click the OK button. To cancel the requested operation, click the Cancel button. For this example, click the Advanced button to further configure the restore to your specifications.

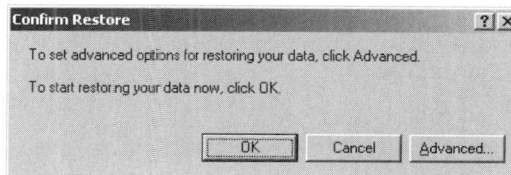

FIGURE 10.25 The Confirm Restore dialog box.

9. The Advanced Restore Options dialog box opens, as shown in Figure 10.26, displaying five check boxes, an OK button, and a Cancel button. Selecting the first check box allows the backup to be restored with the same security permissions as were in place when the backup was made; it is checked by default. This option is only available if the contents of the backup were stored on a New Technology File System (NTFS)-formatted drive. The second check box, when selected, restores all junction points and the file and folder data beneath those junction points. If the backup selected was created on a mounted drive, you must select the second check box. If the third check box is selected, any replicated data sets are marked as the primary data sets, indicating that they will be replicated to any other servers receiving data from your server via File Replication Services (FRS). If other replica sets in your FRS configuration have already been restored, don't select this option. If the backup does not contain FRS data sets, this option is disabled. If the fourth check box is selected, the Microsoft Cluster Services (MSCS) configuration data within the backup is restored and replicated to every node in the cluster. Consider this option carefully, because the Backup Utility does require that the cluster be taken down to complete the restore operation. If the backup package does not contain configuration data for an MSCS cluster, this option is disabled. The fifth check box, if selected, preserves existing mount points on the target server's drive rather than using the ones stored in the backup file. Select the options you want to use, and click the OK button to return to the Confirm Restore dialog box.

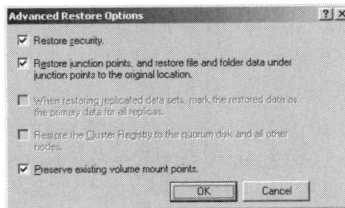

FIGURE 10.26 The Advanced Restore Options dialog box.

10. Click the OK button to start the restore operation. The Restore Progress window (see Figure 10.27) opens to report the progress of the operation. You can click the Cancel button at any time when the operation is running to interrupt it and roll back all changes.

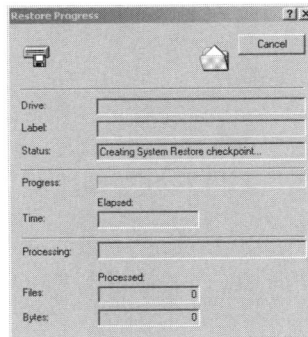

FIGURE 10.27 The Restore Progress window at the beginning of a restore operation.

11. When the operation completes, the Restore Progress window is updated, with a status of Completed. The Cancel button is now the Close button, and a Report button is displayed below the Close button (see Figure 10.28). Click the Report button to open the log for the backup operation.

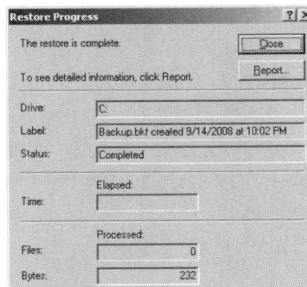

FIGURE 10.28 The Restore Progress window at the completion of a restore operation.

Compressed Folders

You can extract items in compressed folders by copying or dragging them out into uncompressed locations, at which point Windows decompresses them into their original state. If a file exists in the target location with the same name as the compressed file, Windows prompts the user to determine how the conflict should be resolved. The entire compressed folder can also be extracted by right-clicking on the folder and selecting the Extract All menu option to open the Compressed (zipped) Folders Extraction Wizard.

IIS

Restoring backups for the key components of IIS is a fairly straightforward process. The following sections cover the steps necessary to restore backups for the IIS metabase of a Web server in your SharePoint environment and an SSL certificate.

The IIS Metabase

The following steps outline how to restore the IIS metabase via the IIS Manager snap-in for the Microsoft Management Console.

1. Open the IIS Manager management console snap-in on the target server and right-click on the local computer object in the left pane of the console.
2. From the All Tasks menu option, select the Backup/Restore Configuration option.
3. This opens the Configuration Backup/Restore dialog box (see Figure 10.14). Select the backup that you want to restore from the Backups list box and click the Restore button.
4. IIS Manager displays a dialog box like the one in Figure 10.29 informing you that your actions require IIS's Web sites and services to be stopped while the restore operation executes. Click the Yes button to proceed.
5. Once you have clicked the Yes button, the only indication of the running operation that IIS Manager provides is the hourglass icon in place of the normal pointer icon for your mouse. When the metabase restore has completed, IIS displays a dialog box reporting that status, as shown in Figure 10.30.

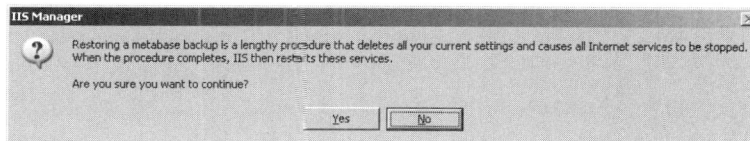

FIGURE 10.29 IIS Manager displays a warning dialog box to inform users of the impact a metabase restore operation has on IIS's sites and services.

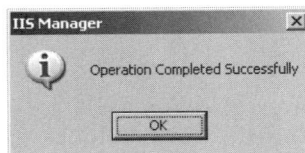

FIGURE 10.30 The dialog box displayed by IIS Manager when a metabase restore operation has successfully completed.

SSL Certificates

To restore an SSL certificate from an exported backup, you may import it in one of two ways: via the Certificate Manager snap-in for the Microsoft Management console or the Directory Security tab for a Web site's Properties in IIS Manager. The option selected should be the same method that you used to originally back up the certificate file. Follow these steps to import an SSL certificate through IIS Manager:

1. Open IIS Manager and right-click on the Web site to which you want to restore the SSL certificate. Select the Properties option from the menu to continue.

These steps assume that the Web site targeted for import does not currently have an SSL certificate installed.

NOTE

2. When the Properties window opens, click the Directory Security tab (see Figure 10.17). When the tab is displayed, click the Server Certificate button in the Secure Communications section to open the Web Server Certificate Wizard.

3. Click the Next button in the Welcome page of the Web Server Certificate Wizard (see Figure 10.18) to proceed.

4. Select the option button next to Import a Certificate from a .PFX File in the Server Certificate page (see Figure 10.31), and click the Next button to continue.

5. Enter a name for the certificate file to be imported in the Path and File Name text field of the Import Certificate page (see Figure 10.32), and click the Next button to continue. To change the storage location of the file, click the Browse button to select the new target location. If you want to allow the imported certificate to be exportable in the future, select the Mark Cert as Exportable check box.

6. Enter the password that was used to encrypt the certificate file when it was exported, and confirm it in the Import Certificate Password page (see Figure 10.33). Then click the Next button to continue.

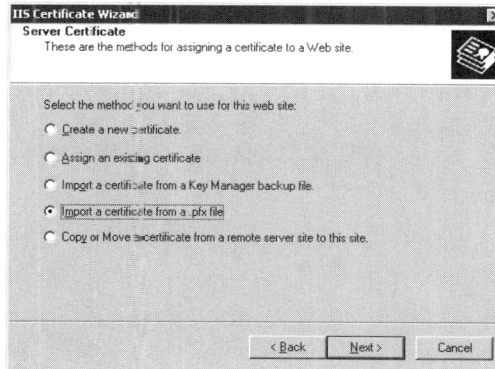

FIGURE 10.31 The Server Certificate page of the IIS Certificate Wizard.

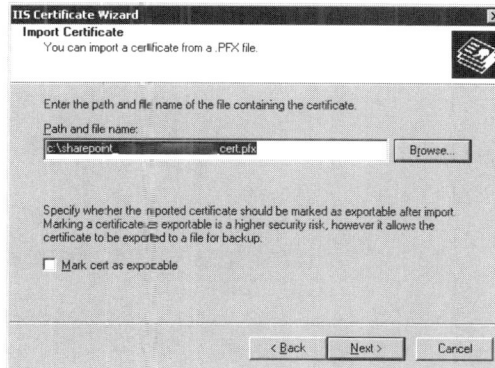

FIGURE 10.32 The Import Certificate page of the IIS Certificate Wizard.

FIGURE 10.33 The Import Certificate Password page of the IIS Certificate Wizard.

7. The SSL Port page opens with the SSL Port This Web Site Should Use text field prepopulated with a port number (see Figure 10.34). Review the value and update it as desired; then click the Next button to continue.

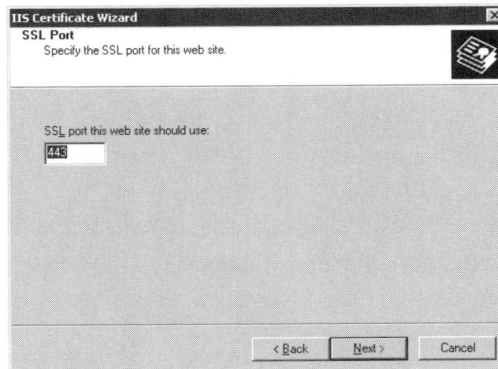

FIGURE 10.34 The SSL Port page of the IIS Certificate Wizard.

8. Review the information in the Imported Certificate Summary page (see Figure 10.35), and click the Next button to import the certificate.

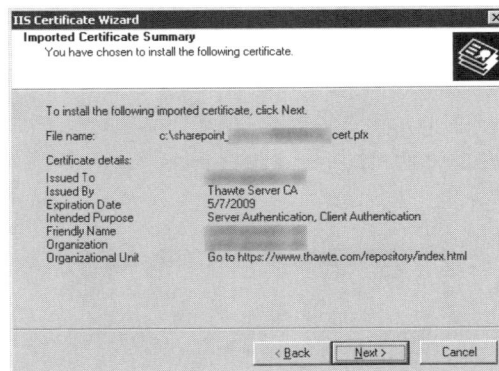

FIGURE 10.35 The Imported Certificate Summary page of the IIS Certificate Wizard.

9. The Wizard displays a message stating that the import was successful (see Figure 10.36). Click the Finish button to close the window.

FIGURE 10.36 The IIS Certificate Wizard reporting a successful import of the SSL certificate.

RESTORING THE WINDOWS REGISTRY

If you've backed up the Windows Registry with the Windows Backup Utility, you should restore it with that tool as well. If you backed up the Registry or parts of it via the Export function within REGEDIT.exe, you can restore those backups into the Registry via the Import function. Simply open REGEDIT.exe and select the Import option from the File menu. The Import Registry File dialog box opens to allow you to select the exported Registry keys you want to import back into the Registry. After you've navigated to the storage location for the target export, click it to select it, and then click the Open button. REGEDIT.exe then imports the backup into the Registry and displays a dialog box stating that the backup was successfully added into the server's Registry. Review the Registry to confirm that the backup was imported as expected, and then close REGEDIT.exe.

> *The simplest way to restore a* .REG *Windows Registry backup file is to ensure that the file resides in the file system of the server you want to apply it to and to double-click on it. When it opens, it is automatically imported into the correct location(s) within the target Windows Registry. It definitely offers a much more hands-on approach, but you should still open the Registry to confirm that your updates were successful.*

NOTE

CONCLUSION

The Windows Server 2003 operating system is the foundation of your SharePoint environment. Every server in your farm must be running it as its base operating system. You need to preserve the key elements of your SharePoint farm stored within the operating system to have a solid, comprehensive disaster recovery solution for your organization's SharePoint resources. If you don't take care to include these items in your backup and restore plans, at a minimum you're incurring additional time and resources spent to re-create them. Or, even worse, you may not be able to re-create them and stand to lose valuable configuration details and resources.

Another best practice previously mentioned in this guide that is especially relevant to this topic is the creation, maintenance, and review of a detailed change log for your SharePoint environment. It can quickly become difficult, if not impossible, to have an accurate picture of what has been installed, modified, or removed from your servers if you don't record those updates for posterity. An accurate change log can be an invaluable asset during a restore of your operating systems or SharePoint farms, telling you exactly what items you need to have in place to return the system to its previous state and how they were configured. It can also aid in the verification of a restored system, to help you know if you have restored or reinstalled all the correct Web parts or hotfixes.

You should also keep in mind that a current change log does you little good unless you know where the Web parts or hotfixes used to modify and update your environment are stored. Although it is all too easy to store these files wherever you please or just delete them when you're done with them, this can pose a serious risk to your system in the event of a disaster. You should store these crucial files in a controlled, centralized location so that you know exactly where to find them and exactly which version should be used to redeploy the correct update. Make sure to include this storage location in your file system backups so its contents are preserved along with the rest of your critical path items, and ensure that the proper personnel can access the location as needed to deploy the packages.

You can go about backing up and restoring the SharePoint-critical components of your Windows Server 2003 operating system in several ways. The simplest and most comprehensive approach to take is to back up your entire server on a regular basis using a tool like the Windows Backup Utility. More importantly, make sure to select an approach that fits your needs, resources, and budget, and then thoroughly test it to ensure that it performs to your specifications. Although it may be expensive to implement tape backups or to purchase third-party tools, it can be even more expensive to have to start over from scratch when you can't restore your system.

Now that you've learned more about backing up and restoring SharePoint-related items within Windows Server 2003, you should be able to answer the following questions. You can find the answers to these questions in Appendix B, "Chapter Review Q&A," on the book's Web site at http://www.courseptr.com/downloads.

1. What is the SharePoint 12 Hive?
2. Can the Windows Backup Utility write backups to tape devices?
3. How can the IIS metabase be backed up?
4. What are some of the drawbacks of backing up files with compressed folders?

11

Windows Server 2003 High Availability

In This Chapter

■ Load Balancing

■ High Availability

I n the mid-1970s, the United States Air Force (USAF) introduced a new aircraft designed to provide U.S. forces on the ground with close-in air support, the A-10 Thunderbolt II, affectionately known as the "Warthog." The A-10 is not a sleek, sexy fighter jet like the F-15 Eagle or F-16 Fighting Falcon, nor is it technologically advanced like the B-2 Stealth bomber. It isn't pretty, but it's effective. The A-10 is slow, at least when compared to burners like the Eagle, and it's less maneuverable. This means it's exposed to counterattacks for longer periods than its fighter brethren, and these attacks come in a much higher volume, meaning that the highest priorities in its design were reliability and durability. Every system in the A-10 critical to keeping it in the air has redundant backups available in case of an error or failure. This is just one aspect of the thought that has gone into keeping the A-10 safely in the air for as long as possible; and the approach works; A-10s have been hit by missiles and hundreds of shells. They've even flown home missing half a wing and survived.

You may be asking yourself, "What does this have to do with Windows Server 2003 High Availability (HA)?" Hopefully the brief description of the A-10's redundant design and durability has gotten you thinking about the steps you could take to introduce similar attributes into your SharePoint environment. What sort of redundant systems do you, or should you, have in place if a key component of your system should fail? In Chapter 10, "Windows Server 2003 Backup and Restore," you were introduced to some of the ways you can back up items in Windows Server

2003 crucial to SharePoint and restore them. This chapter outlines several ways you can create redundant systems for your SharePoint environment so that if a hard drive, server, or more should fail, your users can still access, modify, and work with their business-critical SharePoint content.

HA is not something implemented easily, nor is it a problem that can be solved by a single hardware or software solution. It requires comprehensive analysis, planning, and design of your IT infrastructure from the ground up, not to mention careful consideration of your service and uptime requirements, the budget you have available to meet those requirements, as well as the staff needed to manage and implement your HA processes. While uptime numbers like the "five nines" discussed in Chapter 9, "SQL Server 2005 High Availability," may certainly be attractive to you and your management, the overhead in providing that kind of service is often prohibitive to all but the largest of enterprises. The important thing to do is to review the options discussed in this chapter and determine the HA solution that best fits your needs and budget, and then make sure your service levels are clearly defined and communicated to your customers.

The visual examples provided in this chapter were generated in a testing environment using the following platforms and components. Depending on how your environment is configured, your experiences may vary slightly.

- **Operating system.** Microsoft Windows Server 2003 R2 Enterprise Edition Service Pack (SP) 2
- **Microsoft .NET Framework.** Versions 1.1, 2.0 SP1, 3.0 SP1, and 3.5
- **Database.** Microsoft SQL Server 2005 Developer Edition SP2
- **Web server.** Microsoft Internet Information Services (IIS) 6.0
- **SharePoint.** Microsoft Office SharePoint Server (MOSS) 2007 Enterprise Edition

LOAD BALANCING

One of the best ways to ensure that your SharePoint farm's content is always available to your users is by spreading the responsibility for serving that content across multiple SharePoint frontend servers via a practice known as *load balancing*. SharePoint is designed to allow for the use of multiple frontend servers in a load-balanced configuration, serving up content to users on a single Uniform Resource Locator (URL). Even though users may be making complex requests to SharePoint, the servers are able to answer those requests in a uniform manner, even if during a single session end users are directed to multiple servers for their content. Load balancing can be accomplished by installing a hardware or software solution in front of your SharePoint frontend servers that forwards an HTTP request directed at a single URL to one of the frontend servers. If one of the servers in your load-balanced pool is receiving too many requests or happens to crash completely, the load balancer is able to redirect traffic away from the affected server to the other members of the pool, ensuring a higher level of service continuity than what is possible with a single server.

Load-Balancing Software

Load-balancing software is pretty easy to describe: by installing and configuring an application on the SharePoint frontend servers you want to load-balance, you can distribute client requests across all those servers. It requires no special hardware and usually comes with a lower price tag than hardware-based solutions. In fact, the most common load-balancing software solution for SharePoint, Windows Network Load Balancing (NLB) Services, is available as a free addition to Windows Server 2003. This section guides you through how to enable and configure an NLB cluster to load-balance the HTTP traffic directed at your SharePoint farm's frontend servers. It is by no means the only way you can use a software product to load-balance SharePoint, but in the interest of time, we are focusing on the most prevalent option available.

CAUTION

Even though NLB and the Microsoft Cluster Service (MSCS) share some of the same terms and concepts, they are two distinct technologies intended to provide solutions for different problem sets. MSCS is best suited for applications that require transactions to occur in a synchronous order and be aware of their position within that order, referred to as the application's state. Applications that need to frequently update large amounts of data in a specific sequence, like SQL Server, are excellent candidates for clustering via MSCS. NLB is targeted at applications that operate in a "stateless" manner, like IIS Web servers. The transactions used by these applications have no knowledge of the transactions that came before or after them; each one is treated as an independent operation. Because SharePoint is a stateless Web application, its frontend servers are not good candidates for clustering via MSCS.

About Windows Network Load-Balancing Services

Windows NLB is designed to be a scalable, reliable, high-availability solution for stateless applications that communicate via the Internet Protocol (IP). It allows up to 32 servers to be placed into a server farm cluster to avoid outages or performance losses for a single URL. To configure an NLB cluster, a single URL and its IP address serves as a "virtual" IP that receives all traffic directed at the application and reroutes it to one of the member servers within the NLB cluster. If a member of the cluster fails, NLB automatically removes the server from the cluster and distributes its load among the rest of the servers in the cluster until service is restored on the affected server.

NLB does not require special hardware to configure or use its functionality. No hardware devices or Storage Area Network (SAN) configurations are required. For optimal use, the member servers in the NLB cluster should have two Network Interface Cards (NICs), but NLB can certainly be used if the servers have only one NIC. Each member server must be configured to allow network communication with the server via IP, because NLB relies on this protocol to communicate with the cluster and direct traffic through it.

NLB can be configured to operate in two modes: Unicast and Multicast. All the member servers within an NLB cluster must be set to the same operational mode, regardless of whether Unicast or Multicast is selected.

- **Unicast.** In Unicast mode, the Media Access Control (MAC) address assigned to the NIC for clustered traffic is overridden by a virtual MAC address that the NLB generates. Each server in the cluster uses the same MAC, which means that each member server receives all traffic directed at the cluster. Unicast mode can cause conflicts with network switching hardware, leading to dropped traffic to and from the cluster or to the switch being flooded by traffic it can't redirect.
- **Multicast.** In Multicast mode, a second MAC address is added to the NIC of each member server in the cluster, and the original MAC address for the NIC is retained. The NLB-generated MAC address is used to send and receive traffic directed at the NLB cluster's virtual IP address. The original MAC address is used to send and receive traffic directed specifically at the member server on its own IP address. With Multicast mode, your network administrators can create static entries in the cluster's network switch that point to the ports used by the cluster, removing the risk of flooding your switch.

Whenever possible, Microsoft highly recommends the use of multiple NICs for servers in an NLB cluster. NLB does not require that the number of NICs used by the cluster's member servers be the same across all servers; each server can use a different number of NICs if desired. If the cluster is operating in Unicast mode and only one NIC is being used on a member server, that server is not able to effectively or reliably communicate with other servers for traffic unrelated to the cluster.

Although Unicast mode is enabled by default when creating an NLB cluster, Multicast mode is the operating mode often recommended for NLB clusters. Multicast mode provides more functionality when only a single NIC can be used on member servers in the cluster, because Unicast mode can limit each member server's ability to send and receive traffic other than what is associated with the cluster. Multicast mode may require the creation of static port entries or other additional configuration on your network switch, in which case Unicast mode is the best option to go with, but most networking hardware is now compatible with Multicast.

When planning how to configure your NLB cluster, make sure to consult and involve your organization's network administrators. Not only are they going to be able to provide details on how your network is configured and how that impacts your design, but they should also be able to give you valuable recommendations and constraints based on their knowledge of the network that your SharePoint environment uses.

How to Configure Windows Network Load-Balancing Services

The following instructions detail the steps necessary to install and configure NLB to create a cluster containing two servers. Each server has two NICs installed, and the cluster is going to be configured to operate in Multicast mode. The user executing these steps must be a local administrator on each of the servers in the cluster. The member servers in the cluster must have unique IP addresses assigned to each of their NICs, and an IP address must be available to serve as the cluster's "virtual" address.

1. Log on to the server you want to add to an NLB cluster as an administrator.
2. Click the Start button and navigate to Programs, Administrative Tools, Network Load Balancing Manager.
3. This opens the Network Load Balancing Manager application, as shown in Figure 11.1.

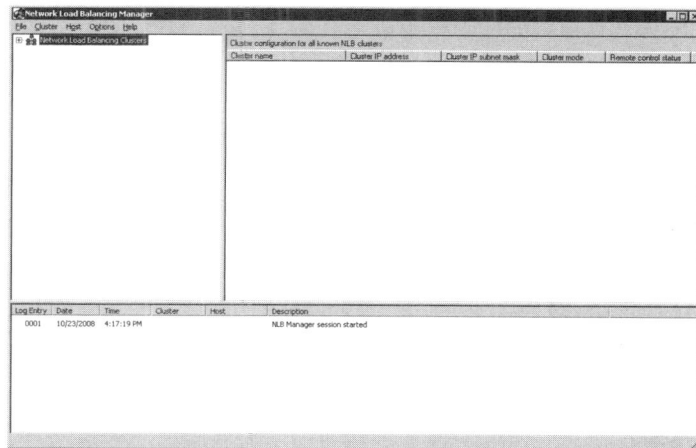

FIGURE 11.1 The Network Load Balancing Manager.

4. From the Cluster menu, select the New option to open the Cluster Parameters window (see Figure 11.2) and create a new NLB cluster.
5. When the Cluster Parameters window opens, enter the IP address and subnet mask for the cluster's virtual address and the Internet address that is mapped to that clustered IP address in the Cluster IP Configuration section.

In the Cluster Operation Mode section, select the Multicast option button. Leave the Allow Remote Control check box unchecked, and click the Next button to open the Cluster IP Addresses window and continue.

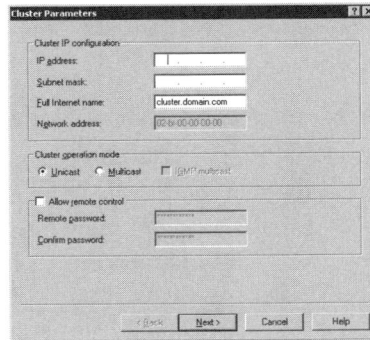

FIGURE 11.2 The Cluster Parameters window.

6. Click the Next button in the Cluster IP Addresses window (see Figure 11.3) without adding additional IP addresses. If you want to add additional IP addresses to the cluster, you may do so here, but it is not necessary for this example.

7. The Port Rules window is now opened, as shown in Figure 11.4. By default, a single rule has already been created encompassing every TCP and UDP port on the clustered IP address. If you want to modify that rule, click the Edit button to open the Add/Edit Port Rule window (shown in Figure 11.5). In this window, you can apply the rule to the entire cluster or a single IP address if there are multiple in the cluster, change the range of ports included in the cluster for the IP address, select the Internet Protocol that the cluster uses, set its Filtering Mode, set its Affinity, or disable the selected range of ports for the cluster. To accept the defaults for the rule, click the Next button to open the Connect window and continue.

NOTE

An NLB cluster's Affinity setting is used to configure how "sticky" a session is between a client and a host within the cluster. If None is selected for a cluster's Affinity, each client session is directed by the load balancer to the next available host in the cluster, regardless of whether the client previously was communicating with a specific host. Selecting Single sets a client to always be directed to the same host within a given session, regardless of its traffic load. The Class C option directs requests from the same TCP/IP Class C address range to a specific host in the cluster. For more information about NLB Affinity settings and SharePoint, see the "Windows NLB and SharePoint" section later in this chapter.

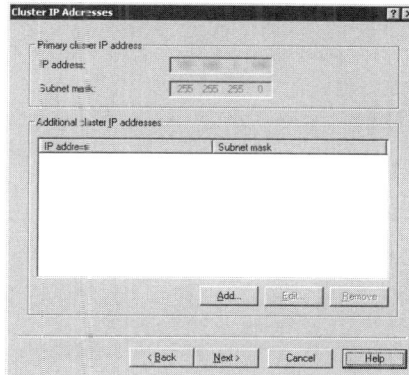

FIGURE 11.3 The Cluster IP Addresses window.

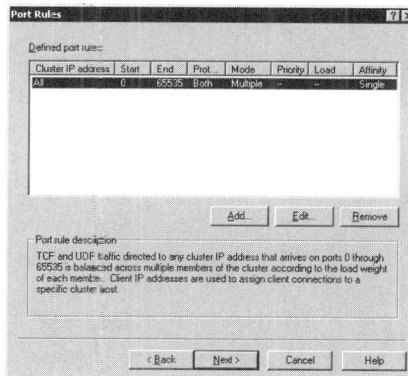

FIGURE 11.4 The Port Rules window.

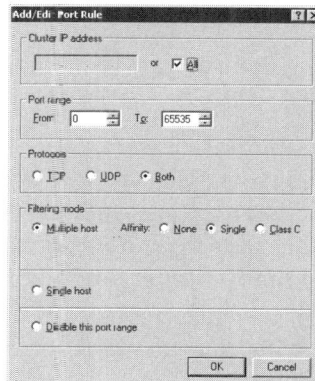

FIGURE 11.5 The Add/Edit Port Rule window.

8. The Connect window opens as shown in Figure 11.6, allowing you to add a host to the new cluster. Enter the host name or its dedicated IP address for the first server in the cluster in the Host text field, and click the Connect button. The Connection Status window is updated to a status of Connecting as the tool attempts to reach the host server, depicted in Figure 11.7. Once it connects to the server, the status is updated to Connected, and the host's NICs are displayed in the Interfaces Available for Configuring a New Cluster list box (see Figure 11.8). Select the NIC on the server to be used by the cluster, and click the Next button to configure the host's interface.

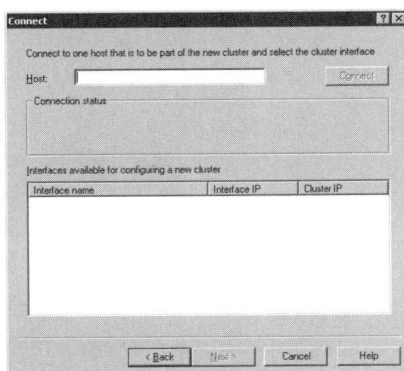

FIGURE 11.6 The Connect window.

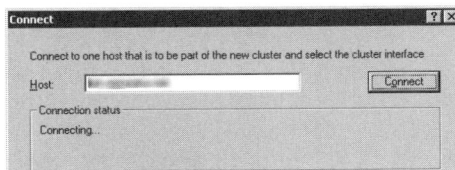

FIGURE 11.7 Attempting to connect to a new host for the cluster.

9. This opens the Host Parameters window (see Figure 11.9), allowing you to configure the host's settings and role within the cluster. Because this is the first host in the cluster, it should have a priority of 1 to uniquely identify it. Confirm that the IP Address and Subnet Mask values in the Dedicated IP Configuration section are correct, and ensure that the proper values are selected in the Initial Host State section. For this example, accept the defaults and click the Finish button to kick off the configuration of the cluster.

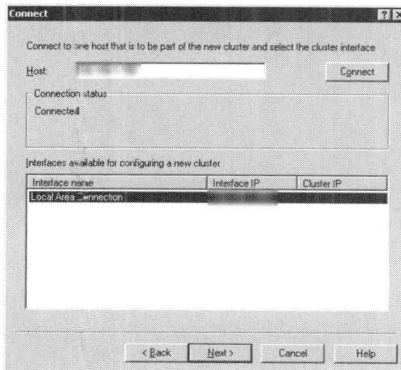

FIGURE 11.8 The Connect window with a connected host and its available NICs.

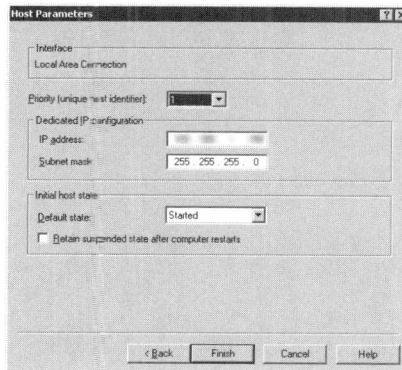

FIGURE 11.9 Configuring a host's network interface in the Host Parameter window.

10. When the cluster configuration operation completes, the cluster is now shown in the Network Load Balancing Manager screen in the left window pane under the Network Load Balancing Clusters entry (see Figure 11.10). To add hosts to the cluster, right-click on the new cluster's name and select the Add Host to Cluster option from the menu. This opens the Connect window, allowing you to complete Steps 8 through 10 to add subsequent hosts to the cluster. The Network Load Balancing Manager also displays a log entry stating `Update <#> succeeded [double-click for details…]`, as shown in Figure 11.11.

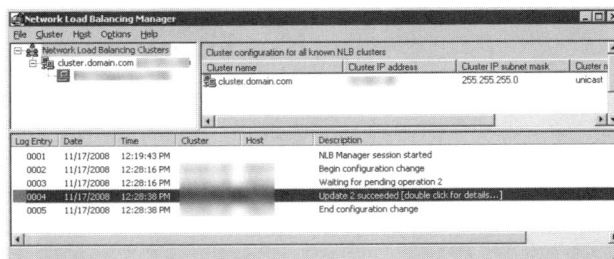

FIGURE 11.10 A cluster shown in the NLB Manager application's window.

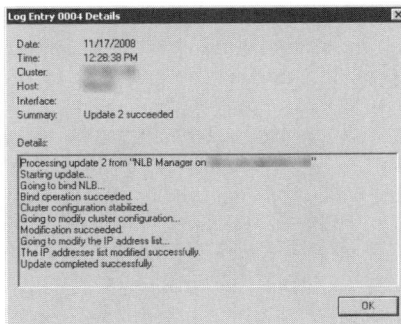

FIGURE 11.11 The details of the cluster's configuration log entry after an NLB cluster has been successfully created.

Windows NLB and SharePoint

When implementing Windows NLB with SharePoint, there are two main issues that you need to keep in mind and consider: operational mode and session affinity. You can configure each of these items in different ways, and your choices can have a definite impact on the functionality and performance of your SharePoint environment.

NLB Operational Mode and SharePoint

Your operational mode decision, between the choice of Unicast or Multicast, is most likely to be decided by the configuration of your environment's networking hardware. If your servers in the NLB cluster are configured with multiple NICs, Unicast is the best-fitting operational mode. If they have only one NIC, Multicast makes the most sense. If you are building your servers from the ground up, the recommended approach is to install more than one NIC and go with Unicast, but these recommendations are based on general situations, and your specific requirements and environment may dictate otherwise. Regardless of the operational mode you select, make sure to apply this setting uniformly across all servers in the NLB cluster; each node must use the same setting, or you'll encounter errors.

If you chose to use Multicast in your cluster, make sure that your network's hardware is compatible. Specifically, your hardware must be able to accept the Address Resolution Protocol (ARP) replies generated by the multicast nodes in the NLB cluster or allow administrators to create a static ARP entry to properly resolve the addresses being used by the cluster. Although most modern networking hardware is now compatible with the functionality and settings required to make NLB work, you may still encounter legacy or niche hardware that is not compatible. You need to confirm that your infrastructure meets the needs of your solution and thoroughly test the full configuration before using it in a production environment.

NLB Session Affinity and SharePoint

Internet traffic, by design, is intended to be stateless. That is, each transaction between a client and a server is supposed to be self-contained and unconnected so that it can be routed by the most efficient means possible regardless of how communication operated in the past. But the reality of the situation is that not all traffic over the Internet is stateless. And while SharePoint is in many ways a typical stateless Internet application, this is not always the case. Some functionality, such as workflows or InfoPath forms, is prone to errors in load-balanced SharePoint environments where clients can communicate with any Web front end server at any point in time. To avoid these errors, each node in your NLB cluster should have Affinity set at Single so a client's repeated traffic becomes "sticky" by being directed back to the same WFE server for each trip. This ensures continuity in these transactions that do require the persistence of state for proper operation.

Advantages of NLB and SharePoint

The most obvious advantage to the use of Windows NLB is its cost. Because SharePoint requires the Windows Server operating system, you already obtained the right to use NLB when you purchased your Windows Server licenses. NLB does not require the additional purchase of expensive, proprietary hardware to enable HA for your SharePoint content Windows NLB also allows administrators to manage it by logging into your SharePoint servers, providing a central location for the administration of your environment's critical platforms.

Drawbacks of NLB and SharePoint

Windows NLB is not a sophisticated load-balancing solution. It can require specific or at times unusual networking hardware to function effectively. Its network bandwidth requirements make it a poor choice for load balancing across diverse locations for geographic redundancy. For a single NLB cluster to be spread across two datacenters, the connection speed between those data centers must have response times of 500 milliseconds or less, a capability that comes at a high cost and is not possible over long distances. This distance constraint negates the purpose of geographic redundancy because the target data centers would be too close together to ensure that at least one could survive a disaster. Another possible solution for multiple sites is to create a separate NLB cluster in each location and direct traffic to one or the other via a Doman Name System (DNS) round robin solution, but this approach does not truly distribute traffic loads between the sites.

Perhaps NLB's biggest drawback is its inability to detect when a host within a cluster is no longer serving live content. If the IIS Web server in one of your SharePoint WFEs has crashed and is no longer sending Web pages to requesting clients, the NLB cluster continues to direct traffic to the Web server until its service is restored or the host is manually removed from the cluster. This can have a definite impact on your environment, because some end users are going to see intermittent errors while that downed server is still being used by the cluster, which can be difficult to troubleshoot. It also requires manual intervention by an administrator, not only to remove the affected server from the cluster, but to determine which server is displaying the errors in the first place. Differentiating between load-balanced servers can be a difficult thing to do when each is generating the same content, adding additional challenges to your ability to provide stable and consistent service via NLB.

LOAD-BALANCING HARDWARE

Hardware load balancers are specialized networking applications designed to route traffic to certain individual servers in a network. You can configure hardware load balancers to distribute network traffic across multiple servers based on a variety of conditions such as connection volume, bandwidth utilization, processor utilization, or overall server performance. Software load balancers add an additional task load to the servers in the cluster, on top of their normal tasks, such as generating the load-balanced content. Hardware load balancers, on the other hand, reside on specialized hardware dedicated to the sole responsibility of distributing traffic to their constituent servers according to their configuration. They are designed, engineered, and tested to efficiently and flexibly spread network traffic across the servers clustered beneath them.

The most obvious benefit to the use of a hardware load balancer is to reduce the workload of your servers, when compared to Windows NLB. Because the servers themselves are not responsible for establishing and managing the NLB cluster, those free cycles can be allocated to other responsibilities such as generating and serving content. They also offer a variety of configuration and management options, although options do vary from manufacturer to manufacturer. Traffic destinations can be determined by affinity, server workload, bandwidth availability, geographic location, or several other factors. Clusters can span network subnets or even data centers. Servers can be automatically or manually removed from active service depending on a range of criteria such as failures to respond or errors being displayed in requested content. Hardware load balancers are offered by several network hardware vendors, such as Cisco, F5, Coyote Point Systems, Barracuda Networks, and many more, each with their own feature sets, capabilities, and limitations. You should work with your organization's network administrator(s) to determine what hardware solution is the best fit for its needs, if you decide to use a hardware load balancer.

Load-Balancing Hardware and SharePoint

Much like Windows NLB, your most effective results for a SharePoint farm using a hardware load balancer occur when client sessions are made to be sticky, via affinity settings. This is a universal requirement and should be tested and implemented (when testing shows that it is beneficial) whenever possible. One difference between hardware load balancers and Windows NLB is that the Unicast/Multicast operating modes are functions unique to NLB; there may be hardware solutions that offer similar functionality, but you should review their documentation and conduct your own testing to determine the behavior of that functionality to find out how it behaves.

SharePoint is supported on all hardware load-balancing solutions, so it is ultimately up to you and your network administrators to determine which one is right for you. When evaluating a hardware load balancer, do not make your choice simply based on the load-balancing functionality of the devices. It is important to also consider each candidate's manageability and flexibility, because networking administration (especially for Web server–based solutions like SharePoint) is a fluid and ever-changing responsibility. Your hardware load balancer should be able to quickly enable configuration changes, effectively identify status changes in the servers beneath it, and make your life as a SharePoint administrator easier, not harder.

As SharePoint's sales and popularity has grown, so has the need to deliver it to end users efficiently and consistently. This has not gone unnoticed by the manufacturers of hardware load balancers, and several have begun to provide information, guidance, and configurations specifically geared toward the load balancing of SharePoint content with their products. This is great news for SharePoint administrators, because it means that the manufacturers have taken care of the extensive testing and monitoring activities necessary to find the configuration sweet spot for running SharePoint behind their devices, allowing you to quickly and often drastically improve the performance of your SharePoint environment with reduced risk to your service quality.

You should still exercise caution when considering a hardware load-balancing device optimized for SharePoint, because the performance gains offered by these products can drastically vary depending on the configuration of your environment and its network. If your SharePoint servers and the client workstations accessing your SharePoint site have high bandwidth connections, you may not see performance gains worth the cost of implementing a SharePoint-optimized load balancer.

Instead, manufacturers have focused on situations where network configurations lead to smaller or slower pipes for data to flow through, such as wide area network (WAN) connections.

Connection speeds for WANs, which often use public communication links to connect local area networks (LANs) across multiple geographic locations, can pale in comparison to LANs. WAN connection speeds can range from 1200 bits per second to as high as, in limited cases, 156 megabits per second. (5 megabits is a more realistic normal ceiling for WAN speeds.) Most LANs use Ethernet connections ranging from 10 megabits per second up to 1 gigabit per second, a drastic increase over WAN capabilities. Client LANs using WiFi wireless connections can range from 11 megabits per second up to 300 megabits per second, depending on the communication protocols in use.

It is easy to understand, given the connection limitations WANs face and the amount of network traffic that an active SharePoint site can generate, why this is a main area of focus for manufacturers. But if your network does not use or include WAN connections, you may not see large performance gains when using a SharePoint-optimized load-balancing device. Does this mean you shouldn't use such a device in your network? Not at all. It's just that you need to evaluate the reasons and requirements you have around load-balancing devices, along with the possible avenues of growth your network might follow, and select your resources accordingly. If your environment is not likely to include WAN connections and there is a more affordable device available that offers all the load-balancing capabilities you need, it is probably a better choice than an expensive purchase for technology that you are not going to see much benefit from.

But if your network does include WAN connections or may in the future, the performance gains advertised by manufacturers are certainly compelling. The data available indicates that you may see, at a minimum, performance twice as fast as SharePoint running without these devices, all the way up to 20 times as great. These devices can also be used to reduce traffic over the WAN in general by caching content across the network, as well as reduce CPU utilization on your SharePoint servers to free them up for more processing activities.

Remember, these numbers are coming from the manufacturers; unfortunately, we do not have the sophisticated and complex hardware configurations available to test this data for ourselves. Take these claims with a grain of salt, and understand that your own results may vary.

CAUTION

Many of the major hardware manufacturers, such as F5, Cisco, and Juniper Networks, offer hardware load-balancing devices that include optimizations specific to SharePoint environments. For more information about these devices, we recommend you contact the individual manufacturer or visit its respective Web site.

LOAD BALANCING AND SHAREPOINT FARM TOPOLOGY

Implementing load balancing to distribute traffic across multiple resources within your SharePoint farm can definitely have a positive impact on the performance of your servers and, most importantly, the end user experience. It can also ensure that your environment can withstand the loss of a server within the farm by sharing the load between multiple resources. But that benefit is not achieved by simply adding more servers to your environment, installing SharePoint on them, and adding them to an NLB cluster. It is important to understand not only the areas within your SharePoint farm where load balancing can be advantageous, but also where it provides little to no value and where it can actually be detrimental to the health of your system.

The WFE Role

The most obvious item within your farm that benefits from load balancing is the Windows SharePoint Services (WSS) Web Application role, often referred to as the WFE role. WFEs are responsible for serving SharePoint's Web pages, content, and functionality to your end users, so if you have a large user base who frequently visit your SharePoint sites or need to make sure that your content is always online and available, you will most certainly want to load-balance your WFEs. The interesting thing about load balancing WFE servers is the performance of your environment as you insert additional WFEs to scale out the farm.

Microsoft has conducted extensive testing of how SharePoint performs under extremely heavy loads, for a variety of typical use cases. What it found is that there is a definitive point where performance gains flatten out as new WFEs are added to a load-balanced farm; in most situations, monitoring shows that throughput (measured in requests per second on each server) stops increasing, or can even decrease, once a certain number of WFEs are added to a farm with a single SQL Server instance for content databases. (For more information on Microsoft's findings, head to the SharePoint Performance and Capacity Planning Resource Center on TechNet, at http://technet.microsoft.com/en-us/office/sharepointserver/bb736741.aspx.) After that point, if your metrics indicate that you need to add more WFEs to a farm, you must also add at least one additional SQL Server database instance to host some of the content databases in your farm. Most SharePoint environments should not require the high numbers of resources mentioned with these limits and recommendations; these upper limits of SharePoint architecture and topology are usually reached only by the largest of organizations or Web sites.

Microsoft states that these results are only the output of its testing and that you may see different results or be able to move beyond the four WFE threshold in your own environment, depending on the type of need. Again, it's imperative that you test your configuration on its own so that you can determine your performance and whether it meets your specific requirements. Performance may vary depending on a variety of factors, as follows:

- **Network configuration.** The unique configuration of your network and its hardware may provide you with performance metrics that vastly differ from Microsoft's.
- **Hardware configuration.** The unique configuration of your server hardware may also provide you with performance metrics that vastly differ from Microsoft's.
- **Caching configuration.** Configuring your farm's servers and content to leverage caching functionality can drastically improve the performance of your Web servers.

Adding More Servers to a SharePoint Farm

Because load balancing is common for SharePoint to improve performance, Microsoft has made the process to add additional servers to a SharePoint farm easy and straightforward. The SharePoint installer should be run on the server to be added to the farm, using the same accounts and configuration as the rest of the servers in the farm, making sure to do a Complete Advanced installation. Once the installer finishes, the SharePoint Products and Technologies Configuration Wizard starts up. Walk through the wizard, making sure to select the Connect to an Existing Farm option, and then connect to the configuration database for the existing farm. Confirm that the server is set to not host the farm's Central Administration site (it can only be hosted on a single server in the farm), and complete the wizard. Log into the Central Administration site, and configure the server with the WFE role that it should play in the farm.

> *Adding a server to a farm does not automatically also add it to the pool of load-balanced servers. This configuration step must still be performed for end users to reach the server via the load-balanced URL.*

One nice thing about SharePoint's ability to add additional servers to a farm is its flexibility. Some solutions, such as server clustering, require that each server within the group has the same hardware and software configurations for the cluster to function properly. Although SharePoint does have some configuration requirements, it is nowhere near this strict. The only limitation SharePoint has is around the processor architecture edition of SharePoint that you're running, x86 (32-bit) or x64 (64-bit). A single SharePoint farm can have both types of architectures, as long as a single processor type is used within a server role in the farm. So if your WFEs run on the x64 version of SharePoint, any new WFEs you add must also be x64. But you can still have an x86 index server in the same farm.

But that is the only real configuration limitation. You can have a variety of processor, RAM, or storage configurations. You can add both virtual and physical servers to your farm. In addition, you can have supporting pieces of software installed on different servers in the farm (and most likely will). Keep in mind that this does not include custom add-ons to your SharePoint farm, such as third-party Web parts or solution packages. If those items have pieces that must be present on a server and cannot be deployed via the farm's Timer Job service, you must manually copy them to each WFE in the server to ensure that end users see the same content regardless of what server they are contacting.

Search Roles

SharePoint servers in a farm can serve a few different roles to add performance and functionality to the farm's search capabilities. The two listed server roles affiliated with searching in a SharePoint farm are Index server and Query server. The Index server is responsible for generating the farm's search index by crawling the target content sources and building the index with the results of that crawl. This role cannot be load-balanced within a SharePoint farm; much like the movie *The Highlander*, there can be only one Index Server per shared services provider (SSP) within a farm. Query servers are tasked with the processing required to execute all requested queries against a copy of the farm's search index stored locally on the server.

> *In WSS, the Index and Query roles are consolidated into a single WSS Search role. This role should only be configured on one server within the farm and not load-balanced.*

NOTE

In a load-balanced farm, it's also possible to assign multiple servers, even those serving as WFEs, the query server role to help distribute the query load evenly.

> *To return your farm's content in search results, the Index server must crawl every site within the farm on a regular basis to keep the index up to date. This can potentially impact your system performance, especially if you have a large amount of content in SharePoint, because your WFEs are trying to serve content to end users at the same time the Index server is crawling it to build the index. To solve this problem, Microsoft suggests establishing a dedicated WFE/Query server in your farm without adding it to the pool of load-balanced WFEs, and then setting it as the Index server's target for crawling. Because the server is not load-balanced, end users should never access it. However, it serves the same content as the load-balanced WFEs, so the search index will be accurate.*

TIP

Another possible solution to consider would be to set an additional role on your farm's index server: WFE. By configuring your index server as a WFE, you can omit it from the load-balanced pool and set it as the dedicated target server for crawls necessary to build the farm's search index. So, in addition to reducing the load on the WFEs in your farm accessed by users by moving the crawl to a separate server, you also improve the performance of your crawls by reducing the network traffic generated. Instead of making a call to a separate server then over to the database server to build an index, the Index server processes the crawl internally and then sends its data to the database, removing one of the network hops required by each operation and speeding up the overall process.

If your infrastructure supports the use of virtual servers, this dedicated server is an excellent candidate for virtualization. Its performance requirements are minimal, because it is not serving content to actual end users; if it is slow, the only impact is that the farm's index is not updated quickly, it does not impact search performance. Using a virtual server allows you to avoid purchasing expensive physical hardware for a little-used member of your farm, instead leveraging existing servers hosting other virtual machines (VMs). This is not required, but it's a recommended architectural best practice.

MOSS Enterprise Application Servers

The Enterprise license of MOSS enables several powerful pieces of SharePoint functionality to end users: the Business Data Catalog (BDC), Excel Calculation Services, and InfoPath Forms Services. Servers can be configured to fill the Application Server role within the farm to host and service this Enterprise functionality to end users. Interestingly, these pieces of functionality work in different ways and have different approaches when it comes to distributing work load within the farm's servers.

Excel Services can be processor-intensive for a server hosting it, because this service is used to make all the calculations and computations necessary to display Excel workbooks that are stored within a SharePoint site and configured to run on the server. Multiple servers within a farm can be assigned the Excel Services role, but those servers should not be added to a load-balancing cluster. SharePoint is able to manage the load for multiple Excel Services servers without requiring additional configuration by an administrator. Servers hosting Excel Services can also be clustered, as opposed to load-balanced, which is covered later in the chapter.

The BDC and InfoPath server roles cannot be load-balanced within a SharePoint farm. By default, SharePoint automatically distributes the workload for these functions across all the SSP servers in the farm. Because SharePoint already handles the load balancing, these server roles do not need to and should not be added into the load-balancing configuration, regardless of the type of load-balancing solution currently in use.

HIGH AVAILABILITY

Load balancing your Web servers is by far the most obvious and effective way to ensure continuous uptime for your SharePoint environment, but it does not necessarily represent a complete HA solution. Because SharePoint requires such a wide range of infrastructure and systems to function, it is important to configure these systems redundantly so they can be as highly available as your load-balanced SharePoint components. The failure of a hard drive or network connection can just as easily impact SharePoint's service levels as the more obvious candidates for HA, SharePoint, and SQL Server. Luckily, the IT industry has been hard at work for years to develop and create stable, redundant infrastructure components that address those problems.

STORAGE

Let's face it, it's impossible to have a server running Windows Server 2003 and not have some sort of storage device attached to it. Hard disk drives, commonly known as hard drives, have been used in computers for over 50 years and have evolved and improved as much as processors have over the years, albeit with much less fanfare. Modern hard drives are designed not only to store large amounts of data (manufactures are now producing drives with capacities over 1TB), but to make reading, writing, and updating that data happen as fast as possible and send the results of those actions back to the user at high speeds. But one thing hasn't changed: drives still fail.

That is not to say that manufacturers have ignored the reliability of their products. That statement could not be further from the truth. Today's hard drives are made to last longer while still withstanding the heavier workloads that interconnected, data-driven computer systems place upon them. They are being made to use less power and reduce noise and to handle sudden movements such as those that could impact the hard drive of a laptop computer. But real-world experience has shown that hard drives are still prone to failure, for a variety of reasons.

To expect otherwise is foolhardy, if not irresponsible. Want proof? Consider the findings offered by Google, probably one of the largest consumers of hard drives in the world. In a whitepaper published in February 2007 (http://labs.google.com/papers/disk_failures.pdf), Google presented data based on analysis of hundreds of thousands of hard drives. It found that, despite the best efforts of manufacturers and system administrators, hard drives are prone to failures caused by a variety of sources, especially as the drives become older. Age is not the only reason for hard drive breakdown, and Google is careful to point out that it should not be the only determining factor. But it's important to keep in mind that as a drive gets older, it is more likely to fail.

When it comes to the business-critical data stored on your servers and in your SharePoint environment, we recommend that as a part of an effective disaster plan, you should not only back up your data on a regular basis, you should also configure the systems you store that data on as redundantly as possible. This helps to make certain that your data is still available if a hard drive fails, and it avoids any outages that may be experienced while a backup is being retrieved from storage and restored. The good news is that modern IT systems have some effective solutions available to them to redundantly store their data.

RAID

A Redundant Array of Independent Disks, more commonly known as a RAID array, is a storage solution that uses two or more actual hard drives to create a reliable storage option for servers. The multiple disks in a RAID array are configured to be presented to a server as a single device, providing a redundant solution that can either copy or distribute data across the disks in the array. There are several types of RAID arrays, each providing different attributes and drawbacks to be considered. Some of the most common are listed here:

- **RAID 0.** With RAID 0, data is "striped," or broken down into blocks, and each block is written to different disks in the array. RAID 0 requires at least two hard disks to implement, and its primary advantage is its ability to read and write data to the disk much more quickly than a single disk. Because data is not duplicated across multiple disks in the array, RAID 0 does not provide fault tolerance for high availability.
- **RAID 1.** In this configuration, data is "mirrored" across each disk in the array so that it is preserved if a drive in the array fails. Writing to the array takes slightly longer than a single disk, because the array is writing to multiple drives (a problem more often seen in software-based RAID solutions than in hardware-based ones). The available storage in the array is also limited to the size of the smallest disk in the array.
- **RAID 5.** This combines a minimum of three disks and ensures that the data on one disk in the array is duplicated on at least one of the other disks in the array. It provides fault tolerance (it can withstand the loss of one disk in the array), and reading data from a RAID 5 is similar in performance to a RAID 0. Writing to a RAID 5 array is a different story, because it takes considerably more time to determine what should be written where within the array. The total storage capacity of a RAID 5 array is the sum of all disks in the array but one.
- **RAID 6.** This is similar in configuration to RAID 5, but it offers additional fault tolerance, allowing the array to survive the loss of two disks in the array. Read performance is equal to that of RAID 5, but writes take even longer. The total storage capacity of a RAID 6 array is the sum of all disks in the array but two.

- **RAID 10 (also known as RAID 1+0).** A combination of RAID 0 and RAID 1, this can also be configured as RAID 0+1. With RAID 1+0, drives in the array are paired, data is mirrored across the pairs, and then the data is striped throughout the array. RAID 0+1 creates two striped sets of data and then mirrors them. The array is able to withstand the loss of a single drive in either configuration, but RAID 1+0 is better positioned to handle the loss of multiple drives in the array. (It can experience the loss of up to 50 percent of the drives in the array and still maintain data integrity.) RAID 1+0 is much more commonly used, due to its ability to recover more quickly than RAID 0+1. It also offers faster read and write operations than RAID 5.

Beyond the configuration of the RAID array, there are also two ways to implement an array: software and hardware.

- **Software RAID.** Some operating systems, including Windows Server 2003, can create RAID arrays by creating logical disks that are then mapped to the physical disks attached to the server. Using a software RAID configuration can reduce costs, but managing the array can impact a server's performance. More importantly, manual intervention is required to fail over the array if there is a hard disk failure within the array, leading to service outages.
- **Hardware RAID.** Hardware RAID controllers are specifically built to manage and operate RAID arrays and can be implemented as expansion cards installed in the server or built into the server's motherboard. They offer numerous advantages over software solutions, such as no use of a server's processing power, better failover options, and better error handling, but they can be expensive.

It's difficult to advocate a specific RAID array configuration for your SharePoint farm, because everyone's requirements, budget, and infrastructure are unique, and these factors impact the decision. Because server roles within a farm use their hard drives in various ways, you may end up with different RAID array configurations within your farm. If your organization has a standard configuration for RAID arrays in its data centers, review those settings to confirm that they meet your requirements. The list that follows outlines several items you should keep in mind when designing your RAID configurations.

- **Use hardware RAID controllers when possible.** Hardware RAID controllers offer so many advantages over software-based controllers, especially where RAID is being used to ensure fault tolerance in disaster recovery solutions. They are more expensive to implement, but they may prove to be worth the investment if they end up saving you big bucks by avoiding productivity-killing downtime for your SharePoint environment.

- **Right-size solutions for WFEs.** WFEs do not necessarily need big-time RAID 1+0 arrays to store their data. In most situations, RAID 1 or RAID 5 is sufficient to provide data preservation and fault tolerance in case of a failure, because SharePoint WFEs do not read or write as much data to their disks as SQL Server 2005 does.
- **Right-size solutions for SQL Server 2005.** As Chapter 8, "SQL Server 2005 Backup and Restore," explained, SharePoint's SQL Server databases mean everything to its survival. Moreover, SharePoint is pretty hard on its databases, performing countless reads, writes, and deletes to them every second under load. So it makes sense to use the most fault-tolerant, high-performing array configuration you can afford for the hard drives of your SQL Server (optimally RAID 1+0, but RAID 5 can also make sense).
- **Use quality hard drives.** An easy way to ensure good performance for your RAID arrays is to use hard drives with fast access times and large amounts of cache built in.
- **Use enough hard drives.** Adding more disks to your arrays is another easy way to improve RAID performance. This gives the array another drive to store content on, provides additional redundancy within the array, and can increase the available disk space (depending on the array configuration).

SAN

The other storage option available (besides just using hard drives in your servers) that makes sense to use with SharePoint is storage area networks, or SANs. SANs let you attach remotely located storage to a server so that the operating system displays and treats the storage as if it were local. SANs are usually best suited to large enterprises due to their high costs to implement, but smaller organizations can also purchase managed SAN storage products from hosting providers, if desired.

SANs can be a viable disaster recovery solution, due to their ability to make storage resources available to servers in multiple locations. SANs are also a good way to make large amounts of storage available in a configurable fashion, which makes them appealing as a storage location for SharePoint's SQL Server databases. Additionally, as you were shown in Chapter 9, SAN storage is required to enable MSCS, a tool that can be important in making SQL Server 2005 highly available.

Although SharePoint's SQL Server databases definitely lend themselves to being stored in a SAN, there are not many other aspects of SharePoint that make a compelling case to do it with. In most cases, the benefits of a SAN are outweighed by the high cost of using such a resource for the relatively small-in-comparison hard drives of a SharePoint server, especially when there are other ways that the data stored there can be backed up or made highly available. Despite the fact that

SANs offer large amounts of storage, it does not really make a lot of sense to store large SharePoint items, like your farm's search index, there because hard disks can better handle the high traffic that SharePoint generates when accessing the index. If you want to use a SAN throughout your environment, it is supported by Microsoft and can certainly be done, but please take the time to performance test your configuration and confirm that the results are acceptable for your organization.

SERVER CLUSTERING AND SHAREPOINT

The most common element of SharePoint to make highly available via a clustering tool such as MSCS is its SQL Server databases. Because the topic of MSCS and SQL Server has already been covered extensively in Chapter 9, review that chapter for information on the subject, if you have not already. Most other elements of SharePoint do not lend themselves to clustering, with one exception: Excel Calculation Services. Earlier in the chapter we mentioned that SharePoint can distribute Excel Calculation Services loads across application servers within a farm without additional configuration, which is definitely true. But Excel Calculation Services can also be clustered, although not with MSCS.

Excel Calculation Services can be clustered using Microsoft's Windows Compute Cluster Server 2003 to create a high-performance computing solution designed to provide an enterprise-level solution for Excel-based calculations. Windows Compute Cluster Server 2003 is used to create a type of cluster much different from those created by MSCS. MSCS clusters are designed to provide high availability and failover capabilities where the resources provided by the cluster are those of the primary active node in the cluster. Think of it as a situation where one person in a boat rows until he gets tired, and then the other person in the boat takes over the rowing duties. Windows Compute Cluster Server clusters pool the processing resources of all their member servers to create a high-performance computing node with much greater capability than those of a single server; with Windows Compute Cluster Server clusters, both people are rowing the boat at the same time.

Similar to MSCS, Windows Compute Cluster Server requires specific hardware and software configurations beyond the capabilities of the resources we have available to write this book. In addition, the use of Windows Compute Cluster Server with Excel Calculation Services is a pretty small niche type of implementation that 99% of organizations are not going to implement, and certainly not as part of a comprehensive disaster recovery plan. Because of those factors, this section does not include a walkthrough of how to configure Excel Calculations Services and Windows Compute Cluster Server. If you want to learn more about this subject, there is a Developer Guide from Microsoft that details an example usage scenario that we recommend you take a look at. It is available at http://msdn.microsoft.com/en-us/library/bb462928.aspx.

NETWORKING AND INFRASTRUCTURE PLANNING

The other element of your SharePoint environment that is vulnerable to hardware failures and outages is your networking hardware and infrastructure. If your network or a component within it should fail, is your environment redundant enough to keep lines of communication open between your users and your SharePoint farm? What about between your SharePoint farm and its database servers, domain controllers, and other crucial remote resources? Don't overlook the vital components that provide the key lines of communication into and out of your environment when planning for high availability.

Work with your network administrator(s) to confirm that the switches, routers, load balancers, and other pieces of the network are redundant, so that the connection to the network remains active if one of those items should fail. Regularly test your network to confirm that communications are being quickly and efficiently routed from point A to point B, and to make sure that all address mappings and configurations are correct so that traffic can get to where it is supposed to.

Your servers can be configured with additional NICs, a setup that can offer a lot of additional benefit to your system. Not only do multiple NICs allow for the use of the Unicast operating mode with Windows NLB, but you can establish specific channels for communication, restricted to a specific IP subnet, between your SharePoint servers and their database instances. This is beneficial to performance, because it gives your farm a network location solely devoted to its own database traffic, the foundation of SharePoint's publishing process. It also provides important security to the process by restricting access to the IP subnet to only the servers using it. Multiple NICs can also be teamed, opening up greater bandwidth into and out of your server for content to flow through.

CONCLUSION

As a SharePoint administrator, it is all too easy to become locked in on the SharePoint or SQL Server components of your environment. But from the perspective of disaster recovery and high availability, that just isn't enough. SharePoint depends on so many systems, devices, and processes to function effectively, and as an administrator it is your responsibility to make sure that those constituent items are just as robust, redundant, and available as your SharePoint systems are. How you are able to do that depends a lot on what kind of operating budget you have available and what your existing resources and systems already are. The good news is that SharePoint and its constituent systems are pretty flexible, so you have a lot of options and flexibility. Often, the hard part is sifting through those options to determine which is best for you.

Something that we have harped on throughout this book and will do so even more in Chapter 14, "SharePoint Disaster Recovery Testing and Maintenance," is the importance of testing and monitoring everything in your environment. It is far better to know ahead of time if a system is failing or needs repair or modification, because that way you have more time to plan the right solution and put it in place. Not to mention, it's a much easier conversation to have with your supervisor and customers than the alternative

The concepts and information in this chapter are designed to get you thinking about the foundational systems of your SharePoint environment and what you can do to make them highly available. The best solution for you depends on your organization, but whether you have a single WSS server accessed by 10 users or a global organization with multiple MOSS Enterprise farms and thousands of users, implementing some, any, or all of the contents of this chapter can only benefit your SharePoint environment.

After completing this chapter on Windows Server 2003 High Availability, you should be able to answer the following questions about their capabilities. You can find the answers to these questions in Appendix B, "Chapter Review Q&A," on the book's Web site at http://www.courseptr.com/downloads.

1. Do you need to purchase a separate license for Windows NLB?
2. What is the difference between Unicast and Multicast operating roles for NLB?
3. What SharePoint server roles can be load-balanced?
4. How does RAID 1+0 differ from RAID 5?
5. What is the difference between Windows Compute Cluster Server and Microsoft Cluster Services?

12

SharePoint Disaster Recovery Planning and Key Concepts

In This Chapter

- The Disaster Recovery Plan Context
- Key Concepts and Terms
- Assessment and Planning

The bulk of the information presented in this book thus far has been technical and focused on specific SharePoint platform capabilities and associated disciplines. Topics such as high availability, farm-level backup and restore operations, SQL Server log shipping, and others have been discussed. Each of these topics is relevant to the concept of SharePoint disaster recovery, but none of them actually addresses the bigger picture of what constitutes a true disaster recovery strategy and the concerns that drive the construction of an end-to-end SharePoint disaster recovery plan.

This chapter shifts the focus away from the technical aspects of SharePoint disaster recovery and toward the bigger picture of general disaster recovery planning, what drives a SharePoint disaster recovery strategy, the questions that must be answered before a technical solution can be formulated, and other related strategic objectives and concerns. This chapter also focuses on the concepts, terminology, and acronyms with which you must be fluent to speak the language of disaster recovery.

The Disaster Recovery Plan Context

This book has spent a tremendous amount of time talking about SharePoint disaster recovery and the technical procedures involved in both preparing for a disaster and recovering from it. To truly understand what drives the process of formulating a disaster recovery plan, though, you need to take a step back and understand the context in which a disaster recovery plan is formed.

Although SharePoint is a technical platform, the functions and capabilities it provides are typically used in day-to-day operations by numerous business users. Business users of a SharePoint farm depend on it for everything from collaboration and sharing to publication and business process automation. Although disaster recovery might be viewed as a "technical exercise" by those responsible for bringing a farm and its functions online following a disaster, the restoration of functionality is critical to those who depend on SharePoint for day-to-day operations.

It is in the nature of SharePoint administrators, solutions architects, and those tasked with operations responsibilities to find technical solutions to technical problems. On the surface, a disaster recovery plan looks like such a problem-solution equation. Disaster recovery plans often appear very straightforward: a disaster happens, and the disaster recovery plan goes into effect. Operations are shifted from the servers that went down to backup servers that are running in an alternate data center. The previously taken backups are restored. That which is broken is fixed. Once all steps are executed, everything works as it did prior to the disaster. Right?

Unfortunately, this view of disaster recovery and disaster recovery planning is somewhat naive. It's a common mistake for SharePoint professionals and information technology professionals in general to think of disaster recovery in strictly technical terms. Simply take enough backups, buy enough extra hardware, and rent space in an additional data center, and all disaster recovery risks are mitigated. Project teams budget for disaster recovery without having any real idea of what's important, what drives an appropriate disaster recovery strategy, and what a business-acceptable strategy really includes or costs.

In reality, the creation of a disaster recovery plan is driven less by technical requirements and more from the potential revenue losses associated with a system outage, damage to property and materials by the absence of an operational system, the loss of communications represented by a downed system, and other similarly important business factors. For these reasons, a properly considered and well-formed disaster recovery plan is a single piece of a larger business continuity plan that addresses not only the technical aspects of bringing a system back into operation, but all the other challenges that accompany it: keeping information secure, the changes in day-to-day operations for personnel during a declared disaster, continuity of communications when normal channels are down, staying in compliance with legal requirements in the event of an outage, and so on.

KEY CONCEPTS AND TERMS

The domain of business continuity planning possesses a somewhat unique set of concepts, terms, and processes. To continue building on the concepts and drivers associated with disaster recovery planning, Figure 12.1 zooms out to look at the larger, more holistic process of business continuity planning and where SharePoint disaster recovery planning fits into it.

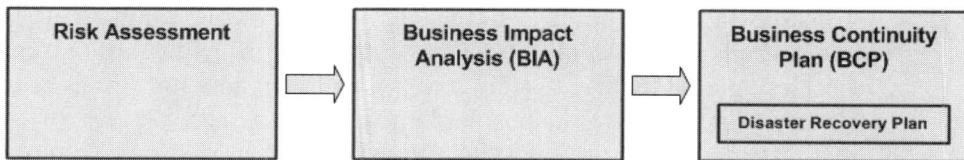

FIGURE 12.1 The stages of business continuity planning.

As illustrated in Figure 12.1, business continuity planning involves three distinct stages:

1. **The risk assessment.** The risk assessment is where disaster recovery planning begins. It entails the analysis of a SharePoint farm and the business processes tied to it from the perspective of vulnerabilities, threats, and general exposures that are introduced simply by having the farm in production and in use by business users. The risks that are identified typically equate to one or more SharePoint functions or usage scenarios. "Collaboration on XYZ project," "business intelligence functions leveraged by executives," and "workflow that is used to approve public communications in the ABC document library" are examples of such functions and scenarios.

2. **The business impact analysis (BIA).** The results of the risk assessment serve as the input to the BIA. The BIA attempts to equate the loss of a particular SharePoint capability or function (such as the loss of business intelligence functions leveraged by executives) with the projected magnitude or expected monetary impact associated with the loss (for example, $10,000 per day in investments). Equating outages to exact losses is difficult at this stage due to all the variables that are typically in play, but the results of the analysis serve as a valuable prioritization tool in the next stage of the business continuity planning process.

3. **The business continuity plan (BCP).** Armed with the results of the BIA, business continuity planners have the data they need to prioritize risk areas and regions of focus that minimize business exposure and loss in the event of a disaster. As described earlier, the BCP that results from this process

addresses both the technological areas included in the disaster recovery plan (such as "restore the system and associated databases from backup") and associated business processes (for example, "have the accounts payable team begin using the new repository at URL http://DRAccountsPayable instead of the standard production URL"). A BCP typically includes other prescriptive advice and workarounds to minimize or mitigate the impact of an outage.

As shown in Figure 12.1, a disaster recovery plan is one component of the ultimate business continuity plan that results from both the risk assessment and BIA of identified risks. Of course, the disaster recovery plan does not simply arise from a determination regarding the potential impact of an outage.

The purposes for which a SharePoint farm is used, along with acceptable outage windows in the event of a disaster, ultimately drive the technological aspects of the disaster recovery plan that an organization crafts and implements. Two key concepts determine what constitutes an "acceptable" outage window:

■ **Recovery time objective (RTO).** The RTO of a disaster recovery plan defines the amount of time that can elapse between the occurrence of a disaster and the affected system being returned to operational status. It is typically during this time that the steps of a disaster recovery plan are executed. A highly critical SharePoint system may have a real-time RTO (that is, the failure of a production system immediately results in a backup system taking over). At the other extreme, a farm that handles tertiary business functions may have an RTO that is measured in weeks to support the acquisition of new hardware and the ultimate rebuild of the farm from scratch.

■ **Recovery point objective (RPO).** Whereas RTOs are forward-looking, an RPO defines the maximum window of data loss that is deemed acceptable in the event of a disaster. In a disaster, an RPO defines the furthest allowable point in the past, relative to the declaration of a disaster, from which data can be restored. As you might expect, a highly critical SharePoint system may have a disaster recovery plan with a near-zero RPO that does not accept any form of data loss. Tertiary systems, on the other hand, may have RPOs that are measured in hours or days.

To illustrate the concepts of RTO and RPO, consider the disaster recovery plan profile shown in Figure 12.2. The requirements in this plan are common of less-critical systems where some amount of data loss and downtime is deemed acceptable in the event of a disaster.

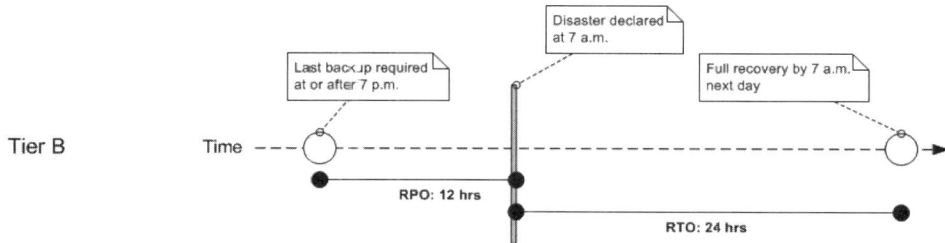

FIGURE 12.2 RPO and RTO for a SharePoint farm of lesser business significance.

In this disaster recovery plan, a disaster occurs and is declared at 7 a.m. The disaster recovery plan mandates an RPO of 12 hours and an RTO of 24 hours. To satisfy the RPO requirement of this plan, a backup or some capture of relevant data and state must have been performed in the 12 hours leading up to the declaration of the disaster. At the same time, the RTO requirement states that the system must be restored to a functional state (qualified within the disaster recovery plan) within 24 hours of the disaster's occurrence.

Figure 12.3 presents a very different set of requirements for recovery when the disaster is declared at 7 a.m. The RTO and RPO shown are more common of a SharePoint farm that is of greater importance to the organization that utilizes it. With an RPO window of 1 hour and an RTO window of 30 minutes, the potential overall outage window is significantly smaller than the one illustrated in Figure 12.2.

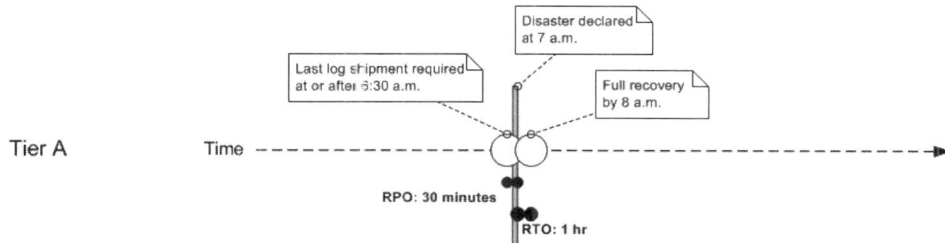

FIGURE 12.3 RPO and RTO for a SharePoint farm of greater business importance.

As you might imagine, implementing a disaster recovery solution to address the RTO and RPO requirements illustrated by the plan shown in Figure 12.3 carries a different set of challenges than meeting the requirements for the plan shown in Figure 12.2. Technical strategies and supplemental equipment requirements vary significantly between the two.

A discussion of the specific means by which you can address the technical and material requirements of a SharePoint disaster recovery plan takes place next in Chapter 13, "SharePoint Disaster Recovery Design and Implementation."

In a perfect world, all disaster recovery strategies would involve no loss of data (that is, have a zero RPO window) and provide instant failover (zero RTO). Unfortunately, the cost of such strategies for SharePoint farms is exceptional and prohibitive for all but the most critical of business uses. As part of their disaster recovery planning, most organizations discover that as RPO and RTO target windows shrink, the cost of an associated disaster recovery strategy goes up. The challenge then becomes balancing data loss and downtime against the total cost of implementing an appropriate and effective disaster recovery strategy.

ASSESSMENT AND PLANNING

The preceding section highlighted the general processes that eventually result in the formation of a SharePoint disaster recovery plan. It was shown that in the early stages of the business continuity planning process, the bulk of the planning and decision making is driven by business owners and those who are capable of assessing the dollar value of the capabilities and functions that a SharePoint farm provides. Technical owners typically have a part to play in this process, but they don't drive it.

This is not to say that disaster recovery planning should be left entirely to business owners until the process eventually flows downstream to those with technical responsibilities. On the contrary, SharePoint technical owners can undertake numerous assessment and planning activities in advance of their involvement in the business continuity planning process. By staying involved in the planning process, SharePoint administrators can ensure that the finished product is viable from both a business and a technical perspective. Otherwise, business owners may base their decisions on incomplete or inaccurate estimates and place unmanageable burdens upon the architecture or costs of your SharePoint environment.

DISCOVERY AND DOCUMENTATION

In the early stages of disaster recovery planning, the goal for SharePoint technical owners is to fully understand and document the farm or farms they're responsible for. If the SharePoint farm isn't yet in production or is still in the planning stages, the expected operational end state should be the target of activities. This sort of analysis and documentation is a worthwhile objective even without the context of disaster recovery planning, but the knowledge and artifacts delivered by the process are a critical input into the design and implementation phases that are discussed in the next chapter.

The Unified Modeling Language (UML) is an excellent tool for communicating the information gathered during this phase of the disaster recovery planning process. Created by the Object Management Group (OMG), the UML provides a set of guidelines and standards for the documentation of application architecture and structure. More information is available at the OMG's UML resource page at http://www.uml.org.

Discovery and documentation should be focused on four key areas: logical architecture, physical deployment, configuration data, and business data.

Logical Architecture

The logical architecture model of a system describes the logical components of the system, the purpose each of the components serves, and how the components interact with one another. It is also common for a system's logical architecture model to identify interfaces and other points of contact between the system and other resources not tied directly to the system.

Whether based strictly on Windows SharePoint Services (WSS) or Microsoft Office SharePoint Server (MOSS), all SharePoint farms possess a number of architectural aspects that should be documented before disaster recovery planning:

- Internet Information Server (IIS) application pools
- SharePoint Web applications
- Zones and associated alternate access mappings
- Web application policies
- Content databases
- Site collections (including host-named site collections)
- Sites
- My Sites

SharePoint farms that are based on MOSS have the additional architectural aspect of one or more shared services providers (SSPs) that implement the Excel Calculation Services, Office SharePoint Search, Business Data Catalog (BDC), and other advanced functions.

Microsoft's TechNet has an excellent section on SharePoint logical architecture design at http://technet.microsoft.com/en-us/library/cc261976.aspx.

When documenting the logical architecture of your SharePoint farm, your focus should be directed primarily to the logical components that are present and how they interact with one another rather than the capture of all details associated with settings and configuration. Some amount of configuration data is typically included within the documented model to accurately describe aspects of the logical architecture, but all of the nitty-gritty configuration and setting data is best inventoried separately as part of SharePoint disaster recovery planning.

Physical Deployment

The physical deployment model of a system describes the system's implementation across a specific set of infrastructure components and hardware. Whereas the logical architecture model of a system is focused primarily on the components of a system and how they interact, the physical deployment model of a system gets into the specifics of the environment in which the system resides and operates.

Most physical deployment models have a number of similar characteristics regardless of the system or application being documented, and SharePoint physical deployment models are no exception. Commonly found elements include

- Physical servers that both SharePoint and SQL Server use
- Storage equipment such as storage area networks (SANs) and network-attached storage (NAS) devices
- Switches and other core networking equipment
- Wide area network (WAN) connections and other remote access links
- Firewalls that are between or touched by SharePoint servers
- Hardware load balancers and other specialty devices
- Other supporting hardware, such as Windows Active Directory (AD) domain controllers

As with the logical architecture model, you should place greater emphasis on identifying the physical components of the SharePoint farm than on capturing every configuration setting associated with the infrastructure and hardware. Some configuration and setting data is naturally included as part of the physical deployment documentation, but an exhaustive treatment of configuration and setting data takes place in the next section, "Configuration Data."

Configuration Data

Configuration data is any data that is required for proper operation of a system, both internally and within its implementation environment. Applications and systems use and store configuration in a variety of ways, such as via files, databases, and the Windows Registry. Typical SharePoint farms leverage numerous configuration settings and settings storage facilities. Just three examples of the many locations and facilities include

- Configuration, Search, and SSP databases
- `Web.config` files for SharePoint Web applications
- IIS's metabase

Each of the examples listed can be targeted with relative ease for automated backup operations. These items represent one type of configuration data that should be captured when focusing on SharePoint disaster recovery planning. Documentation should include a description of each item, the location of the item (such as a database name or full file system path), and how the information represented by the item is used.

The second type of configuration data that must be captured is data that is critical to farm operations but does not lend itself to easy targeting for backup. This can be data that is stored in multiple locations but must remain synchronized across all locations, data that is difficult to access due to its storage location or form, or even data that is dependent on or stored within external systems. Two common examples of data that falls into this overall category are service accounts and passwords that are hashed prior to their storage.

Configuration data that falls into this second category does not lend itself to the same style of capture that was described for data that is easily backed up. Documentation should include the relevant information (such as service account username and password), the purpose of the information, and some indication of how the information is supplied or entered into the SharePoint environment (such as a reference to a Central Administration Web page where an administrator enters the account information).

For reasons of security, many organizations elect to track each of the two types of configuration data separately. Because data falling into the second category typically contains sensitive or restricted information, it is often managed by an organization's computer information security group or personnel operating in a similar role. At a minimum, access to this type of data should be controlled or limited to a defined group of personnel to avoid its misuse.

Business Data

Whereas configuration data is information that a system uses to permit it to operate as designed, business data is information that flows through the system, is processed by the system, and is often stored by the system during the course of day-to-day operations. Business data is the data that end users care about and that normally has a dollar value attached to it during BIA activities. Business data may also be restricted by an organization's internal policies or governed by laws such as the Sarbanes-Oxley Act of 2002 and Health Insurance Portability and Accountability Act (HIPAA).

Fortunately for disaster recovery planners, SharePoint uses a consistent and centralized storage model for nearly all business data. If a business user enters data into SharePoint, in all likelihood that data is stored in a content database. Aside from scenarios that bypass the use of SQL Server (such as implementation of a custom `ISPExternalBinaryProvider` for external Binary Large Object (BLOB) storage within the SharePoint farm), the act of documenting content databases, their site collections, and the data that is contained within them arms you with the information you need to guide the development of a business data recovery strategy.

DEPENDENCIES AND INTERFACES

Judiciously documenting the four areas just discussed provides an overview of the SharePoint farm and how it operates, the environment it operates in, and how SharePoint-based data is consumed and processed. For SharePoint farms that operate independently of all other systems, this is all the information that is needed to prepare for the more formal process of disaster recovery design.

Unfortunately, few organizations use only SharePoint and nothing else. Most organizations using SharePoint also have some combination of e-mail systems, file shares, additional line of business solutions, homegrown applications, and a whole host of additional systems too voluminous to enumerate. Realizing the value of SharePoint when used as a portal or intranet solution, many organizations go to great lengths to integrate SharePoint with these systems.

For purposes of disaster recovery planning, these integration points represent areas that require special attention. A SharePoint farm that is restored to a fully operational state without systems it depends on is not going to be viewed as "fully operational" in the eyes of business users. When documenting the logical architecture, physical architecture, configuration data, and business data associated with a SharePoint farm, particular attention should be paid to interface points with other systems that are leveraged or represented in some form within SharePoint. Examples of such dependencies can include

- Line of business systems that publish data that is consumed through SharePoint's BDC functionality
- Custom user controls and Web Parts that interface with Web services exposed by other systems
- InfoPath forms that include logic to write portions of submitted form data to a non-SharePoint SQL Server database
- A simple Page Viewer Web Part that provides a browser-based view of a file share

Business users would likely judge a full restoration of the associated SharePoint farm without associated external systems as SharePoint being less than fully functional.

Identifying dependencies and interfaces with other systems goes beyond simply documenting a SharePoint farm. It requires an analysis of the purposes of a farm's site collections, an inventory of implemented features (such as InfoPath forms and BDC connections to line-of-business systems), and an understanding of the operations being carried out by custom SharePoint solutions and components running within the farm. Often, this process ultimately consumes more time than the documentation of the SharePoint farm itself. Nevertheless, the knowledge gained by the identification of these dependencies and interfaces is critical to any complete SharePoint disaster recovery plan design.

CONCLUSION

Information technology personnel often regard SharePoint disaster recovery planning as a technical problem that is theirs to solve, but in reality, a disaster recovery plan is just one part of the larger business continuity planning process. If the disaster recovery plan for your SharePoint environment is going to be an effective piece of your organization's overall BCP, you must be ready to invest significant time creating a risk assessment and a BIA. Otherwise, the entire BCP is at risk and fails to provide a necessary and critical service to your business.

Two critical inputs to the disaster recovery planning process come in the form of RTOs and RPOs. These two parameters define the window of available recovery time (RTO) and the window of acceptable data loss (RPO) for a SharePoint farm (or some part of it) when a disaster has been declared. Disaster recovery planners commonly face the challenge of trying to balance downtime and data loss against implementation costs. As RTO and RPO windows shrink, costs associated with appropriate disaster recovery strategies typically rise disproportionately.

A SharePoint disaster recovery design depends on the completion of several business processes to proceed in an informed fashion, but technical owners and those responsible for SharePoint farms can prepare for the design process in a couple of ways. Of greatest importance is the documentation of the SharePoint farm. Detailing the logical architecture, physical deployment, configuration data, and business data aspects of a SharePoint farm provides disaster recovery planners with recovery targets and usage information that are invaluable during the design stage. Also of critical importance in the assessment process is the identification of SharePoint interfaces to other systems and external farm dependencies. Although these non-SharePoint systems may not technically be a part of the SharePoint farm, integration with these systems means that they must be addressed in some fashion during disaster recovery design.

Having completed this chapter, you should now be able to answer the following questions. As with the other chapters, answers to the following questions appear in Appendix B, "Chapter Review Q&A," on the book's Web site at http://www. courseptr.com/downloads.

1. How do a disaster recovery plan and a business continuity plan differ?
2. What is the difference between an RPO and an RTO?
3. How does configuration data differ from business data?
4. Why are interface points with other systems so important to capture during initial analysis?
5. Name some common interface points between SharePoint and other systems that require special analysis and treatment during disaster recovery documentation?

13

SharePoint Disaster Recovery Design and Implementation

In This Chapter

- Scope Definition
- Planning the Recovery Process
- Documenting and Implementing the Disaster Recovery Design

Many administrators of information technology (IT) systems are all too familiar with that famous axiom known as Murphy's Law, which says, "If anything can go wrong, it will." While it may sound fatalistic, having the expectation that one day down the road a mishap of one kind or another will happen to your SharePoint environment is an important perspective to maintain when designing and creating your organization's disaster recovery plan. This isn't something you should generate for the sake of crossing an item off your to-do list or checking a check box in a survey or audit. An effective disaster recovery plan gives you a resource that can be used in all situations, regardless of their scope or importance. By not losing sight of the fact that this strategy is going to be used and not just gather dust somewhere, you are drastically improving your chances for a successful recovery of your business's crucial SharePoint systems and data when the chips are down.

Now that you've been introduced to the concepts and terminology of disaster recovery in Chapter 12, "SharePoint Disaster Recovery Planning and Key Concepts," it's time to start applying those lessons to your organization's requirements and constraints. This chapter is designed to walk you through the process necessary to design and document your disaster recovery plan. You will gain an understanding of the data you need to collect and maintain in your plan, the parameters necessary for not only its design but also its success, and how to record all that data in a consistent, coherent fashion.

SCOPE DEFINITION

It's impossible to plan how you will recover your system in the event of an outage or disaster without understanding what your system is composed of and what its critical components are. For many complex environments, it simply isn't feasible to attempt to fully restore every server, application, or database at the same time; trying to do so would add hours, days, or even weeks to the time it would take to complete this vital restoration activity. That is why the first step you must take when developing your disaster recovery plan is to define its scope and to evaluate and select the essential parts of your system that must be restored in the event of a disaster.

> *It's assumed that you're not designing and developing your SharePoint environment's disaster plan on your own, or only from an IT perspective. As discussed in Chapter 12, a disaster recovery strategy is simply part of a larger business continuity plan (BCP) that's driven primarily by business stakeholders and the cost that is tied to outages in a SharePoint environment. While you, as an administrator, know what infrastructure components you need to have in place to restore your environment, your users are the ones who should determine which sites are business critical, what content should be preserved at all costs, and what the acceptable levels of downtime are for these items. The results of a business impact analysis (BIA) serve as the primary guide when constructing your disaster recovery plan.*

WHAT ARE RECOVERY TARGETS?

Recovery targets are the critical functions and data of your SharePoint environment that need to be restored following the declaration of a disaster. Seems pretty straightforward, doesn't it? Well, thanks in part to the complex and modular nature of a SharePoint environment that is not always the case.

Recovery targets are important because not only do they identify the parts of your system that need to be acknowledged and addressed in some way as a part of your disaster recovery plan, but they are the functions and data that must be restored or replaced as part of a successful recovery operation. A set of recovery targets reads like a checklist, and recovery targets are often used in this fashion during disaster recovery testing to gauge the success or failure of a recovery strategy following its execution.

DEFINING YOUR RECOVERY TARGETS

Recovery targets are defined through the process of mapping the results of a BIA (that is, the data and functionality that business stakeholders have identified as being critical in a SharePoint farm) to elements within the farm that were identified during the discovery and documentation phase described in Chapter 12. Each result from the BIA should translate to one or more technical functions and data elements within the SharePoint farm.

For example, consider a BIA that identifies a SharePoint site housing online actuarial capabilities as being highly critical to daily business operations. Technical analysis and cross-referencing of the site mentioned in the BIA might yield numerous recovery targets including these:

- The content database housing the Report Center SharePoint site containing Excel spreadsheets
- Excel Calculation Services (ECS) for online calculation functionality
- The physical server that is dedicated within the production farm to ECS
- The unattended service account username and password for ECS for several trusted data connections
- A custom trusted data provider resident within the SSP
- Several legacy line of business systems that are accessed through trusted data connections to supply data for the actuarial spreadsheets

As you can see, a seemingly straightforward business function could lead to a cascading list of technical requirements during the definition of recovery targets.

For large SharePoint farms, the recovery targets that are ultimately selected may comprise only a subset of the farm's total functionality. This is especially true if the recovery time objective (RTO) for the functions and data specified are extremely aggressive and the disaster recovery plan involves any substantial manual effort to carry out.

WHAT TO RESTORE

As the results of the BIA are mapped to recovery targets, you may begin to see that some technical functions or data within your farm have a higher priority than others and that some pieces of key technical functionality or data are also required to make their associated business functions available in SharePoint. It's also perfectly normal for some technical functions to be identified as low-priority components that can be restored once your farm's core content and technical functionality have been fully restored and verified. This kind of triage activity can be beneficial, because it helps you to focus your activities and energy on the most important aspects of your environment without getting distracted by targets of lower priority.

Often, this exercise can help you understand that it isn't a good idea to fully restore your production environment immediately after an outage. Another benefit of this analysis is the impact it can have on the architecture, configuration, and governance policies of your SharePoint farm to better position or partition key elements for recoverability based on business value and associated disaster recovery priority. Following are a few other factors that you should keep in mind as you analyze the BIA results and consider the recovery targets that result:

- **Content database distribution.** How are sites and site collections in your farm distributed across content databases? Consider storing high-priority sites in specific or unique content databases to allow more frequent backups to be made on those databases and prevent lesser sites from using resources. Carefully distributing your sites across databases, and even database instances, can make your backup and restore processes much easier to manage and complete.
- **Content.** What types of content or data do users store in different types of sites in your farm? Is the content that users store in their My Sites given the same recovery priority by the BIA as what they store in collaborative team sites? Your organization may already have usage and retention policies that can help to answer these questions about the contents of different types of sites and determine when they should be backed up and restored in the absence of specific directives by the BIA.
- **Search.** What elements of your farm's search infrastructure need to be preserved? When do they need to be restored? It's important to clarify whether resources are to be expended to preserve your farm's search data (that is, it's a recovery target), or if recovery can wait until a new crawl of restored content can be generated and propagated. Given the challenges inherent in using out-of-the-box tools to back up and restore a farm's search components, you may find that the recovery of search functionality complicates (and potentially raises the cost of) a recovery plan.
- **Dependent systems and interfaces.** What applications or configuration items have been identified as recovery targets on your production servers to support the various functions of your SharePoint farm? Some applications provide crucial data or functionality to the users of your SharePoint farm and must be reconnected or also restored as part of your farm's restore effort. Other applications are not identified by the BIA as mission-critical and are therefore not a priority.

What's Out of Scope

It's just as important to establish what's out of scope for your disaster recovery plan as it is to identify what's in scope. This isn't a simple exercise of listing what platforms, applications, systems, or components are not included in your disaster recovery plan. Yes, such actions are definitely part of the scope definition process, but it's also important to determine what other groups are being expected to support and identify those items deemed to be out of scope for your plan. For example, if database administrators (DBAs) external to your group manage your SharePoint databases, it may be possible to declare the disaster recovery of those databases out of scope to your plan because those DBAs will handle them.

Establishing external dependencies within a disaster recovery plan introduces risk and is not the "right" of SharePoint technical owners. Prior to portions of a plan becoming dependent on external systems or personnel, discussions with business owners and stakeholders must take place. Although SharePoint technical owners and personnel are ultimately responsible for meeting the recovery objectives identified through the BIA, business stakeholders are the ones assuming the risk and realizing the ultimate impact of a system outage.

Costs

As professors of economics are often fond of stating, "There's no such thing as a free lunch." Every choice and decision you make around your disaster recovery plan has a direct impact on how much it will cost to implement that plan. Frequent backups can require extensive storage resources, as well as more time to configure, test, and maintain. Opting to restore every aspect of a farm as quickly as possible is certainly possible, but the hardware, software, and workforce resources necessary to pull off such a plan can prove prohibitively high for all but the largest of enterprises. It's key to understand the costs inherent in each aspect of a disaster recovery plan so that you can balance and consider them as part of the plan. You may find that the best solution is not always the right solution for your organization once you introduce costs and expenses into the equation.

PLANNING THE RECOVERY PROCESS

Once you've established the recovery targets based on the BIA, it's time to move on to the steps you must take to actually return your system to acceptable levels of functionality. It's time to start determining the people, hardware, software, and other resources that need to be in place before you can start the recovery process.

During the planning and design process, it's common to discover that the level of recoverability desired by business owners isn't possible with the budget allotted to disaster recovery operations. At this stage, bargaining and compromise are common to reach levels of recoverability and cost that are acceptable to both business stakeholders and SharePoint farm owners.

The following sections outline some of the most common issues you're likely to encounter and need to tackle as part of a complete disaster recovery plan.

INFLUENCING FACTORS

Several diverse dynamics are typically at play within a SharePoint environment that can shape the direction and tactics that are employed as part of a disaster recovery plan. Outlined next are three important areas to consider as you begin the design process.

Other factors commonly arise as a plan evolves, and your design should be able to take those into account, but at a minimum an effective disaster recovery plan is built with strong consideration for the following three aspects:

- **RTO and RPO.** After reading Chapter 12, you should be familiar with the concepts of RTO and RPO and how they impact technical options regarding recoverability. The requirements that are established for each recovery target's RTO and RPO directly affect your plan's design, which must be able to meet those objectives to be effective. RTO and RPO can dictate the type and number of resources you need to have available to execute the plan, the sorts of tools and range of feasible technologies you use to preserve and restore your system, and how you define your success criteria.
- **Your data.** What content, such as business documents or task lists, must be immediately restored to enable your users to remain productive? How is that data stored within your SharePoint environment, and how easily can it be backed up and restored? These considerations impact your plan, the tools you use to implement it, and the infrastructure you put in place to support it.
- **Physical limitations.** The tangible pieces of your infrastructure, such as your data center, storage, backup technology, and networking configuration, can make a real difference in the options you have available to build into your disaster recovery plan. Can your recovery team directly access your servers in the data center if they need to? Do you have enough storage for your backups? Can you architect enough redundancy into your infrastructure from the ground up to make it highly available? These are just some of the physical limitations you need to keep in mind as you design your disaster recovery plan.

COMMON DISASTER RECOVERY TOPOLOGIES

As much as you may want to build your SharePoint farm with geographic redundancy and instantaneous failover to backup systems, those capabilities can come with a top-shelf price tag to match the top-shelf coverage they provide. The following sections are intended to describe three potential disaster recovery topologies for your SharePoint environment and to give you some starting points to base your design on. The primary differentiator for the plans is their cost; each plan is intended to hit a different price point and provide the best or most common functionality available for that budget.

Topology Option 1: Minimal Outage Window

This topology is worthy of consideration if your business demands that your SharePoint farm be able to preserve your data transactions up to the last second possible and have its services fully available as soon as possible after an outage.

This means that the farm must be highly available across all components, provide seamless and automated failovers for continual service, and track every transaction as it's submitted so that it can be backed up and restored. Database instances are hosted within failover clusters to withstand an outage to a host server. Key databases are log-shipped to a remote database instance so that every transaction is backed up and preserved in a separate location. SharePoint Web Front End (WFE) servers are grouped behind a hardware load balancer and distributed across data centers to ensure that content can always be made available to end users regardless of what might befall a single server. All storage in the farm is backed up to tape on an hourly basis, and a high-speed storage area network (SAN) is highly utilized by all platforms. Servers are redundantly hosted in multiple data centers throughout the world so that a local outage does not impact the overall system.

This topology is attractive from a disaster recovery standpoint, as it can offer high levels of service to your end users and withstand the loss of multiple servers or supporting systems within the farm. It distributes responsibilities across physical locations and can restore lost data accurately and quickly. In a worst-case scenario (that is, the loss of a data center), disaster recovery strategies based on this topology have a maximum RPO based on the SQL Server log-shipping interval that is utilized. This is typically measured in minutes. By the same token, RTO is measured in the amount of time it takes to apply shipped transaction logs to the already operational alternate SharePoint farm databases. Again, this is typically measured in minutes.

All of this comes at a high cost. This solution requires specialized hardware, multiple licenses of expensive software like SQL Server, large amounts of high-speed storage, and duplication across those physical locations. It requires large, fast connections between data centers.

The cost is not just limited to the acquisition of the assets. Because of the system's complexity, its configuration is labor-intensive and requires constant monitoring, upkeep, and management to maintain its level of service. That means you have to pay, manage, and train a team of administrators to keep it humming along.

Topology Option 2: Average Outage Window

In this situation, it's important to preserve the system's data and keep it available, but there's a larger window to restore the data in, and tolerances are higher for the data's timeliness. The emphasis is on being able to effectively save and restore the system as a whole to an acceptable percentage while also being cost effective. Disaster recovery plans that implement this type of topology typically have outage windows that are measured in hours, instead of minutes or days.

Databases are backed up fully each night and incrementally throughout the day, and backups are transmitted to a second data center housing a "warm" SharePoint backup farm. The farm can be used for both large-scale restores and the restoration of smaller items like subsites or individual documents that have been cleared from both stages of a site collection's recycle bin. Production WFEs may be load-balanced using a software solution, and all reside in the same data center. SAN storage is available but lightly utilized, and full server backups occur on a weekly basis. The backup SharePoint farm in the alternate data center is typically running on a subset of the hardware that forms the production farm.

Again, this approach offers a number of attractive features for disaster recovery scenarios, including a full farm available for a complete failover should it be needed, but it establishes lower expectations for fidelity and responsiveness than the first topology does. The key focal points of the SharePoint farm, its WFEs and databases, are the main targets for preservation in this topology; think of it as an application of the Pareto principle: it focuses on the 20 percent of your system that is responsible for 80 percent of your functionality.

Going this route does mean that you sacrifice some automation and responsiveness. The failover process to the standby farm is manual and takes time to completely execute. The RPO window associated with this type of topology is dictated by the interval between database backups. If a full nightly backup is taken of all relevant databases and three incremental backups are taken in between, the RPO for this type of topology is typically six hours. More frequent incremental backups can drive this window lower. By the same token, the RTO for this topology is usually dictated by the amount of time it takes to restore database backups. As might be expected, this is typically proportional to the amount of time it takes to execute backups.

Costs for this solution are lower due to its reduced scope and scale, but you're still provisioning and supporting two farms, not to mention the extra effort required to keep them both synchronized and up to date with patches and other software upgrades and updates.

Topology Option 3: Extended Outage Window

Based on the parameters defined for this topology, the goals for its disaster recovery plan are very different from the previous two. It centers more on creating a new farm as a replacement in the event of a disaster than it does on preserving the original farm. Databases are not clustered, and while they're backed up, the backups usually have a larger interval of time between them. If WFEs are load-balanced, it's more for performance reasons than for high availability. Disaster recovery plans based on this topology typically have outage windows that range anywhere from 24 hours to multiple days or, in extreme circumstances, even weeks.

Recovery plans based on this strategy ensure that hardware is on hand when a new farm must be assembled from the ground up as a replacement. They also detail the steps necessary to create the new farm and configure it to meet the setup of the original farm. The emphasis with this topology is on restoring the service provided by the SharePoint farm, rather than its content, to end users.

The most significant drawback to this topology is the potential loss of data and content that may occur if it cannot be restored or is not retrieved from backups and added back into the new farm. Depending on how much time has elapsed since the backup was created, recent changes made by users can be lost and will need to be re-created by hand. RPO windows associated with this topology are dictated by the backup cycle interval, and 24 hours is not uncommon. Because full farm reconstruction is mandated by recovery plans implementing this approach, RTOs are extreme and are often measured in days.

The good news is that hardware and licensing costs are lower, and because only one farm is up and running at a time, maintenance costs are lower as well. Additionally, the actual cost of a recovery operation is reduced, as the looser RTOs mean that less overtime is required to build the new farm and configure it. Significantly more time is spent documenting the highly manual recovery process, though, so the perceived cost savings must be weighed against the dramatically increased hours that go into creating and documenting the disaster recovery plan.

DOCUMENTING AND IMPLEMENTING THE DISASTER RECOVERY DESIGN

Once you've identified the inputs, requirements, and parameters of your plan's design, you can move on to the fun part: putting it into writing and incorporating its elements into your system. This is where the rubber meets the road, where you must explicitly state how your SharePoint environment is prepared for the declaration of a disaster and how it will be restored after such an event. Thoroughly document your plan and store it in an accessible, visible, and reliable location so it can be quickly accessed by anyone who needs to review, revise, or execute it.

If your SharePoint disaster recovery strategy includes one or more alternate data centers or facilities, your recovery plan and any associated documentation should be replicated to those facilities to ensure that they are up to date and available in the event of a disaster.

TIP

Remember, there's always a chance that the author of the plan (you) is not going to be the person who actually executes it, so make sure the plan contains all the information and instructions required to execute it even if the reader isn't intimately familiar with the plan. The recovery plan should clearly state any assumptions it makes about the executor and that person's knowledge of SharePoint and related systems.

ACQUISITION OF RESOURCES

Once you understand your farm's recovery targets and have an appropriate disaster recovery topology, you can start reviewing your available resources and establishing the assets needed to provide or expand your disaster plan. You can also define the resources your plan requires if a disaster is declared and you need to execute your plan. Obviously, it pays to have those items on hand before you actually need them so you can begin to satisfy the requirements of the plan as quickly as possible. The following list outlines the major resource areas you should review for your SharePoint environment and its disaster recovery plan:

- **Determine your physical requirements and resources.** As has already been mentioned, your disaster recovery plan probably identifies some specific pieces of required hardware and infrastructure. Whether the plan's requirements include rack space in multiple data centers, high-speed SAN, hardware for hosting virtualized servers, or tape backup drives, you need to enumerate these items as completely and specifically as possible. Review your network requirements and usage, power consumption, available storage, and redundant devices such as load-balancers and RAID arrays.

- **Acquire your hardware.** Once you know what you need, make sure you have it on hand when it's needed. Don't put this off for a rainy day or the next fiscal year. Disasters don't happen when it's convenient. You can't afford to lose millions in business and productivity because you saved thousands waiting to procure the hardware required by your disaster recovery plan.

- **Acquire and license your software.** If you have a failover farm, make sure to secure the proper software and licensing for that additional farm to stay in full compliance with your providers. Store copies of any required software or media in a location (or locations) that's accessible in the event of a disaster. Work closely with your software manufacturer's licensing representative. Explain exactly how you're using the software, because the representative often has special provisions (at lower price points) for software running in a failover environment.

- **Review your dependent services.** Most SharePoint installations depend heavily on Active Directory (AD) for user authentication, not to mention service accounts and administrative access to servers. Closely examine the disaster recovery plans for your environment's AD domains, Domain Name Services (DNS), Dynamic Host Configuration Protocol (DHCP) services, Simple Mail Transfer Protocol (SMTP) services, and all other services that your SharePoint environment depends on. If these service dependencies have RPO or RTO targets that are out of alignment with those that your SharePoint environment has identified, you might need to make alternate arrangements and spend more money.

ESTABLISHING A DISASTER RECOVERY BASELINE

Baselines determine a desired configuration or setup for a given system at a specific point in time and are used as the basis for comparison for subsequent activities in and changes to that system. Establishing a baseline for your SharePoint farm allows you to solidify a specific configuration point and quality of service that your disaster recovery plan should strive to return the system to after a catastrophe. Baselining your system may not be required for your organization, but doing so gives you a defined target for success and goals that you can drive your plan at. The process can also be repeated at regular intervals, allowing you to quantify how your system has grown and changed over time, which can also provide you with valuable data for future updates to your to-be list. Regardless of whether you baseline your system, you should strive to have a complete picture of its current state and how compatible that state is with your disaster recovery plan.

DOCUMENTING YOUR PROCEDURES FOR AN OUTAGE

Up until now, most of this chapter has focused on the items and details needed for a SharePoint environment's disaster recovery plan to establish the best position possible to deal with the declaration of a disaster. Now this chapter turns its attention to some best practices for actually writing the plan and recording it in a consistent and controlled manner. This is important because the plan must be understandable and complete. Its audience is likely to be under a great deal of pressure when using it and won't have time to spare trying to decipher a dense, ineffective document.

Published Standards for Writing

If your organization already has a common set of standards for official technical documents, your disaster recovery plan should follow them. If not, it may be worth the effort to establish them as a part of this process. When writing a document, it isn't enough to simply outline the steps an executor should take to complete a process. A complete technical document should contain several common types of information, including but not limited to these:

- **Involved parties.** Lists the people associated with the document, such as its author/owner, reviewer(s), and approver(s)
- **Version and revision history.** Details the document's changes over time
- **Effective date.** Records the date that the document became available for use
- **Roles, responsibilities, and capabilities.** Includes a list of the positions that need to be filled to execute the document's instructions, the responsibilities for each of those positions, and the skills a resource must have to fill a position
- **Audience.** Defines who the document is intended for
- **Purpose.** Explains what purpose the document should be used for
- **Scope.** Defines what's in scope and out of scope for the document

- **Covered systems.** Lists the systems or groups that the document applies to
- **Glossary of terms.** Defines common terminology used in the document
- **Prerequisites and dependencies.** Includes any activities or systems that must be completed or in place prior to the document's execution
- **Assumptions.** Details the assumptions made in the document
- **Primary content.** Includes the instructions and procedures the document is intended to cover
- **References.** Lists information, documents, or people external to the document that can be consulted for additional information
- **Training.** Explains how individuals should be trained on the document's content and procedures

Verifying Content

Once you've completed your disaster recovery plan, have a third party review and verify it. If you don't, you risk allowing inconsistencies, omissions, or errors to remain in the document that could directly impact the success of a recovery operation. Consider this book as an example. Every page and every word in it has been reviewed, tested, and verified by at least two separate parties. A copy editor checked it for grammatical consistency and proficiency, and a technical editor checked the technical statements, assertions, walk-throughs, and content written. No matter how much authors check their own work, having outside reviewers drastically improves the quality and accuracy of an author's output. No disaster recovery plan should be allowed to stand without being tested and verified before it's considered complete; otherwise, you chance introducing additional, avoidable risk into your disaster recovery activities.

Lowering the Impact of Recovery

Take whatever precautions you can to lower the impact of your recovery strategy on your SharePoint environment and its users. These steps will vary depending on your situation, but here are two important areas to keep in mind that can make the recovery process go much smoother:

- **Securing your crucial disaster recovery resources.** The need for a secure, centralized store for your software installers, license keys, and other associated bits has already been mentioned, but it bears repeating. Ensure that your disaster recovery personnel can access this storage location, and make sure that its contents are backed up and potentially replicated on a regular basis. If your organization lacks a formal disaster recovery department or group, appoint a specific person with the responsibility of maintaining that store and keeping it current. Identify a backup for that person or group in case the primary is unavailable when a disaster is declared.

■ **Identifying what to secure.** What items, such as service account identities and passwords, software license keys, or data center access, should be secured and unavailable to public access? What items should be commonly available to all resources? Review your system's assets and the security around them to make sure that you are properly balancing your assets' safety measures against the need to access them quickly.

As mentioned in Chapter 12, certain types of privileged configuration data are typically stored separately from other types of data. For configuration data that is deemed secure and stored separately, be sure that your disaster recovery plan identifies how (and from whom) such information should be recovered if a disaster is declared.

DEFINING THE COMMUNICATION PLAN

Your disaster recovery plan should also include a plan for communicating information about the declared outage to everyone associated with your SharePoint environment so that you're presenting a uniform, consistent, and informative front to those constituents. The plan should identify the various players and roles in the recovery action, such as data center technicians, database administrators, management, quality assurance, end user advocates, and end users in general. It should also detail the manner in which these various players should be contacted, who should manage and coordinate the communication effort, and the approvals required before a message can be sent. In addition, the plan should inform key personnel of how they can obtain information on their own, via sources such as conference calls, Web pages, and phone trees. It may also be beneficial to designate a specific meeting area that the team can use in perpetuity until the action is completed so that the team always uses a consistent location. Make sure that all key personnel in a recovery action are identified and assigned specific roles to avoid gaps in knowledge and arguments over areas of responsibility.

DETERMINING SUCCESS

The last thing your SharePoint disaster recovery plan must provide is a coherent, concrete, agreed-upon list of criteria for a successful recovery. As stated earlier in this chapter, this list is often derived directly from the list of recovery targets.

Define the terms of a successful recovery before you ever attempt to conduct one so that there are specific goals your team can drive toward and a point where you can declare victory. Keep your business users' needs in mind during this process. As discussed previously, it does little good to deliver a system that may be fully recovered from a technical standpoint but does not allow business users to get their work done. The success criteria and associated conditions must be agreed upon by all stakeholders in your SharePoint environment and with regard to the recovery targets that the BIA identified. Your plan should also identify a person or group that is responsible for verifying that these criteria have been met and approving the completed recovery effort.

> *You may find it worthwhile to explicitly include a baseline for your SharePoint environment within your disaster recovery plan and use it as a benchmark for a successful recovery. This allows you to solidify a specific configuration and quality of service for your system that your disaster recovery plan should strive to return the system to after a catastrophe, rather than an assorted list of recovery targets.*

TIP

CONCLUSION

Creating a useful, effective disaster recovery plan and documenting it properly is one of the most important aspects of a successful disaster recovery strategy. Documentation isn't one of the more interesting or exciting things that an IT administrator can be tasked with, but it certainly is one of the most crucial. Hopefully this chapter has given you a jumpstart on the process.

The goal is for you to use the recommendations and best practices described in this chapter as a starting point for your organization's SharePoint disaster recovery plan. Don't forget that what has been presented may not cover everything that your team needs to meet the unique requirements of your SharePoint environment. Also keep in mind that your plan should, at a minimum, address all the concepts this chapter has introduced. Once you have developed your disaster recovery plan, the bad news is that you're still not done. The good news is that Chapter 14, "SharePoint Disaster Recovery Testing and Maintenance," walks you through the last steps of the process.

Now that you've learned about the importance of an effective disaster recovery plan and what goes into it, you should be able to answer the following questions about a plan's capabilities. You can find the answers to these questions in Appendix B, "Chapter Review Q&A," on the book's Web site at http://www.courseptr.com/downloads.

1. What are recovery targets?
2. What are some items to consider when evaluating what components of your SharePoint environment to restore?
3. What are some of the ways your organization's RTOs and RPOs can impact the design of your disaster recovery plan?
4. What are some examples of resources that must be acquired or provisioned as part of your disaster recovery plan?
5. How do you know when your disaster recovery plan has been completely executed?

14

SharePoint Disaster Recovery Testing and Maintenance

In This Chapter

- Planning Your Test
- Conducting the Test
- Performing Ongoing Maintenance of Your Disaster Recovery Plan

Hopefully it goes without saying that the content covered in this chapter is the next logical step in your disaster recovery planning process: testing and maintaining your plan. These items are natural and important components of any information technology (IT) project or process, but they're all too often given little attention or resources. Given the potential importance of your SharePoint environment and its contents, you can drastically increase your risk factor and decrease the viability of your system if you don't adequately test and sustain your disaster recovery plan.

Obviously, these two items can occur at different stages in the life cycle of your disaster recovery process, but they're related. Most notably, the first maintenance activities of your plan are likely going to happen after you conduct its first test. Testing your plan should produce several lessons learned, valuable data, and necessary modifications. These naturally lead you into the maintenance phase of the process. Likewise, as you continue ongoing maintenance for your plan, you should re-execute your tests to validate all the changes that you've made to the plan.

PLANNING YOUR TEST

The quality of the testing you do for your disaster recovery plan can be just as crucial to the success of your plan as the quality of its design and contents. If you don't conduct an effective test of your plan, you don't have a comprehensive understanding of how it will be applied and utilized if a disaster is declared involving your SharePoint environment. Testing is the best way to begin identifying potential bottlenecks, weaknesses, and dependencies that you may not have considered during the design process. Testing also provides your team with an outstanding training mechanism. Through execution of the plan, team members are developing a deeper understanding of the plan and gaining realistic experience with it. Testing also helps you to estimate your ability to meet your recovery time objective (RTO) and recovery point objective (RPO) goals, which are of paramount importance to the viability of the disaster recovery plan.

Whenever possible, conduct disaster recovery testing for your SharePoint environment within the context of testing your organization's overall business continuity plan (BCP). Given the interdependencies between technical systems such as SharePoint and the business users who work with them, most of the time it isn't sufficient to simply test your disaster recovery plan in a vacuum. You need to know how your design impacts the rest of the BCP, any consequences the BCP may have for your recovery plans, and any other systems in your organization that depend on the restoration of the SharePoint environment for their own success. This information lets you examine your communication plan and its viability, not to mention allows business users to verify that their expectations and strategies involving the BCP and your SharePoint environment are accurate and realistic. If your testing efforts don't in some way involve stakeholders or resources from the business side of your organization, you should at a minimum convey the results of your testing effort so they're informed of your findings.

DEFINING THE SCOPE OF YOUR OUTAGE

The first step of defining how to create an outage in your SharePoint environment for purposes of testing is to determine the scope of that outage. As with any type of test or activity, the value of your test results is based on how successfully the test covers the key aspects of your system and assesses the effectiveness of your disaster recovery plan. Running a test that doesn't impact SharePoint or isn't likely to actually occur in the real world isn't a productive use of your time and resources. The following list outlines some of the questions you should be asking yourself as you determine what your disaster recovery test will encompass:

- **What are the most likely types of outages your system may experience?** If your SharePoint environment contains mostly read-only content, there may be little reason to test the retrieval of content that was accidentally deleted by end users. If your servers are located in an area of the world prone to certain types of weather patterns or natural disasters (tornados, hurricanes, earthquakes, and so on), does it make sense to simulate one of those events in your test?

- **What are your most valuable recovery targets?** Your test should confirm your plan's ability to restore your system's most important recovery targets. These are likely the items your business users will be looking for first, and your plan must be able to bring them back successfully.

- **What items have minimal RTOs and RPOs?** If you have little time to bring back a resource or need to bring back a resource to a recent state, it's imperative that you test and verify your ability to meet those requirements.

- **What are your most vulnerable recovery targets?** If your SharePoint farm has components that are more likely than others to be impacted by an outage, such as a WAN connection or Internet-facing servers outside your firewall, you should exercise them during the disaster test.

- **What resources are available for testing?** There may be constraints placed on your test by the resources you have available to execute it with. If your production SharePoint farm contains load-balanced Web Front End (WFE) servers but your test environment doesn't, you won't be able to test that high availability aspect of your disaster recovery plan. This evaluation should also include resources external to your SharePoint environment, such as business representatives, data center administrators, or storage area network (SAN) capacity available to your servers.

- **What components or dependent systems in your SharePoint environment are governed by disaster recovery plans other than your own?** Again, consider testing your plan as a part of testing to your organization's overall BCP. If you're testing independently of the BCP, your plan may still have dependencies on other plans that you need to examine. It may not be necessary to test these items, but you must verify that these external plans have been tested or are assured by their owners to reduce the risk to your plan.

ORGANIZING YOUR RESOURCES

The obvious conclusion you may come to when evaluating how to test your SharePoint disaster recovery plan is that your test should, whenever possible, mirror the conditions, configurations, and resources found in your production environment as closely as possible. This is certainly one way to approach your test, but you need to determine if this is the most effective way to test your plan and the most effective use of your resources. Review the requirements and design of your plan, and find an approach for testing that is authentic and challenging without wasting efforts or resources.

Testing Your Systems

Again, your plan's RTO and RPO goals play an important role in deciding what systems or environments to use to conduct your test. If your SharePoint environment is designed to deliver minimal or near-zero RTO and RPO outage windows, it's probably going to involve multiple duplicate systems, such as replicated SharePoint farms in alternate data centers, clustered databases, and redundant storage. In this case, it may make more sense to actually conduct the test by leveraging these failover systems, even though they're in a production environment. This gives you a highly accurate profile of how your system will perform in a disaster by using the actual systems that you'll need to function correctly when something hits the fan. This isn't to say that a duplicate testing environment is a poor solution. Rather, the point is to consider the best testing solution to give you the most accurate and relevant data possible about how your plan, your SharePoint farm, its dependent systems, and all the involved personnel will perform in a disaster. If it makes the most sense for your organization to create a test environment for this activity, by all means do so. But make sure that you think about how your plan, its requirements, and its constituents are best tested, in addition to considering your test's available resources and budget.

Also keep in mind that the physical resources your test requires are not just limited to the SharePoint environment needed to run your test. Just as your production SharePoint environment most likely uses several other systems for monitoring, reporting, networking, and other crucial capabilities, your test environment has equivalent dependencies to consider. For example, if you rely on a monitoring system that generates trouble tickets or pages resources when an outage occurs, make sure that system is also monitoring the SharePoint farm hosting your test. But also configure the monitoring system so that production resources aren't assigned to handle the events generated by your test system during disaster recovery testing, to avoid confusion and service degradation for the production system.

Testing Your People

Whenever possible, make the test as authentic as possible, not just in terms of the IT assets used, but also the team involved in the test. Assign participants to fill each of the key roles dictated by your disaster recovery plan so that the required actions, abilities, and responsibilities of each role can be assessed and evaluated. Also include business owners or their representatives in the test. This can go a long way toward properly setting their expectations in an outage and not only give them an excellent understanding of the communication they can expect when an outage occurs but show them the role(s) they play during plan execution and the overall recovery effort.

Planning for Losses

Seriously consider incorporating certain losses of disaster recovery resources and personnel in your test so that you and your team can understand how to overcome those challenges should something similar occur during an actual outage. Who needs to be informed if the latest set of tape backups is corrupted and an RPO target can't be met? What if a database administrator is on vacation during an outage? Can your plan still be executed to meet its criteria for success without the presence of key resources? By purposely building losses into your test, you can further identify weaknesses and dependencies in your system.

VERIFYING CHECKLISTS AND PREPAREDNESS

The initial test of your system is also an excellent opportunity to verify or develop any checklists that you may need as job aids for the disaster recovery plan. During the planning phase of any project, it's often difficult to capture every necessary activity down to the smallest detail, but it becomes much more feasible to do so during test execution. Creating task and resource lists can make your personnel more effective during an actual outage, improving your disaster recovery team's efficiency and effectiveness while eliminating common mistakes and missteps. It's also much easier to learn these lessons during a test than during an actual disaster when business owners are breathing down your neck and everything has to be executed without surprises and errors.

Testing your disaster recovery plan with the people who are likely to execute it in a production environment is a great training exercise for these resources and can identify other areas for additional improvement. It also educates your partners and service providers on what you'll be counting on them for in the event of an outage in terms of both services and their delivery windows. Remember that your disaster recovery plan is likely going to encompass a group far larger than just your SharePoint team. The more you can do to ensure the preparedness and responsiveness of all parties involved in a recovery effort, the more effective the recovery effort is.

CONDUCTING THE TEST

Remember that the more authentic your test is and the more accurately it re-creates an outage of your SharePoint environment, the more value it gives you and the more predictable and effective your disaster recovery plan becomes. The test isn't an excuse to inconvenience your personnel or make unnecessary requests of your external service providers, but all participants should take the test seriously and act as if it's an actual outage. With business representatives and nontechnical personnel from your organization participating, it's even more important to take the exercise seriously to build their confidence in your plan, your team's ability to execute it, and the stability of your SharePoint environment in general.

ENCOURAGING COMMUNICATION

At all stages of the test, encourage communication among the test's participants and provide them with all the information necessary to fully participate in the test. This starts with the test's kickoff activities, where the participants are introduced to the test SharePoint farm, assigned their roles within it, informed of the outage, and provided with the specific details of the catastrophic event that has occurred in the test environment. All participants must understand their role within the test; otherwise, the test may not be fully implemented or worse, would be executed incorrectly.

Throughout the test, the recovery team should have regular meetings to communicate status and findings. The frequency of meetings can follow the communication requirements of the disaster recovery plan, but you might need to provide updates on a more consistent basis as participants execute, learn, and troubleshoot the plan. Record all the key findings, tips, issues, and communications made during the test so that you can review them once the exercise is completed and incorporate them into the revised plan.

TIP

Because recording information and observations during a test can take a significant amount of time, assign a note-taking observer for each person carrying out some part of the recovery plan. Taking this step ensures that execution of the recovery plan isn't slowed and that the feedback gathered is objective in nature. It also encourages recovery plan participants to stay focused on the work they're doing rather than taking notes.

After the test has been completed, you can take several steps to gather further information about it. Collect any and all notes that participants made during their activities, and survey all contributors to collect general thoughts and responses about the test. Once you've gathered all the data, communicate a summary and findings report to all participants. Make sure that the personnel executing the test are given feedback on their work so they know what they did well during the test and what they need to work on and improve in the event of an actual disaster. Also incorporate the findings into the disaster recovery plan; for more information on maintaining your plan, see the section "Performing Ongoing Maintenance of Your Disaster Recovery Plan" later in this chapter.

OBSERVING THE TEST

In addition to the notes, thoughts, and data generated by the note-taking observers assigned to each of the test's participants, it's important to assign certain members of your team to observe the overall test as it progresses. These independent observers should especially be on the lookout for items that are not addressed but need to be added to the larger disaster recovery plan, different streams of recovery that may conflict with one another, activities that have some dependency on other activities, timing, or some other outside influence. You may find that you're best served by assigning this task to team members closely familiar with the disaster recovery plan so they can spend their time observing the test, as opposed to constantly referencing the plan to confirm one detail or another. This ensures that your less experienced team members are getting more hands-on time with the plan to build their knowledge and expertise.

VALIDATING THE PLAN

The nice thing about testing your disaster recovery plan is that it should already provide you with the criteria you need to evaluate whether you passed. Your SharePoint environment's disaster recovery plan should not only define the benchmarks and goals you need to meet for a successful recovery from an outage, but it should inform you of the RTO and RPO goals you're required to meet to fully satisfy your business owners' requirements. Once the test has completed, validate its output against these standards and determine how successful you were at meeting them. If you're unable to meet the RTO and RPO requirements of your plan, you'll need to perform additional analysis to determine how to remedy that issue and update the plan accordingly.

REDESIGNING THE PLAN

After you've validated your test and reviewed its output, you may need to redesign your plan based on your findings. Although you can't expect your disaster recovery plan to account for every complication or calamity that may arise during the recovery of your SharePoint farm, an effective test of your plan often results in some valuable information and changes to the plan. Your responsibility, once the test is completed, is to refactor the plan based on those conclusions and then retest it to verify the accuracy of your modifications.

PERFORMING ONGOING MAINTENANCE OF YOUR DISASTER RECOVERY PLAN

In life and in IT administration in particular, the only constant is change. One challenging aspect of creating a disaster recovery plan is that the system you're designing against is likely to go through frequent modifications, even during the course of your design process. It is not uncommon that in as soon as six months after your plan is completed and approved, the system you designed it for will have grown, matured, and been updated to the point that the plan is no longer fully relevant. That's why it isn't only important to write your plan in such a way that it can be easily modified and updated, but to re-evaluate and update it on a regular basis to keep it in line with the SharePoint environment it addresses.

ANALYZING YOUR SYSTEMS: AS-IS/TO-BE

One way to anticipate changes that may be required for your SharePoint disaster recovery plan is by creating some key lists that track the current and future state of your environment. Organizations are constantly evaluating their IT systems to determine if they're able to meet their specific needs and learn what modifications, additions, or subtractions they may make to them in the future. Often, this analysis is broken into two sections: As-Is and To-Be. As-Is analysis of a system examines the business's current users, processes, and data and compares it to the existing IT system. This comparison is then used to evaluate how well the system serves the needs and actions of the business and to establish a baseline for the future state of the system. The future state is defined in the To-Be analysis. The To-Be list defines the vision for the business's IT systems of the future, prioritizes features and functionality, and establishes goals that upgrades should meet or exceed.

An effective disaster recovery plan is designed to meet the requirements and conditions set forth by the As-Is list of an organization while keeping an eye toward the state described by the To-Be list. A plan must encompass the current system's entire configuration, workflows, and data but also be flexible enough to either handle or be modified to accommodate the projected future state of the system. If a disaster recovery plan can't grow with your SharePoint farm as its role within your organization grows, and thus its IT footprint grows to match, it quickly loses its effectiveness.

If your organization doesn't have official As-Is and To-Be lists that include your SharePoint environment, consider compiling these items before finalizing your SharePoint disaster recovery plan. You need to have a concrete understanding of your system, its strengths and weaknesses, and its projected future state to effectively know what needs to be preserved and restored and how that could yield changes to your disaster recovery plan in the coming years.

MODIFYING YOUR PLAN

In general, your organization should have procedures that govern the review and update of approved documentation so that all documents are evaluated on a regular basis (for example, every year) and updated accordingly. You may find that, based on how your SharePoint system evolves and grows, your disaster recovery plan requires more frequent care and feeding. Take care to establish certain criteria that can trigger an update to your plan, such as a major release for your system, the deployment of new hardware, or the installation of service packs or version upgrades for your software.

When you do modify the plan, create a new version of its documentation so that you can maintain and track a history of its changes over time. Ensure that the document again goes through a full review and approval process so that all stakeholders are made aware of the changes that have occurred in the system and the disaster recovery plan itself. Allowing the plan to gather dust while the state of your production SharePoint system evolves presents a major risk to the plan's relevance and effectiveness and your ability to actually recover the system in a catastrophe.

EXPECTING AND BUDGETING FOR ONGOING MAINTENANCE

To make changes to your disaster recovery plan, you need to expend at least *some* resources, in the form of the time necessary to redesign the plan to meet the changing needs of your systems as well as any additional hardware or software that the redesigned plan may require. Be prepared for expenses beyond time if the scope of your SharePoint farm grows, because you'll likely require further physical resources such as expanded storage space or more servers, not to mention the possibility of specialized backup and restore software. All these items can add definitive costs to your budget that you may not necessarily anticipate once the disaster recovery plan is in place, but you should expect them as part of your plan's ongoing maintenance. As economic circumstances fluctuate and available budgets grow and shrink, you must make sure that sufficient resources are made available to support ongoing maintenance of the plan.

The yearly cost of disaster recovery maintenance is often tied to the disaster recovery design that is implemented for a SharePoint farm. A best practice for most corporate SharePoint farm owners is to calculate and budget for the cost of ongoing disaster recovery maintenance at the same time they prepare a capital asset request for the acquisition of a SharePoint environment and the initial implementation of its disaster recovery strategy and design.

CONCLUSION

The worst thing you could do once your disaster recovery plan is completed and approved is to put it on a shelf and forget it. As you have hopefully gleaned from this chapter, disaster recovery planning is a process of continuous improvement, not a one-time activity. Just as your users are constantly adding new content, documents, tasks, and more to your SharePoint sites, the system is growing with them, and you need to be confident that you can recover your system in the event of a disaster in spite of those changes.

This may require some vigilance on your part, but there are ways that you can alleviate this burden. Monitor your IT organization's change control process for updates, rollouts, or decommissioning activities that may impact your plan. If your organization doesn't have a defined change control process, implement one as soon as you can. Although this process can create overhead and some extra work for your administrators, it provides an opportunity to review the important changes that are being made to your systems and see how they've changed over time.

Baselining your SharePoint system on a regular basis can also aid in the maintenance of your disaster recovery plan. Comparing a given baseline to the current state of the system allows you to identify changes and additional items that your plan may need to address. It may be best to incorporate a system baseline into your regularly scheduled or triggered maintenance activities for your plan to ensure that it's happening on a consistent basis.

Regardless of how you do it, treat your SharePoint environment's disaster recovery plan as a living document, one in a regular state of modification and improvement like an entry in a wiki, rather than a static resource that changes less than the *Encyclopedia Britannica*. But remember, given the importance of your farm's disaster recovery plan, the quality and accuracy of the information in it should be created, reviewed, tested, and approved more like that of the *Encyclopedia Britannica* than a wiki.

Now that you've seen how to test and maintain your SharePoint disaster recovery plan, you should be able to answer the following questions. You can find the answers to these questions in Appendix B, "Chapter Review Q&A," on the book's Web site at http://www.courseptr.com/downloads.

1. What are some examples of resources that can be removed from a test of your disaster recovery plan to check its effectiveness?
2. What are some of the expected outputs you should have once a test of your plan is completed?
3. Can you describe some of the potential risks of not updating your disaster recovery plan over time?
4. What's the difference between an As-Is and a To-Be list?

15 Conclusion

Now that you've finished this book, you're ready to go out, buy some more hardware, throw it into your environment, and voilà—instant disaster recovery support for SharePoint! Right?

We certainly hope not. In reading this book, particularly the last few chapters, you should now clearly understand that jumping into disaster recovery without a solid plan and open eyes can be more costly in terms of both time and money than having no disaster recovery strategy at all. An effective SharePoint disaster recovery strategy is synthesized from a lot of planning, a lot of hard work, and the discipline to regularly revisit the strategy to ensure that it's still applicable to the environment and business it was crafted for.

When we were contemplating how to approach this book, we knew that it wouldn't be possible to propose a single course of action that would fit every situation or save everyone's farms from loss or disaster. Most SharePoint farms share some common characteristics, and the same holds true for the majority of SharePoint disaster recovery plans. On the other hand, every SharePoint farm is unique in many ways, so there is no "one size fits all" strategy or set of technologies that can be recommended or implemented from the perspective of disaster recovery readiness. Trust us, if there was, we'd be shouting it from the mountain tops. Each company or organization has its own set of tools, dependencies, business partners, internal processes, and way of doing things. There are as many valid approaches to disaster recovery planning and implementation as there are SharePoint environments for each of these groups.

When writing this book, we chose to discuss with you the tools and technologies you most likely already have on hand, as well as the processes and guidance that are central to crafting a SharePoint disaster recovery plan for any given situation or setting. We've run through a range of methods to back up and restore the key components of your SharePoint farm. We've highlighted their warts and pain points just as much as their strengths. The challenge you now face is to evaluate this information and figure out which solution best fits your requirements and budget. As much as we would like to be able to do that for you, we can't.

Where possible, we've also included tips, tricks, and watch-outs that you should keep in mind as the many facets of an end-to-end disaster recovery strategy are planned and addressed. But don't just take our word for it. Try them out yourself with your configurations and your systems. Applying the information in this book for yourself, especially within the context of your unique circumstances, is something that we've encouraged you to consider throughout the book. And now that you've finished it, we'll reiterate that advice once more, with one qualifier: consider everything you've seen throughout this book, put it all together, and then test it end to end. You can use the concepts, technologies, and guidance presented within each chapter of this book quite productively in a piecemeal fashion, but they're far more powerful, cohesive, and complete when leveraged together.

One of SharePoint's biggest assets is its flexibility in how it can be implemented and configured. It's a tool that can be used by the smallest of teams to share documents, but it can also be used by thousands of employees to view and collaborate. This diversity is powerful, but it also makes it difficult to anticipate every configuration and situation. We didn't expect every page of this book to be completely relevant to you, and hopefully you didn't either. But we're confident that this book provides you with the jumping-off point to seriously create the correct disaster recovery plan for your SharePoint environment. Because if you're truly serious about the security and viability of the data, documents, and other content that your users are putting into your SharePoint sites, it's imperative that you protect that content and work to ensure its long-term stability.

Our overall goal has been to supply you with the information required to build a foundation that can be leveraged and adapted to guide disaster recovery planning and implementation in a way that works within your unique environment or organization. There are a finite number of pages in this book, though, and invariably something got missed or some facet or topic didn't get fully addressed or maybe even addressed at all. After reading this book, though, we hope that you feel you have the requisite understanding and knowledge needed to take the next step forward in building and implementing a disaster recovery plan that will work for your SharePoint environment.

The following quote is attributed to Alan Lakein, an acknowledged expert on personal time management:

> *"Planning is bringing the future into the present so that you can*
> *do something about it now."*

These words summarize the essence of disaster recovery planning in a nutshell. Disasters don't happen when it's organizationally convenient, and they strike without warning. The only reasonable course of action is to assume that a disaster *will* happen to your SharePoint environment at some point in the future and work to prepare for that disaster now. After all, hope and ignorance are not recognized as acceptable risk mitigation strategies in any technical group or organization.

Index

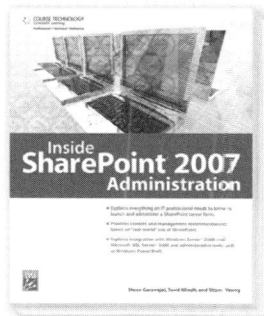

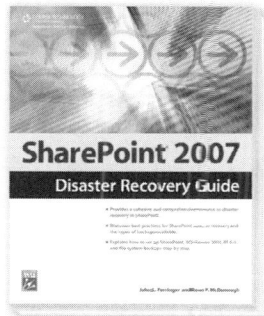

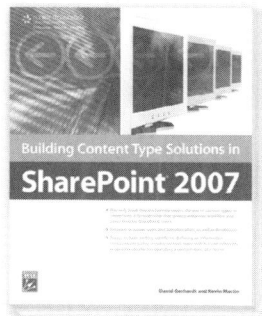

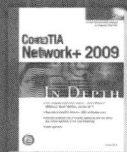